GMS INTENSIVE METHOD
Glossika Mass Sentences

Features: Sound files have A/B/C formats.

A Files	English - Target language 2x
B Files	English - space - Target 1x
C Files	Target language only 1x

every day, with review of 40 sentences, for a total of 1000 sentences in 104 days. Requires less than 20 minutes daily.

 Useful for students with more time to dedicate.

Useful for people with busy schedules and limited study time.

HOW TO USE

1 To familiarise yourself with IPA and spelling, Glossika recommends using the book while listening to A or C sound files and going through all 1000 sentences on your first day. Then you can start your training.

2 Set up your schedule. It's your choice, you can choose 20, 50 or 100 sentences for daily practice. We recommend completing the following four steps.

 Training Step **1**: Try repeating the sentences with the same speed and intonation in the A sound files.

 Training Step **2**: Dictation: use the C sound files (and pausing) to write out each sentence (in script or IPA or your choice). Use the book to check your answers.

 Training Step **3**: Recording: record the sentences as best you can. We recommend recording the same sentences over a 3-day period, and staggering them with new ones.

 Training Step **4**: Use the B sound files to train your interpretation skills. Say your translation in the space provided.

2 Set up your schedule. You can listen to a single GSR file daily or even double up. One book typically takes 3-4 months to complete.

3 You can accompany with the GMS training when you have extra time to practice.

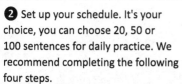

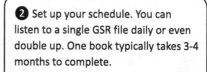

Reminder

Don't forget that if you run into problems, just skip over it! Keep working through the sentences all the way to the end and don't worry about the ones you don't get. You'll probably get it right the second time round. Remember, one practice session separated by *one* sleep session yields the best results!

Glossika Mass Sentences

Russian

Fluency 3

Complete Fluency Course

Michael Campbell

Ksenia Ortyukova

Glossika

Glossika Mass Sentence Method

Russian Fluency 3

This edition published: DEC 2015
via license by Nolsen Bédon, Ltd.
Taipei, Taiwan

Authors: Michael Campbell, Ksenia Ortyukova
Chief Editor: Michael Campbell
Translator: Michael Campbell, Ksenia Ortyukova
Recording: Michael Campbell, Ksenia Ortyukova
Editing Team: Claudia Chen, Sheena Chen
Consultant: Percy Wong
Programming: Edward Greve
Design: Glossika team

glossika.com

Glossika Series

The following languages are available (not all are published in English):

Afroasiatic

AM Amharic
ARE Egyptian Arabic
HA Hausa
IV Hebrew
AR Modern Standard Arabic
ARM Moroccan Arabic

Altaic

AZ Azerbaijani
JA Japanese
KK Kazakh
KR Korean
MN Mongolian
UZ Uzbek

Austroasiatic

KH Khmer
VNN Vietnamese (Northern)
VNS Vietnamese (Southern)

Austronesian

AMP Amis

TYS Atayal
BNN Bunun
ILO Ilokano
SDQ Seediq
TGL Tagalog
THW Thao

Caucasian

Dravidian

KAN Kannada
MAL Malayalam
TAM Tamil
TEL Telugu

IE: Baltic

LAV Latvian
LIT Lithuanian

IE: Celtic

CYM Welsh

IE: Germanic

EN American English
DA Danish
NL Dutch

DE German
IS Icelandic
NO Norwegian
SV Swedish

IE: Indo-Iranian

BEN Bengali
PRS Dari Persian
GUJ Gujarati
HI Hindi
KUR Kurmanji Kurdish
MAR Marathi
NEP Nepali
FA Persian
PAN Punjabi (India)
SIN Sinhala
KUS Sorani Kurdish
TGK Tajik
UR Urdu

IE: Other

SQ Albanian
HY Armenian
EU Basque
EO Esperanto
EL Greek

IE: Romance

PB Brazilian Portuguese
ES Castilian Spanish
CA Catalan
PT European Portuguese
FR French
IT Italian
ESM Mexican Spanish
RO Romanian

IE: Slavic

BEL Belarusian
BOS Bosnian
HR Croatian
CS Czech
MK Macedonian
PL Polish
RU Russian
SRP Serbian
SK Slovak
SL Slovene
UKR Ukrainian

Kartuli

KA Georgian

Niger-Congo

SW Swahili
YO Yoruba

Sino-Tibetan

MY Burmese
YUE Cantonese
ZH Chinese
HAK Hakka
ZS Mandarin Chinese (Beijing)
WUS Shanghainese
MNN Taiwanese
WUW Wenzhounese

Tai-Kadai

LO Lao
TH Thai

Uralic

EST Estonian
FI Finnish
HU Hungarian

Glossika Levels

Many of our languages are offered at different levels (check for availability):

Intro Level	Fluency Level	Expression Level
Pronunciation Courses	Fluency	Business Courses
Intro Course	Daily Life	Intensive Reading
	Travel	
	Business Intro	

Getting Started

For Busy People & Casual Learners

- 20 minutes per day, 3 months per book
- Use the Glossika Spaced Repetition (GSR) MP3 files, 1 per day. The files are numbered for you.
- Keep going and don't worry if you miss something on the first day, you will hear each sentence more than a dozen times over a 5 day period.

For Intensive Study

- 1-2 hours per day, 1 month per book

Log on to our website and download the Self Study Planner at: glossika.com/howto.

Steps:

1. Prepare (GMS-A). Follow the text as you listen to the GMS-A files (in 'GLOSSIKA-XX-GMS-A'). Listen to as many sentences as you can, and keep going even when you miss a sentence or two. Try to focus on the sounds and matching them to the text.
2. Listen (GMS-A). Try to repeat the target sentence with the speaker the second time you hear it.
3. Write (GMS-C). Write down the sentences as quickly as you can, but hit pause when you need to. Check your answers against the text.
4. Record (GMS-C). Listen to each sentence and record it yourself. Record from what you hear, not from reading the text. You can use your mobile phone or computer to do the recording. Play it back, and try to find the differences between the original and your recording.
5. Interpret (GMS-B). Try to recall the target sentence in the gap after you hear it in English. Try to say it out loud, and pause if necessary.

Glossika Mass Sentence Method

Russian

Fluency 3

This GMS Fluency Series accompanies the GMS recordings and is a supplementary course assisting you on your path to fluency. This course fills in the fluency training that is lacking from other courses. Instead of advancing in the language via grammar, GMS builds up sentences and lets students advance via the full range of expression required to function in the target language.

GMS recordings prepare the student through translation and interpretation to become proficient in speaking and listening.

Glossika Spaced Repetition (GSR) recordings are strongly recommended for those who have trouble remembering the content. Through the hundred days of GSR training, all the text in each of our GMS publications can be mastered with ease.

What is Glossika?

From the creation of various linguists and polyglots headed by Michael Campbell, Glossika is a comprehensive and effective system that delivers speaking and listening training to fluency.

It's wise to use Glossika training materials together with your other study materials. Don't bet everything on Glossika. Always use as many materials as you can get your hands on and do something from all of those materials daily. These are the methods used by some of the world's greatest polyglots and only ensures your success.

If you follow all the guidelines in our method you can also become proficiently literate as well. But remember it's easier to become literate in a language that you can already speak than one that you can't.

Most people will feel that since we only focus on speaking and listening, that the Glossika method is too tough. It's possible to finish one of our modules in one month, in fact this is the speed at which we've been training our students for years: 2 hours weekly for 4 weeks is all you need to complete one module. Our students are expected to do at least a half hour on their own every day through listening, dictation, and recording. If you follow the method, you will have completed 10,000 sentence repetitions by the end of the month. This is sufficient enough to start to feel your fluency come out, but you still have a long way to go.

This training model seems to fit well with students in East Asia learning tough languages like English, because they are driven by the fact that they need a better job or have some pressing issue to use their English. This drive makes them want to succeed.

Non-East Asian users of the Glossika Mass Sentence (GMS) methods are split in two groups: those who reap enormous benefit by completing the course, and others who give up because it's too tough to stick to the schedule. If you feel like our training is too overwhelming or demands too much of your time, then I suggest you get your hands on our Glossika Spaced Repetition (GSR) audio files which are designed for people like you. So if you're ambitious, use GMS. If you're too busy or can't stick to a schedule, use GSR.

Glossika Levels

The first goal we have in mind for you is Fluency. Our definition of fluency is simple and easy to attain: speaking full sentences in one breath. Once you achieve fluency, then we work with you on expanding your expression and vocabulary to all areas of language competency. Our three levels correlate to the European standard:

- Introduction = A Levels
- Fluency = B Levels
- Expression = C Levels

The majority of foreign language learners are satisfied at a B Level and a few continue on. But the level at which you want to speak a foreign language is your choice. There is no requirement to continue to the highest level, and most people never do as a B Level becomes their comfort zone.

Glossika Publications

Each Glossika publication comes in four formats:

- Print-On-Demand paperback text
- E-book text (available for various platforms)
- Glossika Mass Sentence audio files
- Glossika Spaced Repetition audio files

Some of our books include International Phonetic Alphabet (IPA) as well. Just check for the IPA mark on our covers.

We strive to provide as much phonetic detail as we can in our IPA transcriptions, but this is not always possible with every language.

As there are different ways to write IPA, our books will also let you know whether it's an underlying pronunciation (phonemic) with these symbols: / /, or if it's a surface pronunciation (phonetic) with these symbols: [ ].

IPA is the most scientific and precise way to represent the sounds of foreign languages. Including IPA in language training guides is taking a step away from previous decades of language publishing. We embrace the knowledge now available to everybody via online resources like Wikipedia which allow anybody to learn the IPA: something that could not be done before without attending university classes.

To get started, just point your browser to Wikipedia's IPA page to learn more about pronouncing the languages we publish.

4 Secrets of the Mass Sentence Method

When learning a foreign language it's best to use full sentences for a number of reasons:

1. Pronunciation—In languages like English, our words undergo a lot of pronunciation and intonation changes when words get strung together in sentences which has been well analyzed in linguistics. Likewise it is true with languages like Chinese where the pronunciations and tones from individual words change once they appear in a sentence. By following the intonation and prosody of a native speaker saying a whole sentence, it's much easier to learn rather than trying to say string each word together individually.

2. Syntax—the order of words, will be different than your own language. Human thought usually occurs in complete ideas. Every society has developed a way to express those ideas linearly by first saying what happened (the verb), or by first saying who did it (the agent), etc. Paying attention to this will accustom us to the way others speak.

3. Vocabulary—the meanings of words, never have just one meaning, and their usage is always different. You always have to learn words in context and which words they're paired with. These are called collocations. To "commit a crime" and to "commit to a relationship" use two different verbs in most other languages. Never assume that learning "commit" by itself will give you the answer. After a lifetime in lexicography, Patrick Hanks "reached the alarming conclusion that words don't have meaning," but rather that "definitions listed in dictionaries can be regarded as presenting meaning potentials rather than meanings as such." This is why collocations are so important.

4. Grammar—the changes or morphology in words are always in flux. Memorizing rules will not help you achieve fluency. You have to experience them as a native speaker says them, repeat them as a native speaker would, and through mass amount of practice come to an innate understanding of the inner workings of a language's morphology. Most native speakers can't explain their own grammar. It just happens.

How to Use GMS and GSR

The best way to use GMS is to find a certain time of day that works best for you where you can concentrate. It doesn't have to be a lot of time, maybe just 30 minutes at most is fine. If you have more time, even better. Then schedule that time to be your study time every day.

Try to tackle anywhere from 20 to 100 sentences per day in the GMS. Do what you're comfortable with.

Review the first 50 sentences in the book to get an idea of what will be said. Then listen to the A files. If you can, try to write all the sentences down from the files as dictation without looking at the text. This will force you to differentiate all the sounds of the language. If you don't like using the A files, you can switch to the C files which only have the target language.

After dictation, check your work for any mistakes. These mistakes should tell you a lot that you will improve on the next day.

Go through the files once again, repeating all the sentences. Then record yourself saying all the sentences. Ideally, you should record these sentences four to five days in a row in order to become very familiar with them.

All of the activities above may take more than one day or one setting, so go at the pace that feels comfortable for you.

If this schedule is too difficult to adhere to, or you find that dictation and recording is too much, then take a more relaxed approach with the GSR files. The GSR files in most cases are shorter than twenty minutes, some go over due to the length of the sentences. But this is the perfect attention span that most people have anyway. By the end of the GSR files you should feel pretty tired, especially if you're trying to repeat everything.

The GSR files are numbered from Day 1 to Day 100. Just do one every day, as all the five days of review sentences are built in. It's that simple! Good luck.

Sentence Mining

Sentence mining can be a fun activity where you find sentences that you like or feel useful in the language you're learning. We suggest keeping your list of sentences in a spreadsheet that you can re-order how you wish.

It's always a good idea to keep a list of all the sentences you're learning or mastering. They not only encompass a lot of vocabulary and their actual usage, or "collocations", but they give you a framework for speaking the language. It's also fun to keep track of your progress and see the number of sentences increasing.

Based on many tests we've conducted, we've found that students can reach a good level of fluency with only a small number of sentences. For example, with just 3000 sentences, each trained 10 times over a period of 5 days, for a total of 30,000 sentences (repetitions), can make a difference between a completely mute person who is shy and unsure how to speak and a talkative person who wants to talk about everything. More importantly, the reps empower you to become a stronger speaker.

The sentences we have included in our Glossika courses have been carefully selected to give you a wide range of expression. The sentences in our fluency modules target the kinds of conversations that you have discussing day-to-day activities, the bulk of what makes up our real-life conversations with friends and family. For some people these sentences may feel really boring, but these sentences are carefully selected to represent an array of discussing events that occur in the past, the present and the future, and whether those actions are continuous or not, even in languages where such grammar is not explicitly marked—especially in these languages as you need to know how to convey your thoughts. The sentences are transparent enough that they give you the tools to go and create dozens of more sentences based on the models we give you.

As you work your way through our Fluency Series the sentences will cover all aspects of grammar without actually teaching you grammar. You'll find most of the patterns used in all the tenses and aspects, passive and active (or ergative as is the case in some languages we're developing), indirect speech, and finally describing events as if to a policeman. The sentences also present some transformational patterns you can look out for. Sometimes we have more than one way to say something in our own language, but maybe only one in a foreign language. And the opposite is true where we may only have one way to say something whereas a foreign language may have many.

Transformation Drills

A transformation is restating the same sentence with the same meaning, but using different words or phrasing to accomplish this. A transformation is essentially a translation, but inside the same language. A real example from Glossika's business module is:

- Could someone help me with my bags?
- Could I get a hand with these bags?

You may not necessarily say "hand" in a foreign language and that's why direct translation word-for-word can be dangerous. As you can see from these two sentences, they're translations of each other, but they express the same meaning.

To express yourself well in a foreign language, practice the art of restating everything you say in your mother language. Find more ways to say the same thing.

There are in fact two kinds of transformation drills we can do. One is transformation in our mother language and the other is transformation into our target language, known as translation.

By transforming a sentence in your own language, you'll get better at transforming it into another language and eventually being able to formulate your ideas and thoughts in that language. It's a process and it won't happen over night. Cultivate your ability day by day.

Build a bridge to your new language through translation. The better you get, the less you rely on the bridge until one day, you won't need it at all.

Translation should never be word for word or literal. You should always aim to achieve the exact same feeling in the foreign language. The only way to achieve this is by someone who can create the sentences for you who already knows both languages to such fluency that he knows the feeling created is exactly the same.

In fact, you'll encounter many instances in our GMS publications where sentences don't seem to match up. The two languages are expressed completely differently, and it seems it's wrong. Believe us, we've not only gone over and tested each sentence in real life situations, we've even refined the translations several times to the point that this is really how we speak in this given situation.

Supplementary Substitution Drills

Substitution drills are more or less the opposite of transformation drills. Instead of restating the same thing in a different way, you're saying a different thing using the exact same way. So using the example from above we can create this substitution drill:

- Could someone help me with my bags?
- Could someone help me with making dinner?

In this case, we have replaced the noun with a gerund phrase. The sentence has a different meaning but it's using the same structure. This drill also allows the learner to recognize a pattern how to use a verb behind a preposition, especially after being exposed to several instances of this type.

We can also combine transformation and substitution drills:

- Could someone help me with my bags?
- Could someone give me a hand with making dinner?

So it is encouraged that as you get more and more experience working through the Glossika materials, that you not only write out and record more and more of your own conversations, but also do more transformation and substitution drills on top of the sentences we have included in the book.

Memory, The Brain, and Language Acquisition

by Michael Campbell

We encounter a lot of new information every day that may or may not need to be memorized. In fact, we're doing it all the time when we make new friends, remembering faces and other information related to our friends.

After some experience with language learning you'll soon discover that languages are just like a social landscape. Except instead of interconnected friends we have interconnected words. In fact, looking at languages in this way makes it a lot more fun as you get familiar with all the data.

Since languages are natural and all humans are able to use them naturally, it only makes sense to learn languages in a natural way. In fact studies have found, and many students having achieved fluency will attest to, the fact that words are much easier to recognize in their written form if we already know them in the spoken form. Remember that you already own the words you use to speak with. The written form is just a record and it's much easier to transfer what you know into written form than trying to memorize something that is only written.

Trying to learn a language from the writing alone can be a real daunting task. Learning to read a language you already speak is not hard at all. So don't beat yourself up trying to learn how to read a complicated script like Chinese if you have no idea how to speak the language yet. It's not as simple as one word = one character. And the same holds true with English as sometimes many words make up one idea, like "get over it".

What is the relationship between memory and sleep? Our brain acquires experiences throughout the day and records them as memories. If these memories are too common, such as eating lunch, they get lost among all the others and we find it difficult to remember one specific memory from the others. More importantly such memories leave no impact or impression on us. However, a major event like a birth or an accident obviously leaves a bigger impact. We attach importance to those events.

Since our brain is constantly recording our daily life, it collects a lot of useless information. Since this information is both mundane and unimportant to us, our brain has a built-in mechanism to deal with it. In other words, our brains dump the garbage every day. Technically speaking our memories are connections between our nerve cells and these connections lose strength if they are not recalled or used again.

During our sleep cycles our brain is reviewing all the events of the day. If you do not recall those events the following day, the memory weakens. After three sleep cycles, consider a memory gone if you haven't recalled it. Some memories can be retained longer because you may have anchored it better the first time you encountered it. An anchor is connecting your memory with one of your senses or another pre-existing memory. During your language learning process, this won't happen until later in your progress. So what can you do in the beginning?

A lot of memory experts claim that making outrageous stories about certain things they're learning help create that anchor where otherwise none would exist. Some memory experts picture a house in their mind that they're very familiar with and walk around that house in a specific pre-arranged order. Then all the objects they're memorizing are placed in that house in specific locations. In order to recall them, they just walk around the house.

I personally have had no luck making outrageous stories to memorize things. I've found the house method very effective but it's different than the particular way I use it. This method is a form of "memory map", or spatial memory, and for me personally I prefer using real world maps. This probably originates from my better than average ability to remember maps, so if you can, then use it! It's not for everybody though. It really works great for learning multiple languages.

What do languages and maps have in common? Everything can be put on a map, and languages naturally are spoken in locations and spread around and change over time. These changes in pronunciations of words creates a word history, or etymology. And by understanding how pronunciations change over time and where populations migrated, it's quite easy to remember a large number of data with just a memory map. This is how I anchor new languages I'm learning. I have a much bigger challenge when I try a new language family. So I look for even deeper and longer etymologies that are shared between language families, anything to help me establish a link to some core vocabulary. Some words like "I" (think Old English "ic") and "me/mine" are essentially the same roots all over the world from Icelandic (Indo-European) to Finnish (Uralic) to Japanese (Altaic?) to Samoan (Austronesian).

I don't confuse languages because in my mind every language sounds unique and has its own accent and mannerisms. I can also use my memory map to position myself in the location where the language is spoken and imagine myself surrounded by the people of that country. This helps me adapt to their expressions and mannerisms, but more importantly, eliminates interference from other languages. And when I mentally set myself up in this way, the chance of confusing a word from another language simply doesn't happen.

When I've actually used a specific way of speaking and I've done it several days in a row, I know that the connections in my head are now strengthening and taking root. Not using them three days in a row creates a complete loss, however actively using them (not passively listening) three days in a row creates a memory that stays for a lifetime. Then you no longer need the anchors and the memory is just a part of you.

You'll have noticed that the Glossika training method gives a translation for every sentence, and in fact we use translation as one of the major anchors for you. In this way 1) the translation acts as an anchor, 2) you have intelligible input, 3) you easily start to recognize patterns. Pattern recognition is the single most important skill you need for learning a foreign language.

A lot of people think that translation should be avoided at all costs when learning a foreign language. However, based on thousands of tests I've given my students over a ten-year period, I've found that just operating in the foreign language itself creates a false sense of understanding and you have a much higher chance of hurting yourself in the long run by creating false realities.

I set up a specific test. I asked my students to translate back into their mother tongue (Chinese) what they heard me saying. These were students who could already hold conversations in English. I found the results rather shocking. Sentences with certain word combinations or phrases really caused a lot of misunderstanding, like "might as well" or "can't do it until", resulted in a lot of guesswork and rather incorrect answers.

If you assume you can think and operate in a foreign language without being able to translate what's being said, you're fooling yourself into false comprehension. Train yourself to translate everything into your foreign language. This again is an anchor that you can eventually abandon when you become very comfortable with the new language.

Finally, our brain really is a sponge. But you have to create the structure of the sponge. Memorizing vocabulary in a language that you don't know is like adding water to a sponge that has no structure: it all flows out.

In order to create a foreign language structure, or "sponge", you need to create sentences that are natural and innate. You start with sentence structures with basic, common vocabulary that's easy enough to master and start building from there. With less than 100 words, you can build thousands of sentences to fluency, slowly one by one adding more and more vocabulary. Soon, you're speaking with natural fluency and you have a working vocabulary of several thousand words.

If you ever learn new vocabulary in isolation, you have to start using it immediately in meaningful sentences. Hopefully sentences you want to use. If you can't make a sentence with it, then the vocabulary is useless.

Vocabulary shouldn't be memorized haphazardly because vocabulary itself is variable. The words we use in our language are only a tool for conveying a larger message, and every language uses different words to convey the same message. Look for the message, pay attention to the specific words used, then learn those words. Memorizing words from a wordlist will not help you with this task.

Recently a friend showed me his wordlist for learning Chinese, using a kind of spaced repetition flashcard program where he could download a "deck". I thought it was a great idea until I saw the words he was trying to learn. I tried explaining that learning these characters out of context do not have the meanings on his cards and they will mislead him into a false understanding, especially individual characters. This would only work if they were a review from a text he had read, where all the vocabulary appeared in real sentences and a story to tell, but they weren't. From a long-term point of view, I could see that it would hurt him and require twice as much time to re-learn everything. From the short-term point of view, there was definitely a feeling of progress and mastery and he was happy with that and I dropped the issue.

Russian Background and Pronunciation

- Classification: Indo-European Language Family - East Slavic Branch
- Writing: Cyrillic

- Consonants:

  /m b p mʲ bʲ pʲ f v fʲ vʲ n d t ts s z l nʲ dʲ tʲ tsʲ sʲ zʲ rʲ lʲ ş z̢ r tɕ ɕ: ʑ: j g k x ɣ xʲ/ Unvoiced stops (p, t, k) are not aspirated /pˀ tˀ kˀ/ different from English. Letters appear in pairs of non-palatal /p/ and palatal /pʲ/.

- Vowels:

  Phonemic /a o e u ɨ i/, phonetic allophones: [ə ɐ æ ɪ ɛ ʊ ʉ ü ɘ ɨ]

- IPA: phonetic transcription displaying all the vowel allophones

- Intonation: stress is unpredictable and marked for learners in this publication
- Word Order: Subject - Verb - Object
- Adjective Order: Adjective - Noun
- Possessive Order: Noun - Genitive
- Adposition Order: Preposition - Noun
- Dependent Clause: Dependent - Noun, Noun - Relative Clause
- Verbs: Tense (present, past), Aspect (perfect, imperfect), Mood (indicative, subjunctive)
- Nouns: 36 declensions: 3 genders, 6 cases, singular/plural
- Pronouns: 1st/2nd/3rd, masculine/feminine/neuter, singular/plural, reflexive, 6 conjugations

Russian Pronunciation

Although Russian is written in the Cyrillic alphabet, the language is written phonemically and has a lot of rules for getting from the phonemic to the phonetic (actual) pronunciation. Without knowledge of where the stress falls in a Russian word, you won't have any way to know what is the actual pronunciation of the vowels, as these change allophonically depending on their relation to the stress. All the sentences in this book are written in phonemic Russian orthography with stress marked, a line of romanization showing the major vowel allophones, and finally a phonetic transcription in International Phonetic Alphabet (IPA) showing both vowel and consonant allophones. It makes little sense to memorize the position of stress in every Russian word, as sometimes the stress changes in each declension or conjugation, and a single adjective may have more than twenty declensions. Instead, get used to where the stress lands by listening to native speakers. The index to this book lists every declension and conjugation that occurs in the body text, together with stress and IPA for your reference.

It's a good idea to familiarize yourself with IPA. A lot of online tools such as Wikipedia can give you a head start, especially articles such as IPA where you can click on individual symbols in the chart, go to their respective pages and hear sample sound files. You can also read the Wikipedia article on Russian Phonology. Once you are familiar with IPA, you will be able to make good use of the surface pronunciations presented in this book. It would be difficult to take into account or even memorize all the phonological changes of Russian so this is why we've transcribed every sentence with all the details for your quick reference.

As in most Slavic languages, all the sounds of Russian can be categorized into one of two classes: palatalized and unpalatalized. Here is a list of all the sounds of Russian for your reference. Vowels are listed separately as stressed and unstressed.

CONSONANTS:

Cyrillic		IPA	
п	пь	p	p^j
б	бь	b	b^j
ф	фь	f	f^j
в	вь	v	v^j
м	мь	m	m^j
т	ть	t	t^j
д	дь	d	d^j
с	сь	s	s^j
з	зь	z	z^j
н	нь	n	n^j
л	ль	l-	l^j-

Cyrillic		IPA	
л	ль	-ɫʲ	-ɫʲ
р	рь	r	rʲ
ш	щ(ь)	ʂ	ɕ
ж	жь	z̪	ʑ
ч		tɕ	
ц	ць	ts	tsʲ
к	кь	k	kʲ
г	гь	g	gʲ
х	хь	x	xʲ
й		j	

STRESSED VOWELS:

Cyrillic	IPA
á	á
э́	ɛ́
ы́	ɨ́
ó	ọ́
ý	ú
я́	ʲá
é	ʲɛ́
и́	ʲí
ё	ʲọ́
ю́	ʲú
Also:	
é_ь as in семь	ʲɛ́_ʲ
я́_ь as in пять	ʲǽ_ʲ
ю́_ь as in йюнь	ʲʉ́_ʲ

PRE-STRESS VOWELS:

Cyrillic	IPA
a-	ɐ-
o-	ɐ-
э-	ɛ-
ы-	ɨ-
у-	ʊ-
я-	ʲɪ-
е-	ʲɪ-
и-	ʲɪ-
ю-	ʲü-

Also, if two unstressed {a} or {o} appear before the stress, the first one becomes a schwa:	
a_a, o_a, o_o, a_o	ə_ɐ

If any unstressed {a} or {o} appear together before the stress, they are both pronounced [ɐ]:	
-aa-, -oa-, -oo-, -ao-	-ɐɐ-

Notice that {a, o} both reduce to [ɐ], and {я, е, и} reduce to ʲɪ/.

POST-STRESS VOWELS:

Cyrillic	IPA
-a	-ə
-o	-ə
-э	-ɛ
-ы	-ɨ
-у	-ʊ
-я	-ʲə/-ʲɪ
-е	-ʲɪ
-и	-ʲɪ

Cyrillic	IPA
-ю	^{j}u

{я} is only pronounced [^{j}ə] if preceded by a vowel. Otherwise it is pronounced [^{j}ɪ].

Forbidden Letter Combinations:

{ши}	ş+^{j}ɪ	→it must be pronounced [şɨ] (the {ши} spelling is allowed)
{жи}	z̧+^{j}ɪ	→it must be pronounced [z̧ɨ] (the {жи} spelling is allowed)
{кы}	k+ɨ	→it must be pronounced [k^{j}ɪ]; the spelling usually reflects this as {ки}
{хы}	x+ɨ	→it must be pronounced [x^{j}ɪ]; the spelling usually reflects this as {хи}

There are other combinations and elisions that occur in Russian. Whenever in doubt regarding Russian pronunciation, be sure to reference the IPA transcription for the most detailed analysis. The romanization provided is easier to read but does not offer as much detail.

Vocabulary: Russian

Prepositions

about	о
above	выше
according to	в соответствии с
across	через
after	после
against	против
among	между
around	около
as	как
as far as	насколько
as well as	а также
at	в
because of	из-за
before	до
behind	за
below	ниже
beneath	под
beside	рядом с
between	между
beyond	вне
but	но
by	по
close to	близко к
despite	несмотря на

down	вниз
due to	из-за
during	во время
except	за исключением
except for	за исключением
far from	далеко от
for	для
from	от
in	в
in addition to	в дополнение к
in front of	перед
in spite of	несмотря на
inside	внутри
inside of	внутри
instead of	вместо
into	в
near	около
near to	рядом с
next	следующий
next to	рядом с
of	из
on	по
on behalf of	от имени
on top of	в верхней части
opposite	напротив
out	из
outside	за пределами
outside of	за пределами
over	за

per	в
plus	плюс
prior to	до
round	около
since	с
than	чем
through	через
till	до
to	к
toward	к
under	под
unlike	в отличие от
until	до
up	вверх
via	через
with	с
within	в
without	без

Pronouns

I	я
you (sg)	ты
he	он
she	она
we	мы
you (pl)	вы
they	они
me (acc)	меня, мне, мной

you (acc)	тебя, тебе, тобой
him (acc)	[н]его, ему, нём
her (acc)	[н]её, ей, ей
us (acc)	нас, нам, нами
you (pl-acc)	вас, вам, вами
them (acc)	[н]их, им, ими
my (gen)	мой, моя, мое, мои...
your (gen)	твой, твоя, твое, твои...
his (gen)	его
her (gen)	её
our (gen)	наш, наше, наша, наши...
your (pl-gen)	ваш, ваше, ваша, ваши...
their (gen)	их
mine (gen)	у меня
yours (gen)	у тебя
his (gen)	у него
hers (gen)	у неё
ours (gen)	у нас
yours (pl-gen)	у вас
theirs (gen)	у них

Interrogatives

how	как
what	что
who	кто
why	почему
how many/much	сколько
how long	как дольго

how often	как часто
which	который
when	когда
where	где

Days

Monday	понедельник
Tuesday	вторник
Wednesday	среда
Thursday	четверг
Friday	пятница
Saturday	суббота
Sunday	воскресенье

Adjectives

a few	несколько
bad	плохой
big	большой
bitter	горький
clean	чистый
correct	правильный
dark	тёмный
deep	глубокий
difficult	трудный
dirty	грязный
dry	сухой
easy	лёгкий
empty	пустой

expensive	дорогой
fast	быстрый
few	несколько
foreign	иностранный
fresh	свежий
full	полный
good	хороший
hard	жесткий
heavy	тяжёлый
inexpensive	недорогой
light	светлый
little	маленький
local	местный
long	длинный
many	многие
much	много
narrow	узкий
new	новый
noisy	шумный
old	старый
part	часть
powerful	мощный
quiet	тихий
salty	соленый
short person	короткий
slow	медленный
small	маленький
soft	мягкий
some	некоторые

sour	кислый
spicy	острый
sweet	сладкий
tall	высокий
thick	толстый
thin	тонкий
very	очень
weak	слабый
wet	мокрый
whole	целое
wide	широкий
wrong	неправильный
young	молодой

Adverbs

absolutely	абсолютно
ago	тому назад
almost	почти
alone	в одиночку
already	уже
always	всегда
anywhere	где угодно
away	прочь
barely	едва
carefully	осторожно
everywhere	везде
fast	быстро
frequently	часто

hard	жёсткий
hardly	вряд ли
here	здесь
home	дома
immediately	немедленно
last night	вчера вечером
lately	за последнее время
later	позже
mostly	главным образом
never	никогда
next week	на следующей неделе
now	в настоящее время
nowhere	нигде
occasionally	иногда
out	из
over there	вон там
pretty	довольно
quickly	быстро
quite	вполне
rarely	редко
really	на самом деле
recently	недавно
right now	прямо сейчас
seldom	редко
slowly	медленно
sometimes	иногда
soon	скоро
still	по-прежнему
then	затем

there	там
this morning	сегодня утром
today	сегодня
together	вместе
tomorrow	завтра
tonight	сегодня вечером
usually	обычно
very	очень
well	хорошо
yesterday	вчера
yet	ещё
afterwards	после того
until...only then	не... до...
afternoon	днём
enough	достаточно
often	часто
certainly	конечно
probably	возможно, может быть
evening	вечером
ever do	когда-нибудь делать
ever have	когда-нибудь сделать
never do	никогда не делать
never have	никогда не сделали
once	когда-то сделал, один раз

Conjunctions

also	также
and	и

because	потому что
but	но
furthermore	более того
however	однако
or (in questions)	или
or else, otherwise	либо
so	так
so that	так что

Glossika Mass Sentences

GMS #2001 - 2100

2001

EN Can you remind me to call Sandra tomorrow?

RU Мо́жешь напо́мнить мне позвони́ть Са́ндре за́втра?

ROM móžiś napómnjɪt' mnjɛ pəzvanít' sándrjɪ závtrə?

IPA mᵂǫ́zj̇ç nɐpᵂǫ́mnʲɪtʲ mnʲɛ pəzvɐnʲítʲ sándrʲɪ záftrə?

2002

EN Who taught you to drive?

RU Кто тебя́ учи́л води́ть?

ROM kto tjɪbjá ućíl vadít'?

IPA ktǫ tʲɪbʲá ʊtçíɫ vɐdʲítʲ?

2003

EN I didn't move the piano by myself. I got somebody to help me.

RU Я не сам передви́нул (♀сама́ передви́нула) пиани́но, мне помогли́.

ROM ja njɪ sam pjɪrɪdvínul (♀samá pjɪrɪdvínulə) pjɪanínə, mnjɛ pəmaglí.

IPA ʲa nʲɪ sam pʲɪrʲɪdvʲínuɫ (♀sɐmá pʲɪrʲɪdvʲínʊlə) pʲɪɐnʲínə, mnʲɛ pəmɐɡlʲí.

2004

EN Diego said the switch was dangerous, and warned me not to touch it.

RU Диéго сказáл, что выключáтель слóман, и предупредил, чтобы я его не трóгал (♀ трóгала).

ROM djɪjégə skazál, što vɪkljućátjel' slómən, i prɪduprɪdíl, štóbɪ ja jɪvó njɪ trógəl (♀ trógələ).

IPA dʲɾʲégə skɐzáł, stɔ vɪklʲütçátʲɪlʲ slómən, ɪ prʲɪdʊprʲɪdʲíł, stɔ́bɨ ʲa ʲɪvʷɔ́ nʲɪ trógəł (♀ trógələ).

2005

EN I was warned not to touch the switch.

RU Меня предупредили не трóгать выключáтель.

ROM mjɪnjá prɪduprɪdíljɪ njɪ trógət' vɪkljućátjel'.

IPA mʲɪnʲá prʲɪdʊprʲɪdʲílʲɪ nʲɪ trógətʲ vɪklʲütçátʲɪlʲ.

2006

EN Stan suggested I ask you for advice.

RU Стэн предложил, чтобы я спросил (♀ спросила) твоегó совéта.

ROM stɛn prɪdlažíl, štóbɪ ja sprasíl (♀ sprasílə) tvajɪvó savjétə.

IPA stɛn prʲɪdlɐʐíł, stɔ́bɨ ʲa sprɐsʲíł (♀ sprɐsʲílə) tfɐʲɪvʷɔ́ sɐvʲétə.

2007

EN I wouldn't advise staying in that hotel. > I wouldn't
advise anybody to stay in that hotel.

RU Я бы не советовал (♀ советовала) останавливаться
в том отеле.

ROM ja bɨ njɪ savjétəvəl (♀ savjétəvələ) əstanávljɪvət'sjɪ v
tom atéljɪ.

IPA ʲa bɨ nʲɪ sɐvʲétəvəɫ (♀ sɐvʲétəvələ) əstɐnávlʲɪvətʲsʲɪ f
tom ɐtélʲɪ.

2008

EN They don't allow parking in front of the building. >
They don't allow people to park in front of the
building.

RU Они не разрешают парковаться перед зданием.

ROM aní njɪ rɪzrɪšájut pərkavát'sjɪ pjérjɪd zdánjɪjɪm.

IPA ɐnʲí nʲɪ rɐzrʲɪšáʲüt pərkɐvátʲsʲɪ pʲérʲɪd zdánʲɪrʲɪm.

2009

EN Parking isn't allowed in front of the building. > You
aren't allowed to park in front of the building.

RU Парковка перед зданием запрещена.

ROM parkóvkə pjérjɪd zdánjɪjɪm zaprɪççɪná.

IPA pɐrkʷófkə pʲérʲɪd zdánʲɪrʲɪm zɐprʲɪççɨná.

2010

EN I made him promise that he wouldn't tell anybody what happened.

RU Я заставил (♀заставила) его пообещать, что он никому не расскажет о том, что произошло. > Я заставил (♀заставила) его пообещать не рассказывать о произошедшем.

ROM ja zastávjıl (♀zastávjılə) jıvó paabjıççát', što on njıkamú njı rısskážıt a tom, što prəjızašló. > ja zastávjıl (♀zastávjılə) jıvó paabjıççát' njı rısskázıvət' a prəjızašjédšım.

IPA ʲa zɐstávʲıɫ (♀zɐstávʲılə) ʲɪvʷǫ́ pɐɐbʲıççátʲ, ştǫ on nʲıkɐmú nʲı rɐsskázı̇t ɐ tǫm, ştǫ prə ʲɪzɐ̇sló. > ʲa zɐstávʲıɫ (♀zɐstávʲılə) ʲɪvʷǫ́ pɐɐbʲıççátʲ nʲı rɐsskázı̇vət ʲ ɐ prə ʲɪzɐ̇sétʂım.

2011

EN Hot weather makes me feel tired.

RU Жара меня утомляет.
ROM žırá mjınjá utamljájıt.
IPA zı̇rá mʲınʲá ʋtɐmlʲǽʲıt.

2012

EN Her parents wouldn't let her go out alone.

RU Её родители не разрешили бы ей пойти одной.
ROM jıjó radítjeljı njı rızrıšíljı bı jej pajtí adnój.
IPA ʲrʲǫ́ rɐdʲítʲılʲı nʲı rɐzrʲışílʲı bı ʲej pɐjtʲí ɐdnój.

2013

EN Let me carry your bag for you.

RU Позвóль мне понестú твою сýмку. > Давáй я помогý тебé донестú сýмку.

ROM pazvól' mnjɛ panjıstí tvajú súmku. > daváj ja pəmagú tjıbjé danjıstí súmku.

IPA pɐzvʷɑ̯lʲ mnʲɛ pɐnʲɪstʲí tɕɐʲú súmkʊ. > dɐváj ʲa pəmɐgú tʲɪbʲé dɐnʲɪstʲí súmkʊ.

2014

EN We were made to wait for two (2) hours.

RU Мы бы́ли вы́нуждены ждать два часá.

ROM mɪ bíljɪ vínuždjɪnɪ ždat' dva ćısá.

IPA mɨ bílʲɪ vínʊʐdʲɪnɨ ʐdatʲ dva tɕɪsá.

2015

EN My lawyer said I shouldn't say anything to the police. > My lawyer advised me not to say anything to the police.

RU Мой адвокáт сказáл, что мне не стóит говорúть чтó-либо полúции. > Мой адвокáт посовéтовал ничегó не говорúть полúции.

ROM moj ədvakát skazál, što mnjɛ njɪ stójɪt gəvarít' štó-ljɪbə palítsɪjɪ. > moj ədvakát pəsavjétəvəl njɪćıvó njɪ gəvarít' palítsɪjɪ.

IPA mʷoj ədvɐkát skɐzál, ʂtʊ mnʲɛ nʲɪ stɑ̯ɪt gəvɐrʲítʲ ʂtɑ̯-lʲɪbə pɐlʲítsʲɪ. > mʷoj ədvɐkát pəsɐvʲétəvəɫ nʲɪtɕɪvʷɑ̯ nʲɪ gəvɐrʲítʲ pɐlʲítsʲɪ.

2016

EN   I was told that I shouldn't believe everything he says.
> I was warned not to believe anything he says.

RU   Мне сказа́ли, что не сто́ит ве́рить всему́, что он
говори́т. > Меня́ предупреди́ли не ве́рить всему́,
что он говори́т.

ROM mnjɛ skazáljɪ, što njɪ stójɪt vjérjɪt' vsjɪmú, što on
gəvarít. > mjɪnjá prɪduprɪdíljɪ njɪ vjérjɪt' vsjɪmú, što
on gəvarít.

IPA mnʲɛ skɐzálʲɪ, ʂtɔ nʲɪ stǫ́ɪt vʲérʲɪtʲ fsʲɪmú, ʂtɔ ǫn
gəvɐrʲít. > mʲɪnʲá prʲɪdʊprʲɪdʲílʲɪ nʲɪ vʲérʲɪtʲ fsʲɪmú, ʂtɔ
ǫn gəvɐrʲít.

2017

EN   If you have a car, you're able to get around more
easily. > Having a car enables you to get around
more easily.

RU   Е́сли у тебя́ есть маши́на, тебе́ про́ще
передвига́ться по го́роду. > Нали́чие маши́ны
де́лает передвиже́ние по го́роду про́ще.

ROM jésljɪ u tjɪbjá jest' mašínə, tjɪbjé próççɪ pjɪrɪdvjɪgát'sjɪ
pa górədu. > nalíćɪjɪ mašínɪ djéləjɪt pjɪrɪdvjɪžjénjɪjɪ
pa górədu próççɪ.

IPA ʲéslʲɪ u tʲɪbʲá ʲestʲ mɐʂínə, tʲɪbʲé próççɪ pʲɪrʲɪdvʲɪgátʲsʲɪ
pɐ gʷórədʊ. > nɐlʲítçɪ̈ɪ mɐʂínɪ dʲéləɪt pʲɪrʲɪdvʲɪzɛ́nʲɪ̈rʲɪ
pɐ gʷórədʊ próççɪ̈.

2018

EN I know I locked the door. I clearly remember locking it. > I remembered to lock the door, but I forgot to shut the windows.

RU Я уве́рен (♀уве́рена), что закры́л (♀закры́ла) дверь. Я чётко по́мню, как закры́л (♀закры́ла) её. > Я закры́л (♀закры́ла) дверь, но забы́л (♀забы́ла) закры́ть о́кна.

ROM ja uvjérjın (♀uvjérjınə), što zakríl (♀zakrílə) dvjer'. ja ćjótkə pómnju, kak zakríl (♀zakrílə) jıjó. > ja zakríl (♀zakrílə) dvjer', no zabíl (♀zabílə) zakrít' óknə.

IPA ʲa ʊvʲérʲɪn (♀ʊvʲérʲɪnə), ʂto zɐkrɨ́ɫ (♀zɐkrɨ́lə) dvʲerʲ. ʲa tɕɕ́tkə pʷómnʲü, kak zɐkrɨ́ɫ (♀zɐkrɨ́lə) ʲɾʲɕ́. > ʲa zɐkrɨ́ɫ (♀zɐkrɨ́lə) dvʲerʲ, no zɐbɨ́ɫ (♀zɐbɨ́lə) zɐkrɨ́tʲ óknə.

2019

EN He could remember driving along the road just before the accident, but he couldn't remember the accident itself.

RU Он по́мнил, как вёл маши́ну до моме́нта ава́рии, но саму́ ава́рию ника́к не мог вспо́мнить.

ROM on pómnjıl, kak vjól mašínu da mamjéntə avárjıjı, no samú avárjıju njıkák njı mog vspómnjıt'.

IPA on pʷómnʲɪɫ, kak vʲɕ́ɫ mɐʂínʊ dɐ mɐmʲéntə ɐvárʲʲɾʲɪ, no sɐmú ɐvárʲɾʲü nʲɪkák nʲɪ mʷog fspʷómnʲɪtʲ.

2020

EN Please remember to mail the letter on your way to work.

RU Пожа́луйста, не забу́дь отпра́вить письмо́ по доро́ге на рабо́ту.

ROM pažálujstə, njı zabúd' atprávjıt' pjıs'mó pa darógjı na rıbótu.

IPA pɐʑálujstə, nʲɪ zɐbúdʲ ɐtrávʲɪtʲ pʲɪsʲmʷ ǿ pɐ dɐrǿgʲɪ na rɐbʷ ǿtʊ.

2021

EN I now regret saying what I said. I shouldn't have said it.

RU Тепе́рь я сожале́ю о том, что сказа́л (♀ сказа́ла). Мне не сто́ило э́того говори́ть.

ROM tjıpjér' ja səžıljéju a tom, što skazál (♀ skazálə). mnjɛ njı stójılə étəvə gəvarít'.

IPA tʲɪpʲérʲ ʲa səʑɪlʲéʲü ɐ tom, ʂtʊ skɐzáɫ (♀ skɐzálə). mnʲɛ nʲɪ stǿɪlə étəvə gəvɐrʲítʲ.

2022

EN It began to get cold, and he regretted not wearing his coat.

RU Начина́ло холода́ть, и он пожале́л, что не наде́л пальто́.

ROM naćınálə həladát', i on pəžıljél, što njı nadjél pal'tó.

IPA nɐtɕɪnálə xəlɐdátʲ, ɪ on pəʑɪlʲéɫ, ʂtʊ nʲɪ nɐdʲéɫ pɐlʲtǿ.

2023

EN We regret to inform you that we cannot offer you the job.

RU Нам о́чень жаль, но мы вы́нуждены отказа́ть вам в приёме на рабо́ту.

ROM nam óćɪn' žal', no mɪ vínuždjɪnɪ ətkazát' vam v prɪjómjɪ na rɪbótu.

IPA nam ọ́tɕɨnʲ z̨alʲ, nọ mɨ vínʊz̨dʲɪnɨ ətkɐzátʲ vam f prʲɪʲẹ́mʲɪ na rɐbʷọ́tʊ.

2024

EN The president went on talking for hours.

RU Речь президе́нта продолжа́лась вот уже́ не́сколько часо́в.

ROM rjeć' prɪzjɪdjéntə prədalžáləs' vot užjɛ́ njɛ́skəl'kə ćɪsóv.

IPA rʲetɕʲ prʲɪzʲɪdʲɛ́ntə prədɐłz̨áləsʲ vʷọt ʊz̨ɨ́ nʲɛ́skəlʲkə tɕɨsọ́f.

2025

EN After discussing the economy, the president then went on to talk about foreign policy.

RU По́сле пробле́м эконо́мики, президе́нт перешёл к обсужде́нию междунаро́дной поли́тики.

ROM póslјɪ prabljɛ́m ɛkanómjɪkjɪ, prɪzjɪdjɛ́nt pjɪrɪšjól k absuždjénjɪju mjɪždunaródnəj palítjɪkjɪ.

IPA pʷọ́slʲɪ prɐblʲɛ́m ɛkɐnọ́mʲɪkʲɪ, prʲɪzʲɪdʲɛ́nt pʲɪrʲɪʂọ́ł k ɐpsʊz̨dʲénʲɪʲʊ̈ mʲɪz̨dʊnɐrọ́dnəj pɐlʲítʲɪkʲɪ.

2026

EN We need to change. We can't go on living like this.

RU Мы должны́ измени́ться, так бо́льше жить нельзя́.

ROM mɪ dalžní jɪzmjɪnít'sjɪ, tak ból'šɪ žɪt' njɪl'zjá.

IPA mɨ dɐɫzɲí ʲɪzmʲɪɲítʲsʲɪ, tak bʷólʲʂɨ zɨ̯tʲ nʲɪlʲzʲá.

2027

EN Don't bother locking the door. I'll be right back.

RU Мо́жешь не закрыва́ть дверь, я ско́ро верну́сь.

ROM móžɪś njɪ zakrɪvát' dvjér', ja skórə vjɪrnús'.

IPA mʷóʐɨ̯ɕ nʲɪ zɐkrɨvátʲ dvʲérʲ, ʲa skʷórə vʲɪrnúsʲ.

2028

EN I lent you some money a few months ago. — Are you sure? I don't remember you lending me money.

RU Я за́нял (♀заня́ла) тебе́ де́ньги не́сколько ме́сяцев наза́д. — Ты уве́рен (♀уве́рена)? Я не по́мню тако́го.

ROM ja zanjál (♀zanjálə) tjɪbjé djén'gjɪ njéskəl'kə mjésjatsɪv nazád. — tɪ uvjérjɪn (♀uvjérjɪnə)? ja njɪ pómnju takóvə.

IPA ʲa zɐɲáɫ (♀zɐɲálə) tʲɪbʲé dʲénʲgʲɪ nʲéskəlʲkə mʲésʲɪtsɨv nɐzát. — tɨ ʊvʲérʲɪn (♀ʊvʲérʲɪnə)? ʲa nʲɪ pʷómnʲü tɐkʷóvə.

2029

EN Did you remember to call your mother? — Oh no, I completely forgot. I'll call her tomorrow.

RU Ты не забы́л (♀забы́ла) позвони́ть ма́ме? — О, нет, я совсе́м забы́л (♀забы́ла)! Позвоню́ ей за́втра.

ROM tɪ njɪ zabíl (♀zabílə) pəzvanít' mámjɪ? — o, njɛt, ja savsjém zabíl (♀zabílə)! pəzvanjú jej závtrə.

IPA tɨ nʲɪ zɐbɨ́ɫ (♀zɐb́ilə) pəzvɐnʲítʲ mámʲɪ? — ɐ, nʲɛt, ʲa sɐfsʲém zɐbɨ́ɫ (♀zɐbílə)! pəzvɐnʲú ʲej záftrə.

2030

EN Chandra joined the company nine (9) years ago and became assistant manager after two (2) years.

RU Чэ́ндра пришёл в компа́нию де́вять лет наза́д и стал ассисте́нтом ме́неджера спустя́ два го́да.

ROM ćéndrə prɪšjól v kampánjɪju djévjat' ljet nazád i stal assjɪstjéntəm mjénjedžɪrə spustjá dva gódə.

IPA tɕéndrə prʲɪʂǫ́ɫ f kɐmpánʲrʲü dʲévʲɪtʲ lʲet nɐzád ɪ staɫ ɐssʲɪstʲéntəm mʲénʲɪdzɨrə spʊstʲá dva gʷǫ́də.

2031

EN A few years later, he went on to become the manager of the company.

RU Че́рез не́сколько лет он стал ме́неджером компа́нии.

ROM ćjérjɪz njéskəl'kə ljet on stal mjénjedžɪrəm kampánjɪjɪ.

IPA tɕérʲɪz nʲéskəlʲkə lʲet on staɫ mʲénʲɪdzɨrəm kɐmpánʲrʲɪ.

2032

EN I tried to keep my eyes open, but I couldn't.

RU Я стара́лся (♀стара́лась) держа́ть глаза́ откры́тыми, но у меня́ ника́к не получа́лось.

ROM ja starálsjı (♀staráləs') djıržát' glazá atkrítımjı, no u mjınjá njıkák njı palućáləs'.

IPA ʲa stɐráts^jı (♀stɐráləs^j) dʲırzát^j glɐzá ɐtkrítɨm^jı, nɐ u m^jın^já n^jıkák n^jı pɐlʊtɕáləs^j.

2033

EN Please try to be quiet when you come home. Everyone will be asleep.

RU Постара́йся, пожа́луйста, быть поти́ше, когда́ вернёшься домо́й. Все уже́ бу́дут спать.

ROM pəstarájsjı, pažálujstə, bıt' patíšı, kagdá vjırnjóssjı damój. vsjɛ užjé búdut spat'.

IPA pəstɐrájs^jı, pɐʐálʊjstə, bɨt^j pɐt^jíʂɨ, kɐgdá v^jırn^jǿɕs^jı dɐm^wój. fs^jɛ ʊʐɨ́ búdʊt spat^j.

2034

EN We couldn't find anywhere to stay. We tried every
hotel in town, but they were all full.

RU Мы не могли́ найти́ ме́сто переночева́ть. Мы
позвони́ли во все оте́ли го́рода, но нигде́ не́ было
свобо́дных номеро́в (мест).

ROM mɪ njɪ maglí najtí mjéstə pjɪrmaćɪvát'. mɪ pəzvaníljɪ
va vsjɛ atjéljɪ górədə, no njɪgdjé njé bɪlo svabódnɪh
namjɪróv (mjest).

IPA mɨ nʲɪ mɐɡlʲí nɐjtʲí mʲéstə pʲɪrʲmɐtɕɪvátʲ. mɨ pəzvɐnʲílʲɪ
vɐ fsʲɛ ɐtʲélʲɪ ɡʷórədə, nǫ nʲɪɡdʲé nʲé bɨlə svɐbʷódnɨx
nɐmʲɪrʷóf (mʲest).

2035

EN The photocopier doesn't seem to be working. — Try
pressing the green button.

RU Ка́жется, копирова́льный аппара́т не рабо́тает. —
Попро́буй нажа́ть на зелёную кно́пку.

ROM kážɪtsjɪ, kəpjɪravál'nɪj əpparát njɪ rɪbótəjɪt. —
papróbuj nažát' na zjɪljónuju knópku.

IPA kázɨtsʲɪ, kəpʲɪrɐválʲnɨj əppɐrát nʲɪ rɐbʷótəʲɪt. —
pɐpróbʊj nɐzátʲ na zʲɪlʲǫ́nʊü knópkʊ.

2036

EN I need to get more exercise. > I need to start
working out more.

RU Мне ну́жно бо́льше занима́ться спо́ртом.

ROM mnjɛ núžnə ból'šɪ zanjɪmát'sjɪ spórtəm.

IPA mnʲɛ núz̟nə bʷólʲsɨ zɐnʲɪmátʲsʲɪ spʷórtəm.

2037

EN He needs to work harder if he wants to make progress.

RU Ему́ ну́жно бо́льше рабо́тать, е́сли он хо́чет доби́ться успе́ха.

ROM jɪmú núžnə ból'šɪ rɪbótət', jéslʲɪ on hóćɪt dabít'sjɪ uspjɛ́hə.

IPA ʲɪmú núz̨nə bʷɔ́lʲs̨ɨ rɐbʷɔ́tətʲ, ʲéslʲɪ ọn xɔ́tɕɪt dɐbʲítʲsʲɪ ʊspʲéxə.

2038

EN My cellphone needs to be charged. > My cellphone needs charging.

RU Мне ну́жно заряди́ть телефо́н.

ROM mnjɛ núžnə zaradít' tjɪljɪfón.

IPA mnʲɛ núz̨nə zɐrʲɪdʲítʲ tʲɪlʲɪfʷón.

2039

EN Do you think my pants need to be washed? > Do you think my pants need washing?

RU Ду́маешь, мне ну́жно постира́ть э́ти штаны́? > Ду́маешь, мои́ штаны́ нужда́ются в сти́рке?

ROM dúməješ, mnjɛ núžnə pastjɪrát' étjɪ štaní? > dúməješ, maí štaní nuždájutsjɪ v stírkjɪ?

IPA dúmə ʲɪ ɕ, mnʲɛ núz̨nə pɐstʲɪrátʲ étʲɪ s̨tɐní? > dúmə ʲɪ ɕ, mɐ ʲí s̨tɐní nʊz̨dáʲ üts ʲɪ f stʲírkʲɪ?

2040

EN They needed help to clean up after the party, so everybody helped clean up.

RU Им нужна́ была́ по́мощь в убо́рке по́сле вечери́нки, поэ́тому все помогли́ убра́ться.

ROM im nužná bılá póməçç' v ubórkjı pósljı vjıćırínkjı, paétəmu vsjɛ pəmaglí ubrát'sjı.

IPA ʲim nʊzná bɨlá pʷóm`əçç`ʲ v ʊbʷórkʲı pʷóslʲı vʲıtɕırʲínkʲı, pʀétəmʊ fsʲɛ pəmʀglʲí ʊbrátʲsʲı.

2041

EN I need your help to move this table. > Do you think you could help me move this table?

RU Мне нужна́ твоя́ по́мощь, что́бы передви́нуть э́тот стол. > Мо́жешь помо́чь мне передви́нуть стол?

ROM mnjɛ nužná tvajá póməçç', štóbı pjırıdvínut' étət stol. > móžıś pamóć' mnjɛ pjırıdvínut' stol?

IPA mnʲɛ nʊzná tfʀʲá pʷóməçç'ʲ, ʂtóbɨ pʲırʲıdvʲínʊtʲ étət stoɫ. > mʷóʑɨtɕ pʀmʷótɕʲ mnʲɛ pʲırʲıdvʲínʊtʲ stoɫ?

2042

EN I don't like him, but he has a lot of problems. I can't help feeling sorry for him.

RU Он мне не нра́вится, но у него́ мно́го пробле́м, и мне его́ жаль.

ROM on mnjɛ njı nrávjıtsjı, no u njıvó mnógə prabljém, i mnjɛ jıvó žal'.

IPA on mnʲɛ nʲı nrávʲıtsʲı, no u nʲıvʷó mnógə prʀblʲém, ı mnʲɛ ʲıvʷó zalʲ.

2043

EN She tried to be serious, but she couldn't help laughing.

RU Она́ попыта́лась быть серьёзной, но не смогла́ сдержа́ть смех.

ROM aná papıtáləs' bıt' sjırjóznəj, no njı smaglá sdjıržát' smjɛh.

IPA ɐná pɐpɪtáləsʲ bɨtʲ sʲɪrʲép̞znəj, nọ nʲɪ smɐglá zdʲɪrzátʲ smʲɛx.

2044

EN I'm sorry I'm so nervous. I can't help it.

RU Извини́, я так не́рвничаю. Ничего́ не могу́ с э́тим поде́лать.

ROM jızvjıní, ja tak njérvnjıćəju. njıćıvó njı magú s étjım padjélət'.

IPA ʲɪzvʲɪnʲí, ʲa tak nʲérvnʲɪtɕəʲü. nʲɪtɕɨvʷɔ́ nʲɪ mɐgú s étʲɪm pɐdʲélətʲ.

2045

EN Do you like getting up early? > Do you like to get up early?

RU Ты лю́бишь ра́но встава́ть?

ROM tı ljúbjıś ránə vstavát'?

IPA tɨ lʲʉ́bʲɪɕ ránə fstɐvátʲ?

2046

EN Vadim hates flying. > Vadim hates to fly.

RU   Вадим ненавидит летать.
ROM vadím njmavídjɪt ljɪtát'.
IPA vɐdʲím nʲmɐvʲídʲɪt ʎɪtátʲ.

2047

EN I love meeting people. > I love to meet people.

RU   Мне нравится встречаться с новыми людьми.
ROM mnjɛ nrávjɪtsjɪ vstrɪćát'sjɪ s nóvɪmjɪ ljud'mí.
IPA mnʲɛ nrávʲɪtsʲɪ fstrʲɪtɕátʲsʲɪ s nóvɨmʲɪ ʎüdʲmʲí.

2048

EN I don't like being kept waiting. > I don't like to be
      kept waiting.

RU   Я не люблю, когда меня заставляют ждать.
ROM ja njɪ ljubljú, kagdá mjmjá zəstavljájut ždat'.
IPA ʲa nʲɪ ʎübʎú, kɐgdá mʲɪnʲá zəstɐvʎǽ̈üt ʐdatʲ.

2049

EN I don't like friends calling me at work. > I don't like friends to call me at work.

RU Мне не нравится, когда друзья звонят мне на работу.

ROM mnjɛ njɪ nrávjɪtsjɪ, kagdá druz'já zvanját mnjɛ na rɪbótu.

IPA mnʲɛ nʲɪ nrávʲɪtsʲɪ, kɐgdá drʊzʲjá zvɐnʲát mnʲɛ na rɐbʷótʊ.

2050

EN Silvia likes living in London.

RU Сильвии нравится жить в Лондоне.

ROM síl'vjɪjɪ nrávjɪtsjɪ žɪt' v lóndənjɪ.

IPA sʲílʲvʲɪrʲɪ nrávʲɪtsʲɪ zɨtʲ v lóndənʲɪ.

2051

EN The office I worked at was horrible. I hated working there.

RU Офис, в котором я работал (♀работала) был ужасен. Я ненавидел (♀ненавидела) там работать.

ROM ófjɪs, v katórəm ja rɪbótəl (♀rɪbótələ) bɪl užásjɪn. ja njɪnavídjɪl (♀njɪnavídjɪlə) tam rɪbótət'.

IPA ófʲɪs, f kɐtórəm ʲa rɐbʷótəɫ (♀rɐbʷótələ) bɨɫ ʊzásʲɪn. ʲa nʲɪnɐvʲídʲɪɫ (♀nʲɪnɐvʲídʲɪlə) tam rɐbʷótətʲ.

2052

EN It's not my favorite job, but I like cleaning the kitchen as often as possible.

RU Э́то не са́мое моё люби́мое заня́тие, но я предпочита́ю убира́ться на ку́хне как мо́жно ча́ще.

ROM étə njı sáməjı majó ljubíməjı zanjátjıjı, no ja prıdpaćıtáju ubjırát'sjı na kúhnjı kak móžnə ćáççı.

IPA étə nʲı sáməʲı mɐʲé̹ l̡übʲíməʲı zɐnʲǽt̡ʲr̡ʲı, no̹ ʲa prʲıtpɐtɕıtáʲü ʋbʲırát̡ʲsʲı na kúxnʲı kak mʷó̹znə tɕáççɨ.

2053

EN I enjoy cleaning the kitchen. > I don't mind cleaning the kitchen.

RU Я люблю́ убира́ться на ку́хне. > Я не про́тив убо́рки на ку́хне.

ROM ja ljubljú ubjırát'sjı na kúhnjı. > ja njı prótjıv ubórkjı na kúhnjı.

IPA ʲa l̡übl̡ʲú ʋbʲırát̡ʲsʲı na kúxnʲı. > ʲa nʲı pró̹t̡ʲıv ʋbʷórkʲı na kúxnʲı.

2054

EN I'd love to meet your family.

RU Я с удово́льствием встре́чусь с твое́й семьёй.

ROM ja s udavól'stvjıjım vstrjéćus' s tvajéj sjımjój.

IPA ʲa s ʋdɐvʷó̹l̡ʲstf̡ʲr̡ʲım fstrʲétɕusʲ s tfɐ̹ʲéj sʲımʲé̹j.

2055

EN Would you prefer to have dinner now or later? — I'd prefer later.

RU Ты бы предпочёл (♀предпочла) поýжинать сейчáс или пóзже? — Лýчше пóзже.

ROM tɪ bɪ prɪdpaćjól (♀prɪdpaćlá) paúžɪnət' sjɪjćás ili póžžɪ? — lúćśɪ póžžɪ.

IPA tɨ bɨ prʲɪtpɐtɕə́ɫ (♀prʲɪtpɐtɕlá) pɐúʐɨnətʲ sʲɪjtɕás ʲiʲi pʷóʐʐɨ? — lútɕɕɨ pʷóʐʐɨ.

2056

EN Would you mind closing the door, please? — Not at all.

RU Ты бы не мог (♀моглá) закрыть дверь? — Да, конéчно.

ROM tɪ bɪ njɪ mog (♀maglá) zakrít' dvjer'? — da, kanjéćnə.

IPA tɨ bɨ nʲɪ mʷok (♀mɐglá) zɐkrʲítʲ dvʲerʲ? — da, kɐnʲétɕnə.

057

EN It's too bad we didn't see Hideki when we were in Tokyo. I would have liked to have seen him again.

RU Как жаль, что мы не ви́дели Хидеки, когда́ бы́ли в Токио. Я бы с удово́льствием встре́тился (♀встре́тилась) с ним сно́ва.

ROM kak žal', što mɪ njɪ vídjeljɪ hidjeki, kagdá bíljɪ v tokio. ja bɪ s udavól'stvjɪjɪm vstrjétjɪlsjɪ (♀vstrjétjɪləs') s nim snóvə.

IPA kak zalʲ, ş̩tǫ mɪ nʲɪ vʲídʲɪlʲɪ xʲidʲekʲi, kɐgdá bíɫʲɪ f tǫkʲio. ʲa bɪ s ʊdɐvʷóɫʲstf̩rʲɪm fstrʲétʲɪɫsʲɪ (♀fstrʲétʲɪləsʲ) s nʲim snǫ́və.

058

EN We'd like to have gone on vacation, but we didn't have enough money.

RU Мы бы хоте́ли пое́хать в о́тпуск, но у нас бы́ло недоста́точно де́нег.

ROM mɪ bɪ hatjéljɪ pajéhət' v ótpusk, no u nas bílə njɪdastátəčnə djénjɪg.

IPA mɪ bɪ xɐtélʲɪ pɐʲéxətʲ v ǫ́tpʊsk, nǫ u nas bíɫə nʲɪdɐstátətçnə dʲénʲɪk.

2059

EN Poor Hanako! I would hate to have been in her position.

RU Бе́дная Ха́нако! Я бы не хоте́л (♀хоте́ла) оказа́ться на её ме́сте.

ROM bjédnəjı hánəkə! ja bı njı hatjél (♀hatjélə) əkazát'sjı na jıjó mjéstjı.

IPA bʲédnəʲı xánəkə! ʲa bɨ nʲı xɐtʲéɫ (♀xɐtʲélə) əkɐzátʲsʲı na ʲrʲɵ mʲéstʲı.

2060

EN I'd love to have gone to the party, but it was impossible.

RU Я бы с удово́льствием пошёл (♀пошла́) на вечери́нку, но э́то бы́ло невозмо́жно.

ROM ja bı s udavól'stvjıjım pašjól (♀pašlá) na vjıċırínku, no étə bílə njıvazmóžnə.

IPA ʲa bɨ s ʊdɐvʷólʲstfʲrʲım pɐʂɵ́ɫ (♀pɐʂlá) na vʲıtɕırʲínkʊ, nọ étə bɨ́lə nʲıvɐzmʷóznə.

2061

EN I prefer driving over traveling by train. > I prefer to drive rather than travel by train.

RU Я бо́льше люблю́ путеше́ствовать на маши́не, чем на по́езде. > Мне бо́льше нра́вится е́здить на маши́не, чем на по́езде.

ROM ja ból'ši ljubljú putjɪšjéstvəvət' na mašínjɪ, ćɪm na pójezdjɪ. > mnje ból'ši nrávjɪtsjɪ jézdjɪt' na mašínjɪ, ćɪm na pójezdjɪ.

IPA ʲa bʷǫ́lʲʂɨ lʲüblʲú puʨɪʂéstfəvətʲ na mɐʂínʲɪ, ʨɛm na pʷǫ́ɪzdʲɪ. > mnʲɛ bʷǫ́lʲʂɨ nrávʲɪtsʲɪ ʲézdʲɪtʲ na mɐʂínʲɪ, ʨɛm na pʷǫ́ɪzdʲɪ.

2062

EN Tamara prefers to live in the country rather than in the city.

RU Тама́ра бо́льше лю́бит жить в дере́вне, чем в го́роде.

ROM tamárə ból'ši ljúbjɪt žɪt' v djɪrjévnjɪ, ćɪm v górədjɪ.

IPA tɐmárə bʷǫ́lʲʂɨ lʲúbʲɪt zɨtʲ v dʲɪrʲévnʲɪ, ʨɛm v gʷǫ́rədʲɪ.

2063

EN   I'd prefer to stay at home tonight rather than go to the movies. > I'd rather stay at home tonight than go to the movies.

RU   Я бы сегодня вечером предпочёл (♀предпочла) остаться дома, а не идти в кино. > Я лучше останусь дома, чем пойду в кино.

ROM ja bɪ sjɪvódnjɪ vjéćɪrəm prɪdpaćjól (♀prɪdpaćlá) astát'sjɪ dómə, a njɪ jɪdtí v kjɪnó. > ja lúćsɪ astánus' dómə, ćɪm pajdú v kjɪnó.

IPA ʲa bɨ sʲɪvʷódnʲɪ vʲétɕɨrəm prʲɪtpɐtɕǫ́ɫ (♀prʲɪtpɐtɕlá) ɐstátʲsʲɪ dǫ́mə, a nʲɪ ʲɪttʲí f kʲɪnǫ́. > ʲa lútɕɕɨ ɐstánʊsʲ dǫ́mə, tɕɛm pɐjdú f kʲɪnǫ́.

2064

EN   I'm tired. I'd rather not go out tonight, if you don't mind.

RU   Я устал (♀устала). Давай лучше сегодня вечером никуда не пойдём, если ты не против.

ROM ja ustál (♀ustálə). daváj lúćsɪ sjɪvódnjɪ vjéćɪrəm njɪkudá njɪ pajdjóm, jésljɪ tɪ njɪ prótjɪv.

IPA ʲa ʊstáɫ (♀ʊstálə). dɐváj lútɕɕɨ sʲɪvʷódnʲɪ vʲétɕɨrəm nʲɪkʊdá nʲɪ pɐjdʲǫ́m, ʲéslʲɪ tɨ nʲɪ prǫ́tʲɪf.

2065

EN I'll fix your car tomorrow. — I'd rather you did it today.

RU Я отремонти́рую твою́ маши́ну за́втра. — Бы́ло бы лу́чше, е́сли бы ты сде́лал э́то сего́дня.

ROM ja ətrɪmantíruju tvajú mašínu závtrə. — bílə bɪ lúćśɪ, jésljɪ bɪ tɪ sdjéləl étə sjɪvódnjɪ.

IPA ʲa ətrʲɪmɛntʲíruʲü tfɛʲú mɛ̞ʂínʊ záftrə. — bílə bɨ lútɕɕɨ, ʲéslʲɪ bɨ tɨ zdʲéləł étə sʲɪvʷ ódnʲɪ.

2066

EN Should I tell them, or would you rather they didn't know? — No, I'll tell them.

RU Мне рассказа́ть им или лу́чше, что́бы они́ не зна́ли? — Не на́до, я сам (♀сама́) им скажу́.

ROM mnjɛ rɪsskazát' im ili lúćśɪ, štóbɪ aní njɪ ználjɪ? — njɪ nádə, ja sam (♀samá) im skažú.

IPA mnʲɛ rəsskɛzátʲ ʲim ʲilʲi lútɕɕɨ, ʂtó̞bɨ ɛnʲí nʲɪ ználʲɪ? — nʲɪ nádə, ʲa sam (♀sɛmá) ʲim skɛ̞ʐú.

2067

EN I'd rather you didn't tell anyone what I said.

RU Лу́чше, что́бы ты никому́ не расска́зывал (♀расска́зывала) то, что я сказа́л (♀сказа́ла).

ROM lúćśɪ, štóbɪ tɪ njɪkamú njɪ rɪsskázɪvəl (♀rɪsskázɪvələ) to, što ja skazál (♀skazálə).

IPA lútɕɕɨ, ʂtó̞bɨ tɨ nʲɪkɛ̞mú nʲɪ rɛsskázɨvəł (♀rɛsskázɨvələ) tɔ, ʂtɔ ʲa skɛ̞záł (♀skɛ̞zálə).

2068

EN I'd prefer to take a taxi rather than walk home.

RU Я бы лу́чше взял (♀взяла́) такси́, чем шёл (♀шла) домо́й пешко́м.

ROM ja bɪ lúćsɪ vzjal (♀vzjálə) taksí, ćɪm šjól (♀šla) damój pjɪškóm.

IPA ʲa bɨ lútɕɕɨ vzʲaɫ (♀vzʲálə) tɐksʲí, tɕɛm ʂǿɫ (♀ʂla) dɛmʷǿj pʲɪʂkʷǿm.

2069

EN I'd prefer to go swimming rather than playing basketball.

RU Я бы предпочёл (♀предпочла́) попла́вать, чем игра́ть в баскетбо́л. > Лу́чше попла́вать, чем игра́ть в баскетбо́л.

ROM ja bɪ prɪdpaćjól (♀prɪdpaćlá) paplávət', ćɪm jɪgrát' v baskjɪtból. > lúćsɪ paplávət', ćɪm jɪgrát' v baskjɪtból.

IPA ʲa bɨ prʲɪtpɐtɕǿɫ (♀prʲɪtpɐtɕlá) pɐplávətʲ, tɕɛm ʲɪgrátʲ v bɛskʲɪtbʷǿɫ. > lútɕɕɨ pɐplávətʲ, tɕɛm ʲɪgrátʲ v bɛskʲɪtbʷǿɫ.

2070

EN Are you going to tell Vladimir what happened or would you rather I told him? — No, I'll tell him.

RU Ты собираешься рассказать Владимиру о произошедшем или лучше, чтобы я рассказал (♀рассказала)? — Нет, я расскажу.

ROM tɪ sabjɪrájeśsjɪ rɪsskazát' vladímjɪru a prəjɪzašjédšɪm ili lúćśɪ, štóbɪ ja rɪsskazál (♀rɪsskazálə)? — njɛt, ja rɪsskažú.

IPA tɨ sɐbʲɪráʲɪɕsʲɪ rəsskɐzátʲ vlɐdʲímʲɪrʊ ɐ prəʲɪzɐʂétʂɨm ʲilʲi lútɕɕɨ, ʂtóbɨ ʲa rəsskɐzáɫ (♀rəsskɐzálə)? — nʲɛt, ʲa rəsskɐzú.

2071

EN Before going out, I called Jianwen.

RU Перед выходом я позвонил (♀позвонила) Цзяньвэну.

ROM pjérjɪd víhədəm ja pəzvaníl (♀pəzvanílə) tszjan'vɛnu.

IPA pʲérʲɪd víxədəm ʲa pəzvɐnʲíɫ (♀pəzvɐnʲílə) tssʲænʲvɛnu.

2072

EN What did you do after finishing school?

RU Чем ты занимался (♀занималась) после окончания школы?

ROM ćɪm tɪ zanjɪmálsjɪ (♀zanjɪmáləs') pósljɪ əkanćánjɪjə škólɪ?

IPA tɕɛm tɨ zɐnʲɪmáɫsʲɪ (♀zɐnʲɪmáləsʲ) pʷóslʲɪ əkɐntɕánʲɪ̯ə ʂkʷólɨ?

2073

EN The burglars got into the house by breaking a window and climbing in.

RU Граби́тели забрали́сь в дом, разби́в окно́.

ROM grıbítjeljı zəbrılís' v dom, rızbív aknó.

IPA grɐbʲítʲɪlʲɪ zəbrɐlʲísʲ v dọm, rɐzbʲív ɐknọ́.

2074

EN You can improve your language skills by reading more.

RU Ты мо́жешь улу́чшить свои́ на́выки чте́ния, е́сли бу́дешь бо́льше чита́ть.

ROM tı móžıś ulúćsıt' svaí návıkjı ćtjénjıjə, jésljı búdjeś ból'šı ćıtát'.

IPA tɨ mʷọ́zj̞ɕ ʊlútɕɕɨtʲ svɐʲí návɨkʲɪ tɕtʲénʲɪɾʲə, ʲéslʲɪ búdʲɪɕ bʷọ́lʲʂɨ tɕɪtátʲ.

2075

EN She made herself sick by not eating properly.

RU Она́ довела́ себя́ до боле́зни тем, что непра́вильно пита́лась.

ROM aná davjılá sjıbjá da baljéznjı tjɛm, što njıprávjıl'nə pjıtáləs'.

IPA ɐná dɐvʲɪlá sʲɪbʲá dɐ bɐlʲéznʲɪ tʲɛm, ʂtọ nʲɪprávʲɪlʲnə pʲɪtáləsʲ.

2076

EN Many accidents are caused by people driving too fast.

RU Большое количество аварий происходит из-за
людей, которые ездят на высокой скорости.

ROM bal'šójı kalíćıstvə avárjıj prajıshódjıt iz-za ljudjéj,
katórıjı jézdjıt na vısókəj skórəstjı.

IPA bɐlʲsǫ́ʲɪ kɐlʲítɕɪstfə ɐvárʲɪj prɐʲɪsxǫ́dʲɪt ʲiz-za lʲüdʲéj,
kɐtórɪ̇ʲɪ ʲézdʲɪt na vɪsǫ́kəj skʷǫ́rəstʲɪ.

2077

EN We ran ten (10) kilometers without stopping.

RU Мы пробежали без остановки десять километров.

ROM mı prabjıžáljı bız əstanóvkjı djésjat' kjılamjétrəv.

IPA mɪ prɐbʲɪzálʲɪ bʲɪz əstɐnǫ́fkʲɪ dʲésʲɪtʲ kʲɪlɐmʲétrəf.

2078

EN It was a stupid thing to say. I said it without thinking.

RU Было глупо так говорить. Я сказал (♀ сказала) это,
не подумав.

ROM bílə glúpə tak gəvarít'. ja skazál (♀ skazálə) étə, njı
padúməv.

IPA bílə glúpə tak gəvɐrʲítʲ. ʲa skɐzáł (♀ skɐzálə) étə, nʲɪ
pɐdúməf.

2079

EN She needs to work without people disturbing her.

RU Ей необходи́мо порабо́тать, что́бы никто́ не
отвлека́л её.

ROM jej njɪəbhadímə pərɪbótət', štóbɪ njɪktó njɪ atvljɪkál
jɪjó.

IPA ʲej nʲɪəbxɐdʲímə pərɐbʷǫ́tətʲ, ṣtǫ́bɨ nʲɪktǫ́ nʲɪ ɐtfʎɪkáɫ
ʲɾʲǫ́.

2080

EN I have enough problems of my own without having to
worry about yours.

RU У меня́ и без тебя́ доста́точно пробле́м.

ROM u mjɪnjá i bɪs tjɪrbjá dastátəćnə prabljém.

IPA u mʲɪnʲá ɪ bʲɪs tʲɪbʲá dɐstátətɕnə prɐbʎʲém.

2081

EN Would you like to meet for lunch tomorrow? —
Sure, let's do lunch.

RU Ты не хо́чешь пойти́ пообе́дать за́втра? —
Коне́чно, дава́й.

ROM tɪ njɪ hóćɪś pajtí paabjédət' závtrə? — kanjéćnə, daváj.

IPA tɨ nʲɪ xǫ́tɕɪɕ pɐjtʲí pɐɐbʲédətʲ záftrə? — kɐnʲétɕnə,
dɐváj.

2082

EN   Are you looking forward to the weekend? — Yes, I
am.

RU   С нетерпе́нием ждёшь выходны́х? — Да.
ROM s njɪtjɪrpjénjɪjɪm ždjóś vɪhadníh? — da.
IPA s nʲɪtʲɪrpʲénʲɾʲɪm ʐɖʲǿɕ vɪxɐdnɪ́x? — da.

2083

EN   Why don't you go out instead of sitting at home all
the time?

RU   Почему́ ты не схо́дишь куда́-нибудь вме́сто того́,
чтоб сиде́ть всё вре́мя до́ма?
ROM paćɪmú tɪ njɪ shódjɪś kudá-njɪbud' vmjéstə tavó, štob
sjɪdjét' vsjó vrjémjɪ dómə?
IPA pɐtɕɪmú tɨ nʲɪ sxǿdʲɪɕ kʊdá-nʲɪbʊdʲ vmʲéstə tɐvʷǿ, ʂtɔp
sʲɪdʲétʲ fsʲǿ vrʲémʲɪ dǿmə?

2084

EN   We got into the exhibition without having to wait in
line.

RU   Мы прошли́ на вы́ставку без о́череди.
ROM mɪ prašlí na vístəvku bɪz óćɪrjedjɪ.
IPA mɨ prɐʂlʲí na vístəfku bʲɪz ǿtɕɪrʲɪdʲɪ.

2085

EN Victor got himself into financial trouble by borrowing too much money.

RU У Ви́ктора фина́нсовые пробле́мы из-за того́, что он занима́л сли́шком мно́го де́нег.

ROM u víktərə fjɪnánsəvɪjɪ prabljémɪ iz-za tavó, što on zanjɪmál slíškəm mnógə djénjɪg.

IPA u vʲíktərə fʲɪnánsəvɨ̈ʲɪ prɐblʲémɨ̈ ʲiz-za tɐvʷó, ʂtɔ ɔn zɐnʲɪmáɫ slʲíʂkəm mnǫ́gə dʲénʲɪk.

2086

EN Ramona lives alone. She's lived alone for fifteen (15) years. It's not strange for her.

RU Рамо́на живёт одна́. Она́ так живёт уже́ пятна́дцать лет. Она́ не нахо́дит э́то стра́нным.

ROM rɪmónə žɪvjót adná. aná tak žɪvjót užjé pjɪtnádtsət' ljet. aná njɪ nahódjɪt étə stránnɪm.

IPA rɐmʷónə zɨ̈vʲǫ́t ɐdná. ɐná tak zɨ̈vʲǫ́t ʊzɨ́ pʲɪtnáttsətʲ lʲet. ɐná nʲɪ nɐxǫ́dʲɪt étə stránnɨ̈m.

2087

EN She's used to it. She's used to living alone.

RU Она́ привы́кла к э́тому. Она́ привы́кла жить одна́.

ROM aná prɪvíklə k étəmu. aná prɪvíklə žɪt' adná.

IPA ɐná prʲɪvíklə k étəmu. ɐná prʲɪvíklə zɨ̈tʲ ɐdná.

2088

EN I bought some new shoes. They felt strange at first because I wasn't used to them.

RU Я купи́л (♀купи́ла) но́вые ту́фли. Снача́ла они́ мне показа́лись не о́чень удо́бными, потому́ что я тогда́ к ним ещё не привы́к (♀привы́кла).

ROM ja kupíl (♀kupílə) nóvɪjɪ túfljɪ. snaćálə aní mnjɛ pəkazáljɪs' njɪ óćɪn' udóbnɪmjɪ, pətamú što ja tagdá k nim jɪ̨ɕjó njɪ prɪvík (♀prɪvíklə).

IPA ʲa kʊpʲíł (♀kʊpʲílə) nóvʲɨɪ túfłʲɪ. snɐtɕálə ɐnʲí mnʲɛ pəkɐzálʲɪsʲ nʲɪ ɵ̨tɕɪnʲ ʊdɵ́bnɨmʲɪ, pətɐmú ʂtɵ ʲa tɐgdá k nʲim ʲɪ̨ɕɵ̨́ nʲɪ prʲɪvík (♀prʲɪvíklə).

2089

EN Our new apartment is on a very busy street. I expect we'll get used to the noise, but for now it's very annoying.

RU На́ша но́вая кварти́ра нахо́дится на о́чень шу́мной у́лице. Я ду́маю, что со вре́менем мы привы́кнем к шу́му, но пока́ что он си́льно раздража́ет.

ROM nášə nóvəjə kvartírə nahódjɪtsjɪ na óćɪn' šúmnəj úljɪtsɪ. ja dúməju, što sa vrjémjenjɪm mɪ prɪvíknjɪm k šúmu, no paká što on síl'nə rɪzdrɪžájɪt.

IPA náʂə nóvəʲə kfɐrtʲírə nɐxɵ́dʲɪtsʲɪ na ɵ̨tɕɪnʲ ʂúmnəj úlʲɪtsɨ. ʲa dúməʉ, ʂtɵ sɐ vrʲémʲɪnʲɪm mɨ prʲɪvíknʲɪm k ʂúmʊ, nɵ pɐká ʂtɵ ɵn sʲílʲnə rəzdrɐʐáʲɪt.

2090

EN Jamaal has a new job. He has to get up much earlier now than before. He finds it difficult because he isn't used to getting up so early.

RU У Джама́ла но́вая рабо́та. Тепе́рь по утра́м ему́ прихо́дится встава́ть гора́здо ра́ньше. И э́то о́чень тяжело́ для него́, потому́ что он не привы́к встава́ть так ра́но.

ROM u džɪmálə nóvəjə rɪbótə. tjɪpjér' pa utrám jɪmú prɪhódjɪtsjɪ vstavát' garázdə rán'šɪ. i étə óćɪn' tjɪžɪló dlja njɪvó, pətamú što on njɪ prɪvík vstavát' tak ránə.

IPA u dzɨmálə nóvəjə rʉbʷótə. tʲɪpʲérʲ pʉ ʊtrám jɪmú prʲɪxódʲɪtsʲɪ fstʌvátʲ gʉrázdə ránʲʂɨ. ɪ étə ótɕɪnʲ tʲɪzɨló dlʲa nʲɪvʷó, pətʉmú ʂtʊ ɔn nʲɪ prʲɪvík fstʌvátʲ tak ránə.

2091

EN Malika's husband is often away. She doesn't mind. She's used to him being away.

RU Муж Мали́ки ча́сто [нахо́дится] в командиро́вках. Но она́ не про́тив. Она́ привы́кла к тому́, что его́ ча́сто не быва́ет до́ма.

ROM muž malíkjɪ ćástə [nahódjɪtsjɪ] v kəmandjɪróvkəh. no aná njɪ prótjɪv. aná prɪvíklə k tamú, što jɪvó ćástə njɪ bɪvájɪt dómə.

IPA muz̪ mʉlʲíkʲɪ tɕástə [nʉxódʲɪtsʲɪ] f kəmʉndʲɪrófkəx. ʊná nʲɪ prótʲɪf. ʊná prʲɪvíklə k tʉmú, ʂtʊ ʲɪvʷó tɕástə nʲɪ bɨvájɪt dómə.

2092

EN Keiko had to get used to driving on the left when she moved back to Japan.

RU Кейко пришлóсь привыкáть к левосторóннему движéнию, когдá онá переéхала обрáтно в Япóнию.

ROM kjejko prišlós' prɪvɪkát' k ljɪvəstarónnjɪmu dvjɪžjénjɪju, kagdá aná pjɪrɪjɛ́hələ abrátnə v jɪpónjɪju.

IPA kʲejkʷo̞ prʲɪʂló̞sʲ prʲɪvɨkátʲ k lʲɪvəstɐró̞nnʲɪmʊ dvʲɪzɛ̞́nʲɪʲʊ̈, kɐgdá ɐná pʲɪrʲɪʲɛ́xələ ɐbrátnə v ʲɪpʷó̞nʲɪʲʊ̈.

2093

EN I'm used to driving on the left because I grew up in England.

RU Я привы́к (♀привы́кла) к левосторóннему движéнию, потомý что я вы́росла в Áнглии.

ROM ja prɪvík (♀prɪvíklə) k ljɪvəstarónnjɪmu dvjɪžjénjɪju, pətamú što ja vírəslə v ánglјɪjɪ.

IPA ʲa prʲɪvɨ́k (♀prʲɪvɨ́klə) k lʲɪvəstɐró̞nnʲɪmʊ dvʲɪzɛ̞́nʲɪʲʊ̈, pətɐmú ʂto̞ ʲa vɨ́rəslə v ánglʲɪʲɪ.

2094

EN I used to drive to work every day, but these days I usually ride my bike.

RU Ра́ньше я е́здил (♀е́здила) на рабо́ту на маши́не, но в после́днее вре́мя я е́зжу на велосипе́де.

ROM rán'šɪ ja jézdjɪl (♀jézdjɪlə) na rɪbótu na mašínjɪ, no v pasljédnjejɪ vrjémjɪ ja jéžžu na vjɪlasjɪpjédjɪ.

IPA rán⁽ʲ⁾sɪ̆ ʲa ʲézdʲɨɫ (♀ʲézdʲɪlə) na rɐbʷótʊ na mɐsín⁽ʲ⁾ɪ, nɔ f pɐslʲédn⁽ʲ⁾ɨ̆ɪ vrʲém⁽ʲ⁾ɪ ʲa ʲézzʊ na vʲɪlɐs⁽ʲ⁾ɪpʲéd⁽ʲ⁾ɪ.

2095

EN We used to live in a small town, but now we live in Los Angeles.

RU Ра́ньше мы жи́ли в ма́леньком городке́, но тепе́рь мы живём в Лос-А́нджелесе.

ROM rán'šɪ mɪ žíljɪ v máljen'kəm gəradkjé, no tjɪpjér' mɪ živjóm v las-ándžɪljesjɪ.

IPA rán⁽ʲ⁾sɪ̆ mɨ̆ zílʲ⁽ʲ⁾ɪ v mál⁽ʲ⁾ɪn⁽ʲ⁾kəm gərɐtkʲé, nɔ tʲɪpʲér⁽ʲ⁾ mɨ̆ zɨ̆vʲémv lɐs-ándzɨ̆l⁽ʲ⁾ɪs⁽ʲ⁾ɪ.

2096

EN We talked about the problem.

RU Мы обсуди́ли пробле́му.

ROM mɪ absudíljɪ prabljému.

IPA mɨ̆ ɐpsʊdʲílʲ⁽ʲ⁾ɪ prɐblʲémʊ.

2097

EN You should apologize for what you said.

RU Тебе́ сле́дует извини́ться за то, что ты сказа́л
(♀ сказа́ла).

ROM tjɪbjé sljédujɪt jɪzvjɪnít'sjɪ za to, što tɪ skazál
(♀ skazálə).

IPA tʲɪbʲé sʲédʊʲɪt ʲɪzvʲɪnʲítʲsʲɪ za tɔ, ʂtɔ tɨ skɐzáɫ
(♀ skɐzálə).

2098

EN You should apologize for not telling the truth.

RU Тебе́ сле́дует извини́ться за то, что ты не сказа́л
(♀ сказа́ла) пра́вду.

ROM tjɪbjé sljédujɪt jɪzvjɪnít'sjɪ za to, što tɪ njɪ skazál
(♀ skazálə) právdu.

IPA tʲɪbʲé sʲédʊʲɪt ʲɪzvʲɪnʲítʲsʲɪ za tɔ, ʂtɔ tɨ nʲɪ skɐzáɫ
(♀ skɐzálə) právdʊ.

2099

EN Have you succeeded in finding a job yet?

RU Как твой по́иски рабо́ты?

ROM kak tvaí pójɪskjɪ rɪbótɪ?

IPA kak tfɐʲí pʷóʲɪskʲɪ rɐbʷótɨ?

2100

EN They insisted on paying for dinner.

RU Они́ настоя́ли на опла́те за у́жин.
ROM aní nəstajáljı na aplátjı za úžın.
IPA ɐnʲí nəstɐˈjælʲɪ na ɐplátʲɪ za úzʲɪn.

GMS #2101 - 2200

2101

EN I'm thinking of buying a house.

RU Я подумываю о покупке дома.
ROM ja padúmɪvəju a pakúpkjɪ dómə.
IPA ʲa pɐdúmɨvəʲü ɐ pɐkúpkʲɪ dómə.

2102

EN I wouldn't dream of asking them for money.

RU Я бы не рискнул (♀рискнула) просить у них денег.
ROM ja bɪ njɪ rɪsknúl (♀rɪsknúlə) prasít' u nih djénjɪg.
IPA ʲa bɨ nʲɪ rʲɪsknúɫ (♀rʲɪsknúlə) prɐsʲítʲ u nʲix dʲénʲɪk.

2103

EN He doesn't approve of swearing.

RU Он не одобряет использование нецензурной лексики. > Он против использования ругательств в речи.
ROM on njɪ ədabrjájɪt jɪspól'zəvənjɪjɪ njɪtsɪnzúrnəj ljéksjɪkjɪ. > on prótjɪv jɪspól'zəvənjɪjɪ rugátjel'stv v rjéćɪ.
IPA on nʲɪ ədɐbrʲǽʲɪt ʲɪspʷóⱡʲzəvənʲrʲɪ nʲɪtsɨnzúrnəj ⱡʲéksʲɪkʲɪ. > on prótʲɪv ʲɪspʷóⱡʲzəvənʲrʲɪ rʊgátʲɪⱡʲstf v rʲétɕɨ.

2104

EN We've decided against moving to Australia.

RU Мы реши́ли не переезжа́ть в Австра́лию.
ROM mı rışíljı njı pjırıjıžžát' v avstráljıju.
IPA mɨ rʲɪşílʲɪ nʲɪ pʲɪrʲɪrʲɪzzátʲ v ɐfstrálʲrʲü.

2105

EN Do you feel like going out tonight?

RU Ты сего́дня в настрое́нии сходи́ть куда́-нибудь?
ROM tı sjıvódnjı v nəstrajénjıjı shadít' kudá-njıbud'?
IPA tɨ sʲɪvʷódnʲɪ v nəstrɐʲénʲrʲɪ sxɐdʲítʲ kudá-nʲɪbʊdʲ?

2106

EN I'm looking foward to meeting her.

RU Я с нетерпе́нием жду встре́чи с ней.
ROM ja s njıtjırpjénjıjım ždu vstrjéćı s njej.
IPA ʲa s nʲɪtʲɪrpʲénʲrʲɪm zdu fstrʲétɕɨ s nʲej.

2107

EN I congratulated Mira on getting a new job.

RU Я поздра́вил (♀поздра́вила) Ми́ру с но́вой рабо́той.
ROM ja pazdrávjıl (♀pazdrávjılə) míru s nóvəj rıbótəj.
IPA ʲa pɐzdrávʲɨɫ (♀pɐzdrávʲɪlə) mʲíru s nóvəj rɐbʷótəj.

2108

EN They accused us of telling lies.

RU Они́ обвини́ли нас во лжи.

ROM aní abvjɪníljɪ nas va lžɪ.

IPA ɐnʲí ɐbvʲɪnʲílʲɪ nas vɐ łzʲ.

2109

EN Nobody suspected the employee of being a spy.

RU Никто́ не подозрева́л сотру́дника в шпиона́же.

ROM njɪktó njɪ pədazrɪvál satrúdnjɪkə v špjɪanážɪ.

IPA nʲɪktó nʲɪ pədɐzrʲɪváł sɐtrúdnʲɪkə f ʂpʲɪɐnázʲ.

2110

EN What prevented you from coming to see us?

RU Что помеша́ло тебе́ (вам) прийти́ к нам?

ROM što pamjɪšálə tjɪbjé (vam) prɪjtí k nam?

IPA ʂto pɐmʲɪʂálə tʲɪbʲé (vam) prʲɪjtʲí k nam?

2111

EN The noise keeps me from falling asleep.

RU Э́тот шум не даёт мне засну́ть.

ROM étət šum njɪ dajót mnjɛ zasnút'.

IPA étət ʂum nʲɪ dɐjót mnʲɛ zɐsnútʲ.

2112

EN The rain didn't stop us from enjoying our vacation.

RU Дождь не помешáл нам насладúться нáшим óтпуском.

ROM dožd' njɪ pamjɪšál nam nəsladít'sjɪ nášɪm ótpuskəm.

IPA dǫẓdʲ nʲɪ pɐmʲɪṣáɫ nam nəslɐdʲítʲsʲɪ náṣɪm ǫ́tpʊskəm.

2113

EN I forgot to thank them for helping me.

RU Я забы́л (♀забы́ла) поблагодорúть их за пóмощь.

ROM ja zabíl (♀zabílə) pəbləgədarít' ih za póməçç'.

IPA ʲa zɐbíɫ (♀zɐbílə) pəbləgədɐrʲítʲ ʲix za pʷǫ́məççʲ.

2114

EN Please excuse me for not returning your call.

RU Извинú, что я не перезвонúл (♀перезвонúла) тебé.

ROM jɪzvjɪní, što ja njɪ pjɪrɪzvaníl (♀pjɪrɪzvanílə) tjɪbjé.

IPA ʲɪzvʲɪnʲí, ṣtǫ ʲa nʲɪ pʲɪrʲɪzvɐnʲíɫ (♀pʲɪrʲɪzvɐnʲílə) tʲɪbʲé.

2115

EN There's no point in having a car if you never use it.

RU Нет смы́сла в том, что у тебя́ есть машúна, éсли ты éю не пóльзуешься.

ROM njɛt smíslə v tom, što u tjɪbjá jest' mašínə, jésljɪ tɪ jéju njɪ pól'zujeśsjɪ.

IPA nʲɛt smíslə f tǫm, ṣtǫ u tʲɪbʲá ʲestʲ mɐṣínə, ʲéslʲɪ tɨ ʲéʲü nʲɪ pʷǫ́lʲzʊʲɪçsʲɪ.

2116

EN There was no point in waiting any longer, so we left.

RU Нé было смы́сла ждать да́льше, поэ́тому мы ушли́.
ROM njé bɪlo smíslə ždat' dál'šɪ, paétəmu mɪ ušlí.
IPA nʲé bɨlə smíslə z̪datʲ dálʲʂɨ, pɐétəmʊ mɨ ʊʂlʲí.

2117

EN There's nothing you can do about the situation, so there's no use worrying about it.

RU Ты ничего́ не мо́жешь сде́лать в да́нной ситуа́ции, поэ́тому нет смы́сла пережива́ть.
ROM tɪ njɪćɪvó njɪ móžɪś sdjélət' v dánnəj sjɪtuátsɪjɪ, paétəmu njet smíslə pjɪrɪžɪvát'.
IPA tɨ nʲɪtɕɪvʷɵ́ nʲɪ mʷɵ́zɨɕ zdʲélətʲ v dánnəj sʲɪtʊátsɨ̈ɪ, pɐétəmʊ nʲet smíslə pʲɪrʲɪzɨvátʲ.

2118

EN I live only a short walk from here, so it's not worth taking a taxi.

RU Я живу́ всего́ в пяти́ мину́тах отсю́да, так что нет смы́сла брать такси́.
ROM ja žɪvú vsjɪvó v pjɪtí mjɪnútəh atsjúdə, tak što njet smíslə brat' taksí.
IPA ʲa zɨvú fsʲɪvʷɵ́ f pʲɪtʲí mʲɪnútəx ɐtsʲúdə, tak ʂtɔ nʲet smíslə bratʲ tɐksʲí.

2119

EN Our flight was very early in the morning, so it wasn't worth going to bed.

RU Наш самолёт был óчень ра́но у́тром, так что нé бы́ло смы́сла ложи́ться спать.

ROM naš səmaljót bɪl óćɪn' ránə útrəm, tak što njé bɪlo smíslə lažít'sjɪ spat'.

IPA naṣ səmɐlʲét bɪɫ ótçin̪ʲ ránə útrəm, tak ṣto n̪ʲé bɪlə smíslə lɐzʲítʲsʲɪ spatʲ.

2120

EN What was the movie like? Was it worth seeing?

RU Как фильм? Сто́ит посмотре́ть?

ROM kak fil'm? stójɪt pəsmatrjét'?

IPA kak fʲilʲm? stój̞ɪt pəsmɐtrʲétʲ?

2121

EN Thieves broke into the house, but there was nothing worth stealing.

RU Граби́тели забрали́сь в дом, но там нé бы́ло ничего́, что мо́жно бы́ло бы укра́сть.

ROM grɪbítjeljɪ zəbrɪlís' v dom, no tam njé bɪlo njɪćɪvó, što móžnə bílə bɪ ukrást'.

IPA grɐbʲítʲɪlʲɪ zəbrɐlʲísʲ v do̞m, no̞ tam n̪ʲé bɪlə n̪ʲɪtçɪvʷó, ṣto̞ mʷóẓnə bílə bɨ ukrástʲ.

2122

EN I had no trouble finding a place to live.

RU У меня́ не́ было пробле́м с по́иском ме́ста, где жить.

ROM u mjɪnjá njé bɪlo prabljém s pójɪskəm mjéstə, gdjɛ žɪt'.

IPA u mʲɪnʲá nʲé bɨlə prɐblʲém s pʷɵ́ɪskəm mʲéstə, gdʲɛ zɨtʲ.

2123

EN Did you have any trouble getting a visa?

RU Бы́ли каки́е-нибудь пробле́мы с получе́нием ви́зы?

ROM bíljɪ kakíjɪ-njɪbud' prabljémɪ s palućjénjɪjɪm vízɪ?

IPA bɨ́lʲɪ kɐkʲjʲɪ-nʲɪbʊdʲ prɐblʲémɨ s pɐlʊtɕénʲrʲɪm vʲízɨ?

2124

EN People often have a lot of trouble reading my handwriting.

RU Обы́чно лю́ди с трудо́м понима́ют мой по́черк.

ROM abíćnə ljúdjɪ s trudóm panjɪmájut moj póćɪrk.

IPA ɐbɨ́tɕnə lʲúdʲɪ s trʊdóm pɐnʲɪmáʲüt mʷoj pʷótɕɪrk.

2125

EN I had trouble finding a place to live. > I had difficulty finding a place to live.

RU У меня́ бы́ли пробле́мы с по́иском ме́ста, где жить. > Бы́ло о́чень сло́жно найти́ ме́сто, где жить.

ROM u mjınjá bíljı prabljémı s pójıskəm mjéstə, gdjɛ žıt'. > bílə óćm' slóžnə najtí mjéstə, gdjɛ žıt'.

IPA u mʲɪnʲá bílʲɪ prɐblʲémɨ s pʷǿʲɪskəm mʲéstə, gdʲɛ zɨtʲ. > bílə ǿtɕinʲ slóznə nɐjtʲí mʲéstə, gdʲɛ zɨtʲ.

2126

EN He spent hours trying to repair the clock.

RU Он потра́тил мно́го вре́мени, пыта́ясь починить часы́.

ROM on patrátjıl mnógə vrjémjenjı, pıtájas' paćmít' ćısí.

IPA ɐn pɐtrátʲɪɫ mnǿgə vrʲémʲɪnʲɪ, pɨtáʲɪsʲ pɐtɕinʲítʲ tɕɨsí.

2127

EN I waste a lot of time daydreaming.

RU Я ча́сто вита́ю в облака́х, и поэ́тому теря́ю мно́го вре́мени впусту́ю .

ROM ja ćástə vjıtáju v əblakáh, i paétəmu tjırjáju mnógə vrjémjenjı vpustúju .

IPA ʲa tɕástə vʲɪtáʲü v əblɐkáx, ɪ pɐétəmu tʲɪrʲǽʲü mnǿgə vrʲémʲɪnʲɪ fpustúʲü .

2128

EN How often do you go swimming?

RU Как ча́сто ты хо́дишь пла́вать?
ROM kak ćástə tı hódjıś plávət'?
IPA kak tɕástə tɨ xǫ́dʲıɕ plávətʲ?

2129

EN When was the last time you went shopping?

RU Когда́ ты после́дний раз ходи́л (♀ходи́ла) в магази́н?
ROM kagdá tı pasljédnjıj raz hadíl (♀hadílə) v məgazín?
IPA kɐgdá tɨ pɐslʲédnʲıj ras xɐdʲíɫ (♀xɐdʲílə) v məgɐzʲín?

2130

EN I have a problem remembering people's names.

RU У меня́ пробле́мы с запомина́нием имён.
ROM u mjınjá prabljémı s zəpamjınánjıjım jımjón.
IPA u mʲınʲá prɐblʲémɨ s zəpɐmʲınánʲrʲım ʲımʲǫ́n.

2131

EN She had no difficulty getting a job.

RU Она́ без труда́ нашла́ но́вую рабо́ту.
ROM aná bıs trudá našlá nóvuju rıbótu.
IPA ɐná bʲıs trudá nɐʂlá nǫ́vuʲü rɐbʷǫ́tu.

2132

EN You won't have any trouble getting a ticket for the game.

RU Ты без труда́ доста́нешь биле́т на игру́.
ROM tɪ bɪs trudá dastánjeś bjɪljét na jɪgrú.
IPA tɨ bʲɪs trʊdá dɐstánʲɪɕ bʲɪlʲét na ʲɪgrú.

2133

EN I think you waste too much time watching television.

RU Я ду́маю ты теря́ешь сли́шком мно́го вре́мени за просмо́тром телеви́зора.
ROM ja dúməju tɪ tjɪrjájeś slíškəm mnógə vrjémjenjɪ za prasmótrəm tjɪljɪvízərə.
IPA ʲa dúmə⁰ü tɨ tʲɪrʲǽʲɪɕ slʲíʂkəm mnǫ́gə vrʲémʲɪnʲɪ za prɐsmʷǫ́trəm tʲɪlʲɪvʲízərə.

2134

EN It's hard to find a place to park downtown.

RU В це́нтре всегда́ о́чень сло́жно найти́ ме́сто для парко́вки.
ROM v tsjéntrjɪ vsjɪgdá óćɪn' slóžnə najtí mjéstə dlja parkóvkjɪ.
IPA f tséntrʲɪ fsʲɪgdá ǫ́tɕɨnʲ slǫ́ʐnə nɐjtʲí mʲéstə dlʲa pɐrkʷǫ́fkʲɪ.

2135

EN   I get lonely if there's nobody to talk to.

RU   Я чу́вствую себя́ одино́ко, е́сли нет кого́-то, с кем
мо́жно поболта́ть.

ROM ja ćústvuju sjɪbjá adjɪnókə, jésljɪ njɛt kavó-tə, s kjɛm
móžnə pəbaltát'.

IPA ʲa tɕúʊstfʊʲü sʲɪbʲá ɐdʲɪnǫ́kə, ʲɛslʲɪ nʲet kɐvʷǫ́-tə, s kʲɛm
mʷǫ́znə pəbɐɫtátʲ.

2136

EN   I need something to open this bottle with.

RU   Мне ну́жно что́-то, с по́мощью чего́ мо́жно
откры́ть э́ту буты́лку.

ROM mnjɛ núžnə štó-tə, s póməççju ćɪvó móžnə atkrít' étu
butílku.

IPA mnʲɛ núznə ʂtǫ́-tə, s pʷǫ́məççʲü tɕɪvʷǫ́ mʷǫ́znə ɐtkrítʲ
étʊ bʊtíɫkʊ.

2137

EN   They gave us some money to buy some food.

RU   Они́ да́ли нам де́нег, чтобы мы могли́ купи́ть
немно́го еды́.

ROM aní dáljɪ nam djénjɪg, štóbɪ mɪ maglí kupít' njɪmnógə
jɪdí.

IPA ɐnʲí dálʲɪ nam dʲénʲɪk, ʂtǫ́bɨ mɪ mɐɡlʲí kʊpʲítʲ nʲɪmnǫ́gə
ʲɪdí.

2138

EN Do you have much opportunity to practice your foreign language?

RU У тебя́ есть возмо́жность практикова́ть язы́к?
ROM u tjıbjá jest' vazmóžnəst' prıktjıkavát' jızík?
IPA u tʲıbʲá ʲestʲ vɐzmʷóʐnəstʲ praktʲıkɐvátʲ ʲızík?

2139

EN I need a few days to think about your proposal.

RU Мне ну́жно не́сколько дней, что́бы поду́мать над твои́м предложе́нием.
ROM mnjɛ núžnə njéskəl'kə dnjej, štóbı padúmət' nad tvaím prıdlažjénjıjım.
IPA mnʲɛ núʐnə nʲéskəlʲkə dnʲej, ʂtóbɨ pɐdúmətʲ nat tfɐʲím prʲıdlɐzénʲrʲım.

2140

EN Since there weren't any chairs for us to sit on, we had to sit on the floor.

RU Нам пришло́сь сиде́ть на полу́, потому́ что нам не хвати́ло сту́льев.
ROM nam prıšlós' sjıdjét' na palú, pətamú što nam njı hvatílə stúljıv.
IPA nam prʲıʂlós̪ʲ s̪ʲıdʲétʲ na pɐlú, pətɐmú ʂtɔ nam nʲı xfɐtʲílə stúlʲıf.

2141

EN I hurried so that I wouldn't be late.

RU Я поторопи́лся (♀поторопи́лась), что́бы не опозда́ть.
ROM ja pətərapílsjı (♀pətərapíləs'), štóbı njı əpazdát'.
IPA ʲa pətərɐpʲíɫsʲɪ (♀pətərɐpʲíləsʲ), ştǫ́bɨ nʲɪ əpɐzdátʲ.

2142

EN Leave early so that you won't miss the bus.

RU Вы́йди пора́ньше, что́бы успе́ть на авто́бус.
ROM víjdjı parán'šı, štóbı uspjét' na avtóbus.
IPA víjdʲɪ pɐránʲşɨ, ştǫ́bɨ ʊspʲétʲ na ɐftǫ́bʊs.

2143

EN She's learning English so that she can study in Australia.

RU Она́ изуча́ет англи́йский, что́бы учи́ться в Австра́лии.
ROM aná jızučájıt anglíjskjıj, štóbı učít'sjı v avstráljıjı.
IPA ɐná ʲɪzʊtɕáʲɪt ɐnglʲíjskʲɪj, ştǫ́bɨ ʊtɕítʲsʲɪ v ɐfstrálʲɪ̯ɪ.

2144

EN We moved to the city so that we could see our children more often.

RU Мы переéхали в гóрод, чтóбы чáще вúдеться с детьмú.

ROM mı pjırıjéhəljı v górəd, štóbı ćáççı vídjet'sjı s djıt'mí.

IPA mɨ pʲɪrʲɨʲéxəlʲɨ v gʷórət, ʂtǫ́bɨ tɕáççɨ vʲídʲɪtʲsʲɨ s dʲɪtʲmʲí.

2145

EN I put on warmer clothes so I wouldn't feel cold.

RU Я надевáю вéщи потеплéе, чтóбы не замёрзнуть.

ROM ja nadjıváju vjéççı patjıpljéjı, štóbı njı zamjórznut'.

IPA ʲa nɐdʲɪváʲü vʲéççɨ pɐtʲɪplʲéʲɨ, ʂtǫ́bɨ nʲɪ zɐmʲǫ́rznuʈʲ.

2146

EN I left Kenji my phone number so he'd be able to contact me.

RU Я остáвил (♀остáвила) свой нóмер телефóна Кенцзи, чтóбы он мог со мной связáться.

ROM ja astávjıl (♀astávjılə) svoj nómjır tjıljıfónə kjentszi, štóbı on mog sa mnoj svjızát'sjı.

IPA ʲa ɐstávʲɨł (♀ɐstávʲɨlə) svʷoj nǫ́mʲɨr tʲɨlʲɨfʷǫ́nə kʲentssʲi, ʂtǫ́bɨ on mʷǫk sɐ mnoj svʲɨzátʲsʲɨ.

2147

EN We whispered so that nobody could hear our conversation.

RU Мы говори́ли шёпотом, что́бы нас никто́ не услы́шал.

ROM mı gəvaríljı šjópətəm, štóbı nas njıktó njı uslíšəl.

IPA mɨ gəvɐrʲílʲɪ s̪ɵ́pətəm, s̪t̪ɵ́bɨ nas nʲɪktó nʲɪ ʊslís̪əɫ.

2148

EN Please arrive early so that we'll be able to start the meeting on time.

RU Пожа́луйста, приходи́те пора́ньше, что́бы мы могли́ нача́ть конфере́нцию во́время.

ROM pažálujstə, prıhadítjı parán'šı, štóbı mı maglí naćát' kanfjırjéntsıju vóvrjemjı.

IPA pɐʐálujstə, prʲɪxɐdʲítʲɪ pɐránʲs̪ɨ, s̪t̪ɵ́bɨ mɨ mɐɡlʲí nɐt̪ɕátʲ kɐnfʲɪrʲénts̪ɨ̈ü vʷɵ́vrʲɪmʲɪ.

2149

EN Sanjit locked the door so that he wouldn't be disturbed.

RU Са́нзит закры́л дверь, что́бы его́ никто́ не беспоко́ил.

ROM sánzjıt zakríl dvjer', štóbı jıvó njıktó njı bjıspakójıl.

IPA sánzʲɪt zɐkrɨ́ɫ dvʲerʲ, s̪t̪ɵ́bɨ ʲɪvʷɵ́ nʲɪktó nʲɪ bʲɪspɐkʷɵ́ʲɪɫ.

2150

EN I slowed down so that the car behind me could pass.

RU Я притормози́л (♀ притормози́ла), что́бы маши́на сза́ди могла́ прое́хать.

ROM ja prɪtərmazíl (♀ prɪtərmazílə), štóbɪ mašínə szádjɪ maglá prajéhət'.

IPA ʲa prʲɪtərmɐzʲíɫ (♀ prʲɪtərmɐzʲílə), ştóbɨ mɐşínə szádʲɪ mɐglá prɐʲéxətʲ.

2151

EN Do you think it's safe to drink this water? > Do you think this water is safe to drink?

RU Ду́маешь, э́ту во́ду мо́жно пить?

ROM dúməješ, étu vódu móžnə pit'?

IPA dúməʲɪɕ, étʊ vʷódʊ mʷóʐnə pʲitʲ?

2152

EN It was impossible to answer the questions on the exam. > They were impossible to answer.

RU Бы́ло невозмо́жно отве́тить на э́ти вопро́сы на экза́мене.

ROM býlə njɪvazmóžnə atvjétjɪt' na étjɪ vaprósɪ na ɛkzámjenjɪ.

IPA býlə nʲɪvɐzmʷóʐnə ɐtʲɕétʲɪtʲ na étʲɪ vɐprósɨ na ɛksámʲɪnʲɪ.

2153

EN It's interesting to talk to Veda. > She's interesting to talk to.

RU С Ве́дой о́чень интере́сно разгова́ривать. > Ве́да - интере́сный собесе́дник.

ROM s vjédəj óćin' jɪntjɪrjésnə rɪzgavárjɪvət'. > vjédə - jɪntjɪrjésnɪj sabjɪsjédnjɪk.

IPA s vʲédəj ótɕinʲ ʲmtʲɪrʲésnə rəzgɐvárʲɪvətʲ. > vʲédə - ʲmtʲɪrʲésnɨj sɐbʲɪsʲédnʲɪk.

2154

EN This is a difficult question for me to answer.

RU На э́тот вопро́с я затрудня́юсь отве́тить. > Мне сло́жно отве́тить на э́тот вопро́с.

ROM na étət vaprós ja zatrudnjájus' atvjétjɪt'. > mnjɛ slóžnə atvjétjɪt' na étət vaprós.

IPA na étət vɐprós ʲa zɐtrʊdnʲǽüsʲ ɐtfʲétʲɪtʲ. > mnʲɛ slóznə ɐtfʲétʲɪtʲ na étət vɐprós.

2155

EN It was nice of you to take me to the airport.

RU Бы́ло о́чень ми́ло с твое́й стороны́ проводи́ть меня́ до аэропо́рта.

ROM bílə óćin' mílə s tvajéj stəraní prəvadít' mjɪnjá da aɛrapórtə.

IPA bílə ótɕinʲ mʲílə s tfʲéj stərɐní prəvɐdʲítʲ mʲɪnʲá dɐ aɛrɐpʷórtə.

2156

EN It's foolish of Liting to quit her job when she needs the money.

RU Ли́тинг поступа́ет о́чень глу́по, уволня́ясь с рабо́ты в тот моме́нт, когда́ она́ нужда́ется в деньга́х.

ROM lítjɪng pastupájɪt óćɪn' glúpə, uvalnjájas' s rɪbótɪ v tot mamjént, kagdá aná nuždájetsjɪ v djɪn'gáh.

IPA lʲítʲɪnk pɐstupáʲɪt ótɕinʲ glúpə, ʊvɐɫnʲǽɪsʲ s rɐbʷótɨ f tɔt mɐmʲént, kɐgdá ɐná nʊzdáʲɪtsʲɪ v dʲɪnʲgáx.

2157

EN I think it was very unfair of him to criticize me.

RU Я ду́маю, с его́ сторо́ны бы́ло нече́стно критикова́ть меня́.

ROM ja dúməju, s jɪvó stərɑní bílə njɪćjésnə krɪtjɪkavát' mjɪnjá.

IPA ʲa dúməʲü, s ʲɪvʷó stərɐní bílə nʲɪtɕésnə krʲɪtʲɪkɐvátʲ mʲɪnʲá.

2158

EN I was sorry to hear that your father is ill.

RU Мне о́чень жаль слы́шать, что твой оте́ц бо́лен.

ROM mnjɛ óćɪn' žal' slíšət', što tvoj atjéts bóljɪn.

IPA mnʲɛ ótɕinʲ zalʲ slíʂətʲ, ʂtɔ tfʷoj ɐtʲéts bʷólʲɪn.

2159

EN Was Adrian surprised to see you?

RU Эдриан был удивлён, когда́ уви́дел тебя́?
ROM édrjɪən bɪl udjɪvljón, kagdá uvídjɪl tjɪbjá?
IPA édrʲɪən bɨɫ ʊdʲɪvlʲǿn, kɐgdá ʊvʲídʲɨɫ tʲɪbʲá?

2160

EN It was a long and tiring trip. We were glad to get
home.

RU Это была́ до́лгая, изнури́тельная пое́здка. Мы
бы́ли ра́ды верну́ться домо́й.
ROM étə bɪlá dólgəjɪ, jɪznurítjel'nəjɪ pajézdkə. mɪ bíljɪ rádɪ
vjɪrnút'sjɪ damój.
IPA étə bɨlá dǿɫgəʲɪ, ʲɪznʊrʲítʲɪlʲnəʲɪ pɐʲéstkə. mɨ bíʲlʲɪ rádɨ
vʲɪrnútʲsʲɪ dɐmʷǿj.

2161

EN If I have any more news, you'll be the first person to
know.

RU Е́сли у меня́ поя́вятся ещё каки́е-нибудь но́вости,
ты бу́дешь пе́рвым (пе́рвой), кто о них узна́ет.
ROM jésljɪ u mjɪnjá pajávjatsjɪ jɪ ɕ ɕjó kakíjɪ-njɪbud' nóvəstjɪ,
tɪ búdjeś pjérvɪm (pjérvəj), kto a nih uznájɪt.
IPA ʲéslʲɪ u mʲɪnʲá pɐʲǽvʲɪtsʲɪ ʲɪ ɕ ɕǿ kɐkʲjʲ ɪ-nʲɪbʊdʲ nǿvəstʲɪ, tɨ
búdʲɪ ɕ pʲérvɨm (pʲérvəj), ktǫ ɐ nʲix ʊznáʲɪt.

2162

EN The next plane to arrive at Gate Four (4) will be Flight five-one-two (512) from Beijing.

RU Сле́дующий самолёт, прибыва́ющий к вы́ходу четы́ре, - рейс 512 из Пеки́на.

ROM sljédujuҫҫɪj səmaljót, prɪbɪvájuҫҫɪj k víhədu ćɪtírjɪ, - rjejs 512 iz pjɪkínə.

IPA slʲédʊʲüҫҫɪj səmɐlʲǫ́t, prʲɪbɪváʲüҫҫɪj k víxədʊ tɕɪtírʲɪ, - rʲejs 512 ʲis pʲɪkʲínə.

2163

EN Everybody was late except me. I was the only one to arrive on time.

RU Все, кро́ме меня́, опозда́ли. Я был еди́нственным (♀была́ еди́нственной), кто прие́хал во́время.

ROM vsjɛ, krómjɪ mjɪnjá, əpazdáljɪ. ja bɪl jɪdínstvjɪnnɪm (♀bɪlá jɪdínstvjɪnnəj), kto prɪjéhəl vóvrjemjɪ.

IPA fsʲɛ, krǫ́mʲɪ mʲɪmʲá, əpɐzdálʲɪ. ʲa bɪɫ ʲɪdʲínstfʲɪnnɪm (♀bɪlá ʲɪdʲínstfʲɪnnəj), ktǫ prʲɪrʲéxəɫ vʷǫ́vrʲɪmʲɪ.

2164

EN Anastasia's a very good student. She's bound to pass the exam.

RU Анастаси́я - о́чень хоро́шая студе́нтка. Она́ непреме́нно сдаст экза́мен.

ROM ənəstasíjə - óćɪn' haróšəjə studjéntkə. aná njɪprɪmjénnə sdast ɛkzámjɪn.

IPA ənəstɐsʲíʲə - ǫ́tɕɪnʲ xɐrǫ́şəʲə stʊdʲéntkə. ɐná nʲɪprʲɪmʲénnə zdast ɛksámʲɪn.

2165

EN I'm likely to get home late tonight.

RU Похо́же, сего́дня я бу́ду до́ма по́здно.
ROM pahóži, sjɪvódnjɪ ja búdu dómə póznə.
IPA pɐxǫ́zɨ̞, sʲɪvʷǫ́dnʲɪ ʲa búdʊ dǫ́mə pʷǫ́znə.

2166

EN I was the second customer to complain to the restaurant manager.

RU Я был (♀была́) уже́ вторы́м клие́нтом, кото́рый пожа́ловался ме́неджеру рестора́на.
ROM ja bɪl (♀bɪlá) užjé vtarím kljɪjéntəm, katórɪj pažáləvəlsjɪ mjénjedžɪru rɪstaránə.
IPA ʲa bɨ̞ɫ (♀bɨ̞lá) ʊzʲɨ̞ ftɐrím kʲɪrʲéntəm, kɐtǫ́rɨ̞j pɐzáləvəɫsʲɪ mʲénʲɪdzɨ̞rʊ rʲɪstɐránə.

2167

EN That chair is not safe to stand on.

RU На э́тот стул встава́ть опа́сно.
ROM na étət stul vstavát' apásnə.
IPA na étət stuɫ fstɐvátʲ ɐpásnə.

2168

EN After such a long trip, you're bound to be tired.

RU Ты наверняка устáл (♀устáла) пóсле такóй дóлгой
поéздки.

ROM tɪ navjɪrnjɪká ustál (♀ustálə) pósljɪ takój dólgəj
pajézdkjɪ.

IPA tɨ nɐvʲɪrnʲɪká ʊstáɫ (♀ʊstálə) pʷósʲlʲɪ tɐkʷój dʷóɫgəj
pɐʲéstkʲɪ.

2169

EN Since the holiday begins this Friday, there's likely
going to be a lot of traffic on the roads.

RU Учи́тывая, что прáздничные дни начинáются в
пя́тницу, весьмá вероя́тно, что движéние на
дорóгах бýдет затрудненó.

ROM uĉítɪvəjə, što práznjɪĉnɪjɪ dni naĉɪnájutsjɪ v pjátnjɪtsu,
vjɪs'má vjɪrajátnə, što dvjɪžjénjɪjɪ na darógəh búdjɪt
zatrudnjɪnó.

IPA ʊtɕítɨvəʲə, ʂtɔ práznʲɪtɕnɨʲɪ dnʲi nɐtɕɪnáʲütsʲɪ f pʲǽtnʲɪtsʊ,
vʲɪsʲmá vʲɪrɐʲátnə, ʂtɔ dvʲɪzénʲɪʲɪ na dɐrógəx búdʲɪt
zɐtrʊdnʲɪnó.

2170

EN This part of town is dangerous. People are afraid to walk here at night.

RU Эта часть го́рода опа́сна. Лю́ди боя́тся ходи́ть там по́здно ве́чером.

ROM étə ćast' górədə apásnə. ljúdjı bajátsjı hadít' tam póznə vjéćırəm.

IPA étə tɕastʲ gʷǫ́rədə ɐpásnə. lʲʉ́dʲı bɐʲǽtsʲı xɐdʲítʲ tam pʷǫ́znə vʲétɕɨrəm.

2171

EN Aleksey was afraid to tell his parents what happened.

RU Алексе́й боя́лся расска́зывать роди́телям о случи́вшемся.

ROM aljıksjéj bajálsjı rısskázıvət' radítjeljım a slućívšımsjı.

IPA ɐlʲʲıksʲéj bɐʲǽɫsʲı rɨsskázɨvətʲ rɐdʲítʲılʲʲım ɐ slʊtɕífsʲɨmsʲı.

2172

EN The sidewalk was icy, so we walked very carefully. We were afraid of falling.

RU Тротуа́р был ско́льзким, так что мы шли о́чень осторо́жно, боя́сь упа́сть.

ROM tratuár bıl skól'zkjım, tak što mı šli óćın' əstaróžnə, bajás' upást'.

IPA trɐtʊár bɨɫ skʷǫ́lʲskʲım, tak ʂtǫ mɨ ʂlʲi ǫ́tɕınʲ əstɐrǫ́znə, bɐʲǽsʲ ʊpástʲ.

2173

EN I don't like dogs. I'm always afraid of getting bitten.

RU Я не люблю собáк. Я всё врéмя боюсь, что они меня покусáют.

ROM ja njɪ ljubljú sabák. ja vsjó vrjémjɪ bajús', što aní mjɪnjá pakusájut.

IPA ʲa nʲɪ ˡʲübˡʲú sɐbák. ʲa fsʲǿ vrʲémʲɪ bɐʲús', ʂtɔ ɐnʲí mʲɪnʲá pɐkʊsáʲüt.

2174

EN I was afraid to go near the dog because I was afraid of getting bitten.

RU Мне было стрáшно проходить мимо собáки, потому что я боялся (♀боялась), что онá меня укусит.

ROM mnjɛ bílə strášnə prəhadít' mímə sabákjɪ, pətamú što ja bajálsjɪ (♀bajáləs'), što aná mjɪnjá ukúsjɪt.

IPA mnʲɛ bílə strášnə prɐxɐdʲítʲ mʲímə sɐbákʲɪ, pətɐmú ʂtɔ ʲa bɐʲǽɫsʲɪ (♀bɐʲáləsʲ), ʂtɔ ɐná mʲɪnʲá ʊkúsʲɪt.

2175

EN Let me know if you're interested in joining the club.

RU Дай мне знать, éсли ты захóчешь вступить в клуб.

ROM daj mnjɛ znat', jésljɪ tɪ zahóćiś vstupít' v klub.

IPA daj mnʲɛ znatʲ, ʲéslʲɪ tɨ zɐxótɕiɕ fstʊpʲítʲ f klup.

2176

EN I tried to sell my car, but nobody was interested in buying it.

RU Я пыта́лся (♀пыта́лась) прода́ть свою́ маши́ну, но никто́ не́ был заинтересо́ван в том, что́бы купи́ть её.

ROM ja pıtálsjı (♀pıtáləs') pradát' svajú mašínu, no njıktó njé bıl zajıntjırısóvən v tom, štóbı kupít' jıjó.

IPA ʲa pɨtát̪sʲɪ (♀pɨtáləsʲ) prɐdátʲ svɐʲú mɐʂínʊ, nɔ nʲɪktɔ̣ nʲɛ́ bɨt̪ zɐʲɪnt̪ʲɪrʲɪsɔ̣vən f tɔ̣m, ʂtɔ̣bɨ kʊpʲítʲ ʲrʲɔ̣.

2177

EN I was interested to hear that Arturo quit his job. — I, on the other hand, was surprised to hear it.

RU Мне бы́ло интере́сно узна́ть, что Арту́ро бро́сил свою́ рабо́ту. — А я, наоборо́т, был удивлён (♀была́ удивлена́) э́тим.

ROM mnjɛ bílə jıntjırjésnə uznát', što artúrə brósjıl svajú rıbótu. — a ja, naabarót, bıl udjıvljón (♀bılá udjıvljıná) étjım.

IPA mnʲɛ bílə ʲɪnt̪ʲɪrʲésnə ʊznátʲ, ʂtɔ̣ ɐrtúrə brɔ̣sʲɪt̪ svɐʲú rɐbʷɔ̣tʊ. — a ʲa, nɐɐbɐrɔ̣t, bɨt̪ ʊdʲɪvlʲɔ̣n (♀bɨlá ʊdʲɪvlʲɪná) ét̪ʲɪm.

2178

EN Ask Anna for her opinion. I'd be interested to know what she thinks.

RU Узнáй мнéние Áнны. Мне бы́ло бы интерéсно узнáть, что онá об э́том дýмает.

ROM uznáj mnjénjıjı ánnı. mnjɛ bílə bı jıntjırjésnə uznát', što aná ab étəm dúməjıt.

IPA ʊznáj mnʲénʲrʲı ánnɨ. mnʲɛ bílə bɨ ʲɪntʲɪrʲésnə ʊznátʲ, ştǫ ɐná ɐb étəm dúməʲɪt.

2179

EN I was sorry to hear that Boris lost his job.

RU Мне бы́ло жаль услы́шать, что Борúс потеря́л рабóту.

ROM mnjɛ bílə žal' uslíšət', što barís patjırjál rıbótu.

IPA mnʲɛ bílə z̪alʲ ʊslíşətʲ, ştǫ bɐrʲís pɐtʲɪrʲáɫ rɐbʷótʊ.

2180

EN I've enjoyed my stay here. I'll be sorry to leave.

RU Мне здесь óчень нрáвится, бýдет жаль уезжáть отсю́да.

ROM mnjɛ zdjes' óćın' nrávjıtsjı, búdjıt žal' ujıžžát' atsjúdə.

IPA mnʲɛ zdʲesʲ ótɕɨnʲ nrávʲɪtsʲɪ, búdʲɪt z̪alʲ ʊʲɪzz̪átʲ ɐtsʲúdə.

2181

EN I'm sorry to call you so late, but I need to ask you
something.

RU Извини́, пожа́луйста, что звоню́ так по́здно, но
мне ну́жно спроси́ть у тебя́ кое-что́.

ROM jızvjıní, pažálujstə, što zvanjú tak póznə, no mnjɛ
núžnə sprasít' u tjıbjá kajı-štó.

IPA ʲɪzvʲɪnʲí, pɐʐálʊjstə, ʂt̪ɔ zvɐnʲú tak pʷǫznə, nǫ mnʲɛ
núzɳə sprɐsʲítʲ u tʲɪbʲá kɐʲɪ-ʂtǫ́.

2182

EN I'm sorry for shouting at you yesterday. > I'm sorry I
shouted at you yesterday.

RU Прости́, что накрича́л (♀накрича́ла) на тебя́ вчера́.
> Прости́, я вчера́ на тебя́ так накрича́л
(♀накрича́ла).

ROM prastí, što nakrıćál (♀nakrıćálə) na tjıbjá vćırá. >
prastí, ja vćırá na tjıbjá tak nakrıćál (♀nakrıćálə).

IPA prɐstʲí, ʂt̪ɔ nɐkrʲɪtɕáɫ (♀nɐkrʲɪtɕálə) na tʲɪbʲá ftɕɨrá. >
prɐstʲí, ʲa ftɕɨrá na tʲɪbʲá tak nɐkrʲɪtɕáɫ (♀nɐkrʲɪtɕálə).

2183

EN We weren't allowed to leave the building. > We were prevented from leaving the building.

RU Нам нельзя́ бы́ло покида́ть зда́ние. > Нам не позво́лили поки́нуть зда́ние.

ROM nam njıl'zjá bílə pakjıdát' zdánjıjı. > nam njı pazvóljıljı pakínut' zdánjıjı.

IPA nam nʲɪlʲzʲá bílə pɐkʲɪdátʲ zdánʲrʲɪ. > nam nʲɪ pɐzvʷólʲɪlʲɪ pɐkʲínʊtʲ zdánʲrʲɪ.

2184

EN Daisuke failed to solve the problem, whereas Aiko succeeded in solving the problem.

RU Да́йсукэ не смог реши́ть пробле́му, в то вре́мя как А́йко удало́сь её разреши́ть.

ROM dájsukɛ njı smog rıšít' prabljému, v to vrjémjı kak ájkə udalós' jıjó rızrıšít'.

IPA dájsʊkɛ nʲɪ smʷɒg rʲɪʂítʲ prɐblʲémʊ, f tɒ vrʲémʲɪ kak ájkə ʊdɐlʷósʲ ʲrʲɵ rɐzrʲɪʂítʲ.

2185

EN Fabio promised to buy me lunch. > Fabio insisted on buying me lunch.

RU Фа́био пообеща́л угости́ть меня́ ла́нчем. > Фа́био настоя́л на том, что́бы он угости́л меня́ ла́нчем.

ROM fábjıə paabjıççál ugastít' mjınjá láncım. > fábjıə nəstajál na tom, štóbı on ugastíl mjınjá láncım.

IPA fábʲɪə pɐɐbʲɪççáɫ ʊgɐstʲítʲ mʲɪnʲá lántɕɪm. > fábʲɪə nəstɐʲáɫ na tɒm, ʂtɒ́bɨ ɒn ʊgɐstʲíɫ mʲɪnʲá lántɕɪm.

2186

EN I saw Donna get into her car and drive away.

RU Я ви́дел (♀ви́дела), как До́нна се́ла в свою́ маши́ну и уе́хала.

ROM ja vídjıl (♀vídjılə), kak dónnə sjélə v svajú mašínu i ujéhələ.

IPA ʲa vʲídʲɪɫ (♀vʲídʲɪlə), kak dónnə sʲélə f svɐʲú mɐʂínʊ ɪ ʊʲéxələ.

2187

EN I saw Fyodor waiting for a bus.

RU Я ви́дел (♀ви́дела) Фёдора, кото́рый ждал авто́бус.

ROM ja vídjıl (♀vídjılə) fjódərə, katórıj ždal avtóbus.

IPA ʲa vʲídʲɪɫ (♀vʲídʲɪlə) fʲǿdərə, kɐtórɨj ʐdaɫ ɐftóbus.

2188

EN I saw him fall off his bike.

RU Я ви́дел (♀ви́дела), как он упа́л с велосипе́да.

ROM ja vídjıl (♀vídjılə), kak on upál s vjılasjıpjédə.

IPA ʲa vʲídʲɪɫ (♀vʲídʲɪlə), kak ɐn ʊpáɫ s vʲɪlɐsʲɪpʲédə.

2189

EN Did you see the accident happen?

RU Вы ви́дели, как произошёл несча́стный слу́чай?

ROM vı vídjeljı, kak prəjızašjól njıśśásnıj slúćəj?

IPA vɨ vʲídʲɪlʲɪ, kak prəʲɪzɐʂǿɫ nʲɪɕɕásnɨj slútɕəj?

2190

EN I saw him walking along the street.

RU Я ви́дел (♀ви́дела) его́ иду́щим по у́лице.
ROM ja vídjıl (♀vídjılə) jıvó jıdúççım pa úljıtsı.
IPA ᴶa vᴶídᴶıɫ (♀vᴶídᴶılə) ᴶɪvʷǫ́ ᴶɪdúççim pɐ úlᴶɪtsɨ.

2191

EN I didn't hear you come in.

RU Я не слы́шал (♀слы́шала), как ты вошёл.
ROM ja njı slíšəl (♀slíšələ), kak tı vašjól.
IPA ᴶa nᴶɪ slíʂəɫ (♀slíʂələ), kak tɨ vɐʂǫ́ɫ.

2192

EN Xenia suddenly felt somebody touch her on the shoulder.

RU Ксе́ния внеза́пно почу́вствовала, как кто́-то косну́лся её плеча́.
ROM ksjénjıjə vnjızápnə paćústvəvələ, kak któ-tə kasnúlsjı jıjó pljıćá.
IPA ksᴶénᴶɾᴶə vnᴶızápnə pɐtɕúʊstfəvələ, kak ktǫ́-tə kɐsnúɫsᴶı ᴶɾᴶǫ́ plᴶɪtɕá.

2193

EN Did you notice anyone go out?

RU Вы не заме́тили, что́бы кто́-то выходи́л?
ROM vı njı zamjétjıljı, štóbı któ-tə vıhadíl?
IPA vɨ nᴶɪ zɐmᴶétᴶɪlᴶɪ, ʂtǫ́bɨ ktǫ́-tə vɨxɐdᴶíɫ?

2194

EN I could hear it raining.

RU Я мог (♀ моглá) слы́шать, как идёт дождь.

ROM ja mog (♀ maglá) slíšət', kak jɪdjót dožd'.

IPA ʲa mʷok (♀ mɐglá) slíşətʲ, kak ʲɪdʲɵ́t doʐdʲ.

2195

EN The missing children were last seen playing near the river.

RU Пропáвших детéй послéдний раз ви́дели игрáющими у реки́.

ROM prapávših djɪtjéj pasljédnjɪj raz vídjeljɪ jɪgrájuççɪmjɪ u rɪkí.

IPA prɐpáfşɨx dʲɪtʲéj pɐslʲédnʲɪj raz vʲídʲɪlʲɪ ʲɪgrájüççɪmʲɪ u rʲɪkʲí.

2196

EN Can you smell something burning?

RU Ты не чýвствуешь зáпах ды́ма?

ROM tɪ njɪ ćústvujeś zápəh dímə?

IPA tɨ nʲɪ tɕúʊstfʊʲɪç zápəx dímə?

2197

EN I found Franz in my room reading my email.

RU Я застáл (♀застáла) в своéй кóмнате Фрáнца за
чтéнием моегó электрóнного письмá.

ROM ja zastál (♀zastálə) v svajéj kómnətjɪ frántsə za
ćtjénjɪjɪm majɪvó ɛljɪktrónnəvə pjɪs'má.

IPA ʲa zɐstáɫ (♀zɐstálə) f svɐʲéj kʷómnətʲɪ frántsə za
tɕtʲénʲrʲɪm mɐʲɪvʷó ɛlʲɪktrónnəvə pʲɪsʲmá.

2198

EN Everyone heard the bomb explode.

RU Все слы́шали, как взорвалáсь бóмба.

ROM vsjɛ slíšəljɪ, kak vzərvalás' bómbə.

IPA fsʲɛ slíʂəlʲɪ, kak vzərvɐlásʲ bʷómbə.

2199

EN I heard someone slamming the door in the middle of
the night.

RU Я слы́шал (♀слы́шала), как ктó-то ломи́лся в
дверь посреди́ нóчи.

ROM ja slíšəl (♀slíšələ), kak któ-tə lamílsjɪ v dvjer' pasrɪdí
nóćɪ.

IPA ʲa slíʂəɫ (♀slíʂələ), kak któ-tə lɐmʲíɫsʲɪ v dvʲerʲ
pɐsrʲɪdʲí nótɕɪ.

2200

EN Heidi hurt her knee playing volleyball.

RU Хэ́йди повреди́ла но́гу, игра́я в волейбо́л.

ROM héjdjɪ pavrɪdílə nógu, jɪgrájə v valjɪjból.

IPA xéjdʲɪ pɐvrʲɪdʲílə nǫ́ɡʊ, ʲɪɡrájʲə v vɐlʲɪjbʷǫ́ɫ.

GMS #2201 - 2300

2201

EN Takahiro's in the kitchen making coffee.

RU Такахи́ро сейча́с на ку́хне де́лает ко́фе.
ROM təkahírə sjɪjćás na kúhnjɪ djéləjɪt kófjɪ.
IPA təkɐxʲírə sʲɪjtɕás na kúxnʲɪ dʲéləʲɪt kʷófʲɪ.

2202

EN A man ran out of the house shouting.

RU Мужчи́на с кри́ками вы́бежал из до́ма.
ROM muśśínə s kríkəmjɪ víbjɪžəl iz dómə.
IPA mʊɕɕínə s krʲíkəmʲɪ vʲíbʲɪzəɫ ʲiz dómə.

2203

EN Do something! Don't just stand there doing nothing.

RU Сде́лай что́-нибудь! Не стой здесь как столб!
ROM sdjéləj štó-njɪbud'! njɪ stoj zdjes' kak stolb!
IPA zdʲéləj ʂtó-nʲɪbʊdʲ! nʲɪ stoj zdʲesʲ kak stoɫp!

2204

EN Did you cut yourself shaving?

RU Ты поре́зался во вре́мя бритья́?
ROM tɪ parjézəlsjɪ va vrjémjɪ brɪt'já?
IPA tɨ pɐrʲézəɫsʲɪ vɐ vrʲémʲɪ brʲɪtʲá?

2205

EN Be careful when crossing the street.

RU Бу́дьте осторо́жны при перехо́де у́лицы.
ROM búd'tjɪ əstaróžnɪ prɪ pjɪrɪhódjɪ úljɪtsɪ.
IPA búdʲtʲɪ əstɐrózṇ̩ prʲɪ pʲɪrʲɪxódʲɪ úlʲɪtsɨ.

2206

EN Having finally found a hotel, we looked for some
place to have dinner.

RU Найдя́ наконе́ц гости́ницу, мы заняли́сь по́исками
ме́ста, где мо́жно пообе́дать.
ROM najdjá nəkanjéts gastínjɪtsu, mɪ zanjɪlís' pójɪskəmjɪ
mjéstə, gdjɛ móžnə paabjédət'.
IPA nɐjdʲá nəkɐnʲéts ɡɐsʲtʲínʲɪtsʊ, mɨ zɐnʲɪlʲísʲ pʷóʲɪskəmʲɪ
mʲéstə, gdʲɛ mʷóžṇə pɐɐbʲédətʲ.

2207

EN After getting off work, she went straight home.

RU По́сле рабо́ты она́ сра́зу верну́лась домо́й.
ROM pósljɪ rɪbótɪ aná srázu vjɪrnúləs' damój.
IPA pʷóslʲɪ rɐbʷótɨ ɐná srázʊ vʲɪrnúləsʲ dɐmʷój.

2208

EN Taking a key out of his pocket, he unlocked the door.

RU Доста́в ключ из карма́на, он откры́л дверь.
ROM dastáv kljuć iz karmánə, on atkríl dvjer'.
IPA dɐstáf klʲutɕ ʲis kɐrmánə, ọn ɐtkrɨ́ɫ dvʲerʲ.

2209

EN Feeling tired, I went to bed early.

RU Я лёг (♀легла́) спать пора́ньше, потому́ что чу́вствовал (♀чу́вствовала) уста́лость.

ROM ja ljóg (♀ljɪglá) spat' parán'šɪ, pətamú što ćústvəvəl (♀ćústvəvələ) ustáləst'.

IPA ʲa lʲ̥k (♀lʲɪglá) spatʲ pɐránʲʂɨ, pətɐmú ʂtɔ tɕúʊstfəvəɫ (♀tɕúʊstfəvələ) ʊstáləstʲ.

2210

EN Being unemployed means he doesn't have much money.

RU Его́ безрабо́тное положе́ние означа́ет, что у него́ нет мно́го де́нег.

ROM jɪvó bjɪzrɪbótnəjɪ pəlažjénjɪjɪ əznaćájɪt, što u njɪvó njɛt mnógə djénjɪg.

IPA ʲɪvʷ̞ bʲɪzrɐbʷótnəʲɪ pəlɐzénʲrʲɪ əznɐtɕáʲɪt, ʂtɔ u nʲɪvʷ̞ nʲɛt mnógə dʲénʲɪk.

2211

EN Not having a car can make getting around difficult in some places.

RU Отсу́тствие маши́ны мо́жет затрудни́ть передвиже́ние в не́которых места́х.

ROM atsútstvjɪjɪ mašínɪ móžɪt zatrudnít' pjɪrɪdvjɪžjénjɪjɪ v njékətərɪh mjɪstáh.

IPA ɐtsútstfrʲɪ mɐʂínɨ mʷóʐɨt zɐtrʊdnʲítʲ pʲɪrʲɪdvʲɪzɛ́nʲrʲɪ v nʲékətərɨx mʲɪstáx.

2212

EN Having already seen the movie twice, I didn't want to go again with my friends.

RU Посмотрéв фильм двáжды, я ужé не захотéл (♀захотéла) идтú смотрéть егó опя́ть с друзья́ми.

ROM pəsmatrjév fil'm dváždı, ja užjé njı zəhatjél (♀zəhatjélə) jıdtí smatrjét' jıvó apját' s druz'jámjı.

IPA pəsmɐtrʲéf fʲilʲm dvázdɨ, ʲa ʊʐɨ́ nʲı zəxɐtʲéɫ (♀zəxɐtʲélə) ʲɪttʲí smɐtrʲétʲ ʲɪvʷǫ́ ɐpʲǽtʲ s druzʲǽmʲɪ.

2213

EN Not being able to speak the local language meant that I had trouble communicating.

RU Незнáние мéстного языкá затрудня́ло процéсс общéния.

ROM njıznánjıjı mjésnəvə jızıká zatrudnjálə pratsjéss abçcjénjıjə.

IPA nʲıznánʲɨ́rʲı mʲésnəvə ʲızɨká zɐtrudnʲálə prɐtséss ɐbçcénʲɨ́rʲə.

2214

EN Being a vegetarian, Mitsuko doesn't eat any kind of meat.

RU Бýдучи вегетариáнкой, Мúтико не ест мя́со.

ROM búdućı vjıgjıtariánkəj, mítjıkə njı jest mjásə.

IPA búdʊtɕɨ vʲɪɡʲɪtɐrʲiánkəj, mʲítʲɪkə nʲı ʲest mʲásə.

2215

EN The police want to talk to anybody who saw the accident.

RU Поли́ция хоте́ла побесе́довать со все́ми, кто стал свиде́телем инциде́нта.

ROM palítsɪjə hatjélə pabjɪsjédəvət' sa vsjémjɪ, kto stal svjɪdjétjeljɪm jɪntsɪdjéntə.

IPA pɐljítsɨʲə xɐtʲélə pɐbjɪsʲédəvətʲ sɐ fsʲémʲɪ, ktǫ stał svʲɪdʲétʲɪlʲɪm ʲɪntsɨdʲéntə.

2216

EN The new city hall isn't a very beautiful building. Most people don't like it.

RU Но́вый си́ти холл не о́чень краси́вое зда́ние. Мно́гим оно́ не нра́вится.

ROM nóvɪj sítjɪ holl njɪ óćɪn' krɪsívəjɪ zdánjɪjɪ. mnógjɪm anó njɪ nrávjɪtsjɪ.

IPA nǫ́vɨj sʲítʲɪ xǫłł nʲɪ ǫ́tɕɨnʲ krɐsʲívəʲɪ zdánʲɪʲ́ɪ. mnǫ́gʲɪm ɐnǫ́ nʲɪ nrávʲɪtsʲɪ.

2217

EN The people were injured in the accident.

RU Бы́ли те, кто пострада́л во вре́мя несча́стного слу́чая.

ROM bíljɪ tjɛ, kto pəstrɪdál va vrjémjɪ njɪśśásnəvə slúćəjə.

IPA bílʲɪ tʲɛ, ktǫ pəstrɐdáł vɐ vrʲémʲɪ nʲɪɕɕásnəvə slútɕəʲə.

2218

EN   Do the police know the cause of the explosion?

RU   Полиция знает причину взрыва?
ROM   palítsɪjə znájɪt prɪcínu vzrívə?
IPA   pɐlʲítsɨʲə znáʲɪt prʲɪtɕínʊ vzrívə?

2219

EN   The police are looking for the stolen car.

RU   Полиция разыскивает украденную машину.
ROM   palítsɪjə rɪzískjɪvəjɪt ukrádjɪnnuju mašínu.
IPA   pɐlʲítsɨʲə rɐzískʲɪvəʲɪt ʊkrádʲɪnnʊʲü mɐʂínʊ.

2220

EN   I need my glasses, but I can't find them.

RU   Мне нужны мои очки, но я никак не могу их найти.
ROM   mnjɛ nužní maí aćkí, no ja njɪkák njɪ magú ih najtí.
IPA   mnʲɛ nʊzɲí mɐʲí ɐtɕkʲí, nɒ ʲa nʲɪkák nʲɪ mɐgú ʲix nɐjtʲí.

2221

EN   I'm going to buy some new jeans today.

RU   Я собираюсь сегодня купить себе джинсы.
ROM   ja sabjɪrájus' sjɪvódnjɪ kupít' sjɪbjé džínsɪ.
IPA   ʲa sɐbʲɪráʲüsʲ sʲɪvʷódnʲɪ kʊpʲítʲ sʲɪbʲé dzʲínsɨ.

2222

EN Did you hear a noise just now?

RU Ты то́лько что слы́шал (♀ слы́шала) шум?
ROM tɪ tól'kə što slíšəl (♀ slíšələ) šum?
IPA tɨ tǫ́lʲkə ştǫ slɨ́şəɫ (♀ slɨ́şələ) şum?

2223

EN I can't work here. There's too much noise.

RU Я не могу́ здесь рабо́тать. Здесь сли́шком шу́мно.
ROM ja njɪ magú zdjes' rɪbótət'. zdjes' slíškəm šúmnə.
IPA ʲa nʲɪ mɐgú zdʲesʲ rɐbʷǫ́tətʲ. zdʲesʲ slʲɨ́şkəm şúmnə.

2224

EN There's a hair in my soup.

RU В моём су́пе во́лос.
ROM v majóm súpjɪ vóləs.
IPA v mɐʲę́m súpʲɪ vʷǫ́ləs.

2225

EN You've got very long hair.

RU У тебя́ дли́нные во́лосы.
ROM u tjɪbjá dlínnɪjɪ vóləsɪ.
IPA u tʲɪbʲá dlʲínnɨʲɪ vʷǫ́ləsɨ.

2226

EN You can stay with us. We have a spare room.

RU Ты мо́жешь оста́ться у нас. У нас есть свобо́дная
ко́мната.

ROM tɪ móžɪś astát'sjɪ u nas. u nas jest' svabódnəjɪ
kómnətə.

IPA tɨ mʷǫ́zɪ̨ç ʋstátʲsʲɪ u nas. u nas ʲestʲ svʋbʷǫ́dnəʲɪ
kʷǫ́mnətə.

2227

EN You can't sit here. There isn't any room.

RU Ты не мо́жешь здесь присе́сть, здесь нет ме́ста.

ROM tɪ njɪ móžɪś zdjes' prɪsjést', zdjes' njɛt mjéstə.

IPA tɨ nʲɪ mʷǫ́zɪ̨ç zdʲesʲ prʲɪsʲéstʲ, zdʲesʲ nʲɛt mʲéstə.

2228

EN I had some interesting experiences while I was
traveling.

RU У меня́ был интере́сный о́пыт во вре́мя
путеше́ствия.

ROM u mjɪnjá bɪl jɪntjɪrjésnɪj ópɪt va vrjémjɪ putjɪšjéstvjɪjɪ.

IPA u mʲɪnʲá bɨɫ ʲɪntʲɪrʲésnɨj ǫ́pɨt vʋ vrʲémʲɪ pʊtʲɪşéstfʲrʲɪ.

2229

EN They offered me the job because I had a lot of experience.

RU Они́ предложи́ли мне рабо́ту, потому́ что у меня́ большо́й о́пыт.

ROM aní prɪdlažíljɪ mnjɛ rɪbótu, pətamú što u mjɪnjá bal'šój ópɪt.

IPA ɐnʲí prʲɪdlɐzʲílʲɪ mnʲɛ rɐbʷótʊ, pətɐmú ʂtɐ u mʲɪnʲá bɐlʲʂój ópɨt.

2230

EN I'm going to go buy a loaf of bread.

RU Я собира́юсь купи́ть буха́нку хле́ба.

ROM ja sabjɪrájus' kupít' buhánku hljébə.

IPA ʲa sɐbʲɪráʲüsʲ kʊpʲítʲ bʊxánkʊ xlʲébə.

2231

EN Enjoy your vacation. I hope you have good weather.

RU Отдохни́ как сле́дует. Наде́юсь, пого́да не подведёт. > Наслажда́йся о́тпуском. Наде́юсь, пого́да бу́дет хоро́шей.

ROM ətdahní kak sljédujɪt. nadjéjus', pagódə njɪ padvjɪdjót. > nəslaždájsjɪ ótpuskəm. nadjéjus', pagódə búdjɪt haróšɪj.

IPA ətdɐxnʲí kak slʲédʊʲɪt. nɐdʲéʲüsʲ, pɐgʷódə nʲɪ pɐdvʲɪdʲét. > nəslɐzdájsʲɪ ótpʊskəm. nɐdʲéʲüsʲ, pɐgʷódə búdʲɪt xɐróʂɨj.

2232

EN Where are you going to put all your furniture?

RU Куда́ ты собира́ешься поста́вить всю свою́ ме́бель?
ROM kudá tɪ sabjɪrájeśsjɪ pastávjɪt' vsju svajú mjébjel'?
IPA kʊdá tɨ sɐbʲɪráʲɪ¢sʲɪ pɐstávʲɪtʲ fsʲu svɐʲú mʲébʲɪlʲʲ?

2233

EN Let me know if you need more information.

RU Дай мне знать, е́сли тебе́ пона́добится бо́льше
    информа́ции.
ROM daj mnjɛ znat', jésljɪ tjɪbjé panádəbjɪtsjɪ ból'šɪ
    jɪnfarmátsɪjɪ.
IPA daj mnʲɛ znatʲ, ʲéslʲɪ tʲɪbʲé pɐnádəbʲɪtsʲɪ bʷǫ́lʲʂɨ
    ʲɪnfɛrmátsɨʲɪ.

2234

EN The news was very depressing.

RU Но́вости бы́ли о́чень плохи́ми. > Но́вости бы́ли
    удруча́ющими.
ROM nóvəstjɪ bíljɪ ó¢ɪn' plahímjɪ. > nóvəstjɪ bíljɪ
    udrućájuççɪmjɪ.
IPA nǫ́vəstʲɪ bɨ́lʲɪ ǫ́tɕɪnʲ plɛxʲímʲɪ. > nǫ́vəstʲɪ bɨ́lʲɪ
    ʊdrʊtɕáʲüççɨmʲɪ.

2235

EN They spend a lot of money on travel.

RU Они потра́тили мно́го де́нег на путеше́ствия.
ROM aní patrátjɪljɪ mnógə djénjɪg na putjɪšjéstvjɪjɪ.
IPA ɐnʲí pɐtrátʲɪlʲɪ mnógə dʲénʲɪg na pʊtʲɪʂéstfʲɪ́ɪ.

2236

EN We had a very good trip.

RU У нас была́ о́чень хоро́шая пое́здка.
ROM u nas bɪlá óćɪn' haróšəjə pajézdkə.
IPA u nas bɪlá ótɕinʲ xɐróʂəʲə pɐʲéstkə.

2237

EN It's a nice day today. > It's nice weather today.

RU Сего́дня о́чень хоро́ший день. > Сего́дня о́чень
хоро́шая пого́да.
ROM sjɪvódnjɪ óćɪn' haróšɪj djen'. > sjɪvódnjɪ óćɪn'
haróšəjə pagódə.
IPA sʲɪvʷódnʲɪ ótɕinʲ xɐróʂij dʲenʲ. > sʲɪvʷódnʲɪ ótɕinʲ
xɐróʂəʲə pɐgʷódə.

2238

EN We had a lot of bags and suitcases. > We had a lot of baggage.

RU У нас бы́ло мно́го су́мок и чемода́нов. > У нас бы́ло мно́го багажа́.

ROM u nas bílə mnógə súmək i ćımadánəv. > u nas bílə mnógə bəgažá.

IPA u nas bɨ́lə mnógə súmək ɪ tɕɨmɐdánəf. > u nas bɨ́lə mnǫ́gə bəgɐʐá.

2239

EN These chairs are mine. > This furniture is mine.

RU Э́то мои́ сту́лья. > Э́то моя́ ме́бель.

ROM étə maí stúljı. > étə majá mjébjel'.

IPA étə mɐjí stúlʲɪ. > étə mɐjá mʲébʲɪlʲ.

2240

EN That's a good suggestion. > That's good advice.

RU Э́то хоро́шее предложе́ние. > Э́то хоро́ший сове́т.

ROM étə haróšıjı prıdlažjénjıjı. > étə haróšıj savjét.

IPA étə xɐrǫ́ʂɨ̈ɪ prʲɪdlɐʐɛ́nʲɪ̯ɪ. > étə xɐrǫ́ʂɨj sɐvʲét.

2241

EN My neighbor drives an SUV.

RU Мой сосе́д е́здит на внедоро́жнике.

ROM moj sasjéd jézdjıt na vnjıdaróžnjıkjı.

IPA mʷoj sɐsʲéd ʲézdʲɪt na vnʲɪdɐrǫ́ʐnʲɪkʲɪ.

2242

EN My neighbor is an FBI agent.

RU Мой сосе́д - аге́нт ФБР.
ROM moj sasjéd - agjént fɛbr.
IPA mʷo̞j sɐsʲét - ɐɡʲént fɛbr.

2243

EN He got a university degree.

RU У него́ университе́тский дипло́м . > Он зако́нчил университе́т.
ROM u njɪvó unjɪvjɪrsjɪtjétskjɪj djɪplóm . > on zakónćɪl unjɪvjɪrsjɪtjét.
IPA u nʲɪvʷo̞ ʊnʲɪvʲɪrsʲɪtʲétskʲɪj dʲɪpló̞m . > o̞n zɐkʷó̞ntɕɪɫ ʊnʲɪvʲɪrsʲɪtʲét.

2244

EN He was an NYU student.

RU Он был студе́нтом Нью-Йо́ркского университе́та.
ROM on bɪl studjéntəm nju-jórkskəvə unjɪvjɪrsjɪtjétə.
IPA o̞n bɪɫ stʊdʲéntəm nʲü-jórkskəvə ʊnʲɪvʲɪrsʲɪtʲétə.

2245

EN If you want to leave early, you have to ask for permission.

RU Éсли ты хóчешь уйти́ ра́ньше, ты дóлжен (♀должна́) отпроси́ться.

ROM jéslʲı tı hóćıś ujtí rán'šı, tı dólžın (♀dalžná) ətprasít'sjı.

IPA ʲéslʲı tɨ xótɕiɕ ʊjtʲí ránʲʂɨ, tɨ dółzɨn (♀dełzná) ətprɐsʲítʲsʲı.

2246

EN I don't think Marco will get the job, because he doesn't have enough experience.

RU Я не ду́маю, что Ма́рко полу́чит э́ту рабо́ту, потому́ что у негó недоста́точно о́пыта.

ROM ja njı dúməju, što márkə palúćıt étu rıbótu, pətamú što u njıvó njıdastátəćnə ópıtə.

IPA ʲa nʲı dúməʲü, ʂtọ márkə pɐlútɕit étu rɐbʷótʊ, pətɐmú ʂtọ u nʲıvʷọ́ nʲıdɐstátətɕnə ópıtə.

2247

EN Can I talk to you? I need some advice.

RU Мóжно с тобóй поговори́ть? Мне ну́жен совéт.

ROM móžnə s tabój pəgəvarít'? mnjɛ núžın savjét.

IPA mʷóʐnə s tɐbʷój pəgəvɐrʲítʲ? mnʲɛ núzɨn sɐvʲét.

2248

EN I'd like some information about hotels in Paris.

RU Я бы хотéл (♀хотéла) получи́ть информáцию об отéлях в Пари́же.

ROM ja bɪ hatjél (♀hatjélə) palućít' jɪnfarmátsɪju ab atéljɪh v paríži.

IPA ʲa bɨ xɐtʲéɬ (♀xɐtʲélə) pɐlʊtɕítʲ ʲɪnfɐrmátsɨü ɐb ɐtélʲɪx f pɐrʲízɨ.

2249

EN English has one (1) alphabet with twenty-six (26) letters.

RU В алфави́те англи́йского языкá двáдцать шесть (26) букв.

ROM v əlfavítjɪ anglíjskəvə jɪzɪká dvádtsət' šɪst' (26) bukv.

IPA v əɬfɐvʲítʲɪ ɐnglʲíjskəvə ʲɪzɨká dváttsətʲ ʂɨstʲ (26) bukf.

2250

EN English has a lot of vocabulary.

RU В англи́йском языкé óчень объёмный вокабуля́р.

ROM v anglíjskəm jɪzɪkjé óćɪn' abjómnɪj vəkabuljár.

IPA v ɐnglʲíjskəm ʲɪzɨkʲé ótɕɪnʲ ɐbʲə́mnɨj vəkɐbʊlʲár.

2251

EN   Today I learned twenty (20) new vocabulary words.

RU   Сегóдня я вы́учил (♀ вы́учила) двáдцать нóвых
     слов.
ROM sjɪvódnjɪ ja víućɪl (♀ víućɪlə) dvádtsət' nóvɪh slov.
IPA sʲɪvʷódnʲɪ ʲa víʊtɕɪɫ (♀ víʊtɕɪlə) dváttsətʲ nóvɨx slǫf.

2252

EN   I've got a new job, and it's hard work.

RU   У меня нóвая рабóта, прихóдится мнóго
     труди́ться.
ROM u mjenja nóvəjə rɪbótə, prɪhódjɪtsjɪ mnógə trudít'sjɪ.
IPA u mʲenʲa nǫ́vəʲə rɐbʷótə, prʲɪxǫ́dʲɪtsʲɪ mnǫ́gə trʊdʲítʲsʲɪ.

2253

EN   I need some money to buy some food.

RU   Мне ну́жны дéньги, чтóбы купи́ть еды́.
ROM mnjɛ núžnɪ djén'gjɪ, štóbɪ kupít' jɪdí.
IPA mnʲɛ núznɪ dʲénʲgʲɪ, ʂtǫ́bɪ kʊpʲítʲ ʲɪdí.

2254

EN We met a lot of interesting people at the party.

RU Мы познакóмились со мнóгими интерéсными
людьмú на вечерúнке.

ROM mɪ pəznakómjɪljɪs' sa mnógjɪmjɪ jɪntjɪrjésnɪmjɪ ljud'mí
na vjɪćɪrínkjɪ.

IPA mɨ pəznɐkʷóm⁽ʲ⁾ɪlʲɨsʲ sɐ mnóɡʲɪmʲɪ ʲɪntʲɪrʲésnɨmʲɪ lʲüdʲmʲí
na vʲɪtɕɨrʲínkʲɪ.

2255

EN I'm going to open a window to get some fresh air.

RU Я собирáюсь открúть окнó, чтóбы провéтрить
помещéние. > Я собирáюсь открúть окнó, чтóбы
впустúть немнóго свéжего вóздуха.

ROM ja sabjɪrájus' atkrít' aknó, štóbɪ pravjétrjɪt'
pamjɪććjénjɪjɪ. > ja sabjɪrájus' atkrít' aknó, štóbɪ
vpustít' njɪmnógə svjéžɪvə vózduhə.

IPA ʲa sɐbʲɪráʲüsʲ ɐtkrítʲ ɐknó, ʂtóbɨ prɐvʲétrʲɪtʲ
pɐmʲɪɕɕénʲɪʲɪ. > ʲa sɐbʲɪráʲüsʲ ɐtkrítʲ ɐknó, ʂtóbɨ
fpustʲítʲ nʲɪmnógə svʲéʑɨvə vʷózduxə.

2256

EN I'd like to give you some advice before you go off to college.

RU Я бы хотéл (♀хотéла) дать тебé нéсколько совéтов пéред тем, как ты уéдешь в кóлледж.

ROM ja bɪ hatjél (♀hatjélə) dat' tjɪbjé njéskəl'kə savjétəv pjérjɪd tjɛm, kak tɪ ujédjeś v kólljɪdž.

IPA ʲa bɨ xɐtʲéɫ (♀xɐtʲélə) datʲ tʲɪbʲé nʲéskəlʲkə sɐvʲétəf pʲérʲɪt tʲem, kak tɨ ʊʲédʲɪɕ f kʷóɫlʲɪdʂ.

2257

EN The tour guide gave us some information about the city.

RU Гид ознакóмил нас с информáцией о гóроде.

ROM gid əznakómjɪl nas s jɪnfarmátsɪjej a górədjɪ.

IPA gʲid əznɐkʷómʲɪɫ nas s ʲɪnfɐrmátsɨʲɪj ɐ gʷórədʲɪ.

2258

EN We've had wonderful weather this last month.

RU Весь прóшлый мéсяц у нас здесь стоя́ла прекрáсная погóда.

ROM vjes' próšlɪj mjésjɪts u nas zdjes' stajálə prɪkrásnəjɪ pagódə.

IPA vʲesʲ próʂlɨj mʲésʲɪts u nas zdʲesʲ stɐʲálə prʲɪkrásnəʲɪ pɐgʷódə.

2259

EN Some children learn very quickly.

RU Некоторые дети быстро схватывают. >
Некоторые дети быстро запоминают.

ROM njékətərıjı djétjı bístrə shvátıvəjut. > njékətərıjı djétjı
bístrə zəpamjınájut.

IPA nʲékətərɨʲı dʲétʲı bístrə sxfátɨvəʲüt. > nʲékətərɨʲı dʲétʲı
bístrə zəpɐmʲɪnáʲüt.

2260

EN Tomorrow there'll be rain in some places, but most of
the country will be dry.

RU Завтра местами ожидается дождь, но большую
часть страны осадки не затронут.

ROM závtrə mjıstámjı ažıdájetsjı dožd', no ból'šuju ćast'
strıní asádkjı njı zatrónut.

IPA záftrə mʲɪstámʲı ɐʐɨdáʲɪtsʲı doʐd̥ʲ, nọ bʷǫ́lʲʂʊʲü tɕastʲ
strɐní ɐsátkʲı nʲı zɐtrǫ́nʊt.

2261

EN I have to go to the bank today. — Is there a bank
near here?

RU Мне сегодня нужно пойти в банк. — Здесь
поблизости есть банк?

ROM mnjɛ sjıvódnjı núžnə pajtí v bank. — zdjes'
pablízəstjı jest' bank?

IPA mnʲɛ sʲıvʷódnʲı núznə pɐjtʲí v bank. — zdʲesʲ
pɐblʲízəstʲı ʲestʲ bank?

2262

EN I don't like going to the dentist. — My sister's a dentist.

RU Я не люблю ходить к стоматологам. — Моя сестра стоматолог.

ROM ja njı ljubljú hadít' k stəmatóləgəm. — majá sjıstrá stəmatóləg.

IPA ʲa nʲɪ lʲüblʲú xɐdʲítʲ k stəmɐtól̩əgəm. — mɐʲá sʲɪstrá stəmɐtól̩ək.

2263

EN I have to go to the bank, and then I'm going to the post office.

RU Мне нужно пойти в банк, а после я собираюсь зайти на почту.

ROM mnjɛ núžnə pajtí v bank, a pósljı ja sabjırájus' zajtí na póćtu.

IPA mnʲɛ núz̧nə pɐjtʲí v bank, a pʷóslʲɪ ʲa sɐbʲɪrájüsʲ zɐjtʲí na pʷótɕtu.

2264

EN Two people were taken to the hospital after the accident.

RU Двое людей были доставлены в больницу после несчастного случая.

ROM dvójı ljudjéj bíljı dastávljını v bal'nítsu pósljı njıśśásnəvə slúćəjə.

IPA dvʷóʲɪ lʲüdʲéj bílʲɪ dɐstávlʲɪnɨ v bɐlʲnʲítsu pʷóslʲɪ nʲɪɕɕásnəvə slútɕəʲə.

2265

EN Flora works eight (8) hours a day, six (6) days a week.

RU Флóра рабóтает по вóсемь часóв в день, шесть дней в недéлю.

ROM flórə rıbótəjıt pa vósjem' ćısóv v djen', šıst' dnjej v njıdjélju.

IPA flǫ́rə rɐbʷǫ́təʲɪt pɐ vʷǫ́sʲɪmʲ tɕɪsóv v dʲenʲ, ʂɪstʲ dnʲej v nʲɪdʲélʲü.

2266

EN What's the longest river in the world?

RU Какáя сáмая длúнная рекá в мúре?

ROM kakájə sáməjə dlínnəjı rıká v mírjı?

IPA kɐkáʲə sáməʲə dlʲínnəʲı rʲıká v mʲírʲı?

2267

EN The earth goes around the sun, and the moon goes around the earth.

RU Земля́ вращáется вокрýг Сóлнца, а Лунá - вокрýг Земли́.

ROM zjımljá vrıççájetsjı vakrúg sóntsə, a luná - vakrúg zjımlí.

IPA zʲımlʲá vrɐ́ççáʲɪtsʲı vɐkrúk sǫ́ntsə, a lʊná - vɐkrúg zʲımlʲí.

2268

EN Have you ever crossed the equator?

RU Ты когда́-нибудь пересека́л (♀пересека́ла) эква́тор?

ROM tɪ kagdá-njɪbud' pjɪrɪsjɪkál (♀pjɪrɪsjɪkálə) ɛkvátər?

IPA tɨ kɐgdá-nʲɪbʊdʲ pʲɪrʲɪsʲɪkáɫ (♀pʲɪrʲɪsʲɪkálə) ɛkfátər?

2269

EN We looked up at all the stars in the sky.

RU Мы посмотре́ли вверх на звёздное не́бо.

ROM mɪ pəsmatrjéljɪ vvjɛrh na zvjóznəjɪ njébə.

IPA mɨ pəsmɐtrʲélʲɪ vvʲɛrx na zvʲǫ́znəʲɪ nʲébə.

2270

EN We must do more to protect the environment.

RU Мы должны́ де́лать бо́льше для того́, что́бы защити́ть окружа́ющую среду́.

ROM mɪ dalžní djélət' ból'šɪ dlja tavó, štóbɪ zaççɪtít' akružájuççuju srɪdú.

IPA mɨ dɐɫzní dʲélətʲ bʷǫ́lʲʂɨ dlʲa tɐvʷǫ́, ʂtǫ́bɨ zɐɕɕɪtʲítʲ ɐkruʑǻʲ ü ɕɕʊʲ ü srʲɪdú.

2271

EN There are millions of stars in space.

RU В ко́смосе миллио́н звёзд.

ROM v kósməsjɪ mjɪlljɪón zvjózd.

IPA f kʷǫ́sməsʲɪ mʲɪɫɫʲɪón zvʲǫ́zt.

2272

EN Milena's brother's in prison for robbery. > He's in jail.

RU Брат Миле́ны в тюрьме́ из-за кра́жи. > Он в тюрьме́.

ROM brat mjɪljénɪ v tjur'mjé iz-za kráʐɪ. > on v tjur'mjé.

IPA brat mʲɪlʲénɨ f tʲürʲmʲέ ʲiz-za krázɨ. > o̜n f tʲürʲmʲέ.

2273

EN Milena went to the prison to visit her brother.

RU Миле́на ходи́ла в тюрьму́ навести́ть бра́та.

ROM mjɪljénə hadílə v tjur'mú navjɪstít' brátə.

IPA mʲɪlʲénə xɐdʲílə f tʲürʲmú nɐvʲɪstʲítʲ brátə.

2274

EN When I finish high school, I want to go to college.

RU Когда́ я око́нчу шко́лу, я хочу́ поступи́ть в ко́лледж.

ROM kagdá ja akónću škólu, ja haćú pastupít' v kólljɪdʐ.

IPA kɐgdá ʲa ɐkʷóntɕʊ ʂkʷólʊ, ʲa xɐtɕú pɐstʊpʲítʲ f kʷóɫlʲɪdʂ.

2275

EN Konstantin is a student at the college where I used to work.

RU Константи́н - студе́нт ко́лледжа, в кото́ром я когда́-то рабо́тал (♀ рабо́тала).

ROM kənstantín - studjént kólljıdžə, v katórəm ja kagdá-tə rıbótəl (♀ rıbótələ).

IPA kənstɐntʲín - stʊdʲént kʷǫ́łlʲıdzə, f kɐtǫ́rəm ʲa kɐgdá-tə rɐbʷǫ́təł (♀ rɐbʷǫ́tələ).

2276

EN I was in class for five (5) hours today.

RU Я был (♀ была́) сего́дня на заня́тиях пять часо́в.

ROM ja bıl (♀ bılá) sjıvódnjı na zanjátjıɉıh pjat' ćısóv.

IPA ʲa bɨł (♀ bɨlá) sʲıvʷódnʲı na zɐnʲǽtʲr̥ʲıx pʲætʲ tɕısǫ́f.

2277

EN Who's the youngest student in the class?

RU Кто са́мый мла́дший студе́нт в кла́ссе?

ROM kto sámıj mládšıj studjént v klássjı?

IPA ktǫ sámɨj mlátʂɨj stʊdʲént f klássʲı?

2278

EN Do you ever have breakfast in bed?

RU Ты когда́-нибудь за́втракаешь в посте́ли?

ROM tı kagdá-njıbud' závtrəkəjeś v pastjéljı?

IPA tɨ kɐgdá-nʲıbʊdʲ záftrəkəʲıɕ f pɐstʲélʲı?

2279

EN What time do you usually finish work?

RU Когда́ ты обы́чно зака́нчиваешь рабо́ту?
ROM kagdá tı abíćnə zakánćıvəjeś rıbótu?
IPA kɐgdá tɨ ɐbʲítɕnə zɐkántɕivəᵏɪɕ rɐbʷǫ́tʊ?

2280

EN Will you be home tomorrow afternoon?

RU Ты бу́дешь до́ма за́втра днём?
ROM tı búdjeś dómə závtrə dnjóm?
IPA tɨ búdʲɪɕ dǫ́mə záftrə dnʲę́m?

2281

EN The economy was bad, so a lot of people were out of work.

RU Из-за плохо́й эконо́мики мно́гие лю́ди оста́лись без рабо́ты.
ROM iz-za plahój ɛkanómjıkjı mnógjıjı ljúdjı astáljıs' bız rıbótı.
IPA ᵏiz-za plɐxój ɛkɐnǫ́mʲıkʲı mnǫ́gʲrʲı lʲúdʲı ɐstálʲısʲ bʲız rɐbʷǫ́tɨ.

2282

EN Do you like strong black coffee?

RU Ты лю́бишь кре́пкий чёрный ко́фе?
ROM tı ljúbjıś krjépkjıj ćjórnıj kófjı?
IPA tɨ lʲúbʲıɕ krʲépkʲıj tɕę́rnɨj kʷǫ́fʲı?

2283

EN Did you like the coffee we had after dinner last
    night?

RU Тебе́ понра́вился ко́фе, кото́рый мы пи́ли вчера́
    ве́чером по́сле у́жина?

ROM tjɪbjé panrávjɪlsjɪ kófjɪ, katórɪj mɪ píljɪ vɕɪrá vjéɕɪrəm
    pósljɪ úžɪnə?

IPA tʲɪbʲé pɐnrávʲɪɫsʲɪ kʷófʲɪ, kɐtórɨj mɨ pʲílʲɪ ftɕɪrá
    vʲétɕɪrəm pʷóslʲɪ úzɨnə?

2284

EN Some people are afraid of spiders.

RU Не́которые боя́тся пауко́в.

ROM njékətərɪjɪ bajátsjɪ paukóv.

IPA nʲékətərɨjɪ bɐʲǽtsʲɪ pɐʊkʷóf.

2285

EN A vegetarian is someone who doesn't eat meat.

RU Вегетариа́нец - тот, кто не ест мя́со.

ROM vjɪgjɪtarɪánjɪts - tot, kto njɪ jɛst mjásə.

IPA vʲɪɡʲɪtɐrʲɪánʲɪts - tot, ktɔ nʲɪ ʲɛst mʲásə.

2286

EN Do you know the people who live next door?

RU Ты зна́ешь тех, кто живёт с тобо́й по сосе́дству?

ROM tɪ znájeś tjɛh, kto žɪvjót s tabój pa sasjédstvu?

IPA tɨ znáʲɪɕ tʲex, ktɔ zɨvʲǿt s tɐbʷój pɐ sɐsʲétstfʊ?

2287

EN History is the study of the past.

RU История - это наука о прошлом.
ROM jɪstórjɪjə - étə naúkə a próšləm.
IPA ᶨɪstǫ́r ᶨɪ́ə - étə nɐúkə ɐ próʂləm.

2288

EN The water in the pool didn't look clean, so we didn't go swimming.

RU Вода в бассейне выглядела грязной, так что мы не поплавали.
ROM vadá v bassjéjnjɪ vɪ́gljadjɪlə grjáznəj, tak što mɪ njɪ paplávəljɪ.
IPA vɐdá v bɐssᶨéjn ᶨɪ vɪ́glᶨɪd ᶨɪlə gr ᶨáznəj, tak ʂtǫ mɨ n ᶨɪ pɐplávəl ᶨɪ.

2289

EN You need patience to teach young children.

RU Нужно терпение, чтобы преподавать маленьким детям.
ROM núžnə tjɪrpjénjɪjɪ, štóbɪ prɪpədavát' máljen'kjɪm djétjɪm.
IPA núz̦nə t ᶨɪrp ᶨén ᶨɪ́ɪ, ʂtǫ́bɨ pr ᶨɪpədɐvát ᶨ mál ᶨɪn ᶨk ᶨɪm d ᶨét ᶨɪm.

2290

EN Paolo and Giuliana got married, but the marriage
didn't last very long.

RU Па́оло и Джулиа́на пожени́лись, но их брак не
продли́лся до́лго.

ROM páələ i džuljıánə pažıníljıs', no ih brak njı pradlílsjı
dólgə.

IPA páələ ı dzʊlʲıánə pɐʐın^jíl^jıs^j, nọ ^jix brak n^jı prɐdl^jíɫs^jı
dọ́ɫgə.

2291

EN A pacifist is a person who is against war.

RU Пацифи́ст - тот, кто про́тив войны́.

ROM patsıfíst - tot, kto prótjıv vajní.

IPA pɐtsıf^jíst - tọt, ktọ prọ́t^jıv vɐjní.

2292

EN Do you think the rich should pay higher taxes?

RU Как ты счита́ешь, бога́тые должны́ плати́ть бо́лее
высо́кие нало́ги?

ROM kak tı śśıtájeś, bagátıjı dalžní platít' bóljejı vısókjıjı
nalógjı?

IPA kak tı ɕɕıtá^jıɕ, bɐgát^jı dɐɫzní plɐt^jít' b^wọ́l^jɪ^jı vısọ́k^jɪ^jı
nɐlọ́g^jı?

2293

EN The government has promised to provide more money to help the homeless.

RU Госуда́рство пообеща́ло вы́делить бо́льше де́нег на по́мощь бе́дным.

ROM gasudárstvə paabjıççálə vídjeljıt' ból'šı djénjıg na póməçç' bjédnım.

IPA gɐsʊdárstfə pɐɐbʲıççálə vídʲılʲıtʲ bʷǫ́lʲs̨ı dʲénʲıg na pʷǫ́məçç' bʲédnɨm.

2294

EN The French are famous for their food.

RU Францу́зы изве́стны свое́й ку́хней.

ROM frıntsúzı jızvjésnı svajéj kúhnjej.

IPA frɐntsúzɨ ʲ ızvʲésnɨ svɐʲéj kúxnʲıj.

2295

EN The Chinese invented printing.

RU Кита́йцы изобре́ли книгопеча́тание.

ROM kjıtájtsı jızabrjéljı knjıgapjıçátənjıjı.

IPA kʲıtájtsɨ ʲ ızɐbrʲélʲı knʲıgɐpʲıtçátənʲrʲı.

2296

EN The dollar is the currency of many countries.

RU До́ллар - э́то валю́та мно́гих стран.

ROM dóllər - étə valjútə mnógjıh stran.

IPA dǫ́łlər - étə vɐlʲútə mnǫ́gʲıx stran.

2297

EN   Life is all right if you have a job, but things are not
     so easy for the unemployed.

RU   Жизнь стаби́льна, е́сли у тебя́ есть рабо́та, но всё
     стано́вится намно́го сложне́е, е́сли ты
     безрабо́тный.

ROM žīzn' stabíl'nə, jéslјı u tјıbjá jest' rıbótə, no vsjó
     stanóvjıtsjı namnógə slažnjéjı, jéslјı tı bjızrıbótnıj.

IPA zɨznʲ stɐbʲílʲnə, ʲéslʲı u tʲıbʲá ʲestʲ rɐbʷótə, nọ fsʲǫ́
     stɐnóvʲıtsʲı nɐmnǫ́gə slɐznʲéʲı, ʲéslʲı tɨ bʲızrɐbʷótnɨj.

2298

EN   It is said that Robin Hood took money from the rich
     and gave it to the poor.

RU   Говоря́т, Ро́бин Гуд отбира́л де́ньги у бога́тых и
     раздава́л их бе́дным.

ROM gəvarját, robin gud atbjırál djén'gjı u bagátıh i
     rızdavál ih bjédnım.

IPA gəvɐrʲát, rọbʲin gud ɐtbʲıráɫ dʲénʲgʲı u bɐgátɨx ı
     rəzdɐváɫ ʲix bʲédnɨm.

2299

EN   Cairo's the capital of Egypt.

RU   Кайр - столи́ца Еги́пта.

ROM kaír - stalítsə jıgíptə.

IPA kɐʲír - stɐlʲítsə ʲıgʲíptə.

2300

EN The Atlantic Ocean is between Africa and America.

RU Атлантический океан находится между Африкой
и Америкой.

ROM ətlantíćıskjıj akjıán nahódjıtsjı mjéždu áfrjıkəj i
amjérjıkəj.

IPA ətlɐnⁱítɕiskʲɪj ɐkʲɪán nɐxóɕdʲɪtsʲɪ mʲéz̪du áfrʲɪkəj ɪ
ɐmʲérʲɪkəj.

GMS #2301 - 2400

2301

EN Sweden is a country in northern Europe.

RU Швéция - э́то странá в сéверной Еврóпе.
ROM švjétsɪjə - étə strɪná v sjévjɪrnəj jɪvrópjɪ.
IPA ʂfʲétsɨʲə - étə strɐná f sʲévʲɪrnəj ʲɪvrópʲɪ.

2302

EN The Amazon is a river in South America.

RU Амазóнка - рекá в Ю́жной Амéрике.
ROM əmazónkə - rɪká v júžnəj amjérjɪkjɪ.
IPA əmɐzónkə - rʲɪká v ʲúznəj ɐmʲérʲɪkʲɪ.

2303

EN Asia is the largest continent in the world.

RU Áзия - э́то сáмый большóй континéнт в мúре.
ROM ázjɪjə - étə sámɪj balʹšój kantjɪnjént v mírjɪ.
IPA ázʲɨʲə - étə sámɨj bɐlʲʂój kɐntʲɪnʲént v mʲírʲɪ.

2304

EN The Pacific is the largest ocean.

RU Тúхий океáн - сáмый большóй океáн.
ROM tíhjɪj akjɪán - sámɪj balʹšój akjɪán.
IPA tʲíxʲɪj ɐkʲɪán - sámɨj bɐlʲʂój ɐkʲɪán.

2305

EN The Rhine is a river in Europe.

RU Рейн - рекá в Еврóпе.
ROM rjejn - rɪká v jɪvrópjɪ.
IPA rʲejn - rʲɪká v ʲɪvrópʲɪ.

2306

EN Kenya is a country in East Africa.

RU Кéния - странá в Востóчной Áфрике.
ROM kjénjɪjə - strɪná v vastóćnəj áfrjɪkjɪ.
IPA kʲénʲrʲə - strʊná v vɐstótɕnəj áfrʲɪkʲɪ.

2307

EN The United States is between Canada and Mexico.

RU Соединённые Штáты (США) нахóдятся мéжду Канáдой и Мéксикой.
ROM sajɪdjɪnjónnɪjɪ štátɪ (sɪša) nahódjatsjɪ mjéždu kanádəj i mjéksjɪkəj.
IPA sʊʲɪdʲɪnʲénnɨʲɪ ʂtátɨ (sɨʂa) nɐxódʲɪtsʲɪ mʲéʐdu kʊnádəj ɪ mʲéksʲɪkəj.

2308

EN The Andes are mountains in South America.

RU Áнды - это гóры в Южной Амéрике.
ROM ándɪ - étə górɪ v júžnəj amjérjɪkjɪ.
IPA ándɨ - étə gʷórɨ v ʲúʐnəj ʊmʲérʲɪkʲɪ.

2309

EN Bangkok is the capital of Thailand.

RU Бангкóк - столи́ца Тайлáнда.
ROM banhkók - stalítsə tajlándə.
IPA bɐnxkʷǫ́k - stɐlʲítsə tɐjlándə.

2310

EN The Alps are mountains in central Europe.

RU А́льпы - гóры в центрáльной Еврóпе.
ROM ál'pɪ - górɪ v tsɪntrál'nəj jɪvrópjɪ.
IPA álʲpɨ - gʷǫ́rɨ f tsɨntrálʲnəj ʲɪvrǫ́pʲɪ.

2311

EN The Sahara is a desert in northern Africa.

RU Сахáра - э́то пусты́ня на сéвере А́фрики.
ROM sahárə - étə pustínjɪ na sjévjerjɪ áfrjɪkjɪ.
IPA sɐxárə - étə pʊstínʲɪ na sʲévʲɪrʲɪ áfrʲɪkʲɪ.

2312

EN The Philippines is a group of islands near Taiwan.

RU Филиппи́ны - э́то гру́ппа островóв óколо Тайвáня.
ROM fjɪlljɪpínɪ - étə grúppə əstravóv ókələ tajvánjɪ.
IPA fʲɪɫlʲɪpʲínɨ - étə grúppə əstrɐvʷǫ́v ǫ́kələ tɐjvánʲɪ.

2313

EN Have you ever been to the south of France?

RU Ты когда́-нибудь быва́л (♀ быва́ла) на ю́ге Фра́нции?

ROM tɪ kagdá-njɪbud' bɪvál (♀ bɪvála) na júgjɪ f[rántsɪjɪ?

IPA tɨ kɐgdá-nʲɪbʊdʲ bɨváɫ (♀ bɨvála) na ʲʉ́gʲɪ frántsɨ̆ʲɪ?

2314

EN I hope to go to the United Kingdom next year.

RU Я наде́юсь побыва́ть в Объединеннёном Короле́встве в сле́дующем году́.

ROM ja nadjéjus' pabɪvát' v abjɪdjɪnjɪnjónəm kəraljéstvjɪ v sljédujuҫcɪm gadú.

IPA ʲa nɐdʲéʲüsʲ pɐbɨvátʲ v ɐbʲɪdʲɪnʲɪnnʲǫ́nəm kərɐʎ́éʋstfʲɪ f sʎ́édʊʲüҫ̧ɨm gɐdú.

2315

EN Scotland, Britain (England), and Wales are all in the United Kingdom.

RU Шотла́ндия, Брита́ния (А́нглия) и Уэ́льс - э́то всё есть Объединённое Короле́вство.

ROM šatlándjɪjɪ, brɪtánjɪjə (ángljɪjɪ) i uél's - étə vsjó jest' abjɪdjɪnjónnəjɪ kəraljéstvə.

IPA ʂɐtlándʲɪ̃ʲɪ, brʲɪtánʲɪ̃ʲə (ánglʲɪ̃ʲɪ) ɪ ʊélʲs - étə fsʲǫ́ ʲestʲ ɐbʲɪdʲɪnʲǫ́nnəʲɪ kərɐʎ́éʋstfə.

2316

EN The Great Wall of China is in China.

RU Вели́кая кита́йская стена́ нахо́дится в Кита́е.
ROM vjɪlíkəjə kjɪtájskəjɪ stjɪná nahódjɪtsjɪ v kjɪtájɪ.
IPA vʲɪlʲíkəʲə kʲɪtájskəʲɪ stʲɪná nɐxódʲɪtsʲɪ f kʲɪtáʲɪ.

2317

EN UCLA is in L.A.

RU УКЛА (Университе́т Калифо́рнии в
Лос-А́нджелесе) нахо́дится в Лос-А́нджелесе.
ROM ukla (unjɪvjɪrsjɪtjét kaljɪfórnjɪjɪ v las-ándžɪljesjɪ)
nahódjɪtsjɪ v las-ándžɪljesjɪ.
IPA ukla (ʊnʲɪvʲɪrsʲɪtʲét kɐlʲɪfʷórnʲɪrʲɪ v lɐs-ándzɨlʲɪsʲɪ)
nɐxódʲɪtsʲɪ v lɐs-ándzɨlʲɪsʲɪ.

2318

EN The Guggenheim Museum is in New York.

RU Музе́й Гуггенха́йма нахо́дится в Нью-Йо́рке.
ROM muzjéj guggjɪnhájmə nahódjɪtsjɪ v nju-jórkjɪ.
IPA mʊzʲéj gʊggʲɪnxájmə nɐxódʲɪtsʲɪ v nʲü-jórkʲɪ.

2319

EN The Acropolis is in Athens.

RU Акро́поль нахо́дится в Афи́нах.
ROM akrópəl' nahódjɪtsjɪ v afínəh.
IPA ɐkrópəlʲ nɐxódʲɪtsʲɪ v ɐfʲínəx.

2320

EN The Kremlin is in Moscow.

RU Кремль нахо́дится в Москве́.
ROM krjeml' nahódjɪtsjɪ v maskvjé.
IPA krʲemlʲ nɐxódʲɪtsʲɪ v mɐskfʲé.

2321

EN The Pentagon is in Washington, D.C.

RU Пентаго́н нахо́дится в Вашингто́не.
ROM pjɪntagón nahódjɪtsjɪ v vašɪngtónjɪ.
IPA pʲɪntɐgʷón nɐxódʲɪtsʲɪ v vɐʂɨngtónʲɪ.

2322

EN The bicycle and the car are means of transportation.

RU Велосипе́ды и автомоби́ли - сре́дства
передвиже́ния.
ROM vjɪlasjɪpjédɪ i əvtəmabíljɪ - srjédstvə pjɪrɪdvjɪžjénjɪjə.
IPA vʲɪlɐsʲɪpʲédɨ ɪ əftəmɐbʲílʲɪ - srʲétstfə pʲɪrʲɪdvʲɪzɛnʲɪrʲə.

2323

EN The police want to interview two (2) men about the robbery last week.

RU Полиция хотела опросить двух человек по поводу кражи на прошлой неделе.

ROM palítsɪjə hatjélə əprasít' dvuh ćɪlavjék pa póvədu kráži na próšləj njɪdjéljɪ.

IPA pɐlʲítsɨˠə xɐtʲélə əprɐsʲítʲ dvux tɕɪlɐvʲék pɐ pʷǫ́vədʊ krázɨ̯ na próʂləj nʲɪdʲélʲɪ.

2324

EN Fortunately, the news wasn't as bad as we expected.

RU К счастью, новости оказались не такими плохими, как мы ожидали.

ROM k śśást'ju, nóvəstjɪ əkazáljɪs' njɪ takímjɪ plahímjɪ, kak mɪ ažɪdáljɪ.

IPA k ɕɕástʲü, nǫ́vəstʲɪ əkɐzálʲɪsʲ nʲɪ tɐkʲímʲɪ plɐxʲímʲɪ, kak mɨ ɐʐɨdálʲɪ.

2325

EN Do the police know how the accident happened?

RU Полиция знает о произошедшем инциденте? Полиция знает как случилось эта авария?

ROM palítsɪjə znájɪt a prəjɪzašjédšɪm jɪntsɪdjéntjɪ? palítsɪjə znájɪt kak slućíləs' étə avárjɪjə?

IPA pɐlʲítsɨˠə znáˠɪt ɐ prəˠɪzɐʂétʂɨm ˠɪntsɨdʲéntʲɪ? pɐlʲítsɨˠə znáˠɪt kak slʊtɕíləsʲ étə ɐvárʲrʲə?

2326

EN I don't like hot weather. Ninety degrees is too hot for me. > I don't like hot weather. Thirty-two (32) degrees is too hot for me.

RU Я не люблю жару. Тридцать два градуса - это для меня слишком (жарко).

ROM ja njı ljubljú žırú. trídtsət' dva grádusə - étə dlja mjınjá slíškəm (žárkə).

IPA ʲa nʲı lʲüblʲú z̯ırú. trʲíttsətʲ dva grádʊsə - étə dlʲa mʲınʲá slʲíşkəm (z̯árkə).

2327

EN I need more than ten (10) dollars. Ten dollars isn't enough. > I need more than six (6) euros. Six euros isn't enough.

RU Мне нужно больше, чем триста рублей. Трёхста рублей недостаточно.

ROM mnjɛ núžnə ból'šı, ćım trístə rubljéj. trjóhstá rubljéj njıdastátəćnə.

IPA mnʲɛ núznə bʷǫlʲşɨ, tɕɛm trʲístə rʊblʲéj. trʲǫ́xstá rʊblʲéj nʲıdɐstátətɕnə.

2328

EN Do you think two (2) days is enough time to visit New York?

RU Ты ду́маешь двух (2) дней доста́точно для того́, чтобы посети́ть Нью-Йо́рк?

ROM tɪ dúməjeś dvuh (2) dnjej dastátəćnə dlja tavó, štóbɪ pasjɪtít' nju-jórk?

IPA tɨ dúməʲɪɕ dvux (2) dnʲej dᴇstátətɕnə dlʲa tᴇvʷǫ́, ʂtǫ́bɨ pᴇsʲɪtʲítʲ nʲü-jǫ́rk?

2329

EN Problems concerning health are health problems.

RU Пробле́мы, каса́ющиеся здоро́вья, - пробле́мы со здоро́вьем.

ROM prabljémɪ, kasájuȼȼɪjesjɪ zdaróvjɪ, - prabljémɪ sa zdaróvjɪm.

IPA prᴇblʲémɨ, kᴇsáʲüȼȼɨⁱsʲɪ zdᴇrǫ́vʲɪ, - prᴇblʲémɨ sᴇ zdᴇrǫ́vʲɪm.

2330

EN Chocolate made from milk is milk chocolate.

RU Шокола́д, кото́рый де́лают с добавле́нием молока́, - моло́чный шокола́д.

ROM šəkalád, katórɪj djélajut s dəbavljénjɪjɪm məlaká, - malóćnɪj šəkalád.

IPA ʂəkᴇlát, kᴇtǫ́rɨj dʲéləʲüt s dəbᴇvlʲénʲrʲɪm məlᴇká, - mᴇlǫ́tɕnɨj ʂəkᴇlát.

2331

EN Someone whose job is to inspect factories is a factory inspector.

RU Тот, чья рабо́та заключа́ется в инспекти́ровании заво́дов, - инспе́ктор заво́дов.

ROM tot, ćja rıbótə zakljućájetsjı v jınspjıktírəvənjıjı zavódəv, - jınspjéktər zavódəv.

IPA to̞t, tɕʲa rɐbʷó̞tə zɐklʲütɕáʲıtsʲı v ʲınspʲıktʲírəvənʲɾʲı zɐvʷó̞dəf, - ʲınspʲéktər zɐvʷó̞dəf.

2332

EN The results of your exams are your exam results.

RU Результа́ты твоего́ экза́мена - э́то экзаменацио́нные результа́ты.

ROM rızul'tátı tvajıvó ɛkzámjınə - étə ɛkzamjınatsıónnıjı rızul'tátı.

IPA rʲızʊlʲtátɨ tfɐʲıvʷó̞ ɛksámʲınə - étə ɛksamʲınɐtsıó̞nnɨʲı rʲızʊlʲtátɨ.

2333

EN A scandal involving an oil company is an oil company scandal.

RU Сканда́л, затра́гивающий нефтяны́е компа́нии, называ́ется нефтяны́м сканда́лом.

ROM skandál, zatrágjıvəjuççıj njıftjıníjı kampánjıjı, nazıvájetsjı njıftjıním skandáləm.

IPA skɐndáɫ, zɐtrágʲıvəʲüççıj nʲıftʲınʲᵻı kɐmpánʲɾʲı, nɐzɨváʲıtsʲı nʲıftʲıním skɐndáləm.

2334

EN A building with five (5) stories is a five-story building.

RU Зда́ние с пятью́ (5) этажа́ми - э́то пятиэта́жное зда́ние.

ROM zdánjɪjɪ s pjɪt'jú (5) ɛtažámjɪ - étə pjɪtjɪɛtážnəjɪ zdánjɪjɪ.

IPA zdánʲrʲɪ s pʲɪtʲú (5) ɛtɐzámʲɪ - étə pʲɪtʲɪɛtáznəʲɪ zdánʲrʲɪ.

2335

EN A man who is thirty (30) years old is a thirty-year-old man.

RU Мужчи́на, кото́рому три́дцать (30) лет, - тридцатиле́тний мужчи́на.

ROM muśśínə, katórəmu trídtsət' (30) ljɛt, - trɪdtsɪtjɪljétnjɪj muśśínə.

IPA mʊççínə, kɐtórəmʊ trʲíttsətʲ (30) lʲet, - trʲɪttsɨtʲɪlʲétnʲɪj mʊççínə.

2336

EN A course that lasts twelve (12) weeks is a twelve-week course.

RU Курс, кото́рый дли́тся двена́дцать (12) неде́ль, - двенадцатинеде́льный курс.

ROM kurs, katórɪj dlítsjɪ dvjɪnádtsət' (12) njɪdjél', - dvjɪmədtsɪtjɪnjɪdjél'nɪj kurs.

IPA kurs, kɐtórɨj dlʲítsʲɪ dvʲɪnáttsətʲ (12) nʲɪdʲélʲ, - dvʲɪnəttsɨtʲɪnʲɪdʲélʲnɨj kurs.

2337

EN A drive that takes two (2) hours is a two-hour drive.

RU Поéздка на машúне в течéние двух (2) часóв -
двухчасовáя поéздка на машúне.

ROM pajézdkə na mašínjɪ v tjɪćjénjɪjɪ dvuh (2) ćɪsóv -
dvuhćɪsavájə pajézdkə na mašínjɪ.

IPA pɐʲéstkə na mɐʂínʲɪ f tʲɪtɕénʲrʲɪ dvux (2) tɕɪsóf -
dvʊxtɕɪsɐváʲə pɐʲéstkə na mɐʂínʲɪ.

2338

EN A question that has two (2) parts is a two-part
question.

RU Вопрóс из двух (2) частéй - двухчáстный вопрóс.

ROM vaprós iz dvuh (2) ćɪstjéj - dvuhćásnɪj vaprós.

IPA vɐprós ʲiz dvux (2) tɕɪstʲéj - dvʊxtɕásnɪj vɐprós.

2339

EN The meeting tomorrow has been canceled. >
Tomorrow's meeting has been canceled.

RU Встрéча, назнáченная на зáвтра, былá отменена́. >
Зáвтрашняя встрéча былá отменена́.

ROM vstrjéćə, naznáćɪnnəjɪ na závtrə, bɪlá atmjɪnjɪná. >
závtrəšnjajɪ vstrjéćə bɪlá atmjɪnjɪná.

IPA fstrʲétɕə, nɐznátɕɪnnəʲɪ na záftrə, bɪlá ɐtmʲɪnʲɪná. >
záftrəʂnʲrʲɪ fstrʲétɕə bɪlá ɐtmʲɪnʲɪná.

2340

EN The storm last week caused a lot of damage. > Last
week's storm caused a lot of damage.

RU Шторм на про́шлой неде́ле принёс мно́жество
разруше́ний. > Неда́вний шторм принёс
мно́жество разруше́ний.

ROM štórm na próšləj njɪdjéljɪ prɪnjós mnóžɪstvə
rɪzrušjénjɪj. > njɪdávnjɪj štorm prɪnjós mnóžɪstvə
rɪzrušjénjɪj.

IPA ştǫrm na prǫ́şləj nʲɪdʲélʲɪ prʲɪnʲǫs mnǫ́zɪstfə rɐzruşénʲɪj.
> nʲɪdávnʲɪj ştǫrm prʲɪnʲǫs mnǫ́zɪstfə rɐzruşénʲɪj.

2341

EN Tourism is the main industry in the region. > The
region's main industry is tourism.

RU Тури́зм - основно́й вид де́ятельности в регио́не. >
Основно́й вид де́ятельности в регио́не - тури́зм.

ROM turízm - əsnavnój vid djéjatjel'nəstjɪ v rɪgjɪónjɪ. >
əsnavnój vid djéjatjel'nəstjɪ v rɪgjɪónjɪ - turízm.

IPA turʲízm - əsnɐvnój vʲid dʲéʲɪtʲɪlʲnəstʲɪ v rʲɪgʲɪǫ́nʲɪ. >
əsnɐvnój vʲid dʲéʲɪtʲɪlʲnəstʲɪ v rʲɪgʲɪǫ́nʲɪ - turʲízm.

2342

EN I bought enough groceries at the supermarket last
night for a week. > I bought a week's worth of
groceries last night.

RU Вчера́ ве́чером в суперма́ркете я купи́л (♀купи́ла)
о́вощи, кото́рых хва́тит на всю неде́лю. > Вчера́
ве́чером я купи́л (♀купи́ла) неде́льный запа́с
овоще́й.

ROM vćɪrá vjéćɪrəm v supjɪrmárkjetjɪ ja kupíl (♀kupílə)
óvəççɪ, katórɪh hvátjɪt na vsju njɪdjélju. > vćɪrá
vjéćɪrəm ja kupíl (♀kupílə) njɪdjél'nɪj zapás əvaççjéj.

IPA ftɕɪrá vʲétɕɪrəm f supʲɪrmárkʲɪtʲɪ ʲa kʊpʲíɫ (♀kʊpʲílə)
óvəççɨ, kɐtórɨx xfátʲɪt na fsʲu nʲɪdʲéɫʲü. > ftɕɪrá
vʲétɕɪrəm ʲa kʊpʲíɫ (♀kʊpʲílə) nʲɪdʲéɫʲnɨj zɐpás əvɐççɨ́j.

2343

EN I haven't been able to rest for even a minute all day.
> I haven't had a minute's rest all day.

RU Сего́дня днём я ни мину́ты не мог (♀могла́)
отдохну́ть. > Сего́дня днём у меня́ не́ было и
мину́тного переры́ва на о́тдых.

ROM sjɪvódnjɪ dnjóm ja ni mjɪnútɪ njɪ mog (♀maglá)
ətdahnút'. > sjɪvódnjɪ dnjóm u mjɪnjá njé bɪlo i
mjɪnútnəvə pjɪrɪrívə na ótdɪh.

IPA sʲɪvʷódnʲɪ dnʲǿm ʲa nʲi mʲɪnútɨ nʲɪ mʷok (♀mɐglá)
ətdɐxnútʲ. > sʲɪvʷódnʲɪ dnʲǿm u mʲɪnʲá nʲɛ́ bɨlə ɪ
mʲɪnútnəvə pʲɪrʲɪrívə na ótdɨx.

344

EN   I don't want you to pay for me. I'll pay for myself.

RU   Я не хочу́, что́бы ты плати́л (♀плати́ла) за меня́. Я сам (♀сама́) за себя́ заплачу́.

ROM ja njı haćú, štóbı tı platíl (♀platílə) za mjınjá. ja sam (♀samá) za sjıbjá zəplaćú.

IPA ʲa nʲɪ xɐtɕú, ʂtóbɨ tɨ plɐtʲíɫ (♀plɐtʲílə) za mʲɪnʲá. ʲa sam (♀sɐmá) za sʲɪbʲá zəplɐtɕú.

345

EN   Do you talk to yourself sometimes?

RU   Ты иногда́ разгова́риваешь сам (♀сама́) с собо́й?

ROM tı jınagdá rızgavárjıvəjeś sam (♀samá) s sabój?

IPA tɨ ʲɪnɐgdá rəzgɐvárʲɪvəʲɪɕ sam (♀sɐmá) s sɐbʷój?

346

EN   If you want more to eat, help yourselves.

RU   Éсли вы хоти́те доба́вки, угоща́йтесь.

ROM jésljı vı hatítjı dabávkjı, ugaɕɕájtjes'.

IPA ʲéslʲɪ vɨ xɐtʲítʲɪ dɐbáfkʲɪ, ʊgɐɕɕájtʲɪsʲ.

347

EN   It's not our fault. You can't blame us.

RU   Э́то не на́ша вина́.Ты не мо́жешь нас вини́ть.

ROM étə njı náśə vjıná.tı njı móžıś nas vjınít'.

IPA étə nʲɪ náʂə vʲɪná.tɨ nʲɪ mʷóʐɨɕ nas vʲɪnʲítʲ.

2348

EN It's our own fault. We should blame ourselves.

RU Это наша вина. Мы должны винить себя.

ROM étə náša vjıná. mı dalžní vjınít' sjıbjá.

IPA étə náşə vʲıná. mɨ dɐɫzʲní vʲmʲítʲ sʲıbʲá.

2349

EN I feel nervous. I can't relax.

RU Я нервничаю. Я не могу расслабиться.

ROM ja njérvnjıćəju. ja njı magú rısslábjıt'sjı.

IPA ʲa nʲérvnʲıtɕəʲü. ʲa nʲı mɐgú rɐsslábʲıtʲsʲı.

2350

EN You have to try and concentrate.

RU Ты должен (♀ должна) постараться сосредоточиться.

ROM tı dólžın (♀ dalžná) pəstarát'sjı səsrıdatóćıt'sjı.

IPA tɨ dóɫzʲin (♀ dɐɫzná) pəstɐrátʲsʲı səsrʲıdɐtótɕɨtʲsʲı.

2351

EN What time should we meet?

RU Во сколько мы сможем встретиться?

ROM va skól'kə mı smóžım vstrjétjıt'sjı?

IPA vɐ skʷóɫʲkə mɨ smʷózɨm fstrʲétʲıtʲsʲı?

2352

EN He got up, washed, shaved, and got dressed.

RU Он проснýлся, умы́лся, побри́лся и одéлся.
ROM on prasnúlsjɪ, umílsjɪ, pabrílsjɪ i adjélsjɪ.
IPA o̞n prɐsnúɫsʲɪ, ʊmɨ́ɫsʲɪ, pɐbrʲíɫsʲɪ ɪ ɐdʲéɫsʲɪ.

2353

EN How long have you and Kenichi known each other?
> How long have you known one another?

RU Как дóлго ты и Кэнъ́йти ужé знáете друг дрýга?
> Скóлько вы ужé знакóмы?
ROM kak dólgə tɪ i kɛnítjɪ užjé znájetjɪ drug drúgə? >
skól'kə vɪ užjé znakómɪ?
IPA kak dɔ́ɫgə tɨ ɪ kɛnʲítʲɪ ʊzʲɪ́ znáʲɪtʲɪ drug drúgə? >
skʷɔ́lʲkə vɨ ʊzʲɪ́ znɐkʷómɨ?

2354

EN Kasumi and Linda don't like each other. > They
don't like one another.

RU Касýми и Ли́нда недолю́бливают друг дрýга. >
Касýми и Ли́нда не нрáвятся друг дрýгу.
ROM kasúmjɪ i líndə njɪdaljúbljɪvəjut drug drúgə. >
kasúmjɪ i líndə njɪ nrávjatsjɪ drug drúgu.
IPA kɐsúmʲɪ ɪ lʲíndə nʲɪdɐlʲúblʲɪvəʲüt drug drúgə. >
kɐsúmʲɪ ɪ lʲíndə nʲɪ nrávʲɪtsʲɪ drug drúgʊ.

2355

EN Do you and Henrik live near each other? > Do you
two (2) live near one another?

RU Вы с Хэнриком ря́дом живёте? > Вы живёте
ря́дом?

ROM vɪ s hénrjɪkəm rjádəm žɪvjótjɪ? > vɪ žɪvjótjɪ rjádəm?

IPA vɨ s xénrʲɪkəm rʲádəm zɨvʲə́tʲɪ? > vɨ zɨvʲə́tʲɪ rʲádəm?

2356

EN I'm not going to do your work for you. You can do it
yourself.

RU Я не собира́юсь де́лать твою́ рабо́ту. Ты мо́жешь
её сде́лать сам (♀ сама́).

ROM ja njɪ sabjɪrájus' djélət' tvajú rɪbótu. tɪ móžɪś jɪjó
sdjélət' sam (♀ samá).

IPA ʲa nʲɪ sɐbʲɪráʲüsʲ dʲélətʲ tfɐʲú rɐbʷótʊ. tɨ mʷózɨɕ ʲrʲə́
zdʲélətʲ sam (♀ sɐmá).

2357

EN The movie itself wasn't very good, but I loved the
music.

RU Сам фильм был не о́чень хоро́шим, но мне
понра́вилась му́зыка.

ROM sam fil'm bɪl njɪ óćɪn' haróšɪm, no mnjɛ panrávjɪləs'
múzɪkə.

IPA sam fʲilʲm bɨɫ nʲɪ ótɕɪnʲ xɐró̜sɨm, nɔ mnʲɛ pɐnrávʲɪləsʲ
múzɨkə.

2358

EN Even Magda herself doesn't think she'll get the new job.

RU Ма́гда да́же сама́ не уве́рена, что полу́чит но́вую рабо́ту.

ROM mágdə dáži samá njı uvjérjınə, što palúćıt nóvuju rıbótu.

IPA mágdə dáz̦ı sɐmá nʲɪ ʊvʲérʲɪnə, ʂtɔ pɐlútɕɪt nǫvʊʲü rɐbʷǫtʊ.

2359

EN She climbed out of the swimming pool and dried herself off with a towel.

RU Она́ вы́лезла из бассе́йна и вы́терлась полоте́нцем.

ROM aná víljızlə iz bassjéjnə i vítjırləs' pəlatjéntsım.

IPA ɐná vílʲɪzlə ʲiz bɐssʲéjnə ɪ vítʲɪrləsʲ pəlɐtʲéntsɪm.

2360

EN I tried to study, but I couldn't concentrate.

RU Я попыта́лся (♀попыта́лась) сесть за учёбу, но не смог (♀смогла́) сосредото́читься.

ROM ja papıtálsjı (♀papıtáləs') sjest' za ućjóbu, no njı smog (♀smaglá) səsrıdatóćıt'sjı.

IPA ʲa pɐpɪtáɫsʲɪ (♀pɐpɪtáləsʲ) sʲestʲ za ʊtɕébu, nǫ nʲɪ smʷok (♀smɐglá) səsrʲɪdɐtǫtɕɪtʲsʲɪ.

2361

EN If somebody attacks you, you need to be able to defend yourself.

RU Éсли кто́-нибудь на тебя́ нападёт, ты до́лжен (♀должна́) уме́ть защити́ть себя́.

ROM jésljı któ-njıbud' na tjıbjá nəpadjót, tı dólžın (♀dalžná) umjét' zaççıtít' sjıbjá.

IPA ʲéslʲɪ ktǫ́-nʲɪbʊdʲ na tʲɪbʲá nəpɐdʲę́t, tɨ dǫ́łzɪ̦n (♀dɐłzṇá) ʊmʲétʲ zɐꞔꞔɨtʲítʲ sʲɪbʲá.

2362

EN You're always rushing around. Why don't you sit down and relax?

RU Ты всё вре́мя торо́пишься. Почему́ бы тебе́ не се́сть и успоко́иться?

ROM tı vsjó vrjémjı tarópjıśsjı. paćımú bı tjıbjé njı sjést' i uspakójıt'sjı?

IPA tɨ fsʲę́ vrʲémʲɪ tɐrópʲɪꞔsʲɪ. pɐtꞔɨmú bɨ tʲɪbʲé nʲɪ sʲéstʲ ɪ ʊspɐkʷǫ́ɪtʲsʲɪ?

2363

EN Some people are very selfish. They think only of themselves.

RU Не́которые лю́ди о́чень эгоисти́чны. Они́ ду́мают то́лько о себе́.

ROM njékətərıjı ljúdjı óćın' ɛgajıstíćnı. aní dúməjut tól'kə a sjıbjé.

IPA nʲékətərɨʲɪ lʲúdʲɪ ǫ́tꞔin ̍ɛgɐʲɪstʲítꞔnɨ. ɐnʲí dúməʲüt tǫ́lʲkə ɐ sʲɪbʲé.

2364

EN We couldn't get back into the house because we had locked ourselves out.

RU Мы не смогли́ войти́ обра́тно в дом, поско́льку дверь была́ за́перта изнутри́.

ROM mɪ njɪ smaglí vajtí abrátnə v dom, paskól'ku dvjer' bɪlá zápjɪrtə jɪznutrí.

IPA mɨ nʲɪ smɐglʲí vɐjtʲí ɐbrátnə v dǫm, pɐskʷǫ́lʲku dvʲerʲ bɨlá zápʲɪrtə ʲɪznʊtrʲí.

2365

EN They're not speaking to each other anymore.

RU Они́ бо́льше не разгова́ривают друг с дру́гом.

ROM aní ból'šɪ njɪ rɪzgavárjɪvəjut drug s drúgəm.

IPA ɐnʲí bʷǫ́lʲʂɨ nʲɪ rəzgɐvárʲɪvəʲüt druk s drúgəm.

2366

EN We'd never met before, so we introduced ourselves to one another.

RU Мы никогда́ не встреча́лись ра́ньше, так что мы предста́вились друг дру́гу.

ROM mɪ njɪkagdá njɪ vstrɪćáljɪs' rán'šɪ, tak što mɪ prɪdstávjɪljɪs' drug drúgu.

IPA mɨ nʲɪkɐgdá nʲɪ fstrʲɪtɕálʲɪsʲ ránʲʂɨ, tak ʂtǫ mɨ prʲɪtstávʲɪlʲɪsʲ drug drúgʊ.

2367

EN A friend of mine is getting married this Saturday.

RU Мой друг жéнится (♀ Моя́ подру́га выхо́дит за́муж) в э́ту суббо́ту.

ROM moj drug žjénjıtsjı (♀ majá padrúgə vıhódjıt zámuž) v étu subbótu.

IPA mʷǫj drug zɛ́nʲɪtsʲɪ (♀ mɐʲá pɐdrúgə vɨxǫ́dʲɪt zámʊz) v étʊ sʊbbʷǫ́tʊ.

2368

EN We took a trip with some friends of ours.

RU Мы отпра́вились в поéздку с нéсколькими на́шими друзья́ми.

ROM mı atprávjıljıs' v pajézdku s njéskəl'kjımjı nášımjı druz'jámjı.

IPA mɨ ɐtprávʲɪlʲɪsʲ f pɐʲéstkʊ s nʲéskəlʲkʲɪmʲɪ nášɨmʲɪ drʊzʲǽmʲɪ.

2369

EN Pietro had an argument with a neighbor of his.

RU Пьéтро поссо́рился с одни́м из свои́х сосéдей.

ROM pjétrə passórjılsjı s adním iz svaíh sasjédjej.

IPA pʲétrə pɐssǫ́rʲɪɫsʲɪ s ɐdnʲím ʲis svɐʲíx sɐsʲédʲɪj.

2370

EN That woman over there is a friend of my sister's.

RU Та же́нщина - подру́га мое́й сестры́.
ROM ta žjénçcɪnə - padrúgə majéj sjɪstrí.
IPA ta zɛ́nçɕɪnə - pɐdrúgə mɐ𐞲éj sʲɪstrí.

2371

EN My sister graduated from college, and is living on her own. > She's living by herself.

RU Моя́ сестра́ око́нчила ко́лледж и сейча́с живёт отде́льно. > Она́ живёт одна́.
ROM majá sjɪstrá akónćɪlə kólljɪdž i sjɪjćás žɪvjót atdjél'nə. > aná žɪvjót adná.
IPA mɐ𐞲á sʲɪstrá ɐkʷɔ́ntɕɪlə kʷɔ́ɫɫʲɪdz̞ ɪ sʲɪjtɕás zʲɪvʲ𐞲ɛ́t ɐtdʲélʲnə. > ɐná zʲɪvʲ𐞲ɛ́t ɐdná.

2372

EN I don't want to share a room with anybody. I want my own room.

RU Я не хочу́ ни с кем дели́ть ко́мнату. Я хочу́ свою́ со́бственную ко́мнату.
ROM ja njɪ haćú ni s kjɛm djɪlít' kómnətu. ja haćú svajú sóbstvjɪnnuju kómnətu.
IPA ʲa nʲɪ xɐtɕú nʲi s kʲɛm dʲɪlʲítʲ kʷɔ́mnətu. ʲa xɐtɕú svɐ𐞲ú sópstfʲɪnnʊʲü kʷɔ́mnətu.

2373

EN It's a shame that the apartment doesn't have its own parking space.

RU Это просто безобразие, что за квартирой не закреплено парковочное место!

ROM étə próstə bjɪzabrázjɪjɪ, što za kvartírəj njɪ zakrɪpljɪnó parkóvəćnəjɪ mjéstə!

IPA étə próstə bʲɪzɐbrázʲr̩ɪ, ştɔ za kfɐrtʲírəj nʲɪ zɐkrʲɪplʲɪnɔ̃ pɐrkʷóvətɕnəʲɪ mʲéstə!

2374

EN Why do you want to borrow my car? Why don't you use your own?

RU Почему ты хочешь одолжить мою машину? Почему бы тебе не воспользоваться своей?

ROM paćɪmú tɪ hóćɪš ədalžít' majú mašínu? paćɪmú bɪ tjɪbjé njɪ vaspól'zəvət'sjɪ svajéj?

IPA pɐtɕɪmú tɨ xótɕɪɕ ədɐɫʐítʲ mɐʲú mɐʂínʊ? pɐtɕɪmú bɨ tʲɪbʲé nʲɪ vɐspʷólʲzəvətʲsʲɪ svɐʲéj?

2375

EN I'd like to have a garden so that I could grow my own vegetables.

RU Я бы хотёл (♀хотёла) иметь свой собственный сад, чтобы выращивать там свои овощи.

ROM ja bɪ hatjél (♀hatjélə) jɪmjét' svoj sóbstvjɪnnɪj sad, štóbɪ vɪráćɕɪvət' tam svaí óvəɕɕɪ.

IPA ʲa bɨ xɐtʲéɫ (♀xɐtʲélə) ʲɪmʲétʲ svʷoj sópstf̬ɨnnɨj sat, ştóbɨ vɨráɕɕɪvətʲ tam svɐʲí óvəɕɕɨ.

2376

EN I traveled around Japan on my own.

RU Я путешéствовал (♀путешéствовала) по Япóнии в одинóчку.

ROM ja putjɪšjéstvəvəl (♀putjɪšjéstvəvələ) pa jɪpónjɪjɪ v adjɪnóćku.

IPA ʲa pʊtʲɪşéstfəvəɫ (♀pʊtʲɪşéstfəvələ) pɐ ʲɪpʷónʲrʲɪ v ɐdʲɪnótɕkʊ.

2377

EN She raises her children as a single mother on her own.

RU Онá мать-одинóчка и растúт ребёнка однá.

ROM aná mət'-adjɪnóćkə i rɪstít rɪbjónkə adná.

IPA ɐná mətʲ-ɐdʲɪnótɕkə ɪ rɐstʲít rʲɪbʲénkə ɐdná.

2378

EN Student drivers are not allowed to drive by themselves.

RU Водúтелям-ученикáм не разрешáется водúть машúну в одинóчку.

ROM vadítjɪljɪm-ućɪnjɪkám njɪ rɪzrɪšájetsjɪ vadít' mašínu v adjɪnóćku.

IPA vɐdʲítʲɪlʲɪm-ʊtɕɪnʲɪkám nʲɪ rɐzrʲɪşáʲɪtsʲɪ vɐdʲítʲ mɐşínʊ v ɐdʲɪnótɕkʊ.

2379

EN Sorry I'm late. There was a lot of traffic.

RU Извини́, я опозда́л (♀опозда́ла). Я попа́л
(♀попа́ла) в про́бку.

ROM jızvjıní, ja əpazdál (♀əpazdálə). ja papál (♀papálə) v
próbku.

IPA ʲızvʲınʲí, ʲa əpɐzdáł (♀əpɐzdálə). ʲa pɐpáł (♀pɐpálə) f
própkʊ.

2380

EN Things are more expensive now. There's been a big
increase in the cost of living.

RU Ве́щи сейча́с намно́го доро́же. Сто́имость
прожива́ния значи́тельно подняла́сь.

ROM vjéççı sjıjćás namnógə daróžı. stójıməst' pražıvánjıjə
znaćítjel'nə padnjılás'.

IPA vʲéççɨ sʲıjtɕás nɐmnógə dɐróʐɨ. stǫ́ʲıməstʲ prɐzɨvánʲrʲə
znɐtɕítʲılʲınə pɐdnʲılásʲ.

2381

EN I wasn't expecting them to come. It was a complete
surprise.

RU Я не ожида́л (♀ожида́ла), что они́ приду́т. Э́то
ста́ло по́лной неожи́данностью.

ROM ja njı ažıdál (♀ažıdálə), što aní prıdút. étə stálə
pólnəj njıažídənnəst'ju.

IPA ʲa nʲı ɐʑɨdáł (♀ɐʑɨdálə), ʂtǫ ɐnʲí prʲıdút. étə stálə
pʷǫ́łnəj nʲıɐʑídənnəstʲü.

2382

EN The new restaurant is very good. I went there last night.

RU Но́вый рестора́н о́чень хоро́ший. Я там был (♀была́) вчера́ ве́чером.

ROM nóvɪj rɪstarán óćɪn' haróšɪj. ja tam bɪl (♀bɪlá) vćɪrá vjéćɪrəm.

IPA nǫ́vɨj rʲɪstɐrán ǫ́tɕɪnʲ xɐrǫ́ʂɨj. ʲa tam bɨɫ (♀bɨlá) ftɕɪrá vʲétɕɨrəm.

2383

EN Is there a flight to Madrid tonight? — There might be, let me check.

RU Сего́дня ве́чером есть рейс до Мадри́да? — Возмо́жно, дава́й я прове́рю.

ROM sjɪvódnjɪ vjéćɪrəm jest' rjejs da madrídə? — vazmóžnə, daváj ja pravjérju.

IPA sʲɪvʷǫ́dnʲɪ vʲétɕɪrəm ʲestʲ rʲejs dɐ mɐdrʲídə? — vɐzmʷǫ́znə, dɐváj ʲa prɐvʲérʲü.

2384

EN If people drove more carefully, there wouldn't be so many accidents.

RU Éсли бы лю́ди води́ли маши́ны аккура́тнее, несча́стных слу́чаев бы́ло бы не так мно́го.

ROM jésljɪ bɪ ljúdjɪ vadíljɪ mašíni akkurátnjejɪ, njɪśśásnɪh slúćəjɪv bɪlo bɪ njɪ tak mnógə.

IPA ʲéslʲɪ bɨ lʲúdʲɪ vɐdʲílʲɪ mɐʂɨnɨ ɐkkʊrátnʲɪʲɪ, nʲɪɕɕásnɨx slútɕəʲɪv bɨlo̞ bɨ nʲɪ tak mnǫ́gə.

2385

EN I heard music, so there must have been somebody at home.

RU Я слы́шал (♀слы́шала) му́зыку, зна́чит, в до́ме кто́-то до́лжен быть.

ROM ja slíšəl (♀slíšələ) múzɪku, znáćɪt, v dómjɪ któ-tə dólžɪn bɪt'.

IPA ʲa slíʂəɫ (♀slíʂələ) múzɨkʊ, znátɕɨt, v dóm̩ʲɪ któ-tə dóɫzɨ̩n bɨtʲ.

2386

EN They live on a big street, so there must be a lot of noise from the traffic.

RU Они́ живу́т о́коло большо́й у́лицы, там должно́ быть оживлённое движе́ние.

ROM aní žɪvút ókələ bal'šój úljɪtsɪ, tam dalžnó bɪt' ažɪvljónnəjɪ dvjɪžjénjɪjɪ.

IPA ɐnʲí zɨvút ókələ bɐlʲʂój úlʲɪtsɨ, tam dɐɫznó bɨtʲ ɐzɨvlʲónnəʲɪ dvʲɪzɛ́nʲɪ̯ʲɪ.

2387

EN That building is now a supermarket. It used to be a movie theater.

RU Э́то зда́ние тепе́рь суперма́ркет. Когда́-то там был кинотеа́тр.

ROM étə zdánjɪjɪ tjɪpjér' supjɪrmárkjɪt. kagdá-tə tam bɪl kjɪnatjɪátr.

IPA étə zdánʲɪ̯ʲɪ tʲɪpʲérʲ sʊpʲɪrmárkʲɪt. kɐgdá-tə tam bɨɫ kʲɪnɐtʲɪátr.

2388

EN There's bound to be a flight to Madrid tonight.

RU Сегóдня вéчером до Мадрúда наверняká есть рейс.
ROM sjɪvódnjɪ vjéćɪrəm da madrídə navjɪrnjɪká jest' rjejs.
IPA sʲɪvʷódnʲɪ vʲétɕɨrəm dɐ mɐdrʲídə nɐvʲɪrnʲɪká ʲestʲ rʲejs.

2389

EN After the lecture, there will be an opportunity to ask questions.

RU Пóсле лéкции бýдет возмóжность задáть вопрóсы.
ROM pósljɪ ljéktsɪjɪ búdjɪt vazmóžnəst' zadát' vaprósɪ.
IPA pʷóslʲɪ lʲéktsɨʲɪ búdʲɪt vɐzmʷóznəstʲ zɐdátʲ vɐprósɨ.

2390

EN I like the place where I live, but it'd be nicer to live by the ocean.

RU Мне нрáвится мéсто, где я живý, но на берегý океáна было бы жить [горáздо] лýчше.
ROM mnjɛ nrávjɪtsjɪ mjéstə, gdjɛ ja žɪvú, no na bjɪrɪgú akjɪánə bɪlo bɪ žɪt' [garázdə] lúćśɪ.
IPA mnʲɛ nrávʲɪtsʲɪ mʲéstə, gdʲɛ ʲa zɨvú, nɒ na bʲɪrʲɪgú ɐkʲɪánə bɨlɒ bɨ zɨtʲ [gɐrázdə] lútɕɕɨ.

2391

EN I was told that there'd be someone to meet me at the airport, but there wasn't.

RU Мне сказáли, что меня́ встрéтят в аэропортý, но меня́ никтó не встрéтил.

ROM mnjɛ skazáljı, što mjınjá vstrjétjıt v aɛrəpartú, no mjınjá njıktó njı vstrjétjıl.

IPA mnʲɛ skɐzálʲı, ştọ mʲınʲá fstrʲétʲıt v aɛrəpɐrtú, nọ mʲınʲá nʲıktọ́ nʲı fstrʲétʲıɫ.

2392

EN She went out without any money.

RU Онá ушлá без дéнег.

ROM aná ušlá bız djénjıg.

IPA ɐná ʊşlá bʲız dʲénʲık.

2393

EN He refused to eat anything.

RU Он отказáлся чтó-либо съéсть.

ROM on ətkazálsjı štó-ljıbə sjést'.

IPA ọn ətkɐzáłsʲı ştọ́-lʲıbə sʲéstʲ.

2394

EN Hardly anybody passed the examination.

RU Почтú никтó не сдал экзáмен.

ROM paćtí njıktó njı sdal ɛkzámjın.

IPA pɐtɕtʲí nʲıktọ́ nʲı zdał ɛksámʲın.

2395

EN If anyone has any questions, I'll be glad to answer them.

RU Éсли у когó-то есть вопрóсы, я бýду рад (♀рáда) на них отвéтить.

ROM jéslϳı u kavó-tə jest' vaprósı, ja búdu rad (♀rádə) na nih atvjétjıt'.

IPA ᶦéslʲı u kɐvʷǫ́-tə ᶦestʲ vɐprǫ́sɨ, ᶦa búdʊ rat (♀rádə) na nʲix ɐtfʲétʲıtʲ.

2396

EN Let me know if you need anything.

RU Дай мне знать, éсли тебé чтó-нибудь понáдобится.

ROM daj mnje znat', jéslϳı tϳıbjé štó-njıbud' panádəbjıtsjı.

IPA daj mnʲɛ znatʲ, ᶦéslʲı tʲıbʲé ştǫ́-nʲıbʊdʲ pɐnádəbʲıtsʲı.

2397

EN I'm sorry for any trouble I've caused.

RU Прости́ меня́ за все неприя́тности, котóрые я тебé достáвил (♀достáвила).

ROM prastí mjınjá za vsje njıprıjátnəstjı, katórıjı ja tjıbjé dastávjıl (♀dastávjılə).

IPA prɐstʲí mʲınʲá za fsʲɛ nʲıprʲɨʲátnəstʲı, kɐtǫ́rɨʲı ᶦa tʲıbʲé dɐstávʲıɫ (♀dɐstávʲılə).

2398

EN Anyone who wants to take the exam should tell me by Friday.

RU Все жела́ющие сдать экза́мен должны́ сообщи́ть мне об э́том до пя́тницы.

ROM vsjɛ žilájuççɪjɪ sdat' ɛkzámjɪn dalžní saabççít' mnjɛ ab étəm da pjátnjɪtsɪ.

IPA fsʲɛ zʲɪláʲüççɨʲɪ zdatʲ ɛksámʲɪn dɐɫzɲí sɐɐbççítʲ mnʲɛ ɐb étəm dɐ pʲǽtnʲɪtsɨ.

2399

EN Someone has forgotten their umbrella.

RU Кто́-то забы́л свой зо́нтик.

ROM któ-tə zabíl svoj zóntjɪk.

IPA któ-tə zɐbíɫ svʷoj zóntʲɪk.

2400

EN We had to walk home because there was no bus.

RU Нам пришло́сь идти́ до до́ма пешко́м, поско́льку не бы́ло авто́бусов.

ROM nam prɪšlós' jɪdtí da dómə pjɪškóm, paskól'ku njɪ bílə avtóbusəv.

IPA nam prʲɪʂlósʲ ʲɪttʲí dɐ dómə pʲɪʂkʷóm, pɐskʷóⱡʲku nʲɪ bíⱡə ɐftóbusəf.

GMS #2401 - 2500

2401

EN She'll have no difficulty finding a job.

RU У неё не возникнет трудностей с поиском работы.
ROM u njɪjó njɪ vazníknjɪt trúdnəstjej s pójɪskəm rɪbótɪ.
IPA u nʲɪ́ɵ̈ nʲɪ vɐznʲíknʲɪt trúdnəstʲɪj s pʷɵ́ʲɪskəm rɐbʷɵ́tɨ.

2402

EN There were no stores open.

RU Там не было открытых магазинов.
ROM tam njɛ́ bɪlo atkrítɪh məgazínəv.
IPA tam nʲɛ́ bɨlə ɐtkrítɨx məgɐzʲínəf.

2403

EN All the tickets have been sold. There are none left.

RU Все билеты были распроданы. Ни одного не осталось.
ROM vsjɛ bjɪljétɪ bíljɪ rɪspródənɪ. ni ədnavó njɪ astáləs'.
IPA fsʲɛ bʲɪlʲétɨ bɨ́lʲɪ rɐspródənɨ. nʲi ədnɐvʷɵ́ nʲɪ ɐstáləsʲ.

2404

EN This money is all yours. None of it is mine.

RU Все э́ти де́ньги - твои́. Моего́ здесь ни копе́йки.
ROM vsje étjı djén'gjı - tvaí. majıvó zdjes' ni kapjéjkjı.
IPA fsʲɛ étʲɪ dʲénʲgʲɪ - tfɐʲí. mɐʲɪvʷǿ zdʲesʲ nʲi kɐpʲéjkʲɪ.

2405

EN None of the stores were open.

RU Ни оди́н из магази́нов не́ был откры́т.
ROM ni adín iz məgazínəv njé bıl atkrít.
IPA nʲi ɐdʲín ʲiz məgɐzʲínəv nʲé bɨɫ ɐtkrít.

2406

EN The house is empty. There's no one living there.

RU Дом пуст. В нём никто́ не живёт.
ROM dom pust. v njóm njıktó njı živjót.
IPA dǫm pust. v nʲǿm nʲɪktǿ nʲɪ zɨ̇vʲǿt.

2407

EN We had nothing to eat.

RU У нас не́ было ничего́ из еды́.
ROM u nas njé bılo njıćıvó iz jıdí.
IPA u nas nʲé bɨɫə nʲɪtɕɨ̇vʷǿ ʲiz ʲɪdí.

2408

EN Herman didn't tell anyone about his plans.

RU Ге́рман никому́ не сообщи́л о его́ пла́нах.
ROM gjérmən njɪkamú njɪ saabççíl a jɪvó plánəh.
IPA gʲérmən nʲɪkɐmú nʲɪ sɐɐbççíɫ ɐ ʲɪvʷó plánəx.

2409

EN No one did what I asked them to do, did they?

RU Никто́ не сде́лал ничего́ из того́, о чём я проси́л
    (♀проси́ла), не так ли?
ROM njɪktó njɪ sdjéləl njɪćɪvó iz tavó, a ćjóm ja prasíl
    (♀prasílə), njɪ tak li?
IPA nʲɪktó nʲɪ zdʲéɫəɫ nʲɪtçɪvʷó ʲis tɐvʷó, ɐ tçǫ́m ʲa prɐsʲíɫ
    (♀prɐsʲílə), nʲɪ tak lʲi?

2410

EN The accident looked serious, but fortunately nobody
    was injured.

RU Ава́рия вы́глядела серьёзной, но, к сча́стью, никто́
    не пострада́л.
ROM avárjɪjə vígljadjɪlə sjɪrjóznəj, no, k śśást'ju, njɪktó njɪ
    pəstrɪdál.
IPA ɐvárʲrʲə vʲíglʲɪdʲɪlə sʲɪrʲǫ́znəj, nǫ, k ççástʲü, nʲɪktǫ́ nʲɪ
    pəstrɐdáɫ.

2411

EN I don't know anything about economics.

RU Я ничего не знаю об экономике.
ROM ja njıćıvó njı znáju ab ɛkanómjıkjı.
IPA ʲa nʲɪtɕɨvʷǫ́ nʲɪ znáʲü ɐb ɛkɐnǫ́mʲɪkʲɪ.

2412

EN We didn't spend much money.

RU Мы не потратили много денег.
ROM mı njı patrátjıljı mnógə djénjıg.
IPA mɨ nʲɪ pɐtrátʲɪlʲʲɪ mnǫ́gə dʲénʲɪk.

2413

EN There's no need to hurry. We've got plenty of time.

RU Нет необходимости спешить. У нас много
времени.
ROM njɛt njıəbhadíməstjı spjıšít'. u nas mnógə vrjémjenjı.
IPA nʲɛt nʲɪəbxɐdʲíməstʲɪ spʲɪşítʲ. u nas mnǫ́gə vrʲémʲɪnʲɪ.

2414

EN There aren't many tourists here. > There aren't a lot
of tourists here.

RU Здесь не много туристов.
ROM zdjes' njı mnógə turístəv.
IPA zdʲesʲ nʲɪ mnǫ́gə tʊrʲístəf.

2415

EN   Do you know many people? > Do you know a lot of
     people?

RU   Ты зна́ешь мно́го люде́й? > Ты знако́м
     (♀знако́ма) со мно́гими людьми́?

ROM tı znájeś mnógə ljudjéj? > tı znakóm (♀znakómə) sa
     mnógjımjı ljud'mí?

IPA tɨ znáʲɪç mnógə ljüdʲéj? > tɨ znɐkʷǫ́m (♀znɐkʷǫ́mə)
     sɐ mnǫ́gʲımʲı ljüdʲmʲí?

2416

EN   Monika's very busy with her job. She has little time
     for other things.

RU   Мо́ника о́чень занята́ рабо́той. У неё остаётся
     ма́ло вре́мени на всё остально́е.

ROM mónjıkə óćın' zanjıtá rıbótəj. u njıjó əstajótsjı málə
     vrjémjenjı na vsjó əstal'nójı.

IPA mʷǫ́nʲıkə ǫ́tɕɪnʲ zɐnʲıtá rɐbʷǫ́təj. u nʲɨ́ʲǫ́ əstɐjǫ́tsʲı málə
     vrʲémʲınʲı na fsʲǫ́ əstɐlʲnǫ́ʲı.

2417

EN   Kimiko has very few friends in London.

RU   У Ки́мико о́чень ма́ло друзе́й в Ло́ндоне.

ROM u kímjıkə óćın' málə druzjéj v lóndənjı.

IPA u kʲímʲıkə ǫ́tɕɪnʲ málə drʊzʲéj v lǫ́ndənʲı.

2418

EN Let's get something to drink. We still have a little time before the train comes.

RU Давáй чтó-нибудь вы́пьем. У нас всё ещё есть немнóго врéмени до прибы́тия пóезда.

ROM daváj štó-njɪbud' vípjɪm. u nas vsjó jɪçcjó jest' njɪmnógə vrjémjenjɪ da prɪbítjɪjə pójɪzdə.

IPA dɐváj s̪t̪ǫ́-nʲɪbʊdʲ vípʲɪm. u nas fsʲǫ́ ʲɪççǫ́ ʲestʲ nʲɪmnǫ́gə vrʲémʲɪnʲɪ dɐ prʲɪbítʲɪ̯ʲə pʷǫ́ɪzdə.

2419

EN He spoke little English, so it was difficult to communicate with him.

RU Он немнóго говори́л по-англи́йски, так что трýдностей в общéнии с ним не возникáло.

ROM on njɪmnógə gəvaríl pa-anglíjskjɪ, tak što trúdnəstjej v abçcjénjɪjɪ s nim njɪ vaznjɪkálə.

IPA ǫn nʲɪmnǫ́gə gəvɐrʲíɫ pɐ-ɐŋglʲíjskʲɪ, tak s̪t̪ǫ trúdnəstʲɪj v ɐbçcén̪ʲr̪ʲɪ s nʲim nʲɪ vɐznʲɪkálə.

2420

EN We have only a little time left.

RU У нас остáлось óчень мáло врéмени.

ROM u nas astáləs' óćɪn' málə vrjémjenjɪ.

IPA u nas ɐstáləsʲ ǫ́t̪ɕ̞ɪnʲ málə vrʲémʲɪnʲɪ.

2421

EN Everybody was surprised that he won. Few people expected him to win.

RU Все бы́ли удивлёны тем, что он вы́играл. Немно́гие ожида́ли от него́ побе́ды.

ROM vsjɛ bíljɪ udjɪvljéni tjɛm, što on víjɪgrǝl. njɪmnógjɪjɪ ažɪdáljɪ at njɪvó pabjédɪ.

IPA fsʲɛ bílʲɪ ʊdʲɪvlʲéni tʲɛm, ʂtǫ ǫn vʲ̥ɪgrǝɫ. nʲɪmnóg̊ʲr̥ʲɪ ɐzɨdálʲɪ ɐt nʲɪvʷǫ́ pɐbʲédɨ.

2422

EN I can't give you a decision yet. I need more time to think about it.

RU Я не могу́ пока́ сообщи́ть тебе́ своё реше́ние. Мне ну́жно бо́льше вре́мени, что́бы всё обду́мать.

ROM ja njɪ magú paká saabççít' tjɪbjé svajó rɪšjénjɪjɪ. mnjɛ núžnǝ ból'šɪ vrjémjenjɪ, štóbɪ vsjó abdúmǝt'.

IPA ʲa nʲɪ mɐgú pɐká sɐɐbççítʲ tʲɪbʲé svɐ̽ʲǫ́ rʲɪ̞ʂénʲr̥ʲɪ. mnʲɛ núz̨nǝ bʷǫ́lʲʂɨ vrʲémʲɪnʲʲɪ, ʂtǫ́bɨ fsʲǫ́ ɐbdúmǝtʲ.

2423

EN It was a very boring place to live. There was little to do.

RU Там бы́ло дово́льно ску́чно жить. Там бы́ло почти́ не́чем заня́ться.

ROM tam bílǝ davól'nǝ skúćnǝ žɪt'. tam bílǝ paćtí njéćɪm zanját'sjɪ.

IPA tam bílǝ dɐvʷǫ́lʲnǝ skútçnǝ zɨtʲ. tam bílǝ pɐtçtʲí nʲétçɪm zɐnʲǽtʲsʲɪ.

2424

EN I don't go out very often. I stay home most days.

RU Я осо́бенно никуда́ не хожу́. Ча́ще всего́ я остаю́сь до́ма.

ROM ja asóbjɪnnə njɪkudá njɪ hažú. ćáççɪ vsjɪvó ja əstajús' dómə.

IPA ʲa ɐsǫ́bʲɪnnə nʲɪkʊdá nʲɪ xɐʐú. tɕáɕɕɪ fsʲɪvᵂǫ́ ʲa əstɐ̈ʲʉ́sʲ dǫ́mə.

2425

EN Some people learn languages more easily than others.

RU Не́которым лю́дям изуче́ние языко́в даётся про́ще, чем други́м.

ROM njékətərɪm ljúdjɪm jɪzućjénjɪjɪ jɪzɪkóv dajótsjɪ próççɪ, ćɪm drugím.

IPA nʲékətərɨm lʲʉ́dʲɪm ʲɪzʊtɕén̠ʲɪ̯ɪ ʲɪzɨkᵂóv dɐ̈ʲə̣́tsʲɪ prǫ́ççɨ, tɕem drʊgʲím.

2426

EN Some of the people I work with are not very friendly.

RU Не́которые лю́ди, с кото́рыми я рабо́таю, не о́чень дружелю́бны.

ROM njékətərɪjɪ ljúdjɪ, s katórɪmjɪ ja rɪbótəju, njɪ óćɪn' družɪljúbnɪ.

IPA nʲékətərɨ̯ɪ lʲʉ́dʲɪ, s kɐtǫ́rɨmʲɪ ʲa rɐbᵂótəʉ, nʲɪ ǫ́tɕɪnʲ drʊʐɨ̣lʲʉ́bnɨ.

2427

EN Have you read any of these books?

RU Ты читáл (♀читáла) какúе-нибудь из э́тих книг?
ROM tɪ ćɪtál (♀ćɪtálə) kakíjɪ-njɪbud' iz étjɪh knig?
IPA tɨ tɕɪtáɫ (♀tɕɪtálə) kɐkʲɨ́ʲɪ-nʲɪbʊdʲ ʲiz étʲɪx knʲik?

2428

EN I was sick yesterday, so I spent most of the day in
    bed.

RU Вчерá я был болён (♀былá больнá), так что
    провёл (♀провелá) бóльшую часть дня в постéли.
ROM vćɪrá ja bɪl baljón (♀bɪlá bal'ná), tak što pravjól
    (♀pravjɪlá) ból'šuju ćast' dnja v pastjéljɪ.
IPA ftɕɪrá ʲa bɨɫ bɐlʲǿɫ (♀bɨlá bɐlʲná), tak ʂtɕ prɐvʲǿɫ
    (♀prɐvʲɪlá) bʷǿlʲʂʊʲü tɕastʲ dnʲa f pɐstélʲɪ.

2429

EN All the flowers in this garden are beautiful.

RU Все цветы́ в садý бы́ли красúвы.
ROM vsjɛ tsvjɪtí v sadú bíljɪ krɪsívɪ.
IPA fsʲɛ tsfʲɪtɨ́ f sɐdú bɨ́lʲɪ krɐsʲívɨ.

2430

EN We're able to solve most of the problems we have.

RU Мы в состоянии решить большинство из проблем, с которыми мы столкнулись.

ROM mı v səstajánjıjı rıšít' bal'šínstvə iz prabljém, s katórımjı mı stalknúljıs'.

IPA mɨ f səstɐʲǽnʲrʲɪ rʲɪşítʲ bɐlʲşínstfə ʲis prɐblʲém, s kɐtórɨmʲɪ mɨ stɐɫknúlʲɪsʲ.

2431

EN Do any of you want to go to a party tonight?

RU Кто-нибудь из вас хочет пойти на вечеринку сегодня вечером?

ROM któ-njıbud' iz vas hóćıt pajtí na vjıćırínku sjıvódnjı vjéćırəm?

IPA któ-nʲɪbʊdʲ ʲiz vas xótɕɨt pɐjtʲí na vʲɪtɕɨrʲínkʊ sʲɪvʷódnʲɪ vʲétɕɨrəm?

2432

EN Half this money is mine, and half of it is yours.

RU Половина из этих денег - моя, половина - твоя.

ROM pəlavínə iz étjıh djénjıg - majá, pəlavínə - tvajá.

IPA pəlɐvʲínə ʲiz étʲɪx dʲénʲɪk - mɐʲá, pəlɐvʲínə - tfɐʲá.

2433

EN   When she got married, she kept it a secret. She didn't tell any of her friends.

RU   Она́ держа́ла в секре́те то, что вы́шла за́муж. Она́ не сказа́ла никому́ из свои́х друзе́й.

ROM   aná djıržálə v sjıkrjétjı to, što víšlə zámuž. aná njı skazálə njıkamú iz svaíh druzjéj.

IPA   ɐná dʲɪrʐálə f sʲɪkrʲétʲɪ to, ʂtɔ víʂlə zámuʂ. ɐná nʲɪ skɐzálə nʲɪkɐmú ʲis svɐʲíx druzʲéj.

2434

EN   Deepak and I have very different ideas. I don't agree with many of his opinions.

RU   У нас с Ди́паком ра́зные взгля́ды. Я не разделя́ю мно́гие из его́ мы́слей.

ROM   u nas s dípəkəm ráznıjı vzgljádı. ja njı rızdjıljáju mnógjıjı iz jıvó mísljej.

IPA   u nas s dʲípəkəm ráznɨʲɪ vzglʲádɨ. ʲa nʲɪ rɐzdʲɪlʲǽʲü mnǫ́gʲɨʲɪ ʲiz ʲɪvʷǫ́ míslʲɪj.

2435

EN   Not all the tourists in the group were Spanish. Some of them were French.

RU   Не все тури́сты в гру́ппе бы́ли испа́нцами. Не́которые из них бы́ли францу́зами.

ROM   njı vsjɛ turístı v grúppjı bíljı jıspántsəmjı. njékətərıjı iz nih bíljı frıntsúzəmjı.

IPA   nʲɪ fsʲɛ turʲístɨ v grúppʲɪ bílʲɪ ʲɪspántsəmʲɪ. nʲékətərɨʲɪ ʲiz nʲix bílʲɪ frɐntsúzəmʲɪ.

2436

EN   I watched most of the movie, but not all of it.

RU   Я посмотре́л (♀посмотре́ла) бо́льшую часть фи́льма, но не весь.

ROM ja pəsmatrjél (♀pəsmatrjélə) ból'šuju ćast' fíl'mə, no njɪ vjes'.

IPA ʲa pəsmɐtrʲéɫ (♀pəsmɐtrʲélə) bʷǫ́lʲʂʊʲü tɕastʲ fʲílʲmə, nǫ nʲɪ vʲesʲ.

2437

EN   I asked some people for directions, but none of them were able to help me.

RU   Я спроси́л (♀спроси́ла) доро́гу у не́скольких челове́к, но никто́ из них не смог мне помо́чь.

ROM ja sprasíl (♀sprasílə) darógu u njéskəl'kjɪh ćɪlavjék, no njɪktó iz nih njɪ smog mnjɛ pamóć'.

IPA ʲa sprɐsʲíɫ (♀sprɐsʲílə) dɐrǫ́gʊ u nʲéskəlʲkʲɪx tɕɪlɐvʲék, nǫ nʲɪktǫ́ ʲiz nʲix nʲɪ smʷǫg mnʲɛ pɐmʷǫ́tɕʲ.

2438

EN   Both restaurants are very good. > Both of these restaurants are very good.

RU   Óба рестора́на о́чень хоро́шие.

ROM óbə rɪstaránə óćɪn' haróšɪjɪ.

IPA ǫ́bə rʲɪstɐránə ǫ́tɕɪnʲ xɐrǫ́ʂʲɪ.

2439

EN Neither restaurant is expensive. > Neither of the restaurants we went to was expensive.

RU Ни оди́н из рестора́нов не явля́ется дороги́м. > Ни оди́н из рестора́нов, в кото́рые мы ходи́ли, не́ был дороги́м.

ROM ni adín iz rıstaránəv njı jıvljájetsjı dəragím. > ni adín iz rıstaránəv, v katórıjı mı hadíljı, njɛ́ bıl dəragím.

IPA nʲi ɐdʲín ʲiz rʲɪstɐránəv nʲɪ ʲɪvlʲǽʲɪtsʲɪ dərɐɡʲím. > nʲi ɐdʲín ʲiz rʲɪstɐránəf, f kɐtórɨʲɪ mɨ xɐdʲílʲɪ, nʲɛ́ bɨɫ dərɐɡʲím.

2440

EN We can go to either restaurant. I don't care.

RU Мы мо́жем пойти́ в любо́й рестора́н. Мне всё равно́.

ROM mı móžım pajtí v ljubój rıstarán. mnjɛ vsjó rıvnó.

IPA mɨ mʷóʐ ɨm pɐjtʲí v lʲübʷój rʲɪstɐrán. mnʲɛ fsʲjǿ rɐvnó.

2441

EN I haven't been to either of those restaurants.

RU Я не́ был (♀была́) ни в одно́м из тех рестора́нов.

ROM ja njɛ́ bıl (♀bılá) ni v adnóm iz tjeh rıstaránəv.

IPA ʲa nʲɛ́ bɨɫ (♀bɨlá) nʲi v ɐdnóm ʲis tʲex rʲɪstɐránəf.

2442

EN I asked two (2) people the way to the station, but neither of them knew.

RU Я спроси́л (♀ спроси́ла) доро́гу до ста́нции у двух челове́к, но ни оди́н из них не знал.

ROM ja sprasíl (♀ sprasílə) darógu da stántsıjı u dvuh ćılavjék, no ni adín iz nih njı znal.

IPA ʲa sprɐsʲíɫ (♀ sprɐsʲílə) dɐrógʊ dɐ stántsɨʲɪ u dvux tɕɪlɐvʲék, nǫ nʲi ɐdʲín ʲiz nʲix nʲɪ znaɫ.

2443

EN Both of us were very tired.

RU Мы о́ба (♀ о́бе) уста́ли.

ROM mı óbə (♀ óbjı) ustáljı.

IPA mɨ ǫ́bə (♀ ǫ́bʲɪ) ʊstálʲɪ.

2444

EN Neither of them want to have children.

RU Никто́ из них не хо́чет име́ть дете́й.

ROM njıktó iz nih njı hóćıt jımjét' djıtjéj.

IPA nʲɪktó ʲiz nʲix nʲɪ xǫ́tɕɨt ʲɪmʲétʲ dʲɪtʲéj.

2445

EN I couldn't decide which of the two (2) shirts to buy. I liked both.

RU Я не мог (♀могла́) реши́ть, каку́ю из руба́шек купи́ть, мне понра́вились о́бе.

ROM ja njɪ mog (♀maglá) rɪšít', kakúju iz rubášɪk kupít', mnjɛ panrávjɪljɪs' óbjɪ.

IPA ʲa nʲɪ mʷok (♀mɐglá) rʲɪṣítʲ, kɐkúʲü ʲiz rʊbáṣɨk kʊpʲítʲ, mnʲɛ pɐnrávʲɪlʲɪsʲ óbʲɪ.

2446

EN I was both tired and hungry when I got home.

RU Я был уста́вшим и голо́дным, когда́ верну́лся домо́й. Я была́ уста́вшей и голо́дной, когда́ верну́лась домо́й.

ROM ja bɪl ustávšɪm i galódnɪm, kagdá vjɪrnúlsjɪ damój. ja bɪlá ustávšɪj i galódnəj, kagdá vjɪrnúləs' damój.

IPA ʲa bɨł ʊstáfṣim ɪ gɐlódnɨm, kɐgdá vʲɪrnúɫsʲɪ dɐmʷój. ʲa bɨlá ʊstáfṣɨj ɪ gɐlódnəj, kɐgdá vʲɪrnúləsʲ dɐmʷój.

2447

EN She said she would contact me, but she neither wrote nor called.

RU Она́ сказа́ла, что свя́жется со мной, но не писа́ла и не звони́ла.

ROM aná skazálə, što svjážɪtsjɪ sa mnoj, no njɪ pjɪsálə i njɪ zvanílə.

IPA ɐná skɐzálə, ṣtø svʲæẓ̇ɪtsʲɪ sɐ mnoj, nø nʲɪ pʲɪsálə ɪ nʲɪ zvɐnʲílə.

2448

EN Either you apologize, or I'll never speak to you again.

RU Или ты извиня́ешься, или я с тобо́й бо́льше не
разгова́риваю.

ROM ili tɪ jɪzvjɪnjáješ́sjɪ, ili ja s tabój ból'šɪ njɪ
rɪzgavárjɪvəju.

IPA ʲilʲi tɨ ʲɪzvʲɪnʲǽʲɪɕsʲɪ, ʲilʲi ʲa s tɐbʷój bʷǫ́lʲs̩i nʲɪ
rəzgɐvárʲɪvəʲü.

2449

EN You could stay at either of these hotels. (2) > You
could stay at any of these hotels. (many)

RU Ты бы мог (♀могла́) останови́ться в одно́м из
э́тих оте́лей. > Ты бы мог (♀могла́) останови́ться
в любо́м из э́тих оте́лей.

ROM tɪ bɪ mog (♀maglá) əstənavít'sjɪ v adnóm iz étjɪh
atéljej. > tɪ bɪ mog (♀maglá) əstənavít'sjɪ v ljubóm
iz étjɪh atéljej.

IPA tɨ bɨ mʷǫk (♀mɐglá) əstənɐvʲítʲsʲɪ v ɐdnǫ́m ʲiz étʲɪx
ɐtélʲɪj. > tɨ bɨ mʷǫk (♀mɐglá) əstənɐvʲítʲsʲɪ v
lʲübʷǫ́m ʲiz étʲɪx ɐtélʲɪj.

2450

EN We couldn't open the door, because neither of us had our key.

RU Мы не могли́ откры́ть дверь, потому́ что ни́ у кого́ из нас не́ было ключе́й.

ROM mɪ njɪ maglí atkrít' dvjer', pətamú što ní u kavó iz nas njé bɪlo kljućjéj.

IPA mɨ nʲɪ mɐglʲí ɐtkrʲítʲ dvʲerʲ, pətɐmú ʂtɐ nʲí u kɐvʷǫ́ ʲiz nas nʲɛ́ bɨlə klʲütɕɨj.

2451

EN All of us enjoyed the party.

RU Нам всем понра́вилась вечери́нка.

ROM nam vsjɛm panrávjɪləs' vjɪćɪrínkə.

IPA nam fsʲɛm pɐnrávʲɪləsʲ vʲɪtɕɪrʲínkə.

2452

EN I'll do all I can to help. > I'll do everything I can to help.

RU Я сде́лаю всё возмо́жное, что́бы помо́чь. > Я сде́лаю всё, что в мои́х си́лах, что́бы помо́чь.

ROM ja sdjéləju vsjó vazmóžnəjɪ, štóbɪ pamóć'. > ja sdjéləju vsjó, što v maíh síləh, štóbɪ pamóć'.

IPA ʲa zdʲéləʲü fsʲǫ́ vɐzmʷóʐnəʲɪ, ʂtóbɨ pɐmʷótɕʲ. > ʲa zdʲéləʲü fsʲǫ́, ʂtɐ v mɐʲíx sʲíləx, ʂtóbɨ pɐmʷótɕʲ.

2453

EN   He thinks he knows everything.

RU   Он ду́мает, что он всё зна́ет.
ROM on dúməjıt, što on vsjó znájıt.
IPA on dúmə^jıt, şto on fs^jǿ zná^jıt.

2454

EN   Our summer vacation was such a disaster. Everything
     that could go wrong went wrong.

RU   Наш ле́тний о́тпуск оберну́лся кошма́ром. Всё,
     что то́лько могло́, пошло́ не так.
ROM naš ljétnjıj atpúsk abjırnúlsjı kašmárəm. vsjó, što
     tól'kə magló, pašló njı tak.
IPA naş l^jétn^jıj ɐtpúsk ɐb^jırnúts^jı kɐşmárəm. fs^jǿ, şto tól^jkə
     mɐgló, pɐşló n^jı tak.

2455

EN   All I've eaten today is a sandwich.

RU   Всё, что я сего́дня съел (♀ съе́ла), - э́то сэ́ндвич.
ROM vsjó, što ja sjıvódnjı sjél (♀ sjélə), - étə séndvjıć.
IPA fs^jǿ, şto ^ja s^jıv^wódn^jı s^jéł (♀ s^jélə), - étə séndv^jıtɕ.

2456

EN   Did you read the whole book?

RU   Ты прочита́л (♀ прочита́ла) всю кни́гу?
ROM tı praćıtál (♀ praćıtálə) vsju knígu?
IPA tɨ prɐtɕıtáł (♀ prɐtɕıtálə) fs^ju kn^jígu?

2457

EN Lakshmi has lived her whole life in India.

RU Ла́кшми про́жил всю свою́ жизнь в И́ндии.

ROM lákšmjɪ próžɪl vsju svajú žɪzn' v índjɪjɪ.

IPA lákşmʲɪ próẓɨɫ fsʲu svɐʲú zɨznʲ v ʲíndʲrʲɪ.

2458

EN I've spent all the money you gave me.

RU Я потра́тил (♀потра́тила) все де́ньги, кото́рые ты мне дал (♀дала́).

ROM ja patrátjɪl (♀patrátjɪlə) vsjɛ djén'gjɪ, katórɪjɪ tɪ mnjɛ dal (♀dalá).

IPA ʲa pɐtrátʲɪɫ (♀pɐtrátʲɪlə) fsʲɛ dʲénʲgʲɪ, kɐtórɨʲɪ tɨ mnʲɛ daɫ (♀dɐlá).

2459

EN When we were on vacation, we went to the beach every day.

RU Когда́ мы бы́ли в о́тпуске, мы ходи́ли на пляж ка́ждый день.

ROM kagdá mɪ bíljɪ v ótpuskjɪ, mɪ hadíljɪ na pljaž káždɪj djen'.

IPA kɐgdá mɨ bílʲɪ v ótpʊskʲɪ, mɨ xɐdʲílʲɪ na plʲaş kázdɨj dʲenʲ.

2460

EN The bus service is very good. There's a bus every ten (10) minutes.

RU Автобусы хо́дят хорошо́. Автобус быва́ет ка́ждые де́сять мину́т.

ROM avtóbusı hódjıt hərašó. avtóbus bıvájıt káždıjı djésjat' mjınút.

IPA ɐftóbʊsɨ xódʲɪt xərɐʂó. ɐftóbʊs bɨváʲɪt kázdɨʲɪ dʲésʲɪtʲ mʲɪnút.

2461

EN We don't see each other very often. About every six (6) months.

RU Мы не ча́сто ви́димся. Приме́рно раз в шесть ме́сяцев.

ROM mı njı ćástə vídjımsjı. prımjérnə raz v šıst' mjésjatsıv.

IPA mɨ nʲɪ tɕástə vʲídʲɪmsʲɪ. prʲɪmʲérnə raz f ʂɨstʲ mʲésʲɪtsɨf.

2462

EN We spent all day at the beach.

RU Мы провели́ на пля́же весь день.

ROM mı pravjılí na pljáži vjes' djen'.

IPA mɨ prɐvʲɪlʲí na plʲǽʐɨ vʲesʲ dʲenʲ.

2463

EN He didn't say a word all night long.

RU Он не сказа́л ни сло́ва за всю ночь.

ROM on njɪ skazál ni slóvə za vsju noć'.

IPA ǫn nʲɪ skɐzáɫ nʲi slǫ́və za fsʲʲu nǫtɕʲ.

2464

EN I've been looking for you all morning long. Where have you been?

RU Я иска́л (♀иска́ла) тебя́ всё у́тро. Где ты был (♀была́)?

ROM ja jɪskál (♀jɪskálə) tjɪbjá vsjó útrə. gdjɛ tɪ bɪl (♀bɪlá)?

IPA ʲa ʲɪskáɫ (♀ʲɪskálə) tʲɪbʲá fsʲʲǫ́ útrə. gdʲɛ tɨ bɨɫ (♀bɨlá)?

2465

EN They never go out. They're at home all the time.

RU Они́ никогда́ никуда́ не выхо́дят. Они́ всё вре́мя сидя́т до́ма.

ROM aní njɪkagdá njɪkudá njɪ vɪhódjɪt. aní vsjó vrjémjɪ sjɪdját dómə.

IPA ɐnʲí nʲɪkɐgdá nʲɪkʊdá nʲɪ vɨxǫ́dʲɪt. ɐnʲí fsʲʲǫ́ vrʲémʲɪ sʲɪdʲát dǫ́mə.

2466

EN Every time I see you, you look different.

RU Ка́ждый раз, когда́ я тебя́ ви́жу, ты вы́глядишь
по-но́вому.

ROM káždıj raz, kagdá ja tjıbjá vížu, tı vígljadjıś
pa-nóvəmu.

IPA kázḍɨj ras, kɐgdá ʲa tʲɪbʲá vʲízu, tɨ vʲɪglʲɪdʲɪ̇ɕ
pɐ-nóvəmu.

2467

EN It was a terrible fire. The whole building got
destroyed.

RU Случи́лся стра́шный пожа́р. Всё зда́ние бы́ло
уничто́жено.

ROM slúćılsjı strášnıj pažár. vsjó zdánjıjı bílə unjıštóžmə.

IPA slútɕɨ̇s̩ʲı strás̩nɨj pɐzár. fsʲɵ́ zdánʲɾʲı bílə unʲɪ̇ʂtózɨ̇nə.

2468

EN I've read every one (1) of those books.

RU Я прочита́л (♀ прочита́ла) ка́ждую из э́тих книг.

ROM ja praćıtál (♀ praćıtálə) kážduju iz étjıh knig.

IPA ʲa prɐtɕitáɫ (♀ prɐtɕitálə) kázdoʲü ʲiz étʲɪx knʲik.

2469

EN None of the rooms was the same. Each was different.

RU Все комнаты были разными. Каждая отличалась от другой.

ROM vsjɛ kómnətɪ bíljɪ ráznɪmjɪ. kážðəjɪ atljɪćáləs' at drugój.

IPA fsʲɛ kʷǫ́mnətɨ bɨ́lʲɪ ráznɨmʲɪ. kázɖəʲɪ ɐtlʲɪtɕáləsʲ ɐt drʊgʷǫ́j.

2470

EN Read each of these sentences carefully.

RU Прочитай каждое из этих предложений внимательно.

ROM praćɪtáj kážðəjɪ iz étjɪh prɪdlažjénjɪj vnjɪmátjel'nə.

IPA prɐtɕɪtáj kázɖəʲɪ ʲiz étʲɪx prʲɪdlɐzɛ́nʲɪj vnʲɪmátʲɪlʲnə.

2471

EN The students were each given a book.

RU Каждому студенту выдали книгу.

ROM kážðəmu studjéntu vídəljɪ knígu.

IPA kázɖəmʊ stʊdʲéntʊ vídəlʲɪ knʲígʊ.

2472

EN There's a train to the city every hour.

RU Поезд до города ходит каждый час.

ROM pójɪzd da górədə hódjɪt kážðɪj ćas.

IPA pʷǫ́jɪzd dɐ gʷǫ́rədə xǫ́dʲɪt kázɖɨj tɕas.

2473

EN Seat belts in cars save lives. Each driver should wear one.

RU Ремни́ безопа́сности в маши́нах сохраня́ют жизнь. Ка́ждый води́тель до́лжен пристёгиваться.

ROM rımní bjızapásnəstjı v mašínəh səhrınjájut žızn'. káždıj vadítjel' dólžın prıstjógjıvət'sjı.

IPA rʲımnʲí bʲızɐpásnəstʲı v mɐʂínəx səxrɐnʲǽʲüt zɨznʲ. kázdɨj vɐdʲítʲılʲ dółzɨn prʲıstʲǿgʲıvətʲsʲı.

2474

EN Write your answer to each question on a separate sheet of paper.

RU Напиши́те отве́ты на ка́ждый вопро́с на отде́льном листе́ бума́ги.

ROM napjıšítjı atvjétı na káždıj vaprós na atdjél'nəm ljıstjé bumágjı.

IPA nɐpʲıʂítʲı ɐtfʲétı na kázdɨj vɐprǿs na ɐtdʲélʲnəm lʲıstʲé bʊmágʲı.

2475

EN The woman who lives next door is a doctor.

RU Же́нщина, кото́рая живёт по сосе́дству, - врач.

ROM žjénɕɕınə, katórəjə živjót pa sasjédstvu, - vrać.

IPA zʲénɕɕɨnə, kɐtórəʲə zɨvʲǿt pɐ sɐsʲétstfʊ, - vratɕ.

2476

EN We know a lot of people who live in the country.

RU Мы зна́ем мно́гих люде́й, кото́рые живу́т в
дере́вне.

ROM mı znájım mnógjıh ljudjéj, katórıjı žıvút v djırjévnjı.

IPA mɨ zná^jɪm mnóg^jɪx ɫʉd^jéj, kɐtóŕɨ^jɪ zɨvút v d^jɪr^jévn^jɪ.

2477

EN Anyone who wants to apply for the job must do so
by Friday.

RU Все, кто хотя́т пода́ть заявле́ние на рабо́ту,
должны́ э́то сде́лать до пя́тницы.

ROM vsjɛ, kto hatját padát' zajıvljénjıjı na rıbótu, dalžní étə
sdjélət' da pjátnjıtsı.

IPA fs^jɛ, ktɐ xɐt^ját pɐdát^j zɐ^jɪvl^jén^jɨ^jɪ na rɐb^wótʊ, dɐɫzɲí étə
zd^jélət^j dɐ p^jǽtn^jɪtsɨ.

2478

EN I don't like stories that have unhappy endings.

RU Я не люблю́ исто́рии с несчастли́выми конца́ми.

ROM ja njı ljubljú jıstórjıjı s njıśśıstlívımjı kantsámjı.

IPA ^ja n^jɪ ɫʉbl^jú ^jɪstór^jɨ^jɪ s n^jɪɕɕɨstl^jívɨm^jɪ kɐntsám^jɪ.

2479

EN The printer that broke down is working again now.

RU Принтер, который сломался, сейчас опять
работает.
ROM príntjɪr, katórɨj slamálsjɪ, sjɪjćás apját' rɪbótəjɪt.
IPA prʲíntʲɪr, kɐtórɨj slɐmáɫsʲɪ, sʲɪjtɕás ɐpʲǽtʲ rɐbʷótəʲɪt.

2480

EN Everything that happened was my fault.

RU Всё, что случилось, - моя вина.
ROM vsjó, što slućíləs', - majá vjɪná.
IPA fsʲǿ, ʂto slʊtɕíləsʲ, - mɐʲá vʲɪná.

2481

EN I've never spoken to the woman who lives next door.

RU Я никогда не разговаривал (♀разговаривала) с
женщиной, которая живёт по соседству.
ROM ja njɪkagdá njɪ rɪzgavárjɪvəl (♀rɪzgavárjɪvələ) s
žjénççɪnəj, katórəjə žɪvjót pa sasjédstvu.
IPA ʲa nʲɪkɐgdá nʲɪ rəzgɐvárʲɪvəɫ (♀rəzgɐvárʲɪvələ) s
ʐénçɕɪnəj, kɐtórəʲə ʐɨvʲǿt pɐ sɐsʲétstfʊ.

2482

EN The building destroyed in the fire has now been rebuilt.

RU Здáние, уничтóженное пожáром, сейчáс восстанóвлено.

ROM zdánjıjı, unjıštóžınnəjı pažárəm, sjıjćás vəsstanóvljınə.

IPA zdánʲɨʲɪ, ʊnʲɪʂtóz̦ɨnnəʲɪ pɐz̦árəm, sʲɪjtɕás vəsstɐnóvlʲɪnə.

2483

EN The shuttle that goes to the airport runs every half hour.

RU Автóбус до аэропóрта хóдит кáждые полчасá.

ROM avtóbus da aɛrapórtə hódjıt káždıjı pəlćısá.

IPA ɐftóbʊs dɐ aɛrɐpʷórtə xódʲɪt kázdɨʲɪ pəɫtɕɪsá.

2484

EN A mystery is something that cannot be explained.

RU Загáдка - э́то то, что не мóжет быть объясненó.

ROM zagádkə - étə to, što njı móžıt bıt' abjısnjınó.

IPA zɐgátkə - étə tɔ, ʂtɔ nʲɪ mʷóz̦ɨt bɨtʲ ɐbʲɪsnʲɪnó.

2485

EN It seems that Earth is the only planet that can support life.

RU Похо́же, что Земля́ - э́то еди́нственная плане́та, на кото́рой есть жизнь.

ROM pahóži, što zjımljá - étə jıdínstvjınnəjı planjétə, na katórəj jest' žızn'.

IPA pɐxǫ́zʲ, ʂtǫ zʲıml̮ʲá - étə ʲıdʲínstf̮ʲınnəʲı pl̮ɐnʲétə, na kɐtǫ́rəj ʲestʲ zɨ̨znʲ.

2486

EN The driver who caused the accident was fined five hundred dollars ($500). > The driver who caused the accident was fined four hundred euros (€400).

RU Води́тель, кото́рый был вино́вником ава́рии, был оштрафо́ван на пятна́дцать ты́сяч рубле́й.

ROM vadítjel', katórıj bıl vjınóvnjıkəm avárjıjı, bıl əštrıfóvən na pjıtnádtsət' tísjıć rubljéj.

IPA vɐdʲítʲıl̮ʲ, kɐtǫ́rɨj bɨł vʲınǫ́vnʲıkəm ɐvárʲɨrʲı, bɨł əʂtrɐfʷǫ́vən na pʲıtnáttsətʲ tísʲıtɕ rublʲéj.

2487

EN We live in a world that is changing all the time.

RU Мы живём в ми́ре, кото́рый постоя́нно меня́ется.

ROM mı žıvjóm v mírjı, katórıj pəstajánnə mjınjájetsjı.

IPA mɨ zʲıvʲǫ́m v mʲírʲı, kɐtǫ́rɨj pəstɐʲánnə mʲınʲǽʲıtsʲı.

2488

EN A woman lives next door. She's a doctor. > The woman who lives next door is a doctor.

RU По сосе́дству со мной живёт же́нщина. Она́ врач. > Же́нщина, кото́рая живёт по сосе́дству, - врач.

ROM pa sasjédstvu sa mnoj žɪvjót žjénççɪnə. aná vrać. > žjénççɪnə, katórəjə žɪvjót pa sasjédstvu, - vrać.

IPA pɐ sɐsʲétstfʊ sɐ mnoj zʲɪvʲэ́t zʲénççɪnə. ɐná vratç. > zʲénççɪnə, kɐtórəˈə zʲɪvʲэ́t pɐ sɐsʲétstfʊ, - vratç.

2489

EN The woman next door is a doctor.

RU Же́нщина по сосе́дству - врач.

ROM žjénççɪnə pa sasjédstvu - vrać.

IPA zʲénççɪnə pɐ sɐsʲétstfʊ - vratç.

2490

EN There was cheese in the refrigerator. Where is it? > Where's the cheese that was in the refrigerator?

RU В холоди́льнике был сыр. Где он? > Где сыр, кото́рый был в холоди́льнике?

ROM v həladíl'njɪkjɪ bɪl sɪr. gdjɛ on? > gdjɛ sɪr, katórɪj bɪl v həladíl'njɪkjɪ?

IPA f xɐlɐdʲílʲnʲɪkʲɪ bɪɫ sɪr. gdʲɛ ɔn? > gdʲɛ sɪr, kɐtórɪj bɪɫ f xɐlɐdʲílʲnʲɪkʲɪ?

2491

EN I wanted to see a woman. She was away on vacation.
> The woman whom I wanted to see was away on
vacation.

RU Я хотéл (♀хотéла) увúдеться с однóй жéнщиной.
Её нé было на мéсте в связú с óтпуском. >
Жéнщины, с котóрой я хотéл (♀хотéла)
увúдеться, нé было на мéсте в связú с óтпуском.

ROM ja hatjél (♀hatjélə) uvídjet'sjɪ s adnój žjénççɪnəj. jɪjó
njé bɪlo na mjéstjɪ v svjɪzí s ótpuskəm. > žjénççɪnɪ, s
katórəj ja hatjél (♀hatjélə) uvídjet'sjɪ, njé bɪlo na
mjéstjɪ v svjɪzí s ótpuskəm.

IPA ʲa xɐtʲéɫ (♀xɐtʲélə) ʊvʲídʲɪtʲsʲɪ s ɐdnój zʲénççɨnəj. ʲrʲǫ́
nʲé bɨlə na mʲéstʲɪ f svʲɪzʲí s ótpʊskəm. > zʲénççɨnɪ, s
kɐtórəj ʲa xɐtʲéɫ (♀xɐtʲélə) ʊvʲídʲɪtʲsʲɪ, nʲé bɨlə na
mʲéstʲɪ f svʲɪzʲí s ótpʊskəm.

2492

EN The woman I wanted to see was away on vacation.

RU Жéнщина, котóрую я хотéл (♀хотéла) увúдеть,
былá не на мéсте в связú с óтпуском.

ROM žjénççɪnə, katóruju ja hatjél (♀hatjélə) uvídjet', bɪlá
njɪ na mjéstjɪ v svjɪzí s ótpuskəm.

IPA zʲénççɨnə, kɐtóruʲü ʲa xɐtʲéɫ (♀xɐtʲélə) ʊvʲídʲɪtʲ, bɨlá nʲɪ
na mʲéstʲɪ f svʲɪzʲí s ótpʊskəm.

2493

EN Have you found the keys that you lost? > Have you found the keys you lost?

RU Ты нашёл (♀нашла́) ключи́, кото́рые потеря́л (♀потеря́ла) ? > Ты нашёл (♀нашла́) потéрянные ключи́?

ROM tı našjól (♀našlá) kljućí, katórıjı patjırjál (♀patjırjálə) ? > tı našjól (♀našlá) patjérjınnıjı kljućí?

IPA tɨ nɐʂ̺ɵ́ɫ (♀nɐʂ̺lá) klʲʉtɕí, kɐtórɨʲı pɐtʲɪrʲáɫ (♀pɐtʲɪrʲálə) ? > tɨ nɐʂ̺ɵ́ɫ (♀nɐʂ̺lá) pɐtʲérʲɪnnɨʲı klʲʉtɕí?

2494

EN The dress that Yuliana bought doesn't fit her very well. > The dress that she bought doesn't fit her very well.

RU Пла́тье, кото́рое Юлиа́на купи́ла, не о́чень идёт ей. > Пла́тье, кото́рое она́ купи́ла, не о́чень ей идёт.

ROM plát'jı, katórəjı juljıánə kupílə, njı óćın' jıdjót jej. > plát'jı, katórəjı aná kupílə, njı óćın' jej jıdjót.

IPA plátʲɪ, kɐtórəʲɪ ʲʉlʲɪánə kʊpʲílə, nʲɪ ótɕɨnʲ ʲɪdʲɵ́t ʲej. > plátʲɪ, kɐtórəʲɪ ɐná kʊpʲílə, nʲɪ ótɕɨnʲ ʲej ʲɪdʲɵ́t.

2495

EN Are these the books that you were looking for? > Are these the books you were looking for?

RU Э́то те кни́ги, кото́рые ты иска́л (♀иска́ла)? > Э́то те са́мые кни́ги, кото́рые ты иска́л (♀иска́ла)?

ROM étə tjɛ knígjı, katórıjı tı jıskál (♀jıskálə)? > étə tjɛ sámıjı knígjı, katórıjı tı jıskál (♀jıskálə)?

IPA étə tʲɛ knʲíɡʲɪ, kɐtórɨ̯ɪ tɨ ʲɪskáɫ (♀ʲɪskálə)? > étə tʲɛ sámɨ̯ɪ knʲíɡʲɪ, kɐtórɨ̯ɪ tɨ ʲɪskáɫ (♀ʲɪskálə)?

2496

EN The woman with whom he fell in love left him after a month. > The woman he fell in love with left him after a month.

RU Же́нщина, в кото́рую он влюби́лся, у́шла от него́ че́рез ме́сяц. > Люби́мая же́нщина ушла́ от него́ че́рез ме́сяц.

ROM žjénççınə, v katóruju on vljubílsjı, úšlə at njıvó ćjérjız mjésjıts. > ljubíməjə žjénççınə ušlá at njıvó ćjérjız mjésjıts.

IPA ʐɛ́nɕɕɨnə, f kɐtóru̯ü ɔn vlʲübʲíɫsʲɪ, úʂlə ɐt nʲɪvʷó tɕérʲɪz mʲésʲɪts. > lʲübʲímə̯ə ʐɛ́nɕɕɨnə ʊʂlá ɐt nʲɪvʷó tɕérʲɪz mʲésʲɪts.

2497

EN The man that I was sitting next to on the plane talked the whole time. > The man I was sitting next to on the plane talked the whole time.

RU Мужчина, с которым я сидел (♀ сидела) рядом в самолёте, говорил всё время. > Мужчина, сидевший рядом со мной в самолёте, говорил всё время.

ROM muśśínə, s katórım ja sjɪdjél (♀ sjɪdjélə) rjádəm v səmaljótjɪ, gəvaríl vsjó vrjémjɪ. > muśśínə, sjɪdjévšɪj rjádəm sa mnoj v səmaljótjɪ, gəvaríl vsjó vrjémjɪ.

IPA mʊɕɕínə, s kɐtórɨm ʲa sʲɪdʲéɫ (♀ sʲɪdʲélə) rʲádəm f səmɐlʲə́tʲɪ, gəvɐrʲíɫ fsʲ ǫ́ vrʲémʲɪ. > mʊɕɕínə, sʲɪdʲéfʂɨj rʲádəm sɐ mnoj f səmɐlʲə́tʲɪ, gəvɐrʲíɫ fsʲ ǫ́ vrʲémʲɪ.

2498

EN Everything that they said was true. > Everything they said was true.

RU Всё, что они сказали, - правда. > Всё, сказанное ими, - правда.

ROM vsjó, što aní skazáljɪ, - právdə. > vsjó, skázənnəjɪ ímjɪ, - právdə.

IPA fsʲ ǫ́, ʂtɐ ɐnʲí skɐzálʲɪ, - právdə. > fsʲ ǫ́, skázənnəʲɪ ʲímʲɪ, - právdə.

2499

EN I gave her all the money that I had. > I gave her all the money I had.

RU Я отда́л (♀отдала́) ей все де́ньги, кото́рые у меня́ бы́ли. > Я отда́л (♀отда́ла) ей все име́вшиеся у меня́ де́ньги.

ROM ja atdál (♀ətdalá) jej vsjɛ djén'gjɪ, katórɪjɪ u mjɪnjá bíljɪ. > ja atdál (♀atdálə) jej vsjɛ jɪmjévšɪjesjɪ u mjɪnjá djén'gjɪ.

IPA ʲa ɐtdáɫ (♀ətdɐlá) ʲej fsʲɛ dʲénʲɡʲɪ, kɐtórɨʲɪ u mʲɪnʲá bílʲɪ. > ʲa ɐtdáɫ (♀ɐtdálə) ʲej fsʲɛ ʲɪmʲéfʂɨʲɪsʲɪ u mʲɪnʲá dʲénʲɡʲɪ.

2500

EN Did you hear the things that they said? > Did you hear what they said?

RU Ты слы́шал (♀слы́шала), что они́ сказа́ли?

ROM tɪ slíšəl (♀slíšələ), što aní skazáljɪ?

IPA tɨ slíʂəɫ (♀slíʂələ), ʂtọ ɐnʲí skɐzálʲɪ?

GMS #2501 - 2600

2501

EN A friend is wearing a dress. You like it. > I like the dress you're wearing.

RU Подру́га оде́та в пла́тье. Оно́ тебе́ нра́вится. > Мне нра́вится пла́тье, кото́рое на тебе́ наде́то.

ROM padrúgə adjétə v plát'jı. anó tjıbjé nrávjıtsjı. > mnjɛ nrávjıtsjı plát'jı, katórəjı na tjıbjé nadjétə.

IPA pɐdrúgə ɐdʲétə f plátʲı. ɐnó tʲıbʲé nrávʲıtsʲı. > mnʲɛ nrávʲıtsʲı plátʲı, kɐtórəʲı na tʲıbʲé nɐdʲétə.

2502

EN A friend is going to see a movie. You want to know the name. > What's the name of the movie you're going to see?

RU Твой друг (♀Твоя́ подру́га) собира́ется посмотре́ть фильм. Ты хо́чешь узна́ть его́ назва́ние. > Как называ́ется фильм, кото́рый ты собира́ешься смотре́ть?

ROM tvoj drug (♀tvajá padrúgə) sabjırájetsjı pəsmatrjét' fil'm. tı hóćıś uznát' jıvó nazvánjıjı. > kak nazıvájetsjı fil'm, katórıj tı sabjırájeśsjı smatrjét'?

IPA tfʷoj druk (♀tfɐʲá pɐdrúgə) sɐbʲıráʲıtsʲı pəsmɐtrʲétʲ fʲilʲm. tɨ xótɕıɕ ʋznátʲ ʲıvʷó nɐzvánʲıʲrʲı. > kak nɐzɨváʲıtsʲı fʲilʲm, kɐtórɨj tɨ sɐbʲıráʲıɕsʲı smɐtrʲétʲ?

2503

EN You wanted to visit a museum. It was closed when you got there. > The museum we were going to visit was closed when we got there.

RU Вы хотéли посети́ть музéй. Но, когда́ вы прие́хали, оказа́лось, что он закры́т. > Музéй, котóрый мы хотéли посети́ть, оказа́лся закры́т, когда́ мы пришли́.

ROM vɪ hatjéljɪ pasjɪtít' muzjéj. no, kagdá vɪ prɪjéhəljɪ, əkazáləs', što on zakrít. > muzjéj, katórɪj mɪ hatjéljɪ pasjɪtít', əkazálsjɪ zakrít, kagdá mɪ prɪšlí.

IPA vɨ xʊtélʲɪ pʊsʲɪtʲítʲ mʊzʲéj. nǫ, kʊgdá vɨ prʲjʲéxəlʲɪ, əkʊzáləsʲ, ştǫ ǫn zʊkrít. > mʊzʲéj, kʊtǫ́rɨj mɨ xʊtélʲɪ pʊsʲɪtʲítʲ, əkʊzáʦʲɪ zʊkrít, kʊgdá mɨ prʲɪʂlʲí.

2504

EN Your friend had to do some work. You want to know if she's finished. > Have you finished the work you had to do?

RU Твоéй подру́ге на́до бы́ло закóнчить кое-каки́е дела́. Ты хóчешь узна́ть закóнчила ли она́ их. > Ты закóнчила все свои́ дела́? Ты доде́лала рабóту?

ROM tvajéj padrúgjɪ nádə bílə zakónčɪt' kəjɪ-kakíjɪ djɪlá. tɪ hóćɪš uznát' zakónćɪlə li aná ih. > tɪ zakónćɪlə vsjɛ svaí djɪlá? tɪ dadjélələ rɪbótu?

IPA tfʊʲéj pʊdrúgʲɪ nádə bílə zʊkʷóntɕɪtʲ kəjɪ-kʊkʲífʲɪ dʲɪlá. tɨ xǫ́tɕɪɕ ʊznátʲ zʊkʷóntɕɪlə lʲi ʊná ʲix. > tɨ zʊkʷóntɕɪlə fsʲɛ svʊʲí dʲɪlá? tɨ dʊdʲélələ rʊbʷótu?

2505

EN You stayed at a hotel. Pavel recommended it to you.
> We stayed at a hotel that Pavel recommended to us.

RU Вы остановились в отеле. Это Павел порекомендовал его вам. > Мы жили в отеле, который нам порекомендовал Павел.

ROM vɪ əstənavíljɪs' v atéljɪ. étə pávjɪl pərɪkəmjɪndavál jɪvó vam. > mɪ žíljɪ v atéljɪ, katórɪj nam pərɪkəmjɪndavál pávjɪl.

IPA vɨ əstənɐvʲílʲɪsʲ v ɐtélʲɪ. étə pávʲɨɫ pərʲɪkəmʲɪndɐváɫ ʲɪvʷ ó vam. > mɨ zʲílʲɪ v ɐtélʲɪ, kɐtǫ́rɨj nam pərʲɪkəmʲɪndɐváɫ pávʲɨɫ.

2506

EN I like the people I work with.

RU Мне нравятся люди, с которыми я работаю.

ROM mnjε nrávjatsjɪ ljúdjɪ, s katórɪmjɪ ja rɪbótəju.

IPA mnʲɛ nrávʲɨtsʲɪ lʲúdʲɪ, s kɐtǫ́rɨmʲɪ ʲa rɐbʷ ǫ́təʝ ü.

2507

EN What's the name of that hotel you told me about?

RU Как называется тот отель, о котором ты мне рассказывал (♀ рассказывала)?

ROM kak nazɪvájetsjɪ tot atél', a katórəm tɪ mnjε rɪsskázɪvəl (♀ rɪsskázɪvələ)?

IPA kak nɐzɨváʲɪtsʲɪ tǫt ɐtélʲ, ɐ kɐtǫ́rəm tɨ mnʲɛ rɐsskázɨvəɫ (♀ rɐsskázɨvələ)?

2508

EN I didn't get the job I applied for.

RU Я не получи́л (♀получи́ла) рабо́ту, на кото́рую отправля́л (♀отправля́ла) резюме́.

ROM ja njɪ palućíl (♀palućílə) rɪbótu, na katóruju ətprɪvljál (♀ətprɪvljálə) rɪzjumjé.

IPA ʲa nʲɪ pɐlʊtɕíɫ (♀pɐlʊtɕílə) rɐbʷótʊ, na kɐtórʊʲü ətprɐvlʲáɫ (♀ətprɐvlʲálə) rʲɪzʲümʲé.

2509

EN Julius is someone you can rely on.

RU Джу́лиус (Ю́лий) - э́то тот челове́к, на кото́рого всегда́ мо́жно положи́ться.

ROM džúljɪus (júljɪj) - étə tot ćɪlavjék, na katórəvə vsjɪgdá móžnə pəlažít'sjɪ.

IPA dzúlʲɪʊs (ʲúlʲɪj) - étə tɐt tɕɪlɐvʲék, na kɐtórəvə fsʲɪgdá mʷóʐnə pəlɐzʲítʲsʲɪ.

2510

EN Who was that man I saw you with in the restaurant?

RU Кто был тот мужчи́на, с кото́рым я ви́дел (♀ви́дела) тебя́ в рестора́не?

ROM kto bɪl tot muśśínə, s katórɪm ja vídjɪl (♀vídjɪlə) tjɪbjá v rɪstaránjɪ?

IPA ktɐ bɨɫ tɐt mʊɕɕínə, s kɐtórɨm ʲa vʲídʲɪɫ (♀vʲídʲɪlə) tʲɪbʲá v rʲɪstɐránʲɪ?

2511

EN They give their children everything they want.

RU Они дают своим детям всё, что те хотят.

ROM aní dajút svaím djétjım vsjó, što tjɛ hatját.

IPA ɐnʲí dɐʲút svɐʲím dʲétʲım fsʲó̞, ʂtọ tʲɛ xɐtʲát.

2512

EN Tell me what you want, and I'll try to get it for you.

RU Скажи мне, чего ты хочешь, и я постараюсь найти это для тебя.

ROM skaží mnjɛ, ćıvó tı hóćıś, i ja pəstarájus' najtí étə dlja tjıbjá.

IPA skɐzí mnʲɛ, tɕivʷó̞ tɨ xó̞tɕiɕ, ɪ ʲa pəstɐráʲüsʲ nɐjtʲí étə dlʲa tʲɪbʲá.

2513

EN Why do you blame me for everything that goes wrong?

RU Почему во всём, что идёт не так, ты винишь меня?

ROM paćımú va vsjóm, što jıdjót njı tak, tı vjıníś mjınjá?

IPA pɐtɕimú vɐ fsʲó̞m, ʂtọ ʲıdʲó̞t nʲɪ tak, tɨ vʲɪnʲíɕ mʲɪnʲá?

2514

EN A widow is a woman whose husband has already passed away.

RU Вдова́ - э́то же́нщина, у кото́рой у́мер муж.

ROM vdavá - étə žjénçcɪnə, u katórəj úmjɪr muž.

IPA vdɐvá - étə zʲénçcinə, u kɐtórəj úmʲɪr muʂ.

2515

EN What's the name of the man whose car you borrowed?

RU Как зову́т мужчи́ну, у кото́рого ты одолжи́л (♀одолжи́ла) маши́ну?

ROM kak zavút muśśínu, u katórəvə tɪ ədalžíl (♀ədalžílə) mašínu?

IPA kak zɐvút mʊçcínʊ, u kɐtórəvə tɨ ədɐɫzʲíɫ (♀ədɐɫzʲílə) mɐʂínʊ?

2516

EN I met someone whose brother I went to school with.

RU Я встре́тил (♀встре́тила) кое-кого́, с чьим бра́том мы вме́сте ходи́ли в шко́лу.

ROM ja vstrjétjɪl (♀vstrjétjɪlə) kəjɪ-kavó, s ćim brátəm mɪ vmjéstjɪ hadíljɪ v škólu.

IPA ʲa fstrʲétʲɪɫ (♀fstrʲétʲɪlə) kəʲɪ-kɐvʷó, s tɕʲim brátəm mɨ vmʲéstʲɪ xɐdʲílʲɪ f ʂkʷólʊ.

2517

EN I met a man who knows you.

RU Я встре́тил (♀встре́тила) мужчи́ну, кото́рый зна́ет
тебя́.

ROM ja vstrjétjɪl (♀vstrjétjɪlə) muśśínu, katórɪj znájɪt
tjɪbjá.

IPA ʲa fstrʲétʲɪɫ (♀fstrʲétʲɪlə) muççínu, kɐtórɨj znáʲɪt tʲɪbʲá.

2518

EN I met a man whose sister knows you.

RU Я встре́тил (♀встре́тила) мужчи́ну, чья сестра́
зна́ет тебя́.

ROM ja vstrjétjɪl (♀vstrjétjɪlə) muśśínu, ćja sjɪstrá znájɪt
tjɪbjá.

IPA ʲa fstrʲétʲɪɫ (♀fstrʲétʲɪlə) muççínu, tɕʲa sʲɪstrá znáʲɪt
tʲɪbʲá.

2519

EN The woman I wanted to see was away on business.

RU Же́нщина, кото́рую я хоте́л (♀хоте́ла) уви́деть,
была́ в командиро́вке.

ROM žjénççɪnə, katóruju ja hatjél (♀hatjélə) uvídjet', bɪlá v
kəmandjɪróvkjɪ.

IPA zʲénççɨnə, kɐtóruʲü ʲa xɐtʲéɫ (♀xɐtʲélə) ʊvʲídʲɪtʲ, bɨlá f
kəmɐndʲɪrófkʲɪ.

2520

EN The people I work with are very nice.

RU Лю́ди, с кото́рыми я рабо́таю, о́чень ми́лые.

ROM ljúdjı, s katórımjı ja rıbótəju, óćın' míljı.

IPA lʲʉ́dʲɪ, s kɐtórʲɪmʲɪ ʲa rɐbʷótəʲü, ótɕɪnʲ mʲílʲɪ.

2521

EN I recently went back to the town where I grew up.

RU Я неда́вно верну́лся (♀верну́лась) в го́род, где я вы́рос (♀вы́росла).

ROM ja njıdávnə vjırnúlsjı (♀vjırnúləs') v górəd, gdjɛ ja vírəs (♀vírəslə).

IPA ʲa nʲɪdávnə vʲɪrnúɫsʲɪ (♀vʲɪrnúləsʲ) v gʷórət, gdʲɛ ʲa vírəs (♀vírəslə).

2522

EN I'd like to live in a place where there's plenty of sunshine.

RU Я бы хоте́л (♀хоте́ла) жить в го́роде, где всегда́ мно́го со́лнца.

ROM ja bı hatjél (♀hatjélə) žıt' v górədjı, gdjɛ vsjıgdá mnógə sóntsə.

IPA ʲa bı xɐtʲéɫ (♀xɐtʲélə) zʲɪtʲ v gʷórədʲɪ, gdʲɛ fsʲɪgdá mnógə sóntsə.

2523

EN Do you remember the day we went to the zoo?

RU Помнишь тот день, когда мы ходили в зоопарк?

ROM pómnjıś tot djen', kagdá mı hadíljı v zaapárk?

IPA pʷǫ́mnʲıȼ tot dʲenʲ, kɐgdá mɨ xɐdʲílʲı v zɐɐpárk?

2524

EN I haven't seen them since the year they got married.

RU Я не видел (♀видела) их с тех пор, как они поженились.

ROM ja njı vídjıl (♀vídjılə) ih s tjɛh por, kak aní pažmíljıs'.

IPA ʲa nʲı vʲídʲıɫ (♀vʲídʲılə) ʲix s tʲɛx pʷor, kak ɐnʲí pɐzɨnʲílʲısʲ.

2525

EN The reason I'm calling you is to ask your advice.

RU Причина, по которой я тебе звоню - это спросить твоего совета.

ROM prıćínə, pa katórəj ja tjıbjé zvanjú - étə sprasít' tvajıvó savjétə.

IPA prʲıȼínə, pɐ kɐtórəj ʲa tʲıbʲé zvɐnʲú - étə sprɐsʲítʲ tfɐʲıvʷó sɐvʲétə.

2526

EN A cemetery is a place where people are buried.

RU Кла́дбище - э́то ме́сто, где хоро́нят люде́й.
ROM kládbjıççı - étə mjéstə, gdjɛ harónjıt ljudjéj.
IPA kládbʲıççɨ - étə mʲéstə, gdʲɛ xɐrónʲıt lʲüdʲéj.

2527

EN I went to see the doctor, who told me to rest for a few days.

RU Я ходи́л (♀ходи́ла) к до́ктору, кото́рый сказа́л мне отдохну́ть па́ру дней.
ROM ja hadíl (♀hadílə) k dóktəru, katórıj skazál mnjɛ ətdahnút' páru dnjej.
IPA ʲa xɐdʲíɫ (♀xɐdʲílə) k dóktərʊ, kɐtórɨj skɐzáɫ mnʲɛ ətdɐxnútʲ páru dnʲej.

2528

EN Do you know anyone who speaks French and Italian?

RU Ты зна́ешь кого́-нибудь, кто говори́т по-францу́зски и по-италья́нски?
ROM tı znájeś kavó-njıbud', kto gəvarít pa-frıntsúzskjı i pa-jıtaljánskjı?
IPA tɨ znáʲıç kɐvʷǫ-nʲıbʊdʲ, ktǫ gəvɐrʲít pɐ-frɐntsússkʲı ı pɐ-ʲıtɐlʲǽnskʲı?

2529

EN Valerio, who speaks French and Italian, works as a tour guide.

RU Валéрио, говорящий на францу́зском и итальянском, рабóтает ги́дом.

ROM valjérjɪə, gəvarjáççɪj na frɪntsúzskəm i jɪtaljánskəm, rɪbótəjɪt gídəm.

IPA vɐlʲérʲɪə, gəvɐrʲǽççɨj na frɐntsússkəm ɪ ʲɪtɐlʲánskəm, rɐbʷǫ́təʲɪt gʲídəm.

2530

EN Wilma works for a company that makes furniture.

RU Ви́лма рабóтает в фи́рме, котóрая выпускáет мéбель.

ROM vílmə rɪbótəjɪt v fírmjɪ, katórəjə vɪpuskájɪt mjébjel'.

IPA vʲíɫmə rɐbʷǫ́təʲɪt f fʲírmʲɪ, kɐtǫ́rəʲə vɨpuskáʲɪt mʲébʲɪlʲ.

2531

EN This morning I met somebody I hadn't seen in ages.

RU Э́тим у́тром я встрéтил (♀ встрéтила) кое-когó, с кем не ви́делся (♀ ви́делась) дóлгое врéмя. (...с кем не ви́делся сто лет).

ROM étjɪm útrəm ja vstrjétjɪl (♀ vstrjétjɪlə) kəjɪ-kavó, s kjem njɪ vídjelsjɪ (♀ vídjɪləs') dólgəjɪ vrjémjɪ. (...s kjem njɪ vídjelsjɪ sto ljet).

IPA étʲɪm útrəm ʲa fstrʲétʲɪɫ (♀ fstrʲétʲɪlə) kəʲɪ-kɐvʷǫ́, s kʲɛm nʲɪ vʲíd̥ʲɪɫsʲɪ (♀ vʲíd̥ʲɪləsʲ) dǫ́ɫgəʲɪ vrʲémʲɪ. (...s kʲɛm nʲɪ vʲíd̥ʲɪɫsʲɪ stǫ lʲet).

2532

EN The population of London, which was once the largest city in the world, is now decreasing.

RU Чи́сленность населе́ния Ло́ндона, когда́-то са́мого большо́го го́рода, тепе́рь идёт на у́быль.

ROM čísljɪnnəst' nasjɪljénjɪjə lóndənə, kagdá-tə sáməvə bal'šóvə górədə, tjɪpjér' jɪdjót na úbɪl'.

IPA tɕíslʲɪnnəstʲ nɐsʲɪlʲénʲrʲə lóndənə, kɐgdá-tə sáməvə bɐlʲşóvə gʷórədə, tʲɪpʲérʲ ʲɪdʲə́t na úbɪlʲ.

2533

EN Few of the people who applied for the job had the necessary qualifications.

RU Всего́ не́сколько челове́к из тех, кто отпра́вил своё резюме́ на э́ту до́лжность, име́ли соотве́тствующую квалифика́цию.

ROM vsjɪvó njéskəl'kə čɪlavjék iz tjɛh, kto atprávjɪl svajó rɪzjumjé na étu dólžnəst', jɪmjéljɪ saatvjétstvujuɕɕuju kvaljɪfjɪkátsɪju.

IPA fsʲɪvʷó nʲéskəlʲkə tɕɨlɐvʲék ʲis tʲex, ktɒ ɐtprávʲɪɫ svɐʲǿ rʲɪzʲümʲé na étʊ dǿɫznəstʲ, ʲɪmʲélʲɪ sɐɐtʲétstfʊʲüɕɕʊʲü kfɐlʲɪfʲɪkátsɨʲü.

2534

EN Camila showed me a picture of her son, who is a
police officer.

RU Камила показала мне фотографию своего сына -
офицера полиции.

ROM kamílə pəkazálə mnjɛ fətagráfjıju svajıvó sínə -
afjıtsjérə palítsıjı.

IPA kʉmʲílə pəkɐzálə mnʲɛ fətɐgráfʲrʲü svɐʲıvʷǫ́ sínə -
ɐfʲıtsérə pɐlʲítsɨʲı.

2535

EN The doctor who examined me couldn't find anything
wrong.

RU Врач, который меня обследовал, не нашёл
никаких болезней.

ROM vrać, katórıj mjınjá absljédəvəl, njı našjól njıkakíh
baljéznjej.

IPA vratɕ, kʉtǫ́rɨj mʲınʲá ɐpslʲédəvəł, nʲı nɐʂǫ́ł nʲıkɐkʲíx
bɐlʲéz)nʲıj.

2536

EN The sun, which is one (1) of millions of stars in the universe, provides us with heat and light.

RU Со́лнце - звезда́ из миллио́нов во Вселе́нной - даёт нам тепло́ и свет. > Со́лнце - одна́ из миллио́нов звёзд во Вселе́нной - даёт нам тепло́ и свет.

ROM sóntsı - zvjızdá iz mjılljıónəv va vsjıljénnəj - dajót nam tjıpló i svjɛt. > sóntsı - adná iz mjılljıónəv zvjózd va vsjıljénnəj - dajót nam tjıpló i svjɛt.

IPA sǫ́ntsɨ - zvʲɪzdá ʲiz mʲɪɫlʲɪǫ́nəv vɐ fsʲɪlʲénnəj - dɐʲę́t nam tʲɪplǫ́ ɪ svʲet. > sǫ́ntsɨ - ɐdná ʲiz mʲɪɫlʲɪǫ́nəv zvʲǫ́zd vɐ fsʲɪlʲénnəj - dɐʲę́t nam tʲɪplǫ́ ɪ svʲet.

2537

EN Mr. Lopez, whom I spoke with at the meeting, is very interested in our plan.

RU Господи́н Ло́пез, с кото́рым я говори́л (♀говори́ла) на собра́нии, о́чень заинтересо́ван в на́шем пла́не.

ROM gəspadín lópjız, s katórım ja gəvaríl (♀gəvarílə) na sabránjıjı, óćın' zajıntjırısóvən v nášım plánjı.

IPA gəspɐdʲín lópʲɪs, s kɐtǫ́rɨm ʲa gəvɐrʲíɫ (♀gəvɐrʲílə) na sɐbránʲrʲɪ, ǫ́tɕɨnʲ zɐʲɪntʲɪrʲɪsǫ́vən v nášɨm plánʲɪ.

2538

EN Fortunately, we had a map that we would have gotten lost without.

RU К счáстью, у нас былá кáрта, без котóрой мы бы заблуди́лись.

ROM k śśást'ju, u nas bɪlá kártə, bɪs katórəj mɪ bɪ zabludíljɪs'.

IPA k ççástʲü, u nas bɨlá kártə, bʲɪs kɐtórəj mɨ bɨ zɐbludʲílʲɪsʲ.

2539

EN This is my friend from Italy that I was telling you about.

RU Это мой друг из Итáлии, о котóром я тебé расскáзывал (♀расскáзывала).

ROM étə moj drug iz jɪtáljɪjɪ, ɐ katórəm ja tjɪbjé rɪsskázɪvəl (♀rɪsskázɪvələ).

IPA étə mʷoj drug ʲiz ʲɪtálʲɪʲ, ɐ kɐtórəm ʲa tʲɪbʲé rɐsskázɨvəł (♀rɐsskázɨvələ).

2540

EN Ten people applied for the job, none of whom were suitable.

RU Дéсять людéй, совсéм не подходя́щих на э́ту дóлжность, отпрáвили свои́ резюмé.

ROM djésjat' ljudjéj, savsjém njɪ pədhadjáççɪh na étu dólžnəst', atprávjɪljɪ svaí rɪzjumjé.

IPA dʲésʲɪtʲ lʲüdʲéj, sɐfsʲém nʲɪ pətxɐdʲáççɨx na étʊ dółznəstʲ, ɐtprávʲɪlʲɪ svɐʲí rʲɪzʲümʲé.

2541

EN Priscilla has two (2) sisters, both of whom were teachers.

RU У Присци́ллы две сестры́, о́бе бы́ли учителя́ми.
ROM u prɪstsíllɪ dvjɛ sjɪstrí, óbjɪ bíljɪ uċɪtjɪljámjɪ.
IPA u prʲɪstsíɫɨ dvʲɛ sʲɪstrí, óbʲɪ bílʲɪ ʊtɕɨtʲɪlʲæmʲɪ.

2542

EN We drove along the road, the sides of which were lined with trees.

RU Мы е́хали по доро́ге, по обе́им сторона́м кото́рой росли́ дере́вья.
ROM mɪ jéhəljɪ pa darógjɪ, pa abjéjɪm stəranám katórəj raslí djɪrjévjɪ.
IPA mɨ ʲéxəlʲɪ pɐ dɐróɡʲɪ, pɐ ɐbʲéʲɪm stərɐnám kɐtórəj rɐslʲí dʲɪrʲévʲɪ.

2543

EN The company has a new business plan, the aim of which is to save money.

RU У компа́нии есть но́вый би́знес-план, цель кото́рого - эконо́мия де́нег.
ROM u kampánjɪjɪ jest' nóvɪj bíznjɪs-plən, tsɪl' katórəvə - ɛkanómjɪjə djénjɪg.
IPA u kɐmpán'ʲrʲɪ ʲestʲ nóvɨj bʲíznʲɪs-plən, tsʲelʲ kɐtórəvə - ɛkɐnómʲrʲə dʲénʲɪk.

2544

EN   Yijuan doesn't have a phone, which makes it difficult to contact her.

RU   У Ицзюа́нь нет телефо́на, и из-за э́того с ней сло́жно связа́ться.

ROM   u jɪtszjuán' njet tjɪljɪfónə, i iz-za étəvə s njej slóžnə svjɪzát'sjɪ.

IPA   u ʲɪtssʲüánʲ nʲet tʲɪlʲɪfʷónə, ɪ ʲiz-za étəvə s nʲej slóʐnə svʲɪzátʲsʲɪ.

2545

EN   Police investigating the crime are looking for three (3) men.

RU   Поли́ция, рассле́дующая преступле́ние, и́щет трои́х мужчи́н.

ROM   palítsɪjə, rɪssljédujuççəjɪ prɪstupljénjɪjɪ, íççɪt traíh mußßín.

IPA   pɐlʲítsʲə, rɐsslʲédüʲüççəʲɪ prʲɪstʊplʲénʲɨ̇ʲɪ, ʲíççɪt trɐʲíx mʊççín.

2546

EN   The road connecting the two (2) towns is very narrow.

RU   Доро́га, соединя́ющая два го́рода, о́чень у́зкая.

ROM   darógə, sajɪdjɪnjájuççəjɪ dva górədə, óćɪn' úzkəjɪ.

IPA   dɐrógə, sɐʲɪdʲɪnʲæ̇ʲüççəʲɪ dva gʷórədə, ótɕɪnʲ úskəʲɪ.

2547

EN I have a large bedroom overlooking the garden.

RU У меня́ больша́я спа́льня, выходя́щая на сад.
ROM u mjɪnjá bal'šájə spál'njɪ, vɪhadjáҫҫəjə na sad.
IPA u mʲɪnʲá bɐlʲṣáʲə spálʲnʲɪ, vɪ̵ɐdʲáҫҫəʲə na sat.

2548

EN The boy injured in the accident was taken to the hospital.

RU Ма́льчик, пострада́вший в ава́рии, был доста́влен в больни́цу.
ROM mál'ćɪk, pəstrɪdávšɪj v avárjɪjɪ, bɪl dastávljɪn v bal'nítsu.
IPA málʲtҫɨk, pəstrɐdáfṣɨj v ɐvárʲrʲɪ, bɨł dɐstávlʲɪn v bɐlʲnʲítsʊ.

2549

EN The police never found the money stolen in the robbery.

RU Поли́ция так и не нашла́ де́ньги, укра́денные во вре́мя ограбле́ния.
ROM palítsɪjə tak i njɪ našlá djén'gjɪ, ukrádjɪnnɪjɪ va vrjémjɪ əgrɪbljénjɪjə.
IPA pɐlʲítsɨʲə tak ɪ nʲɪ nɐṣlá dʲénʲgʲɪ, ʊkrádʲɪnnɨ̵ɪ vɐ vrʲémʲɪ əgrɐblʲénʲrʲə.

2550

EN Most of the goods made in this factory are exported.

RU Большинство товаров, производимых на этой
фабрике, идёт на экспорт.

ROM bal'šmstvó tavárəv, prəjɪzvadímıh na étəj fábrjɪkjɪ,
jɪdjót na ékspərt.

IPA bɐlʲşinstfʷ, tɐvárəf, prəʲɪzvɐdʲímɨx na étəj fábrʲɪkʲɪ,
ʲɪdʲt na ékspərt.

2551

EN There are only a few chocolates left.

RU Осталось всего пару шоколадок.

ROM astáləs' vsjɪvó páru šəkaládək.

IPA ɐstáləsʲ fsʲɪvʷ páru şəkɐládək.

2552

EN I didn't talk much to the man sitting next to me on
the plane.

RU Я не слишком много разговаривал
(♀ разговаривала) с мужчиной, сидящим возле
меня в самолёте.

ROM ja njɪ slíškəm mnógə rɪzgavárjɪvəl (♀ rɪzgavárjɪvələ) s
muššínəj, sjɪdjáççɪm vózljɪ mjɪnjá v səmaljótjɪ.

IPA ʲa nʲɪ slʲíškəm mnógə rəzgɐvárʲɪvəɫ (♀ rəzgɐvárʲɪvələ)
s muççínəj, sʲɪdʲæççɪm vʷzlʲɪ mʲɪnʲá f səmɐlʲt̪ʲɪ.

2553

EN The taxi taking us to the airport broke down.

RU Такси́, кото́рое везло́ нас в аэропо́рт, слома́лось.

ROM taksí, katórəjɪ vjɪzló nas v aɛrapórt, slamáləs'.

IPA tɐksʲí, kɐtórəʲɪ vʲɪzlǫ́ nas v aɛrɐpʷǫ́rt, slɐmáləsʲ.

2554

EN The road damaged in the storm has now been repaired.

RU Доро́га, повреждённая урага́ном, была́ отремонти́рована.

ROM darógə, pavrɪždjónnəjɪ urɪgánəm, bɪlá ətrɪmantírəvənə.

IPA dɐróɡə, pɐvrʲɪʐdʲǫ́nnəʲɪ ʊrɐɡánəm, bɨlá ətrʲɪmɐntʲírəvənə.

2555

EN Most of the suggestions made at the meeting weren't very reasonable.

RU Большинство́ предложе́ний, вы́сказанных на собра́нии, бы́ли не о́чень разу́мными.

ROM bal'šɪnstvó prɪdlažjénjɪj, vískəzənnɪh na sabránjɪjɪ, bíljɪ njɪ óčɪn' rɪzúmnɪmjɪ.

IPA bɐlʲʂɨnstfʷó prʲɪdlɐʐɛ́nʲɪj, vískəzənnɨx na sɐbránʲr̩ʲɪ, bílʲʲɪ nʲɪ ótɕɪnʲ rɛzúmnɨmʲɪ.

2556

EN What was the name of the man arrested by the police?

RU Как зва́ли мужчи́ну, аресто́ванного поли́цией?
ROM kak zválji muśśínu, arıstóvənnəvə palítsıjej?
IPA kak zváļʲı mʊɕɕínʊ, ɐrʲɪstǫ́vənnəvə pɐļʲítsɨ̞ʲɪj?

2557

EN I don't have anything to do. I'm bored.

RU Мне не́чем заня́ться. Мне ску́чно.
ROM mnjɛ njéćım zanját'sjı. mnjɛ skúćnə.
IPA mnʲɛ nʲétɕɨm zɐnʲǽtʲsʲɪ. mnʲɛ skútɕnə.

2558

EN The teacher's explanation was confusing. Most of the students didn't understand it.

RU Объясне́ние учи́теля бы́ло сли́шком запу́танным. Большинство́ студе́нтов его́ не по́няли.
ROM abjısnjénjıjı ućítjeljı bílə slíškəm zapútənnım. bal'šınstvó studjéntəv jıvó njı pónjaljı.
IPA ɐbʲɪsnʲénʲrʲɪ ʊtɕítʲıļʲı bílə sļʲíʂkəm zɐpútənnɨ̞m. bɐļʲʂinstfʷǫ́ stʊdʲéntəv ʲɪvʷǫ́ nʲɪ pʷǫ́nʲɪļʲɪ.

2559

EN The kitchen hadn't been cleaned in ages. It was really disgusting.

RU На ку́хне не убира́лись года́ми. Э́то бы́ло пои́стинне отврати́тельное зре́лище.

ROM na kúhnjı njı ubjıráljıs' gadámjı. étə bílə paístjınnjı ətvrıtítjel'nəjı zrjéljıççı.

IPA na kúxnʲɪ nʲɪ ʊbʲɪrálʲɪsʲ ɡɐdámʲɪ. étə bɨ́lə pɐʲístʲɪnnʲɪ ətfrɐtʲítʲɪlʲnəʲɪ zrʲélʲɪ̥ççɨ̇.

2560

EN You don't have to get annoyed just because I'm a few minutes late.

RU Ты не до́лжен (♀должна́) зли́ться то́лько потому́, что я опозда́л (♀опозда́ла) на не́сколько мину́т.

ROM tı njı dólžın (♀dalžná) zlít'sjı tól'kə pətamú, što ja əpazdál (♀əpazdálə) na njéskəl'kə mjınút.

IPA tɨ nʲɪ dóɫzɨn (♀dɐłzná) zlʲítʲsʲɪ tólʲkə pətɐmú, şt̯ọ ʲa əpɐzdáł (♀əpɐzdálə) na nʲéskəlʲkə mʲɪnút.

2561

EN I've been working very hard all day, and now I'm exhausted.

RU Я рабо́тал (♀рабо́тала) весь день и тепе́рь чу́вствую себя́ изнурённым (♀изнурённой).

ROM ja rıbótəl (♀rıbótələ) vjes' djen' i tjırpjér' ćústvuju sjıbjá jıznurjónnım (♀jıznurjónnəj).

IPA ʲa rɐbʷótəł (♀rɐbʷótələ) vʲesʲ dʲenʲ ɪ tʲɪrpʲérʲ tɕúʊstfʊʲü sʲɪbʲá ʲɪznʊrʲénnɨm (♀ʲɪznʊrʲénnəj).

2562

EN Vitale is very good at telling funny stories. He can be very amusing.

RU Витáле óчень хорóш в расскáзывании смешны́х истóрий. Он мóжет быть óчень забáвным.

ROM vjɪtáljɪ óćɪn' haróš v rɪsskázɪvənjɪjɪ smjɪšnɪ́h jɪstórjɪj. on móžɪt bɪt' óćɪn' zabávnɪm.

IPA vʲɪtálʲɪ ótɕinʲ xɐróş v rɐsskázɪvənʲrʲɪ smʲɪşnɪ́x ʲɪstórʲɪj. ɐn mʷóżɨt bɨtʲ ótɕinʲ zɐbávnɪm.

2563

EN He's one of the most boring people I've ever met. He never stops talking, and he never says anything interesting.

RU Он одúн из сáмых скýчных людéй, котóрых я когдá-либо встречáл (♀встречáла). Он ни на минýту не замолкáет и при э́том не говорúт ничегó интерéсного.

ROM on adín iz sámɪh skúćnɪh ljudjéj, katórɪh ja kagdá-ljɪbə vstrɪćál (♀vstrɪćálə). on ni na mjɪnútu njɪ zəmalkájɪt i prɪ étəm njɪ gəvarít njɪćɪvó jɪntjɪrjésnəvə.

IPA ɐn ɐdʲín ʲis sámɨx skútɕnɨx lʲüdʲéj, kɐtórɨx ʲa kɐgdá-lʲɪbə fstrʲɪtɕáł (♀fstrʲɪtɕálə). ɐn nʲi na mʲɪnútʊ nʲɪ zəmɐɫkáʲɪt ɪ prʲɪ étəm nʲɪ gəvɐrʲít nʲɪtɕivʷó ʲɪntʲɪrʲésnəvə.

2564

EN As the movie went on, it became more and more boring.

RU По ме́ре продолже́ния фильм станови́лся всё бо́лее и бо́лее ску́чным.

ROM pa mjérjɪ prədalžjénjɪjə fil'm stənavílsjɪ vsjó bóljejɪ i bóljejɪ skúćnɪm.

IPA pɐ mʲérʲɪ prədɐɫzɛ́nʲrʲə fʲilʲm stənɐvʲíɫsʲɪ fsʲǿ bʷǿlʲrʲɪ ɪ bʷǿlʲrʲɪ skútɕnɨm.

2565

EN The dinner smells good.

RU У́жин вку́сно па́хнет.

ROM úžɪn vkúsnə páhnjɪt.

IPA úzɨn fkúsnə páxnʲɪt.

2566

EN This milk tastes a little strange.

RU Э́то молоко́ на вкус о́чень стра́нное.

ROM étə məlakó na vkus óćɪn' stránnəjɪ.

IPA étə məlɐkʷǿ na fkus ǿtɕɨnʲ stránnəʲɪ.

2567

EN I can't eat this. I just tried it and it tastes awful!

RU Я не могу́ э́то есть. Я то́лько что попро́бовал
(♀попро́бовала), и на вкус э́то про́сто ужа́сно!

ROM ja nji magú étə jest'. ja tól'kə što papróbəvəl
(♀papróbəvələ), i na vkus étə próstə užásnə!

IPA ʲa nʲɪ mɐgú étə ʲestʲ. ʲa tólʲkə şto pɐpróbəvəł
(♀pɐpróbəvələ), ɪ na fkus étə próstə ʊzásnə!

2568

EN Why do you look all wet? Have you been out in the
rain?

RU Почему́ ты весь мо́крый (♀вся мо́края)? Ты попа́л
(♀попа́ла) под дождь?

ROM paćimú tɪ vjes' mókrɪj (♀vsja mókrəjɪ)? tɪ papál
(♀papálə) pad dožd'?

IPA pɐtɕimú tɨ vʲesʲ mʷókrɨj (♀fsʲa mʷókrəʲɪ)? tɨ pɐpáł
(♀pɐpálə) pɐd dozdʲ?

2569

EN There's no point in doing a job if you don't do it
properly.

RU Нет смы́сла де́лать рабо́ту, е́сли ты не де́лаешь её
пра́вильно.

ROM njet smíslə djélət' rɪbótu, jésljɪ tɪ njɪ djéləjeś jɪjó
právjɪl'nə.

IPA nʲet smíslə dʲélətʲ rɐbʷótʊ, ʲéslʲɪ tɨ nʲɪ dʲéləʲɪç ʲɪ́ʁǫ
právʲɪlʲnə.

2570

EN They'll be away for the next few weeks.

RU Их не бу́дет сле́дующие не́сколько неде́ль.
ROM ih njɪ búdjɪt sljédujuççɪjɪ njéskəl'kə njɪdjél'.
IPA ʲix nʲɪ búdʲɪt slʲédʊʲüççɨʲɪ nʲéskəlʲkə nʲɪdʲélʲ.

2571

EN Two people were seriously injured in the accident.

RU Дво́е челове́к серьёзно пострада́ли в ава́рии.
ROM dvójɪ ćɪlavjék sjɪrjóznə pəstrɪdáljɪ v avárjɪjɪ.
IPA dvʷǫ́ʲɪ tɕɪlɐvʲék sʲɪrʲǫ́znə pəstrɐdálʲɪ v ɐvárʲɪ̯ɪ.

2572

EN We didn't go out because it was raining heavily.

RU Мы никуда́ не пошли́, потому́ что шёл си́льный
дождь.
ROM mɪ njɪkudá njɪ pašlí, pətamú što šjól síl'nɪj doždʼ.
IPA mɨ nʲɪkʊdá nʲɪ pɐʂlʲí, pətɐmú ʂtɐ ʂǫ́ɫ sʲílʲnɨj doʐdʲ.

2573

EN Even though Rosetta still makes mistakes, her English is already very fluent.

RU Не смотря́ на то, что Розе́тта всё ещё допуска́ет оши́бки, она́ уже́ доста́точно бе́гло говори́т по-англи́йски.

ROM njɪ smatrjá na to, što razjéttə vsjó jɪçcjó dapuskájɪt ašíbkjɪ, aná užjé dastátəćnə bjéglə gəvarít pa-anglíjskjɪ.

IPA nʲɪ smɐtrʲá na tɔ, ʂtɔ rɐzʲéttə fsʲɵ́ ʲɪçcɵ́ dɐpʊskáʲɪt ɐʂípkʲɪ, ɐná ʊʐɨ́ dɐstátətɕnə bʲéglə gəvɐrʲít pɐ-ɐnglʲíjskʲɪ.

2574

EN The shoes I tried on fit me perfectly.

RU Ту́фли, кото́рые я поме́рил (♀ поме́рила), бы́ли мне в са́мый раз.

ROM túfljɪ, katórɪjɪ ja pamjérjɪl (♀pamjérjɪlə), bíljɪ mnjɛ v sámɪj raz.

IPA túflʲɪ, kɐtórɨ̯ɪ ʲa pɐmʲérʲɨɫ (♀pɐmʲérʲɪlə), bílʲɪ mnʲɛ f sámɨj ras.

2575

EN We know how to learn languages incredibly quickly.

RU Мы зна́ем, как невероя́тно бы́стро изуча́ть языки́.

ROM mɪ znájɪm, kak njɪvjɪrajátnə bístrə jɪzućát' jɪzɪkí.

IPA mɨ znáʲɪm, kak nʲɪvʲɪrɐʲátnə bístrə ʲɪzʊtɕát ʲɪzɨkʲí.

2576

EN Two people got seriously injured in the accident.

RU Два человéка получи́ли серьёзные ранéния в результáте авáрии.

ROM dva ćɪlavjékə palućíljɪ sjɪrjóznɪjɪ rɪnjénjɪjə v rɪzul'tátjɪ avárjɪjɪ.

IPA dva tɕɪlɐvʲékə pɐlʊtɕílʲɪ sʲɪrʲǫ́znɨʲɪ rɐnʲénʲrʲə v rʲɪzʊlʲtátʲɪ ɐvárʲrʲɪ.

2577

EN The conference was badly organized.

RU Конферéнция былá плóхо организóвана.

ROM kanfjɪrjéntsɪjɪ bɪlá plóhə ərganjɪzóvənə.

IPA kɐnfʲɪrʲéntsɨʲɪ bɨlá plǫ́xə ərgɐnʲɪzǫ́vənə.

2578

EN The movie was unnecessarily long. It could have been much shorter.

RU Фильм был изли́шне дóлгим. Он мог быть горáздо корóче.

ROM fil'm bɪl jɪzlíšnjɪ dólgjɪm. on mog bɪt' garázdə karóćɪ.

IPA fʲilʲm bɨɫ ʲɪzlʲíʂnʲɪ dǫ́ɫgʲɪm. ǫn mʷɐg bɨtʲ gɐrázdə kɐrǫ́tɕɨ.

2579

EN Esteban always wears nice clothes. He's always well
    dressed.

RU Эстебан всегда́ но́сит хоро́шую оде́жду. Он всегда́
    хорошо́ оде́т.

ROM éstjɪbən vsjɪgdá nósjɪt haróšuju adjéždu. on vsjɪgdá
    hərašó adjét.

IPA éstʲɪbən fsʲɪgdá nós̪ʲɪt xɐróṣʊʲü ɐdʲéz̪dʊ. о̝n fsʲɪgdá
    xərɐṣó ɐdʲét.

2580

EN Elisa has a lot of responsibility in her job, but she
    isn't very well paid.

RU Эли́за за мно́гое отвеча́ет на рабо́те, но ей за э́то
    не сли́шком хорошо́ пла́тят.

ROM ɛlízə za mnógəjɪ atvjɪćájɪt na rɪbótjɪ, no jej za étə njɪ
    slíškəm hərašó plátjɪt.

IPA ɛlʲízə za mnóɡəʲɪ ɐtɕʲɪtçáʲɪt na rɐbʷótʲɪ, no̝ ʲej za étə nʲɪ
    slʲíṣkəm xərɐṣó plátʲɪt.

2581

EN You're speaking too quietly, I can hardly hear you.

RU Ты сли́шком ти́хо говори́шь, я с трудо́м слы́шу
    тебя́.

ROM tɪ slíškəm tíhə gəvaríś, ja s trudóm slíšu tjɪbjá.

IPA tɨ slʲíṣkəm tʲíxə gəvɐrʲíɕ, ʲa s trʊdóm slíṣʊ tʲɪbʲá.

2582

EN You look the same now as you looked fifteen (15) years ago. You've hardly changed!

RU Ты вы́глядишь та́кже, как пятна́дцать лет наза́д. Ты почти́ не измени́лся (♀ измени́лась).

ROM tɪ vígljadjɪś tákžɪ, kak pjɪtnádtsət' ljɛt nazád. tɪ paćtí njɪ jɪzmjɪnílsjɪ (♀ jɪzmjɪníləs').

IPA tɨ vʲíglʲɪdʲɪɕ tákʂɨ, kak pʲɪtnáttsətʲ lʲɛt nɐzát. tɨ pɐtɕtʲí nʲɪ ʲɪzmʲɪnʲílsʲɪ (♀ ʲɪzmʲɪnʲíləsʲ).

2583

EN Our new boss is not very popular. Hardly anyone likes her.

RU Наш но́вый босс не по́льзуется большо́й популя́рностью. Она́ почти́ никому́ не нра́вится.

ROM naš nóvɪj boss njɪ pól'zujetsjɪ bal'šój papuljárnəst'ju. aná paćtí njɪkamú njɪ nrávjɪtsjɪ.

IPA naʂ nóvɨj bʷɵss nʲɪ pʷólʲzʊʲɪtsʲɪ bɐlʲʂój pɐpʊlʲárnəstʲʉ. ɐná pɐtɕtʲí nʲɪkɐmú nʲɪ nrávʲɪtsʲɪ.

2584

EN It was very crowded in the room. There was hardly anywhere to sit.

RU Ко́мната была́ перепо́лнена. Бы́ло едва́ где сесть.

ROM kómnətə bɪlá pjɪrɪpólnjɪnə. bílə jɪdvá gdjɛ sjést'.

IPA kʷómnətə bɨlá pʲɪrʲɪpʷólnʲɪnə. bílə ʲɪdvá gdʲɛ sʲéstʲ.

2585

EN I hate this town. There's hardly anything to do and hardly anywhere to go for fun.

RU Ненави́жу э́тот го́род. Здесь почти́ не́чем заня́ться и ма́ло куда́ мо́жно пойти́.

ROM njɪnavížu étət górəd. zdjes' paćtí njéćɪm zanját'sjɪ i málə kudá móžnə pójtjɪ.

IPA nʲɪnɐvʲízʊ étət gʷórət. zdʲesʲ pɐtɕtʲí nʲétɕɪm zɐnʲǽtʲsʲɪ ɪ málə kʊdá mʷóznə pʷójtʲɪ.

2586

EN The story was so stupid. > It was such a stupid story.

RU Исто́рия была́ тако́й глу́пой. > Э́то была́ така́я глу́пая исто́рия.

ROM jɪstórjɪjə bɪlá takój glúpəj. > étə bɪlá takájə glúpəjə jɪstórjɪjə.

IPA ʲɪstórʲɪʲə bɪlá tɐkʷój glúpəj. > étə bɪlá tɐkáʲə glúpəʲə ʲɪstórʲɪʲə.

2587

EN They are so nice. > They are such nice people.

RU Они́ о́чень хоро́шие. > Они́ таки́е хоро́шие лю́ди.

ROM aní óćɪn' haróšɪjɪ. > aní takíjɪ haróšɪjɪ ljúdjɪ.

IPA ɐnʲí ótɕɪnʲ xɐróʂɪʲɪ. > ɐnʲí tɐkʲíʲɪ xɐróʂɪʲɪ lʲúdʲɪ.

2588

EN We had such a good time on vacation that we didn't want to come home.

RU Мы так хорошо́ провели́ вре́мя в о́тпуске, что не хоте́ли возвраща́ться домо́й.

ROM mɪ tak hərašó pravjɪlí vrjémjɪ v ótpuskjɪ, što njɪ hatjéljɪ vəzvrɪҫҫát'sjɪ damój.

IPA mɨ tak xərɐʂó prɐvʲɪlʲí vrʲémʲɪ v ótpʊskʲɪ, ştọ nʲɪ xɐtélʲɪ vəzvrɐҫҫátʲsʲɪ dɐmʷój.

2589

EN She speaks English so well you would think it was her native language.

RU Она́ говори́т по-англи́йски так хорошо́, что вы могли́ бы поду́мать, бу́дто э́то её родно́й язы́к.

ROM aná gəvarít pa-anglíjskjɪ tak hərašó, što vɪ maglí bɪ padúmət', búdtə étə jɪjó radnój jɪzík.

IPA ɐná gəvɐrʲít pɐ-ɐnglʲíjskʲɪ tak xərɐʂó, ştọ vɨ mɐglʲí bɨ pɐdúmətʲ, búttə étə ʲɨʲé̞ rɐdnój ʲɪzík.

2590

EN The music was so loud that you could hear it from miles away.

RU Му́зыка была́ насто́лько гро́мкой, что её мо́жно бы́ло услы́шать издалека́.

ROM múzɪkə bɪlá nastól'kə grómkəj, što jɪjó móžnə bílə uslíšət' jɪzdaljɪká.

IPA múzɨkə bɨlá nɐstólʲkə grómkəj, ştọ ʲɨʲé̞ mʷóʐnə bɨlə ʊslíʂətʲ ʲɪzdɐlʲɪká.

2591

EN   I haven't seen her for such a long time.

RU   Я не ви́дел (♀ви́дела) её в тече́ние дли́тельного
     вре́мени. > Я не ви́дел (♀ви́дела) её так давно́.

ROM ja njɪ vídjɪl (♀vídjɪlə) jɪjó v tjɪćjénjɪjɪ dlítjel'nəvə
     vrjémjenjɪ. > ja njɪ vídjɪl (♀vídjɪlə) jɪjó tak davnó.

IPA ʲa nʲɪ vʲídʲɪɫ (♀vʲídʲɪlə) ʲɾʲé̞ f tʲɪtɕénʲɾʲɪ dlʲítʲɪlʲnəvə
     vrʲémʲɪnʲɪ. > ʲa nʲɪ vʲídʲɪɫ (♀vʲídʲɪlə) ʲɾʲé̞ tak dɐvnó̞.

2592

EN   I didn't know it was such a long way.

RU   Я не знал (♀зна́ла), что э́то был тако́й до́лгий
     путь.

ROM ja njɪ znal (♀ználə), što étə bɪl takój dólgjɪj put'.

IPA ʲa nʲɪ znaɫ (♀ználə), ʂtɔ étə bɨɫ tɐkʷój dó̞ɫgʲɪj putʲ.

2593

EN   You're lazy. You don't work hard enough.

RU   Ты лени́в (♀лени́ва). Ты рабо́таешь не доста́точно
     усе́рдно.

ROM tɪ ljɪnív (♀ljɪnívə). tɪ rɪbótəjeś njɪ dastátəćnə
     usjérdnə.

IPA tɨ lʲɪmʲíf (♀lʲɪmʲívə). tɨ rɐbʷótəʲɪɕ nʲɪ dɐstátətɕnə
     ʊsʲérdnə.

2594

EN Is Raj going to apply for the job? Does he have enough experience? > Is he experienced enough for the job?

RU Радж собира́ется отпра́вить своё резюме́ на э́ту до́лжность? У него́ доста́точно о́пыта? > Он доста́точно о́пытен для э́той рабо́ты?

ROM radž sabjɪrájetsjɪ atprávjɪt' svajó rɪzjumjɛ́ na ɛ́tu dólžnəst'? u njɪvó dastátəćnə ópɪtə? > on dastátəćnə ópɪtjɪn dlja ɛ́təj rɪbótɪ?

IPA radʂ sɐbʲɪráʲɪtsʲɪ ɐtprávʲɪtʲ svɐʲɵ́ rʲɪzʲʉmʲɛ́ na ɛ́tʊ dǫ́ɫʐnəstʲ? u nʲɪvʷǫ́ dɐstátətɕnə ǫ́pɨtə? > ǫn dɐstátətɕnə ǫ́pɨtʲɪn dlʲa ɛ́təj rɐbʷǫ́tɨ?

2595

EN They're too young to get married. > They're not old enough to get married.

RU Они́ сли́шком мо́лоды, что́бы жени́ться. > Они́ не доста́точно взро́слые, что́бы жени́ться.

ROM aní slíškəm móldɪ, štóbɪ žɪnít'sjɪ. > aní njɪ dastátəćnə vzróslɪjɪ, štóbɪ žɪnít'sjɪ.

IPA ɐnʲí slʲíʂkəm mʷǫ́lədɨ, ʂtǫ́bɨ zɨnʲítʲsʲɪ. > ɐnʲí nʲɪ dɐstátətɕnə vzrǫ́slɨʲɪ, ʂtǫ́bɨ zɨnʲítʲsʲɪ.

2596

EN It's too far to walk home from here.

RU Наш дом сли́шком далеко́, что́бы идти́ отсю́да пешко́м.

ROM naš dom slíškəm daljıkó, štóbı jıdtí atsjúdə pjıškóm.

IPA naʂ dom slʲíʂkəm dɐlʲıkʷǫ́, ʂtǫ́bɨ ʲıttʲí ɐtsʲúdə pʲıʂkʷǫ́m.

2597

EN These apples aren't ripe enough to eat.

RU Э́ти я́блоки ещё не созре́ли, что́бы их есть.

ROM étjı jábləkjı jıççjó njı sazrjéljı, štóbı ih jest'.

IPA étʲı ʲábləkʲı ʲıççǫ́ nʲı sɐzrʲélʲı, ʂtǫ́bɨ ʲix ʲestʲ.

2598

EN The situation is too complicated to explain.

RU Э́ту ситуа́цию сли́шком сло́жно объясни́ть.

ROM étu sjıtuátsıju slíškəm slóžnə abjısnít'.

IPA étʊ sʲıtʊátsɨʲü slʲíʂkəm slǫ́znə ɐbʲısnʲítʲ.

2599

EN You're standing too close to the camera. Can you move a little farther away?

RU Ты стóишь слúшком блúзко к кáмере. Ты мóжешь отойтú подáльше?

ROM tɪ stójɪś slíškəm blízkə k kámjerjɪ. tɪ móžɪś ətajtí padál'šɪ?

IPA tɨ stǫ́ʲɪç slʲíʂkəm blʲískə k kámʲɪrʲɪ. tɨ mʷǫ́ʐɨç ətɐjtʲí pɐdálʲʂɨ?

2600

EN The instructions were very complicated. They could have been simpler.

RU Инстрýкции бы́ли óчень слóжными. Онú моглú бы быть прóще.

ROM jɪnstrúktsɪjɪ bíljɪ óćɪn' slóžnɪmjɪ. aní maglí bɪ bɪt' próççɪ.

IPA ʲɪnstrúktsɨʲɪ bɨ́lʲʲɪ ǫ́tɕɨnʲ slǫ́ʐnɨmʲɪ. ɐnʲí mɐɡlʲí bɨ bɨtʲ próɕɕɨ.

GMS #2601 - 2700

2601

EN It takes longer by train than car.

RU На поезде это занимает больше времени, чем на машине.

ROM na pójezdjı étə zanjımájıt ból'šı vrjémjenjı, ćım na mašínjı.

IPA na pʷǫ́ʲızdʲı étə zɐnʲımáʲıt bʷǫ́lʲşɨ vrʲémʲınʲı, tɕem na mɐşínʲı.

2602

EN Walter did worse than I did on the test.

RU Уолтер написал тест хуже, чем я.

ROM uóltjır napjısál tjɛst húžı, ćım ja.

IPA ʋǫ́ɫtʲır nɐpʲısáɫ tʲɛst xúzɨ, tɕem ʲa.

2603

EN My friends arrived earlier than I expected.

RU Мой друзья приехали раньше, чем я ожидал (♀ожидала).

ROM maí druz'já prıjéhəljı rán'šı, ćım ja ažıdál (♀ažıdálə).

IPA mɐʲí druzʲá prʲɨʲéxəlʲı ránʲşɨ, tɕem ʲa ɐzɨdáɫ (♀ɐzɨdálə).

2604

EN The buses run more often than the trains.

RU Автобусы хо́дят ча́ще, чем поезда́.

ROM avtóbusı hódjıt ćáççı, ćım pajızdá.

IPA ɐftóbusɨ xód^jıt tɕáɕɕɨ, tɕɛm pɐ^jızdá.

2605

EN There were a lot of people on the bus. It was more crowded than usual.

RU В автобусе бы́ло мно́го наро́ду (люде́й). Он был заби́т бо́льше обы́чного.

ROM v avtóbusjı bílə mnógə naródu (ljudjéj). on bıl zabít ból'šı abíćnəvə.

IPA v ɐftóbus^jı bílə mnógə nɐródʊ (l^jüd^jéj). ǫn bɨł zɐb^jít b^wół^jşɨ ɐbítɕnəvə.

2606

EN Could you speak a bit more slowly?

RU Ты не мог (♀могла́) бы говори́ть чуть поме́дленнее? > Не могли́ бы вы говори́ть немно́го ме́дленнее?

ROM tı njı mog (♀maglá) bı gəvarít' ćut' pamjédljennjejı? > njı maglí bı vı gəvarít' njımnógə mjédljennjejı?

IPA tɨ n^jı m^wǫk (♀mɐglá) bɨ gəvɐr^jít^j tɕut^j pɐm^jédl^jınn^jɪ́ɪ? > n^jı mɐgl^jí bɨ vɨ gəvɐr^jít^j n^jımnógə m^jédl^jınn^jɪ́ɪ?

2607

EN This bag is slightly heavier than the other one.

RU Э́та су́мка немно́го тяжеле́е, чем друга́я.

ROM étə súmkə njɪmnógə tjɪžɪljéjɪ, ćɪm drugájə.

IPA étə súmkə nʲɪmnógə tʲɪzʲɨlʲéʲɪ, tɕɛm druɡáʲə.

2608

EN Her illness was far more serious than we thought at first.

RU Её боле́знь была́ гора́здо серьёзнее, чем мы ду́мали снача́ла.

ROM jɪjó baljézn' bɪlá garázdə sjɪrjóznjejɪ, ćɪm mɪ dúməljɪ snaćálə.

IPA ʲrʲǿ bɐlʲéznʲ bɨlá ɡɐrázdə sʲɪrʲǿznʲɨrʲɪ, tɕɛm mɨ dúməlʲɪ snɐtɕálə.

2609

EN I've waited long enough and I'm not waiting any longer.

RU Я ждал (♀ждала́) доста́точно до́лго и бо́льше ждать не собира́юсь.

ROM ja ždal (♀ždalá) dastátəćnə dólgə i ból'šɪ ždat' njɪ sabjɪrájus'.

IPA ʲa zdał (♀zdɐlá) dɐstátətɕnə dǿłɡə ɪ bʷǿlʲʂɨ zdatʲ nʲɪ sɐbʲɪráʲüsʲ.

2610

EN We expected their house to be very big, but it's no bigger than ours.

RU Мы ду́мали, что их дом о́чень большо́й, но он не бо́льше на́шего. (...но он не бо́льше чем наш).

ROM mɪ dúməljɪ, što ih dom óćɪn' bal'šój, no on njɪ ból'šɪ nášɪvə. (...no on njɪ ból'šɪ ćɪm naš).

IPA mɨ dúməlʲɪ, ʂtɔ ʲix dɔm ótɕɪnʲ bɐlʲsój, nɔ ɔn nʲɪ bʷólʲʂɨ náʂɨvə. (...nɔ ɔn nʲɪ bʷólʲʂɨ tɕɛm naʂ).

2611

EN This hotel is better than the other one, and it's no more expensive.

RU Э́тот оте́ль лу́чше того́ и при э́том не доро́же. Э́тот оте́ль лу́чше чем тот и при э́том не доро́же.

ROM étət atél' lúćsɪ tavó i prɪ étəm njɪ daróžɪ. étət atél' lúćsɪ ćɪm tot i prɪ étəm njɪ daróžɪ.

IPA étət ɐtélʲ lútɕɕɨ tɐvʷó ɪ prʲɪ étəm nʲɪ dɐrózɨ. étət ɐtélʲ lútɕɕɨ tɕɛm tɔt ɪ prʲɪ étəm nʲɪ dɐrózɨ.

2612

EN What time should we leave? — The sooner the better.

RU Когда́ нам лу́чше выходи́ть? — Чем скоре́е, тем лу́чше.

ROM kagdá nam lúćsɪ vɪhadít'? — ćɪm skarjéjɪ, tjɛm lúćsɪ.

IPA kɐgdá nam lútɕɕɨ vɨxɐdʲítʲ? — tɕɛm skɐrʲéʲɪ, tʲɛm lútɕɕɨ.

2613

EN   When you're traveling, the less luggage you have the better.

RU   Когда́ вы путеше́ствуете, чем ме́ньше у вас багажа́, тем лу́чше.

ROM kagdá vi putjišjéstvujetji, ćim mjén'ši u vas bəgažá, tjɛm lúćśɪ.

IPA kɐgdá vɨ pʊtʲɪʂéstfʊ ʲɪtʲɪ, tɕɛm mʲénʲʂɨ u vas bɐgɐzá, tʲɛm lútɕɕɨ.

2614

EN   The sooner we leave, the earlier we'll arrive.

RU   Чем скоре́е мы вы́йдем, тем ра́ньше доберёмся.

ROM ćim skarjéji mi víjdjim, tjɛm rán'ši dabjirjómsji.

IPA tɕɛm skɐrʲéʲɪ mɨ vʲíjdʲɪm, tʲɛm ránʲʂɨ dɐbʲɪrʲ ém sʲɪ.

2615

EN   The more I thought about the plan, the less I liked it.

RU   Чем бо́льше я ду́мал (♀ду́мала) о пла́не, тем ме́ньше он мне нра́вился.

ROM ćim ból'ši ja dúməl (♀dúmələ) a plánji, tjɛm mjén'ši on mnjɛ nrávjilsji.

IPA tɕɛm bʷ ᶅ ᵻ ʲa dúməɫ (♀dúmələ) ɐ plánʲɪ, tʲɛm mʲénʲʂɨ ɔn mnʲɛ nrávʲɪtsʲɪ.

2616

EN The shopping mall wasn't as crowded as usual. >
The shopping mall was less crowded than usual.

RU В торго́вом це́нтре бы́ло не так лю́дно, как
обы́чно. > В торго́вом це́нтре бы́ло ме́нее лю́дно,
чем обы́чно.

ROM v targóvəm tsjéntrjı bı́lə njı tak ljúdnə, kak abı́ćnə. >
v targóvəm tsjéntrjı bı́lə mjénjejı ljúdnə, ćım abı́ćnə.

IPA f tɐrgʷɵ́vəm ʦéntrʲɪ bı́lə nʲɪ tak lʲúdnə, kak ɐbı́ʦnə. >
f tɐrgʷɵ́vəm ʦéntrʲɪ bı́lə mʲénʲrʲɪ lʲúdnə, ʨɛm ɐbı́ʦnə.

2617

EN I don't know as many people as you do. > I know
fewer people than you do.

RU Я не зна́ю, так мно́го люде́й, как вы (ты). > Я
зна́ю, ме́ньше люде́й, чем вы (ты).

ROM ja njı znáju, tak mnógə ljudjéj, kak vı (tı). > ja
znáju, mjén'šı ljudjéj, ćım vı (tı).

IPA ʲa nʲɪ znáʲü, tak mnógə lʲüdʲéj, kak vɨ (tɨ). > ʲa znáʲü,
mʲénʲʂɨ lʲüdʲéj, ʨɛm vɨ (tɨ).

2618

EN I'm sorry I'm late. I got here as fast as I could.

RU Прости́, я опозда́л (♀опозда́ла). Я прие́хал
(♀прие́хала) сюда́ так бы́стро, как то́лько мог
(♀могла́).

ROM prastí, ja əpazdál (♀əpazdálə). ja prɪjéhəl
(♀prɪjéhələ) sjudá tak bístrə, kak tól'kə mog
(♀maglá).

IPA prɐstʲí, ʲa əpɐzdáɫ (♀əpɐzdálə). ʲa prʲɪ́ɹʲéxəɫ
(♀prʲɪ́ɹʲéxələ) sʲüdá tak bístrə, kak tóɫʲkə mʷok
(♀mɐglá).

2619

EN You're free to have as much food as you want.

RU Вы мо́жете свобо́дно есть сто́лько еды́, ско́лько
хоти́те.

ROM vɪ móžɪtjɪ svabódnə jest' stól'kə jɪdí, skól'kə hatítjɪ.

IPA vɨ mʷóz̩tʲɪ svɐbʷódnə ʲestʲ stóɫʲkə ʲɪdí, skʷóɫʲkə
xɐtʲítʲɪ.

2620

EN Could you send me the money as soon as possible?

RU Не могли́ бы вы вы́слать мне де́ньги как мо́жно
скоре́е?

ROM njɪ maglí bɪ vɪ víslət' mnje djén'gjɪ kak móžnə
skarjéjɪ?

IPA nʲɪ mɐglʲí bɨ vɨ víslətʲ mnʲɛ dʲénʲgʲɪ kak mʷóznə
skɐrʲéʲɪ?

2621

EN Gas is twice as expensive as it was a few years ago.

RU Газ в два ра́за доро́же, чем не́сколько лет наза́д.
ROM gaz v dva rázə daróži, ćim njéskəl'kə ljɛt nazád.
IPA gaz v dva rázə dɐróʐɨ, tɕɛm nʲéskəlʲkə lʲet nɐzát.

2622

EN Satomi's salary is the same as mine. > Satomi gets the same salary as me.

RU Зарпла́та Сато́ми така́я же, как у меня́. > Сато́ми получа́ет таку́ю же зарпла́ту, как и я.
ROM zarplátə satómjı takájə ži, kak u mjınjá. > satómjı palućájıt takúju ži zarplátu, kak i ja.
IPA zɐrplátə sɐtómʲı tɛkáʲə zɨ, kak u mʲınʲá. > sɐtómʲı pɐlʊtɕáʲıt tɛkúʲü zɛ zɐrplátʊ, kak ı ʲa.

2623

EN They have more money than we do. > They have more money than us.

RU У них бо́льше де́нег, чем у нас.
ROM u nih ból'šı djénjıg, ćim u nas.
IPA u nʲix bʷólʲʂɨ dʲénʲık, tɕɛm u nas.

2624

EN I can't run as fast as he can. > I can't run as fast as him.

RU Я не могу́ бежа́ть та́кже бы́стро, как он.

ROM ja njɪ magú bjɪžát' tákžɪ bístrə, kak on.

IPA ʲa nʲɪ mɐgú bʲɪzátʲ tákṣɨ bístrə, kak on̪.

2625

EN The movie we just watched was the most boring movie I've ever seen.

RU Фильм, кото́рый мы то́лько что посмотре́ли, са́мый ску́чный из всех, кото́рые я когда́-либо ви́дел (♀ ви́дела).

ROM fil'm, katórɪj mɪ tól'kə što pəsmatrjéljɪ, sámɪj skúćnɪj iz vsjɛh, katórɪjɪ ja kagdá-ljɪbə vídjɪl (♀ vídjɪlə).

IPA fʲilʲm, kɐtórɪj mɨ tólʲkə ṣtɔ pəsmɐtrʲélʲɪ, sámɪj skútɕnɪj ʲiz fsʲex, kɐtórɨʲɪ ʲa kɐgdá-lʲɪbə vʲídʲɨɫ (♀ vʲídʲɪlə).

2626

EN Why does she always come to see me at the worst possible time?

RU Почему́ она́ всегда́ прихо́дит ко мне в са́мый неподходя́щий моме́нт?

ROM paćɪmú aná vsjɪgdá prɪhódjɪt ka mnjɛ v sámɪj njɪpədhadjáççɪj mamjént?

IPA pɐtɕɨmú ɐná fsʲɪgdá prʲɪxódʲɪt kɐ mnʲɛ f sámɨj nʲɪpətxɐdʲǽɕɕɪj mɐmʲént?

2627

EN He's the most patient person I've ever met.

RU Он са́мый терпели́вый челове́к, кото́рого я
когда́-либо встреча́л (♀ встреча́ла).

ROM on sámɪj tjɪrpjɪlívɪj ćɪlavjék, katórəvə ja kagdá-ljɪbə
vstrɪćál (♀ vstrɪćálə).

IPA on sámɨj tʲɪrpʲɪlʲívɨj tɕɪlɐvʲék, kɐtórəvə ʲa kɐgdá-lʲɪbə
fstrʲɪtɕáɫ (♀ fstrʲɪtɕálə).

2628

EN His eldest son is sixteen (16) years old.

RU Его́ ста́ршему сы́ну шестна́дцать лет .

ROM jɪvó stáršɪmu sínu šɪsnádtsət' ljɛt .

IPA ʲɪvʷó stárʂɨmʊ sínʊ ʂɨsnáttsətʲ lʲɛt .

2629

EN What's the most important decision you've ever had
to make? — It was moving to another country.

RU Како́е са́мое ва́жное реше́ние, кото́рое тебе́
когда́-либо приходи́лось де́лать? — Э́то был
перее́зд в другу́ю страну́.

ROM kakójɪ sáməjɪ vážnəjɪ rɪšjénjɪjɪ, katórəjɪ tjɪbjé
kagdá-ljɪbə prɪhadíləs' djélət'? — étə bɪl pjɪrɪjézd v
drugúju strɪnú.

IPA kɐkʷóʲɪ sáməʲɪ vázṇəʲɪ rʲɪʂénʲɪʲ, kɐtórəʲɪ tʲɪbʲé
kɐgdá-lʲɪbə prʲɪxɐdʲíləsʲ dʲélətʲ? — étə bɨɫ pʲɪrʲɪʲézd v
drʊgúʲü strɐnú.

2630

EN When we went to Munich, our guide spoke English fluently.

RU Когда́ мы е́здили в Мю́нхен, наш гид бе́гло говори́л по-англи́йски.

ROM kagdá mɪ jézdjɪljɪ v mjúnhjɪn, naš gid bjéglə gəvaríl pa-anglíjskjɪ.

IPA kɐgdá mɨ ᶨézdʲɪlʲɪ v mʲúnxʲɪn, naʂ gʲid bʲéglə gəvɐrʲít pɐ-ɐnglʲíjskʲɪ.

2631

EN I met a friend of mine on my way home.

RU Я встре́тил своего́ дру́га (♀ встре́тила свою́ подру́гу) по пути́ домо́й .

ROM ja vstrjétjɪl svajɪvó drúgə (♀ vstrjétjɪlə svajú padrúgu) pa putí damój .

IPA ᶨa fstrʲétʲɪt svɐᶨɪvˠó drúgə (♀ fstrʲétʲɪlə svɐᶨú pɐdrúgʊ) pɐ pʊtʲí dɐmˠój .

2632

EN Walter hardly ever watches TV, and rarely reads newspapers.

RU Уо́лтер почти́ никогда́ не смо́трит телеви́зор и ре́дко чита́ет газе́ты .

ROM uóltjɪr paćtí njɪkagdá njɪ smótrjɪt tjɪljɪvízər i rjédkə ćɪtájɪt gazjéti .

IPA ʊˠóɫtʲɪr pɐtɕtʲí nʲɪkɐgdá nʲɪ smˠótrʲɪt tʲɪlʲɪvʲízər ɪ rʲétkə tɕɪtáᶨɪt gɐzʲétɨ .

2633

EN The traffic isn't usually as bad as it was this morning.

RU Обы́чно про́бок не так мно́го, как сего́дня у́тром.
ROM abíćnə próbək njı tak mnógə, kak sjıvódnjı útrəm.
IPA ɐbítɕnə próbək nʲɪ tak mnógə, kak sʲɪvʷódnʲɪ útrəm.

2634

EN I'll be there next week, but I probably won't see you.

RU Я бу́ду там на сле́дующей неде́ле, но, вероя́тно, я
с тобо́й не уви́жусь .
ROM ja búdu tam na sljédujuççıj njıdjéljı, no, vjırajátnə, ja
s tabój njı uvížus' .
IPA ʲa búdʊ tam na slʲédʊʲüççɪj nʲɪdʲélʲɪ, nọ, vʲɪrɐʲátnə, ʲa s
tɐbʷój nʲɪ ʊvʲízʊsʲ .

2635

EN Gerardo and Feliciana have both applied for the job.

RU Джера́рдо и Фелисиа́на о́ба отпра́вили резюме́ для
э́той рабо́ты.
ROM džırárdə i fjıljısjıánə óbə atprávjıljı rızjumjé dlja étəj
rıbótı.
IPA dzʲɪrárdə ɪ fʲɪlʲɪsʲɪánə óbə ɐtprávʲɪlʲɪ rʲɪzʲümʲé dlʲa étəj
rɐbʷótɨ.

2636

EN He always says he won't be late, but he always is.

RU Он постоя́нно говори́т, что не опозда́ет, но всегда́ опа́здывает.

ROM on pəstajánnə gəvarít, što njı əpazdájıt, no vsjıgdá apázdıvəjıt.

IPA o̞n pəstɐʲánnə gəvɐrʲít, ʂto̞ nʲɪ əpɐzdáʲɪt, no̞ fsʲɪgdá ɐpázdɨvəʲɪt.

2637

EN Yevgeniy doesn't work here anymore. He left last month. But Alan still works here.

RU Евге́ний здесь бо́льше не рабо́тает. Он ушёл в про́шлом ме́сяце. Но А́лан всё ещё рабо́тает здесь .

ROM jıvgjénjıj zdjes' ból'šı njı rıbótəjıt. on ušjól v próšləm mjésjatsı. no álən vsjó jıççjó rıbótəjıt zdjes' .

IPA ʲɪvgʲénʲɪj zdʲesʲ bʷó̞lʲʲʂɨ nʲɪ rɐbʷótəʲɪt. o̞n ʊʂ̧ó̞ɫ f próʂləm mʲésʲɪtsɨ. no̞ álən fsʲó̞ ʲɪççó̧̞ rɐbʷótəʲɪt zdʲesʲ .

2638

EN We used to be good friends, but we aren't anymore. > We're no longer friends.

RU Мы бы́ли хоро́шими друзья́ми, но тепе́рь нет . > Мы уже́ бо́льше не друзья́.

ROM mı bíljı haróšımjı druz'jámjı, no tjıpjér' njet . > mı užjé ból'šı njı druz'já.

IPA mɨ bílʲʲɪ xɐró̞ʂɨmʲʲɪ druzʲʲǽmʲɪ, no̞ tʲɪpʲérʲ nʲɛt . > mɨ ʊʐɨ́ bʷó̞lʲʲʂɨ nʲɪ druzʲʲá.

2639

EN Have you gone to the bank yet? > Not yet.

RU Вы ужé сходи́ли в банк? > Пока́ нет. Ещё нет.
ROM vɪ užjé shadíljɪ v bank? > paká njɛt. jɪççjó njɛt.
IPA vɨ ʊʑ́ sxɐdʲílʲɪ v bank? > pɐká nʲɛt. ʲɪççǿ nʲɛt.

2640

EN Violetta lost her job six (6) months ago and hasn't found another job yet.

RU Виолéтта потеря́ла рабóту шесть мéсяцев наза́д и пока́ ещё не нашла́ другýю .
ROM vjɪaljéttə patjɪrjálə rɪbótu šɪst' mjésjatsɪv nazád i paká jɪççjó njɪ našlá drugúju .
IPA vʲɪɐlʲéttə pɐtʲɪrʲálə rɐbʷótʊ ʂɪstʲ mʲésʲɪtsɨv nɐzád ɪ pɐká ʲɪççǿ nʲɪ nɐʂlá drʊgúʲü .

2641

EN She said she would be here an hour ago, and she still hasn't arrived.

RU Она́ сказа́ла, что бýдет здесь ещё час наза́д, но до сих пор не прие́хала .
ROM aná skazálə, što búdjɪt zdjes' jɪççjó ćas nazád, no da sih por njɪ prɪjéhələ .
IPA ɐná skɐzálə, ʂtɐ búdʲɪt zdʲesʲ ʲɪççǿ tɕas nɐzát, nɐ dɐ sʲix pʷɔr nʲɪ prʲɪɾʲéxələ .

2642

EN Have you written him yet? — Yes, and he still hasn't replied.

RU Ты уже́ написа́л (♀написа́ла) ему́? — Да, но он до сих пор не отве́тил .

ROM tɪ užjé napjɪsál (♀napjɪsálə) jɪmú ? — da, no on da sih por njɪ atvjétjɪl .

IPA tɨ ʋzɨ́ nɐpʲɪsáɫ (♀nɐpʲɪsálə) ʲɪmú ? — da, nɔ ɔn dɐ sʲix pʷɔr nʲɪ ɐtʲfʲétʲɪɫ .

2643

EN Should I tell him what happened, or does he already know?

RU Мне сле́дует ему́ сказа́ть, что произошло́, или он уже́ зна́ет?

ROM mnjɛ sljédujɪt jɪmú skazát', što prəjɪzašló, ili on užjé znájɪt?

IPA mnʲɛ slʲédʋʲɪt ʲɪmú skɐzátʲ, ʂtɔ prəˈɪzɐʂló, ʲɪlʲi ɔn ʋzɨ́ znáʲɪt?

2644

EN I've just had lunch, and I'm already hungry.

RU Я то́лько что пообе́дал (♀пообе́дала) и уже́ сно́ва го́лоден (♀голодна́).

ROM ja tól'kə što paabjédəl (♀paabjédələ) i užjé snóvə gólədjɪn (♀gəladná).

IPA ʲa tɔ́lʲkə ʂtɔ pɐɐbʲédəɫ (♀pɐɐbʲédələ) ɪ ʋzɨ́ snóvə gʷólədʲɪn (♀gəlɐdná).

2645

EN Would you like to eat with us, or have you already eaten?

RU Хо́чешь, пое́сть с на́ми, или ты уже́ пое́л (♀пое́ла)?

ROM hóćıś, pajést' s námjı, ili tı užjé pajél (♀pajélə)?

IPA xǫ́tɕɪ̇ɕ, pɐʲéstʲ s námʲı, ʲilʲi tɨ ʊzɨ́ pɐʲéɫ (♀pɐʲélə)?

2646

EN The plane is still waiting on the runway and hasn't taken off yet.

RU Самолёт всё ещё ждёт на взлётной полосе́ и пока́ не вы́летел .

ROM səmaljót vsjó jıɕɕjó ždjót na vzljótnəj pəlasjé i paká njı víljetjıl .

IPA səmɐlʲét fsʲǫ́ ʲıɕɕǫ́ zdʲǫ́t na vzlʲǫ́tnəj pəlɐsʲé ı pɐká nʲı vílʲɪtʲɪɫ .

2647

EN Has his flight landed yet? > Not yet, it should land in about thirty (30) minutes.

RU Его́ рейс уже́ приземли́лся? > Нет ещё, он до́лжен приземли́ться приме́рно че́рез три́дцать мину́т .

ROM jıvó rjejs užjé prızjımlílsjı? > njet jıɕɕjó, on dólžın prızjımlít'sjı prımjérnə ćjérjız trídtsət' mjınút .

IPA ʲıvˠǫ́ rʲejs ʊzɨ́ prʲızʲımlʲíɫsʲı? > nʲet ʲıɕɕǫ́, ǫn dǫ́ɫzɨn prʲızʲımlʲítʲsʲı prʲımʲérnə tɕérʲıs trʲíttsətʲ mʲınút .

648

EN He always wears a coat, even in hot weather.

RU Он всегда́ но́сит пальто́, да́же в жа́ркую пого́ду.

ROM on vsjıgdá nósjıt pal'tó, dáži v žárkuju pagódu.

IPA on fsʲɪgdá nǫ́sʲɪt pɐlʲtǫ́, dázʲɨ v zárkʊʲü pɐgʷǫ́dʊ.

649

EN They weren't very friendly to us. They didn't even say hello.

RU Они́ к нам бы́ли не о́чень доброжела́тельны. Да́же не поздоро́вались.

ROM aní k nam bíljı njı óćın' dəbražılátjel'nı. dáži njı pəzdaróvəljıs'.

IPA ɐnʲí k nam bílʲʲɪ nʲɪ ǫ́tɕɨnʲ dəbrɐzɨlátʲɪlʲʲnɨ. dázʲɨ nʲɪ pəzdɐrǫ́vəlʲʲɪsʲ.

650

EN I got up very early, but my teacher got up even earlier.

RU Я вста́л (♀вста́ла) о́чень ра́но, но мой учи́тель вста́л ещё ра́ньше.

ROM ja vstál (♀vstálə) óćın' ránə, no moj ućítjel' vstál jıççjó rán'šı.

IPA ʲa fstáł (♀fstálə) ǫ́tɕɨnʲ ránə, nǫ mʷoj ʊtɕítʲɪlʲʲ fstáł ʲɪɕɕǫ́ ránʲʂɨ.

2651

EN I knew I didn't have much money, but I have even less than I thought.

RU Я знал (♀знáла), что у меня́ нет мнóго дéнег, но у меня́ оказáлось дáже мéньше, чем я дýмал (♀дýмала).

ROM ja znal (♀ználə), što u mjɪnjá njɛt mnógə djénjɪg, no u mjɪnjá əkazáləs' dáži mjén'šɪ, ćɪm ja dúməl (♀dúmələ).

IPA ʲa znał (♀ználə), ştọ u mʲɪnʲá nʲet mnógə dʲénʲɪk, nọ u mʲɪnʲá əkɐzáləsʲ dázɪ̣ mʲénʲşɨ̣, tɕem ʲa dúməł (♀dúmələ).

2652

EN Even though she can't drive, she still bought a car.

RU Хотя́ онá не умéет води́ть, онá всё равнó купи́ла маши́ну.

ROM hatjá aná njɪ umjéjɪt vadít', aná vsjó rɪvnó kupílə mašínu.

IPA xɐtʲá ɐná nʲi ʊmʲéʲɪt vɐdʲítʲ, ɐná fsʲǿ rɐvnó kʊpʲílə mɐşínʊ.

653

EN I'll probably see you tomorrow. But even if I don't see you tomorrow, I'm sure we'll see each other before the weekend.

RU Возмо́жно я тебя́ за́втра уви́жу. Но да́же е́сли мы с тобо́й не уви́димся за́втра, я уве́рен (♀ уве́рена), мы встре́тимся до выходны́х.

ROM vazmóžnə ja tjɪbjá závtrə uvížu. no dáži jésljɪ mɪ s tabój njɪ uvídjɪmsjɪ závtrə, ja uvjérjɪn (♀ uvjérjɪnə), mɪ vstrjétjɪmsjɪ da vɪhadníh.

IPA vɐzmʷǫznə ʲa tʲɪbʲá záftrə ʊvʲízu. nǫ dázɨ ʲéslʲɪ mɨ s tɐbʷój nʲɪ ʊvʲídʲɪmsʲɪ záftrə, ʲa ʊvʲérʲɪn (♀ ʊvʲérʲɪnə), mɨ fstrʲétʲɪmsʲɪ dɐ vɨxɐdnɨ́x.

654

EN We're going to the beach tomorrow, even if it's raining.

RU Мы собира́емся пое́хать на пляж за́втра, да́же е́сли бу́дет идти́ дождь.

ROM mɪ sabjɪrájemsjɪ pajéhət' na pljaž závtrə, dáži jésljɪ búdjɪt jɪdtí dožd'.

IPA mɨ sɐbʲɪrá ⁱmsʲɪ pɐʲéxətʲ na plʲaz̩ záftrə, dázɨ ʲéslʲɪ búdʲɪt ʲɪtʲtʲí dozd̩ʲ.

2655

EN I didn't get the job, although I was well qualified. > I didn't get the job in spite of being well qualified.

RU Я не получи́л (♀получи́ла) рабо́ту, хотя́ и соотве́тствовал (♀соотве́тствовала) всем тре́бованиям. > Я не получи́л (♀получи́ла) рабо́ту несмотря́ на то, что соотве́тствовал (♀соотве́тствовала) всем тре́бованиям.

ROM ja njı palućíl (♀palućílə) rıbótu, hatjá i saatvjétstvəvəl (♀saatvjétstvəvələ) vsjem trjébəvənjıjım. > ja njı palućíl (♀palućílə) rıbótu njısmatrjá na to, što saatvjétstvəvəl (♀saatvjétstvəvələ) vsjem trjébəvənjıjım.

IPA ʲa nʲɪ pɐlʊt͡ɕíɫ (♀pɐlʊt͡ɕílə) rɐbʷótʊ, xɐtʲá ɪ sɐɐtfʲétstfəvəɫ (♀sɐɐtfʲétstfəvələ) fsʲem trʲébəvənʲɪʲrʲɪm. > ʲa nʲɪ pɐlʊt͡ɕíɫ (♀pɐlʊt͡ɕílə) rɐbʷótʊ nʲɪsmɐtrʲá na tɔ, ʂtɔ sɐɐtfʲétstfəvəɫ (♀sɐɐtfʲétstfəvələ) fsʲem trʲébəvənʲɪʲrʲɪm.

2656

EN Although she wasn't feeling well, she still went to work. > In spite of not feeling well, she still went to work.

RU Хотя́ она́ пло́хо себя́ чу́вствовала, она́ всё равно́ пошла́ на рабо́ту. > Несмотря́ на то, что она́ пло́хо себя́ чу́вствовала, она́ всё равно́ пошла́ на рабо́ту.

ROM hatjá aná plóhə sjıbjá ćústvəvələ, aná vsjó rıvnó pašlá na rıbótu. > njısmatrjá na to, što aná plóhə sjıbjá ćústvəvələ, aná vsjó rıvnó pašlá na rıbótu.

IPA xɐtʲá ɐná plóxə sʲɪbʲá tɕúʊstfəvələ, ɐná fsʲé rɐvnó pɐslá na rɐbʷótʊ. > nʲɪsmɐtrʲá na tọ, ʂtọ ɐná plóxə sʲɪbʲá tɕúʊstfəvələ, ɐná fsʲé rɐvnó pɐslá na rɐbʷótʊ.

2657

EN I didn't get the job despite the fact that I was extremely qualified.

RU Я не получи́л (♀получи́ла) рабо́ту несмотря́ на то, что соотве́тствовал (♀соотве́тствовала) всем тре́бованиям.

ROM ja njı palućíl (♀palućílə) rıbótu njısmatrjá na to, što saatvjétstvəvəl (♀saatvjétstvəvələ) vsjem trjébəvənjıjım.

IPA ʲa nʲɪ pɐlʊtɕíɫ (♀pɐlʊtɕílə) rɐbʷótʊ nʲɪsmɐtrʲá na tọ, ʂtọ sɐɐtfʲétstfəvəɫ (♀sɐɐtfʲétstfəvələ) fsʲem trʲébəvənʲɪrʲɪm.

2658

EN I couldn't sleep despite being very tired. > Even though I was really tired, I couldn't sleep.

RU Я не мог (♀могла́) засну́ть несмотря́ на то, что о́чень уста́л (♀уста́ла). > Хотя́ я о́чень уста́л (♀уста́ла), я не мог (♀могла́) засну́ть.

ROM ja njı mog (♀maglá) zasnút' njısmatrjá na to, što óćın' ustál (♀ustálə). > hatjá ja óćın' ustál (♀ustálə), ja njı mog (♀maglá) zasnút'.

IPA ʲa nʲı mʷok (♀mɐglá) zɐsnútʲ nʲısmɐtrʲá na tɔ, ʂtɔ ótɕinʲ ʊstáł (♀ʊstálə). > xɐtʲá ʲa ótɕinʲ ʊstáł (♀ʊstálə), ʲa nʲı mʷok (♀mɐglá) zɐsnútʲ.

2659

EN I didn't get the job though I had all the necessary qualifications.

RU Я не получи́л (♀получи́ла) рабо́ту, хотя́ и соотве́тствовал (♀соотве́тствовала) всем тре́бованиям.

ROM ja njı palućíl (♀palućílə) rıbótu, hatjá i saatvjétstvəvəl (♀saatvjétstvəvələ) vsjem trjébəvənjıjım.

IPA ʲa nʲı pɐlʊtɕíł (♀pɐlʊtɕílə) rɐbʷótu, xɐtʲá ı sɐɐtfʲétstfəvəł (♀sɐɐtfʲétstfəvələ) fsʲem trʲébəvənʲrʲım.

2660

EN She only accepted the job because of the salary, which was very high.

RU Она́ согласи́лась на э́ту рабо́ту то́лько из-за за́работной пла́ты, кото́рая оказа́лась о́чень высо́кой.

ROM aná səglasíləs' na étu rıbótu tól'kə iz-za zárəbətnəj plátı, katórəjə əkazáləs' óćın' vısókəj.

IPA ɐná səglɐsʲíləsʲ na étʊ rɐbʷótʊ tólʲkə ʲiz-za zárəbətnəj plátɨ, kɐtórəʲə əkɐzáləsʲ ótɕɪnʲ vɪsókəj.

2661

EN She accepted the job in spite of the salary, which was rather low.

RU Она́ согласи́лась на э́ту рабо́ту несмотря́ на за́работную пла́ту, кото́рая была́ дово́льно ни́зкой.

ROM aná səglasíləs' na étu rıbótu njısmatrjá na zárəbətnuju plátu, katórəjə bılá davól'nə nízkəj.

IPA ɐná səglɐsʲíləsʲ na étʊ rɐbʷótʊ nʲɪsmɐtrʲá na zárəbətnʊʲü plátʊ, kɐtórəʲə bɨlá dɐvʷólʲnə nʲískəj.

2662

EN I'll send you a map and directions in case you can't find our house.

RU Я вы́шлю тебе́ ка́рту с указа́телями на слу́чай, е́сли ты не смо́жешь найти́ наш дом.

ROM ja víšlju tjɪbjé kártu s ukazátjeljamjɪ na slúćəj, jéslɪ tɪ njɪ smóžɪś najtí naš dom.

IPA ʲa víʂlʲü tʲɪbʲé kártʊ s ʊkɐzátʲɪlʲɪmʲɪ na slútɕəj, ʲéslʲɪ tɨ nʲɪ smʷóʑɪɕ nɐjtʲí naʂ dǫm.

2663

EN I'll remind him of the meeting in case he's forgotten.

RU Я напо́мню ему́ о собра́нии на слу́чай, е́сли он забы́л.

ROM ja napómnju jɪmú a sabránjɪjɪ na slúćəj, jésljɪ on zabíl.

IPA ʲa nɐpʷómnʲü ʲɪmú ɐ sɐbránʲɪr̝ɪ na slútɕəj, ʲéslʲɪ ǫn zɐbɨ́ɫ.

2664

EN I'll leave my phone on just in case my mother calls.

RU Я оста́влю мой телефо́н на слу́чай, е́сли моя́ ма́ма бу́дет звони́ть.

ROM ja astávlju moj tjɪljɪfón na slúćəj, jésljɪ majá mámə búdjɪt zvanít'.

IPA ʲa ɐstávlʲü mʷoj tʲɪlʲɪfʷón na slútɕəj, ʲéslʲɪ mɐʲá mámə búdʲɪt zvɐnʲítʲ.

2665

EN I'll give you my phone number in case you need to
contact me.

RU Я дам тебе́ мой но́мер телефо́на на слу́чай, е́сли
тебе́ пона́добится со мной связа́ться.

ROM ja dam tjɪbjé moj nómjɪr tjɪljɪfónə na slúćəj, jésljɪ
tjɪbjé panádəbjɪtsjɪ sa mnoj svjɪzát'sjɪ.

IPA ʲa dam tʲɪbʲɛ́ mʷǫj nómʲɪr tʲɪlʲɪfʷǫ́nə na slútɕəj, ʲɛslʲɪ
tʲɪbʲɛ́ pɐnádəbʲɪtsʲɪ sɐ mnoj svʲɪzátʲsʲɪ.

2666

EN You should register your bike in case it's stolen.

RU Ты до́лжен (♀должна́) зарегистри́ровать свой
велосипе́д на слу́чай, е́сли его́ украду́т.

ROM tɪ dólžɪn (♀dalžná) zarɪgjɪstrírəvət' svoj vjɪlasjɪpjéd
na slúćəj, jésljɪ jɪvó ukrɪdút.

IPA tɨ dǫ́łzʲɪn (♀dɐłzná) zɐrʲɪgʲɪstrʲírəvətʲ svʷǫj vʲɪlɐsʲɪpʲéd
na slútɕəj, ʲɛslʲɪ ʲɪvʷǫ́ ʊkrɐdút.

2667

EN You should tell the police if you have any
information about the crime.

RU Ты до́лжен (♀должна́) сказа́ть поли́ции, е́сли у
тебя́ есть информа́ция о преступле́нии.

ROM tɪ dólžɪn (♀dalžná) skazát' palítsɪjɪ, jésljɪ u tjɪbjá jest'
jɪnfarmátsɪjə a prɪstupljénjɪjɪ.

IPA tɨ dǫ́łzʲɪn (♀dɐłzná) skɐzátʲ pɐlʲítsɨʲɪ, ʲɛslʲɪ u tʲɪbʲá ʲestʲ
ʲɪnfɐrmátsɨʲə ɐ prʲɪstʊplʲénʲɪʲɪ.

2668

EN The club is for members only. You can't go in unless you're a member.

RU Клуб то́лько для его́ чле́нов. Ты не мо́жешь пойти́, е́сли то́лько ты не явля́ешься его́ чле́ном.

ROM klub tól'kə dlja jıvó ćljénəv. tı njı móžıś pajtí, jésljı tól'kə tı njı jıvljáještjı jıvó ćljénəm.

IPA klup tǫ́lʲkə dlʲa ʲɪvʷǫ́ tɕlʲénəf. tɨ nʲɪ mʷǫ́ʑɨɕ pɐjtʲí, ʲéslʲɪ tǫ́lʲkə tɨ nʲɪ ʲɪvlʲǽʲɪɕsʲɪ ʲɪvʷǫ́ tɕlʲénəm.

2669

EN I'll see you tomorrow unless I have to work late.

RU Я уви́жусь с тобо́й за́втра, е́сли то́лько не придётся задержа́ться на рабо́те допоздна́.

ROM ja uvížus' s tabój závtrə, jésljı tól'kə njı prıdjótsjı zadjıržát'sjı na rıbótjı dəpazná.

IPA ʲa ʊvʲízʊsʲ s tɐbʷój záftrə, ʲéslʲɪ tǫ́lʲkə nʲɪ prʲɪdʲétsʲɪ zɐdʲɪrʑátʲsʲɪ na rɐbʷótʲɪ dəpɐzná.

2670

EN You can borrow my car as long as you promise not to drive too fast. > You can borrow my car provided that you don't drive too fast.

RU Ты мо́жешь одолжи́ть мою́ маши́ну, е́сли то́лько пообеща́ешь не води́ть сли́шком бы́стро. > Ты мо́жешь взять на вре́мя мою́ маши́ну при усло́вии, что не бу́дешь води́ть сли́шком бы́стро.

ROM tɪ móžɪś ədalžít' majú mašínu, jéslʲɪ tólʹkə paabjɪççájeś njɪ vadít' slíškəm bístrə. > tɪ móžɪś vzjat' na vrjémjɪ majú mašínu prɪ uslóvjɪjɪ, što njɪ búdjeś vadít' slíškəm bístrə.

IPA tɨ mʷóʐɨ̞ç ədɐɫʐʲítʲ mɐʲú mɐʂínʊ, ʲéslʲɪ tólʲkə pɐɐbʲɪççáʲɪç nʲɪ vɐdʲítʲ slʲíʂkəm bístrə. > tɨ mʷóʐɨ̞ç vzʲǽtʲ na vrʲémʲɪ mɐʲú mɐʂínʊ prʲɪ ʊslóvʲrʲɪ, ʂtɐ nʲɪ búdʲɪç vɐdʲítʲ slʲíʂkəm bístrə.

2671

EN I don't care which hotel we stay at as long as the room is clean. > Provided that the room's clean, I don't really care which hotel we stay at.

RU Мне всё равно́, в како́м оте́ле мы остано́вимся, гла́вное, что́бы ко́мнаты бы́ли чи́стые. > При усло́вии, что ко́мнаты бу́дут чи́стые, мне всё равно́, в како́м оте́ле мы остано́вимся.

ROM mnjɛ vsjó rɪvnó, v kakóm atéljɪ mɪ əstanóvjɪmsjɪ, glávnəjɪ, štóbɪ kómnətɪ bíljɪ ćístɪjɪ. > prɪ uslóvjɪjɪ, što kómnətɪ búdut ćístɪjɪ, mnjɛ vsjó rɪvnó, v kakóm atéljɪ mɪ əstanóvjɪmsjɪ.

IPA mnʲɛ fsʲə́ rɐvnó, f kɐkʷóm ɐtélʲɪ mɨ əstɐnʷóvʲɪmsʲɪ, glávnəʲɪ, ʂtóbɨ kʷómnətɨ bílʲɪ tɕístɨʲɪ. > prʲɪ ʊslʷóvʲɪʲɪ, ʂtɐ kʷómnətɨ búdʊt tɕístɨʲɪ, mnʲɛ fsʲə́ rɐvnó, f kɐkʷóm ɐtélʲɪ mɨ əstɐnʷóvʲɪmsʲɪ.

2672

EN I'm not going unless it stops raining.

RU Я не пойду́, пока́ дождь не прекрати́тся.

ROM ja njɪ pajdú, paká dožd' njɪ prɪkrɪtítsjɪ.

IPA ʲa nʲɪ pɐjdú, pɐká doʐdʲ nʲɪ prʲɪkrɐtʲítsʲɪ.

2673

EN Ayman slipped as he was getting off the bus.

RU А́ймэн поскользну́лся, когда́ заходи́л в авто́бус.

ROM ájmɛn pəskal'znúlsjɪ, kagdá zəhadíl v avtóbus.

IPA ájmɛn pəskɐlʲznúɫsʲɪ, kɐgdá zəxɐdʲíɫ v ɐftʷóbʊs.

2674

EN   We met Yuko as we were leaving the hotel.

RU   Мы встре́тили Ю́ко, когда́ уезжа́ли из оте́ля.
ROM   mı vstrjétjıljı júkə, kagdá ujıžžáljı iz atéljı.
IPA   mɨ fstrʲétʲɪlʲɪ ʲúkə, kɐgdá ʊʲɪzʑálʲɪ ʲiz ɐtélʲɪ.

2675

EN   I had to leave just as the meeting was getting started.

RU   Мне пришло́сь уе́хать, когда́ собра́ние ещё то́лько
      начина́лось.
ROM   mnjɛ prıšlós' ujéhət', kagdá sabránjıjı jıççjó tól'kə
      naćmáləs'.
IPA   mnʲɛ prʲɪşlós̬ ʊʲéxətʲ, kɐgdá sɐbránʲɪ̬ʲɪ ʲɪççǿ tǫ́lʲkə
      nɐtɕináləsʲ.

2676

EN   The phone rang just as I sat down.

RU   Телефо́н зазвони́л, как то́лько я сел (♀се́ла).
ROM   tjıljıfón zəzvaníl, kak tól'kə ja sjɛl (♀sjélə).
IPA   tʲɪlʲʲifʷón zəzvɐnʲít, kak tǫ́lʲkə ʲa sʲɛt (♀sʲélə).

2677

EN The thief was difficult to identify, as he was wearing a mask.

RU Во́ра бы́ло сло́жно вы́числить, поско́льку он был в ма́ске.

ROM vórə bílə slóžnə víćısljıt', paskól'ku on bıl v máskjı.

IPA vʷǫ́rə bílə slǫ́znə vítɕɨslʲɨtʲ, pɐskʷǫ́lʲku on bɨɫ v máskʲɨ.

2678

EN I couldn't contact David as he was on a business trip in Japan and his cellphone doesn't work there.

RU Я не смог (♀смогла́) связа́ться с Дэ́видом, поско́льку он был в командиро́вке в Япо́нии, и его́ телефо́н там не рабо́тал.

ROM ja njı smog (♀smaglá) svjızát'sjı s dévjıdəm, paskól'ku on bıl v kəmandjıróvkjı v jıpónjıjı, i jıvó tjıljıfón tam njı rıbótəl.

IPA ʲa nʲɨ smʷok (♀smɐglá) svʲɨzátʲsʲɨ s dévʲɨdəm, pɐskʷǫ́lʲku on bɨɫ f kəmɐndʲɨrǫ́fkʲɨ v ʲɨpʷǫ́nʲɨ̯ɨ, ɨ ʲɨvʷǫ́ tʲɨlʲɨfʷǫ́n tam nʲɨ rɐbʷǫ́təɫ.

2679

EN Some sports, like motorcycle racing, can be dangerous.

RU Нékоторые вúды спóрта, врóде гóнок на мотоцúклах, мóгут быть опáсными.

ROM njékətərıjı vídı spórtə, vródjı gónək na mətatsíkləh, mógut bıt' apásnımjı.

IPA nʲékətərɨʲɪ vʲídɨ spʷórtə, vrǫ́dʲɪ gʷǫ́nək na mətɐtsíkləx, mʷǫ́gʊt bɨtʲ ɐpásnɨmʲɪ.

2680

EN You should have done it as I showed you. > You should have done it like this.

RU Ты дóлжен был (♀ должнá былá) всё сдéлать так, как я тебé показáл (♀ показáла). > Ты дóлжен был (♀ былá должнá) сдéлать э́то вот так.

ROM tı dólžın bıl (♀ dalžná bılá) vsjó sdjélət' tak, kak ja tjıbjé pəkazál (♀ pəkazálə). > tı dólžın bıl (♀ bılá dalžná) sdjélət' étə vot tak.

IPA tɨ dǫ́łzɨn bɨł (♀ dɐłzná bɨlá) fsʲǫ́ zdʲélətʲ tak, kak ʲa tʲɨbʲé pəkɐzáł (♀ pəkɐzálə). > tɨ dǫ́łzɨn bɨł (♀ bɨlá dɐłzná) zdʲélətʲ étə vʷǫt tak.

2681

EN   As always, you're late to class. > You're late to
     class, as usual.

RU   Ты, как всегда́, опозда́л (♀опозда́ла) на заня́тия.
     > Ты опозда́л (♀опозда́ла) на заня́тия, как
     всегда́.
ROM tɪ, kak vsjɪgdá, əpazdál (♀əpazdálə) na zanjátjɪjə. >
     tɪ əpazdál (♀əpazdálə) na zanjátjɪjə, kak vsjɪgdá.
IPA tɨ, kak fsʲɪgdá, əpɐzdáɫ (♀əpɐzdálə) na zɐnʲǽtʲrʲə. >
     tɨ əpɐzdáɫ (♀əpɐzdálə) na zɐnʲǽtʲrʲə, kak fsʲɪgdá.

2682

EN   Jiyeong works as the manager in his company.

RU   Джиёнг рабо́тает в свое́й компа́нии ме́неджером.
ROM džɪjóng rɪbótəjɪt v svajéj kampánjɪjɪ mjénjedžɪrəm.
IPA dzʲɨ́ɵ̯ng rɐbʷótəʲɪt f svɐʲéj kɐmpánʲrʲɪ mʲénʲɪdzɨ̡rəm.

2683

EN   Euna has to make important decisions, just like the
     manager.

RU   Ю́на должна́ принима́ть ва́жные реше́ния наравне́
     с ме́неджером.
ROM júnə dalžná prɪnjɪmát' vážnɪjɪ rɪšjénjɪjə nərɪvnjé s
     mjénjedžɪrəm.
IPA ʲúnə dɐɫzná prʲɪnʲɪmátʲ váznɨ̡ɪ rʲɪʂénʲrʲə nərɐvnʲé s
     mʲénʲɪdzɨ̡rəm.

2684

EN That house looks like it's going to fall down. > That house looks as if it's going to fall down.

RU Э́тот дом вы́глядит так, как бу́дто он вот-вот ру́хнет. > Э́тот дом вы́глядит так, как бу́дто он вот-вот ру́хнет.

ROM étət dom vígljadjıt tak, kak búdtə on vət-vot rúhnjıt. > étət dom vígljadjıt tak, kak búdtə on vət-vot rúhnjıt.

IPA étət dom víglʲɪdʲɪt tak, kak búttə on vət-vʷot rúxnʲɪt. > étət dom víglʲɪdʲɪt tak, kak búttə on vət-vʷot rúxnʲɪt.

2685

EN Iris is very late, isn't she? It looks like she isn't coming. > It looks as if she isn't coming. > It looks as though she isn't coming.

RU А́йрис запа́здывает, пра́вда? Похо́же, она́ не придёт. > Похо́же, она́ бу́дто уже́ и не придёт. > Ка́жется, она́ уже́ не придёт.

ROM ájrjıs zapázdıvəjıt, právdə? pahóžı, aná njı prıdjót. > pahóžı, aná búdtə užjé i njı prıdjót. > kážıtsjı, aná užjé njı prıdjót.

IPA ájrʲɪs zɐpázdɨvəʲɪt, právdə? pɐxóʐɨ, ɐná nʲɪ prʲɪdʲét. > pɐxóʐɨ, ɐná búttə ʊʐɨ ɪ nʲɪ prʲɪdʲét. > kázɨtsʲɪ, ɐná ʊʐɨ nʲɪ prʲɪdʲét.

2686

EN We took an umbrella because it looked like it was going to rain.

RU Мы взя́ли с собо́й зо́нтик, потому́ что вы́глядело так, как бу́дто пойдёт дождь.

ROM mɪ vzjáljɪ s sabój zóntjɪk, pətamú što vígljadjɪlə tak, kak búdtə pajdjót dožd'.

IPA mɨ vzʲǽlʲɪ s sɐbʷój zóntʲɪk, pətɐmú ʂtɔ víglʲɪdʲɪlə tak, kak búttə pɐjdʲɛ́t dɔʐd̥ʲ.

2687

EN Do you hear music coming from next door? It sounds like they're having a party.

RU Ты слы́шишь му́зыку, доноса́щуюся из-за сосе́дней двери́? Похо́же, у них вечери́нка.

ROM tɪ slɪ́šɪś múzɪku, dənasjáççujusjɪ iz-za sasjédnjej dvjɪrí? pahóžɪ, u nih vjɪćɪrínkə.

IPA tɨ slɨ́ʂɪç múzɨkʊ, dənɐsʲáççʊ̈jüsʲɪ ʲiz-za sɐsʲédnʲɪj dvʲɪrʲí? pɐxóʐɨ, u nʲix vʲɪtɕɨrʲínkə.

2688

EN After the interruption, the speaker went on talking as if nothing had happened.

RU После того, как его прервали, докладчик продолжил говорить, как будто ничего не произошло.

ROM póslji tavó, kak jıvó prırváljı, dakládćık pradólžıl gəvarít', kak búdtə njıćıvó njı prəjızašló.

IPA pʷǫsl̪ʲɪ tɐvʷǫ́, kak ʲɪvʷǫ́ prʲɪrvál̪ʲɪ, dɐkláttɕɪk prɐdǫ́łz̦ɪł gəvɐrʲít̪ʲ, kak búttə n̪ʲɪtɕɪvʷǫ́ n̪ʲɪ prəʲɪzɐșlǫ́.

2689

EN When I told them my plan, they looked at me as though I was crazy.

RU Когда я рассказал (♀рассказала) им свой план, они посмотрели на меня как на сумасшедшего (♀сумасшедшую).

ROM kagdá ja rısskazál (♀rısskazálə) im svoj plan, aní pəsmatrjéljı na mjınjá kak na sumasšjédšıvə (♀sumasšjédšuju).

IPA kɐgdá ʲa rəsskɐzáł (♀rəsskɐzálə) ʲim svʷǫj plan, ɐn̪ʲí pəsmɐtrʲél̪ʲɪ na m̪ʲɪn̪ʲá kak na sumɐșșétsɨvə (♀sumɐșșétsʊʲü).

2690

EN She's always asking me to do things for her, as if I didn't have enough to do already.

RU Она́ всегда́ проси́ла меня́ де́лать для неё всё, как бу́дто бы у меня́ и так не́ было доста́точно дел без неё.

ROM aná vsjıgdá prasílə mjınjá djélət' dlja njıjó vsjó, kak búdtə bı u mjınjá i tak njé bılo dastátəćnə djɛl bız njıjó.

IPA ɐná fsʲɪgdá prɐsʲílə mʲɪnʲá dʲélətʲ dlʲa nʲɪ́ɪ̯ǿ fsʲǿ, kak búttə bɪ u mʲɪnʲá ɪ tak nʲé bɪlə dɐstátətɕnə dʲɛɫ bʲɪz nʲɪ́ɪ̯ǿ.

2691

EN Sachiko is going away for a week in September.

RU Са́тико уезжа́ет на неде́лю в сентябре́.

ROM sátjıkə ujıžžájıt na njıdjélju v sjıntjıbrjé.

IPA sátʲɪkə ʊɪ̯ɪzʐáʲɪt na nʲɪdʲélʲü f sʲɪntʲɪbrʲé.

2692

EN Where have you been? I've been waiting for ages.

RU Где ты был (♀была́)? Я тебя́ уже́ ты́щу лет жду.

ROM gdjɛ tı bıl (♀bılá)? ja tjıbjá užjé tíççu ljɛt ždu.

IPA gdʲɛ tɨ bɨɫ (♀bɨlá)? ʲa tʲɪbʲá ʊzʲɪ́ tíççʊ lʲɛt z̯du.

2693

EN I fell asleep during the movie. > I fell asleep while I was watching the movie.

RU Я уснýл (♀уснýла) во врéмя фи́льма. > Я уснýл (♀уснýла), когдá смотрéл (♀смотрéла) фильм.

ROM ja usnúl (♀usnúlə) va vrjémjɪ fíl'mə. > ja usnúl (♀usnúlə), kagdá smatrjél (♀smatrjélə) fil'm.

IPA ʲa ʊsnúɫ (♀ʊsnúlə) vɐ vrʲémʲɪ fʲílʲmə. > ʲa ʊsnúɫ (♀ʊsnúlə), kɐgdá smɐtrʲéɫ (♀smɐtrʲélə) fʲilʲm.

2694

EN We met some really nice people during our vacation.

RU Мы познакóмились с нéкоторыми действи́тельно прия́тными людьми́ во врéмя óтпуска.

ROM mɪ pəznakómjɪljɪs' s njékətərɪmjɪ djɪjstvítjel'nə prɪjátnɪmjɪ ljud'mí va vrjémjɪ ótpuskə.

IPA mɪ pəznɐkʷómʲɪlʲɪsʲ s nʲékətərɪmʲɪ dʲɪjstfʲítʲɪlʲnə prʲɪʲátnɪmʲɪ lʲüdʲmʲí vɐ vrʲémʲɪ ótpuskə.

2695

EN I'll call you sometime during the afternoon.

RU Я позвоню́ тебé кáк-нибудь пóсле обéда.

ROM ja pəzvanjú tjɪbjé kák-njɪbud' pósljɪ abjédə.

IPA ʲa pəzvɐnʲú tʲɪbʲé kák-nʲɪbʊdʲ pʷóslʲɪ ɐbʲédə.

2696

EN It rained for three (3) days without stopping.

RU Дождь шёл три дня без остановки.
ROM dožd' šjól tri dnja bız əstanóvkjı.
IPA do̞ʐd̪ʲ ʂ�̪ł trʲi dnʲa bʲɪz əstɐnó̞fkʲɪ.

2697

EN There was a phone call for you while you were out.

RU Тебе звонили, пока тебя не было.
ROM tjıbjé zvaníljı, paká tjıbjá njé bılo.
IPA t̪ʲɪbʲé zvɐnʲílʲɪ, pɐká t̪ʲɪbʲá nʲé bɨlə.

2698

EN I'll be in London next week, and I hope to see John while I'm there.

RU Я буду в Лондоне на следующей неделе и надеюсь увидеться с Джоном, пока я там.
ROM ja búdu v lóndənjı na sljédujuççıj njıdjéljı i nadjéjus' uvídjet'sjı s džónəm, paká ja tam.
IPA ʲa búdʊ v ló̞ndənʲɪ na sʲlʲédʊʲüççɨj nʲɪdʲélʲɪ ɪ nɐdʲéʲüsʲ ʊvʲídʲɪtʲsʲɪ s dzó̞nəm, pɐká ʲa tam.

2699

EN I sent the package to them today, so they should receive it by Monday. > They should receive it no later than Monday.

RU Я отправлю им посылку сегодня, так что они должны получить её до понедельника. > Они должны получить её не позднее понедельника.

ROM ja atprávlju im pasílku sjıvódnjı, tak što aní dalžní palućít' jıjó da panjıdjél'njıkə. > aní dalžní palućít' jıjó njı paznjéjı panjıdjél'njıkə.

IPA ʲa ɐtprávlʲü ʲim pɐsíłku sʲɪvʷódnʲɪ, tak ʂtɔ ɐnʲí dɐłzní pɐlʊtɕít' ʲɾʲɵ́ dɐ pɐnʲɪdʲélʲnʲɪkə. > ɐnʲí dɐłzní pɐlʊtɕít' ʲɾʲɵ́ nʲɪ pɐznʲéʲɪ pɐnʲɪdʲélʲnʲɪkə.

2700

EN I have to be home by five [o'clock] (5:00). > I have to be home no later than five [o'clock] (5:00).

RU Я должен (♀ должна) быть дома к пяти часам. > Я должен (♀ должна) быть дома не позднее пяти часов.

ROM ja dólžın (♀ dalžná) bıt' dómə k pjıtí ćısám. > ja dólžın (♀ dalžná) bıt' dómə njı paznjéjı pjıtí ćısóv.

IPA ʲa dółzjin (♀ dɐłzná) bitʲ dómə k pʲɪtʲí tɕɪsám. > ʲa dółzjin (♀ dɐłzná) bitʲ dómə nʲɪ pɐznʲéʲɪ pʲɪtʲí tɕɪsóf.

GMS #2701 - 2800

2701

EN I slept until noon this morning. > I didn't get up until noon this morning.

RU Я сегóдня спал (♀спалá) до полýдня. > Я сегóдня не вставáл (♀вставáла) с постéли до полýдня.

ROM ja sjɪvódnjɪ spal (♀spalá) da palúdnjɪ. > ja sjɪvódnjɪ njɪ vstavál (♀vstaválə) s pastjéljɪ da palúdnjɪ.

IPA ʲa sʲɪvʷódnʲɪ spaɫ (♀spɐlá) dɐ pɐlúdnʲɪ. > ʲa sʲɪvʷódnʲɪ nʲɪ fstɐváɫ (♀fstɐválə) s pɐstélʲɪ dɐ pɐlúdnʲɪ.

2702

EN Pablo will be away until Saturday. > Pablo will be back by Saturday.

RU Пáбло не бýдет до суббóты. > Пáбло вернётся в суббóту.

ROM páblə njɪ búdjɪt da subbótɪ. > páblə vjɪrnjótsjɪ v subbótu.

IPA páblə nʲɪ búdʲɪt dɐ subbʷótɨ. > páblə vʲɪrnʲ jɪ́tsʲɪ f subbʷótʊ.

2703

EN I have to work until eleven pm (11:00) > I'll have finished my work by eleven pm (11:00).

RU Я до́лжен (♀ должна́) рабо́тать до оди́ннадцати часо́в но́чи. > Я зако́нчу рабо́ту к оди́ннадцати часа́м но́чи.

ROM ja dólžɪn (♀ dalžná) rɪbótət' da adínnədtsətjɪ ćɪsóv nóćɪ. > ja zakónću rɪbótu k adínnədtsətjɪ ćɪsám nóćɪ.

IPA ʲa dółzʲɪn (♀ dɐłzṇá) rɐbʷǫ́tətʲ dɐ ɐdʲínnəttsətʲɪ tɕɪsóv nǫ́tɕɪ. > ʲa zɐkʷǫ́ntɕʊ rɐbʷǫ́tʊ k ɐdʲínnəttsətʲɪ tɕɪsám nǫ́tɕɪ.

2704

EN It's too late to go to the bank now. By the time we get there, it'll be closed.

RU Сейча́с уже́ сли́шком по́здно идти́ в банк. К тому́ вре́мени, как мы туда́ доберёмся, он уже́ бу́дет закры́т.

ROM sjɪjćás užjé slíškəm póznə jɪdtí v bank. k tamú vrjémjenjɪ, kak mɪ tudá dabjɪrjómsjɪ, on užjé búdjɪt zakrít.

IPA sʲɪjtɕás ʊʐʲé slʲíškəm pʷóznə ʲɪttʲí v bank. k tɐmú vrʲémʲɪnʲɪ, kak mɪ tʊdá dɐbʲɪrʲǫ́msʲɪ, ǫn ʊʐʲé búdʲɪt zɐkrít.

2705

EN By the time we get to the movies, it'll have already started.

RU К тому́ вре́мени, как мы пришли́ в кино́, фильм уже́ на́чался.

ROM k tamú vrjémjenjı, kak mı prıšlí v kjınó, fil'm užjé náćəlsjı.

IPA k tɐmú vrʲémʲɪnʲı, kak mɨ prʲɪʂlʲí f kʲɪnó, fʲilʲm ʊʐɨ́ nátɕəɫsʲı.

2706

EN Silvio's car broke down on his way to his friend's house. By the time he arrived, everybody had left.

RU Маши́на Си́львио слома́лась на пути́ к до́му его́ дру́га. К тому́ вре́мени, как он дое́хал, все уже́ уе́хали.

ROM mašínə síl'vjıə slamáləs' na putí k dómu jıvó drúgə. k tamú vrjémjenjı, kak on dajéhəl, vsjɛ užjé ujéhəljı.

IPA mɐʂínə sʲílʲʲvʲıə slɐmáləsʲ na pʊtʲí k dómʊ ʲɪvʷó drúgə. k tɐmú vrʲémʲɪnʲı, kak ɞn dɐʲéxəɫ, fsʲɛ ʊʐɨ́ ʊʲéxəlʲı.

2707

EN I'll see you AT noon, ON Wednesday, ON the twenty-fifth, IN December.

RU Я уви́жусь с тобо́й днём, в сре́ду, два́дцать пя́того, в декабре́.

ROM ja uvížus' s tabój dnjóm, v srjédu, dvádtsət' pjátəvə, v djıkabrjé.

IPA ʲa ʊvʲízʊsʲ s tɐbʷój dnʲǫ́m, f srʲédʊ, dváttsətʲ pʲátəvə, v dʲɪkɐbrʲé.

2708

EN I'll see you IN the morning, ON May thirty-first (31st), twenty-fourteen (2014).

RU Я уви́жусь с тобо́й у́тром, три́дцать пе́рвого ма́я, две ты́сячи четы́рнадцатого го́да.

ROM ja uvížus' s tabój útrəm, trídtsət' pjérvəvə májə, dvjɛ tísjaćı ćıtírnədtsətəvə gódə.

IPA ʲa ʊvʲízʊsʲ s tɐbʷój útrəm, trʲíttsətʲ pʲérvəvə máʲə, dvʲɛ tísʲɪtɕɪ tɕɪtírnəttsətəvə gʷódə.

2709

EN I have to work IN the afternoons.

RU Я до́лжен (♀должна́) рабо́тать ежедне́вно во второ́й полови́не дня.

ROM ja dólžın (♀dalžná) rıbótət' jıžıdnjévnə va vtarój pəlavínjı dnja.

IPA ʲa dǫ́łzın (♀dɐłzná) rɐbʷótətʲ ʲɪzɨdnʲévnə vɐ ftɐrój pəlɐvʲínʲɪ dnʲa.

2710

EN The train will be leaving IN a few minutes.

RU Поезд отправляется через несколько минут.
ROM pójızd ətprıvljájetsjı ćjérjız njéskəl'kə mjınút.
IPA pʷǫ́ⁱzd ətprɐvlʲǽʲɪtsʲɪ tɕérʲɪz nʲéskəłʲkə mʲɪnút.

2711

EN I'll be back IN a week.

RU Я вернусь через неделю.
ROM ja vjırnús' ćjérjız njıdjélju.
IPA ʲa vʲɪrnúsʲ tɕérʲɪz nʲɪdʲélʲü.

2712

EN They're getting married in six (6) months' time.

RU Они собираются пожениться через шесть месяцев.
ROM aní sabjırájutsjı pažınít'sjı ćjérjız šıst' mjésjatsıv.
IPA ɐnʲí sɐbʲɪrájütsʲɪ pɐʐɪnʲítʲsʲɪ tɕérʲɪs ʂɪstʲ mʲésʲɪtsɨf.

2713

EN Everything began and ended ON time.

RU Всё началось и закончилось вовремя.
ROM vsjó nəćılós' i zakónćıləs' vóvrjemjı.
IPA fsʲǫ́ nətɕɪlǫ́sʲ ɪ zɐkʷǫ́ntɕɨləsʲ vʷǫ́vrʲɪmʲɪ.

2714

EN If I say ten o'clock (10:00), then I mean, be ON time.

RU Если я говорю́ де́сять часо́в, зна́чит, будь во́время.

ROM jésljɪ ja gəvarjú djésjat' ćɪsóv, znáćɪt, bud' vóvrjemjɪ.

IPA ʲéslʲɪ ʲa gəvɐrʲú dʲésʲɪtʲ tɕɪsóf, znátɕɪt, budʲ vʷóvrʲɪmʲɪ.

2715

EN Will you be home IN time for dinner? > No, I'll be
    late.

RU Ты бу́дешь домо́й к обе́ду во́время? > Нет, я
    опозда́ю.

ROM tɪ búdjeś damój k abjédu vóvrjemjɪ? > njɛt, ja
    əpazdáju.

IPA tɨ búdʲɪɕ dɐmʷój k ɐbʲédʊ vʷóvrʲɪmʲɪ? > nʲɛt, ʲa
    əpɐzdáʲü.

2716

EN We got on the train just IN time.

RU Мы успе́ли на по́езд как раз во́время.

ROM mɪ uspjéljɪ na pójɪzd kak raz vóvrjemjɪ.

IPA mɨ ʊspʲélʲɪ na pʷóʲɪzt kak raz vʷóvrʲɪmʲɪ.

2717

EN I hit the brakes just IN time and didn't hit the child.

RU Я надави́л (♀ надави́ла) на тормоза́ как раз во́время и не сби́л (♀ сби́ла) ребёнка.

ROM ja nədavíl (♀ nədavílə) na tərmazá kak raz vóvrjemjı i njı sbíl (♀ sbílə) rıbjónkə.

IPA ʲa nədɐvʲíɫ (♀ nədɐvʲílə) na tərmɐzá kak raz vʷǫ́vrʲɪmʲɪ ɪ nʲɪ sbʲíɫ (♀ sbʲílə) rʲɪbʲę́nkə.

2718

EN At first we didn't get along very well, but in the end we became good friends.

RU Внача́ле мы не о́чень ла́дили, но в конце́ концо́в ста́ли хоро́шими друзья́ми.

ROM vnaćáljı mı njı óćın' ládjıljı, no v kantsjé kantsóv stáljı haróšımjı druz'jámjı.

IPA vnɐtɕálʲɪ mɨ nʲɪ ǫ́tɕɪnʲ ládʲɪlʲɪ, nǫ f kɐntsɨ́ kɐntsǫ́f stálʲɪ xɐrǫ́ʂɪmʲɪ druʒʲǽmʲɪ.

2719

EN I'm going away at the beginning of January. > I'm going away at the beginning of the year.

RU Я уезжа́ю в нача́ле января́. > Я уезжа́ю в нача́ле го́да.

ROM ja ujıžžáju v naćáljı jınvarjá. > ja ujıžžáju v naćáljı gódə.

IPA ʲa ʊʲɪʐʐǽʉ v nɐtɕálʲɪ ʲɪnvɐrʲá. > ʲa ʊʲɪʐʐǽʉ v nɐtɕálʲɪ gʷǫ́də.

2720

EN I'm coming back at the end of December. > I'm coming back at the end of the year.

RU Я возвращáюсь в концé декабря́. > Я возвращáюсь в концé гóда.

ROM ja vəzvrıççájus' v kantsjé djıkabrjá. > ja vəzvrıççájus' v kantsjé gódə.

IPA ʲa vəzvrɐççáʲüsʲ f kɐntsɨ́ dʲɪkɐbrʲá. > ʲa vəzvrɐççáʲüsʲ f kɐntsɨ́ gʷódə.

2721

EN The hotel we're going to is on a small island in the middle of a lake.

RU Гостúница, в котóрую мы éдем, нахóдится на небольшóм óстрове в цéнтре óзера.

ROM gastínjıtsə, v katóruju mı jédjım, nahódjıtsjı na njıbal'šóm óstrəvjı v tsjéntrjı ózjırə.

IPA gɐstʲínʲıtsə, f kɐtóruʲü mɨ ʲédʲım, nɐxódʲıtsʲı na nʲıbɐlʲşóm óstrəvʲı f tséntrʲı ózʲırə.

2722

EN There's somebody at the door, could you please answer it?

RU Ктó-то стучи́т в дверь, ты не мог (♀моглá) бы откры́ть?

ROM któ-tə stuçít v dvjer', tı njı mog (♀maglá) bı atkrít'?

IPA któ-tə stʊtçít v dvʲerʲ, tɨ nʲı mʷok (♀mɐglá) bɨ ɐtkrítʲ?

2723

EN I like to sit in the back row at the movies.

RU Я люблю сидеть на задних рядах в кинотеатрах.
ROM ja ljubljú sjɪdjét' na zádnjɪh radáh v kjɪnatjɪátrəh.
IPA ʲa lʲübʲú sʲɪdʲétʲ na zádnʲɪx rʲɪdáx f kʲɪnɐtʲɪátrəx.

2724

EN I just started working in the sales department.

RU Я только начал (♀ начала) работать в отделе
продаж.
ROM ja tól'kə náɕəl (♀ nəɕɪlá) rɪbótət' v atdjéljɪ pradáž.
IPA ʲa tólʲkə nátɕəɫ (♀ nətɕɪlá) rɐbʷótətʲ v ɐtdʲélʲɪ prɐdáʂ.

2725

EN Our apartment is on the second floor of the building.

RU Наша квартира на втором этаже здания.
ROM nášə kvartírə na vtaróm ɛtažjé zdánjɪjə.
IPA nášə kfɐrtʲírə na ftɐróm ɛtɐʐɪ́ zdánʲɪrʲə.

2726

EN They drive on the left in Britain, Japan, and Singapore.

RU Левосторо́ннее движе́ние в Великобрита́нии, Япо́нии и Сингапу́ре.

ROM ljɪvəstarónnjeɪ dvjɪžjénjɪjɪ v vjɪljɪkabrɪtánjɪjɪ, jɪpónjɪjɪ i sjɪŋgapúrjɪ.

IPA ˈljɪvəstɐrónnˈrˈɪ dvˈɪzɛ́nˈrˈɪ v vˈɪlˈɪkɐbrˈɪtánˈrˈɪ, ˈɪpʷónˈrˈɪ ɪ sˈɪŋgɐpúrˈɪ.

2727

EN I stopped to get gas on the way home from work.

RU Я останови́лся (♀ останови́лась) зали́ть бензи́н по пути́ с рабо́ты домо́й.

ROM ja əstənavílsjɪ (♀ əstənavíləs') zalít' bjɪnzín pa putí s rɪbótɪ damój.

IPA ˈja əstənɐvˈíɫsˈɪ (♀ əstənɐvˈíləsˈ) zɛlˈítˈ bˈɪnzˈín pɐ putˈí s rɐbʷótɨ dɐmʷój.

2728

EN The plant is in the corner of the room.

RU Расте́ния в углу́ ко́мнаты.

ROM rɪstjénjɪjə v uglú kómnətɪ.

IPA rɐstˈénˈrˈə v ʊglú kʷómnətɨ.

2729

EN The mailbox is on the corner of the street.

RU Почто́вый я́щик на углу́ у́лицы.
ROM paštóvıj jáççık na uglú úljıtsı.
IPA pɐʂtóvɨj ʲǽççɨk na ʊglú úlʲɪtsɨ.

2730

EN Have you ever been in the hospital?

RU Ты когда́-нибудь лежа́л (♀лежа́ла) в больни́це?
ROM tı kagdá-njıbud' ljıžál (♀ljıžálə) v bal'nítsı?
IPA tɨ kɐgdá-nʲɪbʊdʲ lʲɪʐáɫ (♀lʲɪʐálə) v bɐlʲnʲítsɨ?

2731

EN Have you ever been in prison? > Have you ever been in jail?

RU Ты когда́-нибудь сиде́л (♀сиде́ла) в тюрьме́? > Ты когда́-нибудь сиде́л (♀сиде́ла) за решёткой?
ROM tı kagdá-njıbud' sjıdjél (♀sjıdjélə) v tjur'mjé? > tı kagdá-njıbud' sjıdjél (♀sjıdjélə) za rıšjótkəj?
IPA tɨ kɐgdá-nʲɪbʊdʲ sʲɪdʲéɫ (♀sʲɪdʲélə) f tʲürʲmʲé? > tɨ kɐgdá-nʲɪbʊdʲ sʲɪdʲéɫ (♀sʲɪdʲélə) za rʲɪʂǫ́tkəj?

2732

EN My brother's in college, and I'm still in high school.
> He's in medical school, but I want to go to law
school.

RU Мой брат в колледже, а я всё ещё в старшей
школе. Он учится на медицинском, но я хочу
пойти на юридический.

ROM moj brat v kólljedžı, a ja vsjó jıççjó v stáršıj škóljı.
on úćıtsjı na mjıdjıtsínskəm, no ja haćú pajtí na
jurıdíćıskjıj.

IPA mᵂǫj brat f kᵂǫ́łⱡʲɪdzɨ̰, a ʲa fsʲǫ́ ʲɪççǫ̰ f stárṣɨj ʂkᵂǫ́łʲɪ.
ǫn útçɪtsʲɪ na mʲɪdʲɪtsínskəm, nǫ ʲa xɐtçú pɐjtʲí na
ʲürʲɪdʲítçɨskʲɪj.

2733

EN We went ON a cruise last week, and there weren't
many people ON the ship.

RU Мы отправились в круиз на прошлой неделе, на
корабле было немного людей.

ROM mı atprávjıljıs' v kruíz na próšləj njıdjéljı, na kərıbljé
bílə njımnógə ljudjéj.

IPA mɨ ɐtprávʲɪlʲɪsʲ f kruʲíz na prǫ́ʂləj nʲɪdʲélʲɪ, na kərɐbⱡʲé
bɨ́lə nʲɪmnǫ́gə ⱡʲüdʲéj.

2734

EN There were no seats left when we got ON the train.

RU В поезде уже не осталось мест, когда мы зашли.

ROM v pójezdjı užjé njı astáləs' mjɛst, kagdá mı zašlí.

IPA f pᵂǫ́ʲɪzdʲɪ ʊʐɨ̰ nʲɪ ɐstáləsʲ mʲɛst, kɐgdá mɨ zɐʂⱡʲí.

2735

EN The bus was very crowded when we got ON.

RU Автобус был переполнен, когда мы зашли.
ROM avtóbus bıl pjırıpólnjın, kagdá mı zašlí.
IPA ɐftóbʊs bɨɫ pʲɪrʲɪpʷóɫnʲɪn, kɐgdá mɨ zɐʂlʲí.

2736

EN I had an aisle seat ON the plane. > I had an aisle
seat ON the flight.

RU В самолёте у меня было место у прохода.
ROM v səmaljótjı u mjınjá bílə mjéstə u prahódə.
IPA f səmɐlʲǫ́tʲɪ u mʲɪnʲá bɨ́lə mʲéstə u prɐxǫ́də.

2737

EN Nuria passed me ON her bike yesterday.

RU Нурия передала мне свой велосипед на прошлой
неделе.
ROM núrjıjə pjırıdalá mnjɛ svoj vjılasjırpjéd na próšləj
njıdjéljı.
IPA núrʲɨ́ə pʲɪrʲɪdɐlá mnʲɛ svʷoj vʲɪlɐsʲɪpʲéd na prǫ́šləj
nʲɪdʲélʲɪ.

2738

EN My friends are IN China. They'll be going back TO
Italy next week.

RU Мои́ друзья́ в Кита́е. Они́ возвраща́ются в Ита́лию
на сле́дующей неде́ле.

ROM maí druz'já v kjɪtájɪ. aní vəzvrɪҫҫájutsjɪ v jɪtáljɪju na
sljédujuҫҫɪj njɪdjéljɪ.

IPA mɐʲí druzʲá f kʲɪtáʲɪ. ɐnʲí vəzvrɐҫҫáʲütsʲɪ v ʲɪtálʲɾʲü na
slʲédʊʲüҫҫɨj nʲɪdʲélʲɪ.

2739

EN My parents are AT the zoo. My aunt is going TO the
zoo to meet them there.

RU Мои́ роди́тели в зоопа́рке. Моя́ тётя собира́ется
пойти́ в зоопа́рк, что́бы встре́титься с ни́ми там.

ROM maí radítjeljɪ v zaapárkjɪ. majá tjótjɪ sabjɪrájetsjɪ pajtí
v zaapárk, štóbɪ vstrjétjɪt'sjɪ s nímjɪ tam.

IPA mɐʲí rɐdʲítʲɪlʲɪ v zɐɐpárkʲɪ. mɐʲá tʲǫ́tʲɪ sɐbʲɪráʲɪtsʲɪ pɐjtʲí
v zɐɐpárk, ʂtǫ́bɨ fstrʲétʲɪtʲsʲɪ s nʲímʲɪ tam.

2740

EN Sir, I'm in a hurry to catch my flight ON time. When
will we arrive AT the airport?

RU Сэр, я спешу́, что́бы успе́ть на рейс во́время.
Когда́ мы прие́дем в аэропо́рт?

ROM sɛr, ja spjɪšú, štóbɪ uspjét' na rjejs vóvrjemjɪ. kagdá
mɪ prɪjédjɪm v aɛrapórt?

IPA sɛr, ʲa spʲɪšú, ʂtǫ́bɨ ʊspʲétʲ na rʲejs vʷǫ́vrʲɪmʲɪ. kɐgdá
mɨ prʲɪʲʲédʲɪm v aɛrɐpʷǫ́rt?

2741

EN Four of us got INTO a car and the others got ONTO a bus.

RU Четверо из нас сéли в машúну, остальнéые сéли в автóбус.

ROM ćjétvjırə iz nas sjéljı v mašínu, əstal'níjı sjéljı v avtóbus.

IPA tɕétɕʲırə ʲiz nas sʲélʲı v mɐʂínu, əstɐlʲnɕʲı sʲélʲı v ɐftǫ́bʊs.

2742

EN Since it was too hot to sit in the sun, we found a table IN the shade.

RU Поскóльку сидéть на сóлнце бéыло слúшком жáрко, мы нашлú стóлик в тенú.

ROM paskól'ku sjıdjét' na sóntsı bílə slíškəm žárkə, mı našlí stóljık v tjıní.

IPA pɐskʷǫ́lʲkʊ sʲıdʲétʲ na sǫ́ntsɨ bílə slʲíʂkəm zárkə, mɨ nɐʂlʲí stǫ́lʲık f tʲınʲí.

2743

EN Don't go out IN the rain, or else you'll get all wet.

RU Не ходú под дождём, а то промóкнешь.

ROM njı hadí pad daždjóm, a to pramóknjeś.

IPA nʲı xɐdʲí pɐd dɐzdʲǫ́m, a tǫ prɐmʷǫ́knʲıɕ.

2744

EN When filling out forms, be sure to print your name IN capital letters so it's legible.

RU Заполняя бланки, пишите ваше имя заглавными буквами разборчиво.

ROM zəpalnjájə blánkjɪ, pjɪšítjɪ váši ímjɪ zaglávnɪmjɪ búkvəmjɪ rɪzbórćɪvə.

IPA zəpɐłnʲǽʲə blánkʲɪ, pʲɪsítʲɪ váʂɪ ʲímʲɪ zɐglávnɨmʲɪ búkfəmʲɪ rɐzbʷórtɕɪvə.

2745

EN Have you ever been IN love with somebody?

RU Ты когда-нибудь влюблялся (♀влюблялась) в кого-нибудь?

ROM tɪ kagdá-njɪbud' vljubljálsjɪ (♀vljubljáləs') v kavó-njɪbud'?

IPA tɨ kɐgdá-nʲɪbʊdʲ vlʲüblʲǽɫsʲɪ (♀vlʲüblʲáləsʲ) f kɐvʷó-nʲɪbʊdʲ?

2746

EN IN my opinion, the movie wasn't that great.

RU По-моему, фильм не такой уж и хороший.

ROM pa-mójɪmu, fil'm njɪ takój už i haróšɪj.

IPA pɐ-mʷóʲɪmʊ, fʲilʲm nʲɪ tɐkʷój uz̪ ɪ xɐróʂɨj.

2747

EN IN my mother's opinion, the food AT this restaurant is the best.

RU По мнéнию моéй мáмы, в э́том ресторáне лýчшая едá.

ROM pa mnjénjıju majéj mámı, v étəm rıstaránjı lúćśəjı jıdá.

IPA pɐ mnʲénʲrʲü mɐʲéj mámɨ, v étəm rʲɪstɐránʲɪ lútɕɕəʲɪ ʲɪdá.

2748

EN Latifa left school AT the age OF seventeen (17). > She left school AT seventeen (17).

RU Латúфа брóсила шкóлу в вóзрасте семнáдцати лет. > Онá брóсила шкóлу в семнáдцать.

ROM latífə brósjılə škólu v vózrəstjı sjımnádtsətjı ljɛt. > aná brósjılə škólu v sjımnádtsət'.

IPA lɐtʲífə brós̬ʲɪlə s̬kʷólʊ v vʷózrəstʲɪ s̬ʲɪmnáttsətʲɪ lʲɛt. > ɐná brós̬ʲɪlə s̬kʷólʊ f s̬ʲɪmnáttsətʲ.

2749

EN We took off an hour ago, and now we're flying AT a speed OF nine hundred (900) kilometers per hour AT an altitude OF ten thousand (10,000) meters.

RU Мы взлете́ли час наза́д и сейча́с лети́м со ско́ростью девятьсо́т киломе́тров в час на высоте́ десяти́ ты́сяч ме́тров.

ROM mɪ vzljɪtjéljɪ ćas nazád i sjɪjćás ljɪtím sa skórəst'ju djɪvjɪt'sót kjɪlamjétrəv v ćas na vɪsatjé djɪsjɪtí tísjɪć mjétrəv.

IPA mɨ vzlʲɪtélʲɪ tɕas nɐzád ɪ sʲɪjtɕás lʲɪtʲím sɐ skʷórəstʲü dʲɪvʲɪtʲsót kʲɪlɐmʲétrəv f tɕas na vɨsɐtʲé dʲɪsʲɪtʲí tʲísʲɪtɕ mʲétrəf.

2750

EN The train was traveling AT a speed OF one hundred twenty (120) miles per hour when the driver lost control. > The train was traveling AT a speed OF two hundred (200) kilometers per hour when the driver lost control.

RU По́езд шёл со ско́ростью две́сти киломе́тров в час, когда́ машини́ст потеря́л контро́ль.

ROM pójɪzd šjól sa skórəst'ju dvjéstjɪ kjɪlamjétrəv v ćas, kagdá mašɪníst patjɪrjál kantról'.

IPA pʷóʲɪzt ʂ̠ɵɫ sɐ skʷórəstʲü dvʲéstʲɪ kʲɪlɐmʲétrəv f tɕas, kɐgdá mɐʂɨnʲíst pɐtʲɪrʲáɫ kɐntrólʲ.

2751

EN Water boils AT a temperature OF one hundred degrees (100°) Celsius.

RU Водá кипи́т при температýре ста грáдусов по Цéльсию.

ROM vadá kjɪpít prɪ tjɪmpjɪrɪtúrjɪ sta grádusəv pa tsjél'sjɪju.

IPA vɐdá kʲɪpʲít prʲɪ tʲɪmpʲɪrɐtúrʲɪ sta grádʊsəf pɐ tsélʲsʲɪ̈rʲü.

2752

EN Some singers go ON a world tour every year.

RU Нéкоторые певцы́ отправля́ются на гастрóли по всемý ми́ру кáждый год.

ROM njékətərɪjɪ pjɪvtsí ətprɪvljájutsjɪ na gastróljɪ pa vsjɪmú míru káždɪj god.

IPA nʲékətərɨ̈ʲɪ pʲɪftsí ətprɐvlʲǽʲütsʲɪ na gɐstrólʲɪ pɐ fsʲɪmú mʲírʊ kázdɨ̈j gʷɵt.

2753

EN I didn't hear the news ON the radio, nor ON the television; I saw it ON the internet.

RU Я узнáл (♀узнáла) о новостя́х не по рáдио и не по телеви́зору, я прочитáл (♀прочитáла) о них в интернéте.

ROM ja uznál (♀uználə) a nəvastjáh njɪ pa rádjɪə i njɪ pa tjɪljɪvízəru, ja praćɪtál (♀praćɪtálə) a nih v jɪntjɪrnjétjɪ.

IPA ʲa ʊznáł (♀ʊnálə) ɐ nəvɐstʲáx nʲɪ pɐ rádʲɪə ɪ nʲɪ pɐ tʲɪlʲɪvʲízərʊ, ʲa prɐtɕɪtáł (♀prɐtɕɪtálə) ɐ nʲix v ʲɪntʲɪrnʲétʲɪ.

2754

EN I've never met the woman IN charge OF marketing, but I've spoken to her ON the phone a few times.

RU Я никогда́ не встреча́лся (♀ встреча́лась) с же́нщиной, отвеча́ющей за ма́ркетинг, но я разгова́ривал (♀ разгова́ривала) с ней по телефо́ну.

ROM ja njɪkagdá njɪ vstrɪćálsjɪ (♀ vstrɪćáləs') s žjénççɪnəj, atvjɪćájuççɪj za márkjetjɪng, no ja rɪzgavárjɪvəl (♀ rɪzgavárjɪvələ) s njej pa tjɪljɪfónu.

IPA ʲa nʲɪkɐgdá nʲɪ fstrʲɪtɕáɫsʲɪ (♀ fstrʲɪtɕáləsʲ) s zʲénɕɕɪnəj, ɐtfʲɪtɕáʲüɕɕɪj za márkʲɪtʲɪnk, nɔ ʲa rəzgɐvárʲɪvəɫ (♀ rəzgɐvárʲɪvələ) s nʲej pɐ tʲɪlʲʲɪfʷónʊ.

2755

EN There's no train service today because all the railroad workers are ON strike.

RU Поезда́ сего́дня не хо́дят, поско́льку все железнодоро́жные рабо́чие (рабо́тники) на забасто́вке.

ROM pajɪzdá sjɪvódnjɪ njɪ hódjɪt, paskól'ku vsjɛ žɪljɪznədaróžnɪjɪ rɪbóćɪjɪ (rɪbótnjɪkjɪ) na zəbastóvkjɪ.

IPA pɐʲɪzdá sʲɪvʷódnʲɪ nʲɪ xódʲɪt, pɐskʷóɫʲkʊ fsʲɛ zʲɪlʲɪznədɐrʲóznɨʲɪ rɐbʷótɕɪʲɪ (rɐbʷótnʲɪkʲɪ) na zəbɐstʷófkʲɪ.

2756

EN She's put ON a lot of weight this year, so she wants to go ON a diet.

RU Она́ набрала́ вес в э́том году́, поэ́тому она́ хо́чет сесть на дие́ту.

ROM aná nəbrılá vjɛs v étəm gadú, paétəmu aná hóćıt sjest' na djıjétu.

IPA ɐná nəbrɐlá vʲɛs v étəm gɐdú, pɐétəmʊ ɐná xótɕɨt sʲestʲ na dʲrʲétʊ.

2757

EN While I was watching F1 racing yesterday, I saw one of the cars catch ON fire.

RU Когда́ я вчера́ смотре́л (♀смотре́ла) го́нки фо́рмулы оди́н, я уви́дел (♀уви́дела), как одна́ из маши́н загоре́лась.

ROM kagdá ja vćırá smatrjél (♀smatrjélə) gónkjı fórmulı adín, ja uvídjıl (♀uvídjılə), kak adná iz mašín zəgarjéləs'.

IPA kɐgdá ʲa ftɕɪrá smɐtrʲéɫ (♀smɐtrʲélə) gʷónkʲɪ fʷórmʊlɪ ɐdʲín, ʲa ʊvʲídʲɪɫ (♀ʊvʲídʲɪlə), kak ɐdná ʲiz mɐʂín zəgɐrʲéləsʲ.

2758

EN   Sometimes my job can be really stressful, but ON the
     whole I like the people and enjoy the job.

RU   Иногда́ моя́ рабо́та мо́жет быть о́чень
     напряжённой, но в це́лом мне нра́вятся лю́ди и я
     получа́ю удово́льствие от рабо́ты.

ROM jınagdá majá rıbótə móžıt bıt' óćın' napražjónnəj, no v
     tsjéləm mnjɛ nrávjatsjı ljúdjı i ja palućáju
     udavól'stvjıjı at rıbótı.

IPA ʲɪnɐgdá mɐʲá rɐbʷótə mʷóʑɨt bɨtʲ ótɕɪnʲ nɐprʲɪʑónnəj,
     no f tséləm mnʲɛ nrávʲɪtsʲɪ lʲúdʲɪ ɪ ʲa pɐlʊtɕáʲü
     ʊdɐvʷólʲstfʲrʲɪ ɐt rɐbʷótɨ.

2759

EN   I didn't mean to annoy you, I didn't do it ON purpose.

RU   Я не хоте́л (♀хоте́ла) тебя́ оби́деть, я сде́лал
     (♀сде́лала) э́то ненаро́чно.

ROM ja njı hatjél (♀hatjélə) tjıbjá abídjet', ja sdjéləl
     (♀sdjélələ) étə njınaróćnə.

IPA ʲa nʲɪ xɐtʲéɫ (♀xɐtʲélə) tʲɪbʲá ɐbʲídʲɪtʲ, ʲa zdʲéɫət
     (♀zdʲélələ) étə nʲɪnɐrótɕnə.

2760

EN   He bumped INTO me ON accident.

RU   Он случа́йно со мной столкну́лся.

ROM on slućájnə sa mnoj stalknúlsjı.

IPA on slʊtɕájnə sɐ mnoj stɐɫknúɫsʲɪ.

2761

EN He bumped INTO me BY mistake.

RU Он по ошибке со мной столкнулся.
ROM on pa ašíbkjı sa mnoj stalknúlsjı.
IPA ǫn pɐ ɐ̞şípkʲɪ sɐ mnǫj stɐɫknúɫsʲɪ.

2762

EN All of my contact information is ON my business
card, but it's easiest to get ahold of me BY email or
cellphone.

RU Вся моя контактная информация содержится в
моей визитке, но проще всего связаться со мной
по электронной почте или телефону.
ROM vsja majá kantáktnəjı jınfarmátsıjə sadjéržıtsjı v majéj
vjızítkjı, no próçcı vsjıvó svjızát'sjı sa mnoj pa
ɛljıktrónnəj póćtjı ili tjıljıfónu.
IPA fsʲa mɐ̞ʲá kɐntáktnəʲɪ ʲɪnfɐrmátsʲɪ̞ə sɐdʲérzʲɪtsʲɪ v mɐ̞ʲéj
vʲɪzʲítkʲɪ, nǫ próçcɨ fsʲɪvʷǫ́ svʲɪzátʲsʲɪ sɐ mnǫj pɐ
ɛlʲɪktrǫ́nnəj pʷǫ́tɕtʲɪ ʲilʲi tʲɪlʲɪfʷǫ́nʊ.

2763

EN I didn't bring enough cash, so could I pay BY credit
card?

RU Я не взял (♀взяла) с собой достаточно наличных,
я могу расплатиться кредитной картой?
ROM ja njı vzjal (♀vzjılá) s sabój dastátəćnə nalíćnıh, ja
magú rısplatít'sjı krıdítnəj kártəj?
IPA ʲa nʲɪ vzʲaɫ (♀vzʲɪlá) s sɐbʷój dɐstátətɕnə nɐlʲítɕnɨx, ʲa
mɐgú rəsplɐtʲítʲsʲɪ krʲɪdʲítnəj kártəj?

2764

EN You don't need to fix that BY hand, I can write a computer program to help you. > You don't need to fix that manually.

RU Тебе́ не ну́жно нала́живать э́то вручну́ю, я могу́ написа́ть компью́терную програ́мму, что́бы помо́чь тебе́. > Тебе́ не ну́жно нала́живать э́то вручну́ю.

ROM tjɪbjé njɪ núžnə naláživət' étə vrućnúju, ja magú napjɪsát' kampjútjɪrnuju pragrámmu, štóbɪ pamóć' tjɪbjé. > tjɪbjé njɪ núžnə naláživət' étə vrućnúju.

IPA tʲɪbʲé nʲɪ núz̪nə nɐláz̪ɨvətʲ étə vrʊt͡ɕnúʲü, ʲa mɐgú nɐpʲɪsátʲ kɐmpʲütʲɪrnʊʲü prɐgrámmʊ, ʂtóbɨ pɐmʷót͡ɕʲ tʲɪbʲé. > tʲɪbʲé nʲɪ núz̪nə nɐláz̪ɨvətʲ étə vrʊt͡ɕnúʲü.

2765

EN My father sometimes goes to work by taxi, and I go to work by bus.

RU Мой па́па иногда́ е́здит на рабо́ту на такси́, а я е́зжу на рабо́ту на авто́бусе.

ROM moj pápə jɪnagdá jézdjɪt na rɪbótu na taksí, a ja jéžžu na rɪbótu na avtóbusjɪ.

IPA mʷoj pápə ʲɪnɐgdá ʲézdʲɪt na rɐbʷótʊ na tɐksʲí, a ʲa ʲézʐʊ na rɐbʷótʊ na ɐftóbʊsʲɪ.

2766

EN Olga's father is an oil tycoon, and goes to work BY helicopter and BY plane.

RU Отéц Óльги - нефтянóй магнáт, он добирáется до рабóты на вертолёте и самолёте.

ROM atjéts ól'gjɪ - njɪftjɪnój magnát, on dabjɪrájetsjɪ da rɪbótɪ na vjɪrtaljótjɪ i səmaljótjɪ.

IPA ɐtʲéts ólʲgʲɪ - nʲɪftʲɪnój mɐgnát, ɒn dɐbʲɪráʲɪtsʲɪ dɐ rɐbʷótɨ na vʲɪrtɐlʲétʲɪ ɪ səmɐlʲétʲɪ.

2767

EN It's a two-hour drive to the airport BY car, but it's only forty (40) minutes by high-speed rail.

RU На машúне до аэропóрта добирáться два часá, но на экспрéссе всегó сóрок минýт.

ROM na mašínjɪ da aɛrapórtə dabjɪrát'sjɪ dva ćɪsá, no na ɛksprjéssjɪ vsjɪvó sórək mjɪnút.

IPA na mɐʂínʲɪ dɐ aɛrɐpʷórtə dɐbʲɪrátʲsʲɪ dva tɕɪsá, nɒ na ɛksprʲéssʲɪ fsʲɪvʷó sórək mʲɪnút.

2768

EN I arrived ON the seven-o'clock (7:00) train.

RU Я приéхал (♀приéхала) на семичасовóм пóезде.

ROM ja prɪjéhəl (♀prɪjéhələ) na sjɪmjɪćɪsavóm pójezdjɪ.

IPA ʲa prʲɪ̯éxəł (♀prʲɪ̯éxələ) na sʲɪmʲɪtɕɪsɐvʷóm pʷóʲɪzdʲɪ.

2769

EN The door's not broken, so it must have been opened by somebody with a key.

RU Дверь не сло́мана, так что её мо́жно откры́ть ключо́м.

ROM dvjer' njɪ slómənə, tak što jɪjó móžnə atkrít' kljućóm.

IPA dvʲerʲ nʲɪ slómənə, tak stǫ ʲɾʲę mʷǫzɲə ɐtkrítʲ klʲütçǫm.

2770

EN My salary has increased from two thousand dollars ($2000) a month to twenty-five hundred ($2500). > My salary's increased BY five hundred dollars ($500). > My salary has increased from fifteen hundred fifty euros (€1550) a month to nineteen hundred (€1900). > My salary's increased BY three hundred fifty euro (€350).

RU Моя́ зарпла́та увели́чилась с ты́сячи пятисо́т е́вро в ме́сяц до ты́сячи девятиста́. > Моя́ зарпла́та увели́чилась на четы́реста е́вро.

ROM majá zarplátə uvjɪlícɪləs' s tísjaćɪ pjɪtjɪsót jévrə v mjésjɪts da tísjaćɪ djɪvjɪtjɪstá. > majá zarplátə uvjɪlícɪləs' na ćɪtírjɪstə jévrə.

IPA mɐʲá zɐrplátə ʊvʲɪlʲítçiləsʲ s tísʲɪtçi pʲɪtʲɪsǫt ʲévrə v mʲésʲɪts dɐ tísʲɪtçi dʲɪvʲɪtʲɪstá. > mɐʲá zɐrplátə ʊvʲɪlʲítçiləsʲ na tçɪtírʲɪstə ʲévrə.

2771

EN I finished the race three (3) meters ahead of you. > I won the race BY three (3) meters.

RU Я завереши́л (♀завереши́ла) соревнова́ние по бе́гу, опереди́в тебя́ на три́ста ме́тров. > Я вы́играл (♀вы́играла) соревнова́ние по бе́гу с отры́вом в три́ста ме́тров.

ROM ja zavjɪrɪšíl (♀zavjɪrɪšílə) sərɪvnaványjɪjɪ pa bjégu, apjɪrɪdív tjɪbjá na trístə mjétrəv. > ja víjɪgrəl (♀víjɪgrələ) sərɪvnaványjɪjɪ pa bjégu s atrívəm v trístə mjétrəv.

IPA ʲa zɐvʲɪrʲɪʂíɫ (♀zɐvʲɪrʲɪʂílə) sərʲɪvnɐvánʲrʲɪ pɐ bʲégʊ, ɐpʲɪrʲɪdʲíf tʲɪbʲá na trʲístə mʲétrəf. > ʲa vʲɪgrəɫ (♀vʲɪgrələ) sərʲɪvnɐvánʲrʲɪ pɐ bʲégʊ s ɐtrívəm f trʲístə mʲétrəf.

2772

EN Some American companies give college graduates a check FOR five thousand dollars ($5000) AS a signing bonus.

RU Не́которые америка́нские компа́нии даю́т выпускника́м университе́тов чек на пять ты́сяч до́лларов в ка́честве пре́мии.

ROM njékətərɪjɪ amjɪrɪkánskjɪjɪ kampánjɪjɪ dajút vɪpusknjɪkám unjɪvjɪrsjɪtjétəv ćɪk na pjat' tísjɪć dóllərəv v káćɪstvjɪ prjémjɪjɪ.

IPA nʲékətərɨʲɪ ɐmʲɪrʲɪkánskʲrʲɪ kɐmpánʲrʲɪ dɐʲút vɨpʊsknʲɪkám ʊnʲɪvʲɪrsʲɪtʲétəf tɕɛk na pʲætʲ tʲísʲɪtɕ dóɫlərəv f kátɕɪstfʲɪ prʲémʲrʲɪ.

2773

EN I wrote a check FOR five hundred dollars ($500) to
the insurance company. > I wrote a check FOR four
hundred euros (€400) to the insurance company.

RU Я вы́писал (♀вы́писала) чек на четы́реста е́вро
страхово́й компа́нии.

ROM ja vípjɪsəl (♀vípjɪsələ) ćɪk na ćɪtírjɪstə jévrə strɪhavój
kampánjɪjɪ.

IPA ʲa vípʲɪsəɫ (♀vípʲɪsələ) tɕɛk na tɕitírʲɪstə ʲévrə
strəxɐvʷój kɐmpánʲrʲɪ.

2774

EN The company grew quickly due to a strong demand
FOR its products.

RU Компа́ния расширя́лась бы́стрыми те́мпами
благодаря́ большо́му спро́су на её проду́кцию.

ROM kampánjɪjə rɪsšɪrjáləs' bístrɪmjɪ tjémpəmjɪ bləgədarjá
bal'šómu sprósu na jɪjó pradúktsɪju.

IPA kɐmpánʲrʲə rɛşşɪrʲáləsʲ bístrɪmʲɪ tʲémpəmʲɪ bləgədɐrʲá
bɐɫʲşómʊ sprósʊ na ʲrʲǫ prɐdúktsɨü.

2775

EN There's no need FOR impolite behavior.

RU Нет необходи́мости вести́ себя́ неве́жливо.

ROM njɛt njɪəbhadíməstjɪ vjɪstí sjɪbjá njɪvjéžljɪvə.

IPA nʲɛt nʲɪəbxɐdʲíməstʲɪ vʲɪstʲí sʲɪbʲá nʲɪvʲéʑḷɪvə.

2776

EN The advantage OF living alone is that you have more freedom.

RU Когда́ живёшь оди́н, то твоё преиму́щество в том, что у тебя́ бо́льше свобо́ды.

ROM kagdá živjóś adín, to tvajó prijimúççistvə v tom, što u tjibjá ból'ši svabódi.

IPA kɐgdá z̢ɨv̢ɛ́ɕ ɐd̢ín, tо̧ tfɛ̢ɛ́ pr̢ɾ̢imúççɨstfə f tо̧m, s̢tо̧ u t̢ɨb̢á b^wól̢s̢ɨ svɐb^wódɨ.

2777

EN In fact, there are many advantages TO living alone.

RU Факти́чески, существу́ет мно́го преиму́ществ в жи́зни одному́.

ROM faktíćiskji, suççistvújit mnógə prijimúççistv v žíznji ədnamú.

IPA fɛkt̢ítçisk̢ɨ, suççɨstfú̢ɨt mnógə pr̢ɾ̢imúççɨstf v z̢ízn̢ɨ ədnɐmú.

2778

EN The authorities are still baffled by the cause of the explosion.

RU Вла́сти до сих пор не мо́гут разобра́ться в причи́нах взры́ва.

ROM vlástji da sih por nji mógut rizabrát'sji v pričínəh vzrívə.

IPA vlást̢ɨ dɐ s̢ix p^wо̧r n̢ɨ m^wógut rəzɐbrát̢s̢ɨ f pr̢ɨtçínəx vzrívə.

2779

EN I have all the photos OF my family in my cellphone.

RU У меня́ есть все фотогра́фии мое́й семьи́ в моём моби́льном телефо́не.

ROM u mjɪnjá jest' vsjɛ fətagráfjɪjɪ majéj sjɪmí v majóm mabíl'nəm tjɪljɪfónjɪ.

IPA u mʲɪnʲá ʲestʲ fsʲɛ fətɐgráfʲrʲɪ mɐʲéj sʲɪmʲí v mɐʲǫ́m mɐbʲílʲnəm tʲɪlʲɪfʷǫ́nʲɪ.

2780

EN I think we're lost. We need to get a map OF this city. — I'll search FOR an app.

RU Мне ка́жется, мы заблуди́лись. Нам ну́жно доста́ть ка́рту э́того го́рода. — Я поищу́ моби́льное приложе́ние.

ROM mnjɛ kážɪtsjɪ, mɪ zabludíljɪs'. nam núžnə dastát' kártu étəvə górədə. — ja pajɪççú mabíl'nəjɪ prɪlažjénjɪjɪ.

IPA mnʲɛ kázʲɨtsʲɪ, mɨ zɐbludʲílʲɪsʲ. nam núznə dɐstátʲ kártʊ étəvə gʷǫ́rədə. — ʲa pɐʲɪççú mɐbʲílʲnəʲɪ prʲɪlɐzʲénʲrʲɪ.

2781

EN There's always an increase IN the number OF traffic accidents around New Year's.

RU Коли́чество доро́жно-тра́нспортных происше́ствий всегда́ увели́чивается под но́вый год.

ROM kalíçɪstvə daróžna-tránspərtnɪh prajɪsšjéstvjɪj vsjɪgdá uvjɪlíçɪvəjetsjɪ pad nóvɪj god.

IPA kɐlʲítçɪstfə dɐróznɐ-tránspərtnɨx prɐʲɪşşéstfʲɪj fsʲɪgdá ʊvʲɪlʲítçɪvəʲɪtsʲɪ pɐd nóvɪj gʷǫt.

2782

EN The last twenty (20) years has seen a tremendous decrease IN crime.

RU В последние двадцать лет наблюдается значительное снижение количества преступлений.

ROM v pasljédnjɪjɪ dvádtsət' ljet nabljudájetsjɪ znaćítjel'nəjɪ snjɪžjénjɪjɪ kalíćɪstvə prɪstupljénjɪj.

IPA f pɐslʲédnʲɪɾʲɪ dváttsətʲ lʲɛt nɐblʲüdáʲɪtsʲɪ znɐtɕítʲɪlʲnəʲɪ snʲɪzɛ́nʲɪɾʲɪ kɐlʲítɕɨstfə prʲɪstʊplʲénʲɪj.

2783

EN It was a bad year for the company as it faced a huge drop IN sales.

RU Для компании это был плохой год, поскольку ей пришлось пережить стремительное падение продаж.

ROM dlja kampánjɪjɪ étə bɪl plahój god, paskól'ku jej prɪšlós' pjɪrɪžít' strɪmítjel'nəjɪ padjénjɪjɪ pradáž.

IPA dlʲa kɐmpánʲɪɾʲɪ étə bɨl plɐxój gʷɒt, pɐskʷólʲkʊ ʲej prʲɪʂlósʲ pʲɪrʲɪzítʲ strʲɪmʲítʲɪlʲnəʲɪ pɐdʲénʲɪɾʲɪ prɐdáʂ.

2784

EN Since the accident was my fault, I had to pay for the damage to the other car.

RU Поскольку авария произошла по моей вине, я должен (♀должна) выплатить компенсацию владельцу машины.

ROM paskól'ku avárjıjə prəjızašlá pa majéj vjınjé, ja dólžın (♀dalžná) víplətjıt' kampjınsátsıju vladjél'tsu mašínı.

IPA pɐskʷólʲkʊ ɐvárʲɾʲə prəʲɪzɐʂlá pɐ mɐʲéj vʲɪnʲé, ʲa dółzʲɪn (♀dɐłzṇá) víplətʲɪtʲ kɐmpʲɪnsátsɨü vlɐdʲélʲtsʊ mɐʂínɨ.

2785

EN A lot of my friends are getting married this year. I've been getting lots of invitations TO wedding banquets.

RU В этом году многие мои друзья женятся и выходят замуж. Я получаю много приглашений на свадебные торжества.

ROM v étəm gadú mnógjıjı maí druz'já žjénjatsjı i vıhódjıt zámuž. ja palućáju mnógə prıglašjénjıj na svádjıbnıjı taržıstvá.

IPA v étəm gɐdú mnógʲɾʲɪ mɐʲí druzʲá zʲénʲɪtsʲɪ ɪ vɨxódʲɪt zámʊʂ. ʲa pɐlʊtɕáʲü mnógə prʲɪglɐʂénʲɪj na svádʲɪbnɨʲɪ tɐrzɪstfá.

2786

EN The scientists have been working ON a solution TO the problem FOR many years.

RU Учёные работают над решением этой проблемы многие годы.

ROM ućjóniji ribótəjut nad rišjénjijim étəj prabljémı mnógjiji gódı.

IPA ʊtɕę́nɨ́ɪ rɐbʷǫ́tə́ʲüt nad rʲɪʂén̠ʲrʲɪm ɛ́təj prɐblʲémɨ mnǫ́ɡʲrʲɪ ɡʷǫ́dɨ.

2787

EN I was very surprised BY her reaction TO my simple suggestion.

RU Я был (♀ была) очень удивлён (♀ удивлена) её реакцией на моё простое предложение.

ROM ja bıl (♀ bılá) óćın' udjıvljón (♀ udjıvljıná) jıjó rıáktsıjej na majó prastójı prıdlažjénjıjı.

IPA ʲa bɨɫ (♀ bɨlá) ǫ́tɕɪn̠ʲ ʊdʲɪvlʲę́n (♀ ʊdʲɪvlʲɪmá) ʲrʲę́ rʲɪáktsɨ́ɪj na mɐʲę́ prɐstǫ́ɪ prʲɪdlɐzén̠ʲrʲɪ.

2788

EN His attitude toward his job is so positive that he
increases his sales every month.

RU Его отноше́ние к свое́й рабо́те насто́лько
позити́вное, что он увели́чивает прода́жи ка́ждый
ме́сяц.

ROM jıvó ətnašjénjıjı k svajéj rıbótjı nastól'kə pazjıtívnəjı,
što on uvjılíćıvəjıt pradáži káždıj mjésjıts.

IPA ⁱıvʷǫ́ ətnɐʂénʲrʲı k svɐʲéj rɐbʷǫ́tʲı nɐstǫ́lʲkə pɐzʲıtʲívnəʲı,
ʂtǫ ǫn ʊvʲılʲítɕıvəʲıt prɐdázı̣ kázdị̇j mʲésʲıts.

2789

EN Do you have a good relationship WITH your parents?

RU У тебя́ хоро́шие отноше́ния с твои́ми роди́телями?

ROM u tjıbjá haróšıjı ətnašjénjıjə s tvaímjı radítjeljamjı?

IPA u tʲıbʲá xɐróʂị̇ı ətnɐʂénʲrʲə s tfɐʲímʲı rɐdʲítʲılʲımʲı?

2790

EN The police want to question a suspect in connection
with the murder.

RU Поли́ция хо́чет зада́ть вопро́с подозрева́емому о
соуча́стии в уби́йстве.

ROM palítsıjə hóćıt zadát' vaprós pədazrıvájıməmu a
saućástjıjı v ubíjstvjı.

IPA pɐlʲítsị̇ə xǫ́tɕıt zɐdátʲ vɐprǫ́s pədɐzrʲıváʲıməmʊ ɐ
sɐʊtɕástʲrʲı v ʊbʲíjstfʲı.

2791

EN The police believe there's a connection between the two (2) murders, based on DNA evidence.

RU Поли́ция подозрева́ет связь ме́жду двумя́ уби́йствами на основа́нии результа́тов ДНК (дэ-эн-ка́).

ROM palítsıjə pədazrıvájıt svjaz' mjéʐdu dvumjá ubíjstvəmjı na əsnavánjıjı rızul'tátəv dnk (dɛ-ɛn-ká).

IPA pɐlʲítsɫʲə pədɐzrʲɪváʲɪt svʲæzʲ mʲézdʊ dvʊmʲá ʊbʲíjstfəmʲɪ na əsnɐvánʲrʲɪ rʲɪzʊlʲtátəv dnk (dɛ-ɛn-ká).

2792

EN There are minor differences between many European languages.

RU Существу́ют незначи́тельные разли́чия ме́жду мно́гими европе́йскими языка́ми.

ROM suççıstvújut njıznaćítjel'nıjı rızlíćıjə mjéʐdu mnógjımjı jıvrapjéjskjımjı jızıkámjı.

IPA suççɪstfúʲʊt nʲɪznɐtɕítʲɪlʲnʲɪ rɛzlʲítɕʲə mʲézdʊ mnógʲɪmʲɪ ʲɪvrɐpʲéjskʲɪmʲɪ ʲɪzɫkámʲɪ.

2793

EN It was really kind of you to help me. I really
    appreciate it.

RU С твоéй сторонь́ э́то бы́ло óчень мѝло помóчь
    мне. Я действѝтельно э́то ценю́.

ROM s tvajéj stərɑní étə bílə óćɪn' mílə pamóć' mnjɛ. ja
    djɪjstvítjel'nə étə tsɪnjú.

IPA s tɐᵊʲéj stərɐní étə bílə ótɕɪn̯ʲ mʲílə pɐmʷótɕʲ mnʲɛ. ʲa
    dʲɪjstⱼítʲɪʲnə étə tsɪnʲú.

2794

EN He donated half his wealth to charity, which was
    very generous of him.

RU Он отдáл своё состоя́ние на благотворѝтельность,
    что бы́ло óчень великодýшно с егó сторонь́.

ROM on atdál svajó səstajánjɪjɪ na bləgətvarítjel'nəst', što
    bílə óćɪn' vjɪljɪkadúšnə s jɪvó stərɑní.

IPA ɔn ɐtdáɫ svɐᵊʲǫ̵ səstɐʲǽnʲɪ̯ɪ na bləgɐtfɐrʲítʲɪʲnəstʲ, ʂtǫ
    bílə ótɕɪnʲ vʲɪʲɪkɐdúʂnə s ʲɪvʷǫ̵ stərɐní.

2795

EN Always be polite and nice to strangers. They might
be the boss at your next job.

RU Всегда́ бу́дьте ве́жливы и приве́тливы с
незнако́мцами. Кто́-то мо́жет оказа́ться ва́шим
нача́льником на сле́дующем рабо́чем ме́сте.

ROM vsjıgdá búd'tjı vjéžljıvı i prıvjétljıvı s
njıznakómtsəmjı. któ-tə móžıt əkazát'sjı vášım
naćál'njıkəm na sljéduju¢çım rıbóćım mjéstjı.

IPA fsʲɪgdá búdʲtʲɪ vʲézɭʲɪvɨ ɪ prʲɪvʲétlʲɪvɨ s
nʲɪznɐkʷómtsəmʲɪ. któ-tə mʷózɨt əkɐzátʲsʲɪ vášɪm
nɐtɕálʲnʲɪkəm na slʲédʊʲüɕɕɪm rɐbʷótɕɪm mʲéstʲɪ.

2796

EN Rashid is really angry about what his brother said.

RU Раши́д о́чень зли́тся из-за того́, что сказа́л его́
брат.

ROM rıšíd óćın' zlítsjı iz-za tavó, što skazál jıvó brat.

IPA rɐʂíd ótɕɪnʲ zlʲítsʲɪ ʲiz-za tɐvʷó, ʂtɐ skɐzáɫ ʲɪvʷó brat.

2797

EN He's upset with him because he wants to put their
parents in a nursing home.

RU Он в нём разочаро́ван, потому́ что тот хо́чет
отда́ть роди́телей в дом престаре́лых.

ROM on v njóm rızəćıróvən, pətamú što tot hóćıt atdát'
radítjeljej v dom prıstarjélıh.

IPA on v nʲóm rəzətɕɪróvən, pətɐmú ʂtɐ tɐt xótɕɨt ɐtdátʲ
rɐdʲítʲɪlʲɪj v dɐm prʲɪstɐrʲélɨx.

2798

EN In fact, his sister was even more furious when she heard it.

RU Фактически, егó сестрá оказáлась ещё бóлее рассéржена, когдá услы́шала э́то.

ROM faktíćɪskjɪ, jɪvó sjɪstrá əkazáləs' jɪççjó bóljejɪ rɪssjéržɪnə, kagdá uslíšələ étə.

IPA fᵻktʲítɕɪskʲɪ, ʲɪvʷ ó sʲɪstrá əkɐzáləsʲ ʲɪççɛ́ bʷɔ̧lʲrʲɪ rɐssʲérzʲɪnə, kɐgdá ʊslíʂələ étə.

2799

EN Are you excited about going to Europe next week?

RU Ты рад (♀рáда), что éдешь в Еврóпу на слéдующей недéле?

ROM tɪ rad (♀rádə), što jédjeś v jɪvrópu na sljédujuççɪj njɪdjéljɪ?

IPA tɨ rat (♀rádə), ʂtɔ̧ ʲédʲɪç v ʲɪvrópʊ na sʲédʊʲüççɨj nʲɪdʲélʲɪ?

2800

EN Actually, I'm upset about not getting invited to the most important conference.

RU На са́мом де́ле, я расстро́ен (♀расстро́ена) из-за того́, что не́ был приглашён (♀не была́ приглашена́) на са́мую ва́жную конфере́нцию.

ROM na sáməm djéljı, ja rısstrójın (♀rısstrójınə) iz-za tavó, što njé bıl prıglašjón (♀njɛ bılá prıglašıná) na sámuju vážnuju kanfjırjéntsıju.

IPA na sáməm dʲélʲı, ʲa rɐsstrǫ́ʲın (♀rɐsstrǫ́ʲınə) ʲiz-za tɐvʷǫ́, ştǫ nʲɛ́ bɨł prʲɪglɐ̨ɛ́n (♀nʲɛ bɨlá prʲɪglɐ̨ɛ̨iná) na sámʊʲü vázṇʊʲü kɐnfʲɪrʲéntsɨʲü.

GMS #2801 - 2900

2801

EN I'm sorry to hear that.

RU Мне о́чень жаль э́то слы́шать.
ROM mnjɛ óćın' žal' étə slíšət'.
IPA mnʲɛ ɔ́tɕinʲ zalʲ étə slíʂətʲ.

2802

EN Were you nervous about giving a speech in a foreign language?

RU Ты не́рвничал (♀ не́рвничала) по по́воду выступле́ния на иностра́нном языке́?
ROM tı njérvnjıćəl (♀ njérvnjıćələ) pa póvədu vıstupljénjıjə na jınastránnəm jızıkjé?
IPA tɨ nʲérvnʲıtɕəɫ (♀ nʲérvnʲıtɕələ) pɐ pʷɔ́vədʊ vɨstʊplʲénʲrʲə na ʲınɐstránnəm ʲɨzɨkʲé?

2803

EN I was very pleased with the audience's reception of my speech.

RU Мне бы́ло о́чень прия́тно то, как аудито́рия приняла́ моё выступле́ние.
ROM mnjɛ bílə óćın' prıjátnə to, kak audjıtórjıjə prınjılá majó vıstupljénjıjı.
IPA mnʲɛ bílə ɔ́tɕinʲ prʲrʲátnə tọ, kak ɐʊdʲɨtɔ́rʲrʲə prʲınʲılá mɐʲɵ́ vɨstʊplʲénʲrʲɨ.

2804

EN Everybody was shocked by the news on September
eleventh (11th), two thousand one (2001).

RU Все бы́ли шоки́рованы но́востью оди́ннадцатого
(11) сентября́ две ты́сячи пе́рвого (2001) го́да.

ROM vsjɛ bíljɪ šakírəvənɪ nóvəst'ju adínnədtsətəvə (11)
sjɪntjɪbrjá dvjɛ tísjaćɪ pjérvəvə (2001) gódə.

IPA fsʲɛ bíłʲɪ ʂɐkʲírəvənɨ nóvəstʲü ɐdʲínnəttsətəvə (11)
sʲɪntʲɪbrʲá dvʲɛ tísʲɪtɕɨ pʲérvəvə (2001) gʷódə.

2805

EN I was very impressed with his speech. He's an
eloquent speaker.

RU Я был (♀была́) о́чень впечатлён (♀впечатлена́)
его́ выступле́нием (ре́чью). Он красноречи́вый
ора́тор .

ROM ja bɪl (♀bɪlá) óćɪn' vpjɪćɪtljón (♀vpjɪćɪtljɪná) jɪvó
vɪstupljénjɪjɪm (rjéćju). on krɪsnarɪćívɪj arátər .

IPA ʲa bɨ́ł (♀bɨ́łá) ótɕɪnʲ fpʲɪtɕɪtlʲén (♀fpʲɪtɕɪtlʲɪná) ʲɪvʷó
vɨstʊplʲénʲɨ́ʲɪm (rʲétɕʲü). ǫn krəsnɐrʲɪtɕívɨj ɐrátər .

2806

EN I didn't enjoy my last job. When I got fed up with it, I asked to resign.

RU Мне не нравился (♀нравилась) моя последняя работа. И когда мне всё это надоело, я уволился (♀уволилась).

ROM mnjɛ njɪ nrávjɪlsjɪ (♀nrávjɪləs') majá pasljédnjajɪ rɪbótə. i kagdá mnjɛ vsjó étə nədajélə, ja uvóljɪlsjɪ (♀uvóljɪləs').

IPA mnʲɛ nʲɪ nrávʲɪɫsʲɪ (♀nrávʲɪləsʲ) mɐʲá pɐslʲédnʲrʲɪ rɐbʷɵ́tə. ɪ kɐgdá mnʲɛ fsʲɵ́ étə nədɐʲélə, ʲa ʊvʷɵ́lʲɪɫsʲɪ (♀ʊvʷɵ́lʲɪləsʲ).

2807

EN I'm sorry about the mess. I'll clean it up later.

RU Извини за беспорядок. Я приберусь позже .

ROM jɪzvjɪní za bjɪsparjádək. ja prɪbjɪrús' pózžɪ .

IPA ʲɪzvʲɪnʲí za bʲɪspɐrʲádək. ʲa prʲɪbʲɪrúsʲ pʷózʑ̩ .

2808

EN I'm sorry for shouting at you yesterday. > I'm sorry I shouted at you yesterday. — Thank you for apologizing to me.

RU Я прошу́ проще́ния за то, что накрича́л (♀накрича́ла) на тебя́ вчера́. > Извини́, что накрича́л (♀накрича́ла) на тебя́ вчера́. — Хорошо́, извине́ния при́няты.

ROM ja prašú praççjénjɪjə za to, što nakrɪćál (♀nakrɪćálə) na tjɪbjá vćɪrá. > jɪzvjɪní, što nakrɪćál (♀nakrɪćálə) na tjɪbjá vćɪrá. — hərašó, jɪzvjɪnjénjɪjə prínjɪtɪ.

IPA ʲa prɐʂú prɐççénʲrʲə za tọ, ʂtọ nɐkrʲɪtçáł (♀nɐkrʲɪtçálə) na tʲɪbʲá ftçɪrá. > ʲɪzvʲɪnʲí, ʂtọ nɐkrʲɪtçáł (♀nɐkrʲɪtçálə) na tʲɪbʲá ftçɪrá. — xərɐʂó, ʲɪzvʲɪnʲénʲrʲə prʲínʲɪtɨ.

2809

EN I feel sorry for the loser. > I pity the loser.

RU Я чу́вствую жа́лость к проигра́вшему. > Мне жаль проигра́вшего.

ROM ja ćústvuju žáləst' k prajɪgrávšɪmu. > mnjɛ žal' prajɪgrávšɪvə.

IPA ʲa tçúʊstfʊʲü záləstʲ k prɐʲɪgráfʂɪmʊ. > mnʲɛ zaḷʲ prɐʲɪgráfʂɨvə.

2810

EN Are you scared of spiders? > Are you afraid of spiders? > Are spiders scary? > Are spiders frightening?

RU Ты боишься пауков ? > Пауки страшные? > Пауки пугающие?

ROM tɪ baíśsjɪ paukóv ? > paukí strášnɪjɪ? > paukí pugájuȼȼɪjɪ?

IPA tɨ bɐʲíȼsʲɪ pɐʊkʷóf ? > pɐʊkʲí strásnɨʲɪ? > pɐʊkʲí pʊgáʲüȼȼɨʲɪ?

2811

EN Do you fear spiders? > Do spiders scare you? > Do spiders frighten you?

RU Ты боишься пауков? > Тебя пугают пауки?

ROM tɪ baíśsjɪ paukóv? > tjɪbjá pugájut paukí?

IPA tɨ bɐʲíȼsʲɪ pɐʊkʷóf? > tʲɪbʲá pʊgáʲüt pɐʊkʲí?

2812

EN I'm terrified of spiders. > Spiders terrify me.

RU Я боюсь пауков. > Пауки меня пугают.

ROM ja bajús' paukóv. > paukí mjenja pugájut.

IPA ʲa bɐʲúsʲ pɐʊkʷóf. > pɐʊkʲí mʲenʲa pʊgáʲüt.

2813

EN The giant spider in The Hobbit scared me to death!

RU Гига́нтский пау́к в «Хо́ббите» напуга́л меня до
сме́рти!

ROM gjɪgántskjɪj paúk v «hóbbjɪtjɪ» napugál mjenja da
smjértjɪ!

IPA gʲɪgántskʲɪj pɐúk f «xópbʲɪtʲɪ» nɐpʊgáł mʲenʲa dɐ
smʲértʲɪ!

2814

EN Some children feel proud of their parents, while
others are ashamed of them.

RU Не́которые де́ти гордя́тся свои́ми роди́телями, а
други́е стыдя́тся их .

ROM njékətərɪjɪ djétjɪ gardjátsjɪ svaímjɪ radítjeljamjɪ, a
drugíjɪ stɪdjátsjɪ ih .

IPA nʲékətərɨʲɪ dʲétʲɪ gɐrdʲǽtsʲɪ svɐʲímʲɪ rɐdʲítʲɪlʲɪmʲɪ, a
drʊgʲɨʲɪ stɨdʲǽtsʲɪ ʲix .

2815

EN Many children make their parents proud, while some
make their parents ashamed.

RU Мно́гие де́ти заставля́ют роди́телей горди́ться
и́ми, в то вре́мя как не́которые вызыва́ют лишь
чу́вство стыда́.

ROM mnógjɪjɪ djétjɪ zəstavljájut radítjeljej gardít'sjɪ ímjɪ, v
to vrjémjɪ kak njékətərɪjɪ vɪzɪvájut liś ćústvə stɪdá.

IPA mnógʲɨʲɪ dʲétʲɪ zəstɐvlʲǽʲüt rɐdʲítʲɪlʲɪj gɐrdʲítʲsʲɪ ʲímʲɪ, f
tɒ vrʲémʲɪ kak nʲékətərɨʲɪ vɨzɨváʲüt lʲiɕ tɕúʊstfə stɨdá.

2816

EN Don't be jealous or envious of that popular girl in school.

RU Не завидуй этой популярной девочке в школе.
ROM njɪ zavíduj étəj papuljárnəj djévəćkjɪ v škóljɪ.
IPA nʲɪ zɐvʲíduj étəj pɐpʊlʲárnəj dʲévətɕkʲɪ f ʂkʷɡ́lʲɪ.

2817

EN The police remained suspicious of the suspect's motives.

RU Полиция отнеслась с подозрением к мотивам подозреваемого.
ROM palítsɪjə atnjɪslás' s pədazrjénjɪjɪm k matívəm pədazrɪvájɪməvə.
IPA pɐlʲítsɨʲə ɐtnʲɪslásʲ s pədɐzrʲénʲrʲɪm k mɐtʲívəm pədɐzrʲɪváʲɪməvə.

2818

EN The audience was critical of the music performance.

RU Публика была настроена критически к музыкальному исполнению.
ROM públjɪkə bɪlá nastrójɪnə krɪtíćɪskjɪ k muzɪkál'nəmu jɪspalnjénjɪju.
IPA públʲɪkə bɨlá nɐstrɡ́ʲɪnə krʲɪtʲítɕɪskʲɪ k mʊzɨkálʲnəmʊ ʲɪspɐɫnʲénʲrʲ̈ʉ.

2819

EN Many countries are not tolerant of foreigners.

RU Мно́гие стра́ны не терпи́мы к иностра́нцам.

ROM mnógjɪjɪ stránɪ njɪ tjɪrpímɪ k jɪnastrántsəm.

IPA mnǫ́gʲɪ̯r̯ʲɪ stránɨ nʲɪ tʲɪrpʲímɨ k ʲɪnɐstrántsəm.

2820

EN Are you aware of the seriousness of this crime?

RU Зна́ете ли вы о серьёзности э́того преступле́ния ?
Вам изве́стно о серьёзности э́того преступле́ния?

ROM znajétjɪ li vɪ a sjɪrjóznəstjɪ étəvə prɪstupljénjɪjə ? vam
jɪzvjésnə a sjɪrjóznəstjɪ étəvə prɪstupljénjɪjə?

IPA znɐ̯ʲétʲɪ lʲi vɨ ɐ sʲɪrʲǫ́znəstʲɪ étəvə prʲɪstʊplʲénʲɪ̯r̯ʲə ? vam
ʲɪzvʲésnə ɐ sʲɪrʲǫ́znəstʲɪ étəvə prʲɪstʊplʲénʲɪ̯r̯ʲə?

2821

EN I wasn't conscious during the operation. The doctors
had given me anesthesia.

RU Я не́ был (♀ не была́) в созна́нии во вре́мя
опера́ции. Я был (♀ была́) под нарко́зом.

ROM ja njé bɪl (♀ njɛ bɪlá) v saznánjɪjɪ va vrjémjɪ
apjɪrátsɪjɪ. ja bɪl (♀ bɪlá) pad narkózəm.

IPA ʲa nʲé bɨł (♀ nʲɛ bɨlá) f sɐznánʲɪ̯r̯ʲɪ vɐ vrʲémʲɪ ɐpʲɪrátsɨ̯ɪ.
ʲa bɨł (♀ bɨlá) pɐd nɐrkʷózəm.

2822

EN I'm fully confident that you're capable of passing the exam.

RU Я абсолю́тно уве́рен (♀уве́рена), что ты спосо́бен (♀спосо́бна) сдать экза́мен.

ROM ja əbsaljútnə uvjérjɪn (♀uvjérjɪnə), što tɪ spasóbjɪn (♀spasóbnə) sdat' ɛkzámjɪn.

IPA ʲa əpsɐlʲútnə ʊvʲérʲɪn (♀ʊvʲérʲɪnə), ʂtʊ tɨ spɐsópʲɪn (♀spɐsópnə) zdatʲ ɛksámʲɪn.

2823

EN The paper I wrote for class was full of obvious mistakes.

RU Рабо́та, кото́рую я написа́л (♀написа́ла) для уро́ка была́ полна́ очеви́дных оши́бок.

ROM rɪbótə, katóruju ja napjɪsál (♀napjɪsálə) dlja urókə bɪlá palná aćɪvídnɪh ašíbək.

IPA rɐbʷótə, kɐtóruʲü ʲa nɐpʲɪsáɫ (♀nɐpʲɪsálə) dlʲa ʊrókə bɨlá pɐlná ɐtɕɪvʲídnɨx ɐʂíbək.

2824

EN He's late again. It's typical of him to keep everybody waiting.

RU Он опя́ть опозда́л. Э́то типи́чно для него́, заставля́ть всех ждать.

ROM on apját' əpazdál. étə tjɪpíčnə dlja njɪvó, zəstavlját' vsjɛh ždat'.

IPA ɔn ɐpʲætʲ əpɐzdáɫ. étə tʲɪpʲítɕnə dlʲa nʲɪvʷó, zəstɐvlʲætʲ fsʲex ʐdatʲ.

2825

EN I'm tired of eating the same food every day. Let's try something different.

RU Я устáл (♀устáла) от однóй и той же едьí кáждый день. Давáй попрóбуем чтó-то нóвое.

ROM ja ustál (♀ustálə) at adnój i toj zị jɪdí káždɪj djen'. daváj papróbujɪm štó-tə nóvəjɪ.

IPA ˡa ʊstáɫ (♀ʊstálə) ɐt ɐdnój ɪ toj zɨ ˡɪdí kázdɨj dˡenˡ. dɐváj pɐpróbʊˡɪm ʂtó̞-tə nó̞vəˡɪ.

2826

EN She told me she's arriving tonight. — Are you sure of it?

RU Онá сказáла мне, что приезжáет сегóдня вéчером. — Ты увéрен (♀увéрена) в э́том ?

ROM aná skazálə mnjɛ, što prɪjɪžžájɪt sjɪvódnjɪ vjéćɪrəm. — tɪ uvjérjɪn (♀uvjérjɪnə) v étəm ?

IPA ɐná skɐzálə mnˡɛ, ʂtọ prˡrˡɪzz̞ájɪt sˡɪvʷó̞dnˡɪ vˡétɕɪrəm. — tɨ ʊvˡérˡɪn (♀ʊvˡérˡɪnə) v étəm ?

2827

EN Shakira got married to an American, and now she's married with two (2) children.

RU Шакúра вьíшла зáмуж за америкáнца, тепéрь онá зáмужем, и у них двóе детéй .

ROM šɪkírə víšlə zámuž za amjɪrɪkántsə, tjɪpjér' aná zámužɪm, i u nih dvójɪ djɪtjéj .

IPA ʂɨkˡírə víʂlə zámʊʐ za ɐmˡɪrˡɪkántsə, tˡɪpˡérˡ ɐná zámʊz̞ɨm, ɪ u nˡix dvʷó̞ˡɪ dˡɪtˡéj .

2828

EN The customs in their country are similar to ours.

RU Таможенное управление в их стране очень похоже
    на наше.

ROM tamóžɪnnəjɪ uprɪvljénjɪjɪ v ih strɪnjé óćɪn' pahóžɪ na
    nášɪ.

IPA tɐmʷóz̪ɪnnəᶴɪ ʊprɐvlʲénʲr̥ɪ v ᶴix strɐnʲé ótɕinʲ pɐxóz̪ɪ na
    nás̪ɪ.

2829

EN The film was completely different from what I'd been
    expecting.

RU Фильм полностью отличался от того, что я
    ожидал (♀ожидала).

ROM fil'm pólnəst'ju atljɪćálsjɪ at tavó, što ja ažɪdál
    (♀ažɪdálə).

IPA fʲilʲm pʷólnəstʲü ɐtlʲɪtɕáɫsʲɪ ɐt tɐvʷó, şt̥o ᶴa ɐz̪ɪdáɫ
    (♀ɐz̪ɪdálə).

2830

EN If you're dependent on your parents, it means you still need them for money. If not, then you're financially independent.

RU Éсли вы зави́сите от ва́ших роди́телей, э́то означа́ет, вы нужда́етесь в них из-за де́нег. Éсли нет, то вы фина́нсово незави́симы .

ROM jésljı vı zavísjıtjı at vášıh radítjeljej, étə əznaćájıt, vı nuždájetjes' v nih iz-za djénjıg. jésljı njɛt, to vı fjınánsəvə njızavísjımı .

IPA ʲéslʲɪ vɨ zɐvʲísʲɪtʲɪ ɐt vášɨx rɐdʲítʲɪlʲɪj, étə əznɐtɕáʲɪt, vɨ nʊzdáʲɪtʲɪsʲ v nʲix ʲɪz-za dʲénʲɪk. ʲéslʲɪ nʲɛt, tɔ vɨ fʲmánsəvə nʲɪzɐvʲísʲɪmɨ .

2831

EN When we got to the Eiffel Tower, it was crowded with tourists.

RU Когда́ мы добрали́сь до Э́йфелевой ба́шни, там бы́ло полно́ тури́стов.

ROM kagdá mı dəbrılís' da éjfjeljıvəj bášnjı, tam bílə palnó turístəv.

IPA kɐgdá mɨ dəbrɐlʲísʲ dɐ éjfʲɪlʲɪvəj bášnʲɪ, tam bílə pɐlnó tʊrʲístəf.

2832

EN Italy is famous for its art, cuisine, architecture, history, and fashion. It's rich in culture.

RU Италия славится своим искусством, кухней, архитектурой, историей и модой. Эта страна полна культурного наследия.

ROM jıtáljıjə slávjıtsjı svaím jıskússtvəm, kúhnjej, arhjıtjıktúrəj, jıstórjıjej i módəj. étə strıná palná kul'túrnəvə nasljédjıjə.

IPA ʲıtálʲrʲə slávʲıtsʲı svɐʲím ʲıskússtfəm, kúxnʲıj, ɐrxʲıtʲıktúrəj, ʲıstǫ́rʲrʲıj ı mʷǫ́dəj. étə strɐná pɐɫná kʊlʲtúrnəvə nɐslʲédʲrʲə.

2833

EN The police are still trying to determine who was responsible for the murders.

RU Полиция до сих пор пытается определить, кто несёт ответственность за убийства .

ROM palítsıjə da sih por pıtájetsjı aprıdjılít', kto njısjót atvjétstvjınnəst' za ubíjstvə .

IPA pɐlʲítsʲə dɐ sʲix pʷǫr pıtáʲıtsʲı ɐprʲıdʲılʲít, ktǫ nʲısʲét ɐtfʲétstfʲınnəstʲ za ʊbʲíjstfə .

2834

EN Have you responded to your boss's email?

RU Ты отве́тил (♀ отве́тила) на имэ́ил (электро́нное письмо́) своего́ бо́сса?

ROM tɪ atvjétjɪl (♀ atvjétjɪlə) na jɪméjɪl (ɛljɪktrónnəjɪ pjɪs'mó) svajɪvó bóssə?

IPA tɨ ɐtʲɛtʲɪʈ (♀ ɐtʲɛtʲɪlə) na ʲɪmɛʲɪʈ (ɛʲɪktrónnəʲɪ pʲɪsʲmʷó) svɐʲɪvʷó bʷóssə?

2835

EN I can't understand this, can you explain it to me?

RU Я не могу́ поня́ть э́то, ты мо́жешь мне объясни́ть?

ROM ja njɪ magú panját' étə, tɪ móžɪś mnjɛ abjɪsnít'?

IPA ʲa nʲɪ mɐgú pɐnʲǽtʲ étə, tɨ mʷóʐɨɕ mnʲɛ ɐbʲɪsnʲítʲ?

2836

EN Let me describe to you how it happened.

RU Позво́ль мне рассказа́ть тебе́ , как э́то произошло́ .

ROM pazvól' mnjɛ rɪsskazát' tjɪbjé , kak étə prəjɪzašló .

IPA pɐzvʷólʲ mnʲɛ rəsskɐzátʲ tʲɪbʲé , kak étə prəʲɪzɐʂló .

2837

EN His lawyer refused to answer the policeman's question.

RU Его адвокат отказался отвечать на вопрос полицейского .

ROM jıvó ədvakát ətkazálsjı atvjıćát' na vaprós paljıtsjéjskəvə .

IPA ʲɪvʷǫ́ ədvɐkát ətkɐzáɫsʲɪ ɐtʃʲɪtɕátʲ na vɐprǫ́s pɐlʲɪtsʲíjskəvə .

2838

EN Don't worry, they think you're funny. They weren't laughing at you, they were laughing at your joke.

RU Не волнуйся, они думают, что ты забавный (♀забавная). Они смеялись не над тобой, а над твоей шуткой.

ROM njı valnújsjı, aní dúməjut, što tı zabávnıj (♀zabávnəjı). aní smjıjáljıs' njı nad tabój, a nad tvajéj šútkəj.

IPA nʲɪ vɐɫnújsʲɪ, ɐnʲí dúmə ʲüt, ştɔ tɨ zɐbávnɪj (♀zɐbávnə ʲɪ). ɐnʲí smʲɪ ʲɾʲǽlʲɪs ʲ nʲɪ nat tɐbʷój, a nat tfɐ ʲéj şútkəj.

2839

EN The suspect was shouting at the police very loudly.

RU Подозреваемый очень громко кричал на полицейских.

ROM pədazrıvájımıj óćın' grómkə krıćál na paljıtsjéjskjıh.

IPA pədɐzrʲɪvá ʲɪmɪj ǫ́tɕɨn ʲ grǫ́mkə krʲɪtɕáɫ na pɐlʲɪtsʲíjskʲɪx.

2840

EN The police pointed their guns at the suspect and told him to lie on the ground.

RU Полицейские напра́вили ору́жие на подозрева́емого и сказа́ли ему́ лечь на зе́млю .

ROM paljɪtsjéjskjɪjɪ naprávjɪljɪ arúžɪjɪ na pədazrɪvájɪmǝvǝ i skazáljɪ jɪmú ljeć' na zjémlju .

IPA pɐlʲɪtsɨ́jskʲɾ̩ʲɪ nɐprávʲɪlʲʲɪ ɐrúzɨ̩ʲɪ na pədɐzrʲɪváv́ʲɪmǝvǝ ɪ skɐzálʲɪ ʲɪmú lʲetɕʲ na zʲémlʲü .

2841

EN But the man reached for his pockets, and that's when the police started shooting at him.

RU Но челове́к потяну́лся к карма́нам, и и́менно тогда́ поли́ция начала́ стреля́ть в него́ .

ROM no ćɪlavjék patjɪnúlsjɪ k karmánǝm, i ímjɪnnǝ tagdá palítsɪjǝ nǝćɪlá strɪ́ljáť v njɪvó .

IPA nǫ tɕɪlɐvʲék pɐtʲɪnúɫsʲɪ k kɐrmánǝm, ɪ ʲímʲɪnnǝ tɐgdá pɐlʲítsɨ̩ǝ nǝtɕɪlá strʲɪ́lʲʲǽtʲ v nʲɪvʷǫ́ .

2842

EN And then onlookers started shouting to each other.

RU А зате́м очеви́дцы ста́ли крича́ть друг дру́гу.

ROM a zatjém aćɪvídtsɪ stáljɪ krɪćáť drug drúgu.

IPA a zɐtʲém ɐtɕɪvʲíttsɨ stálʲɪ krʲɪtɕátʲ drug drúgʊ.

2843

EN Somebody threw a shoe at the politician.

RU Кто́-то бро́сил боти́нок в поли́тика.
ROM któ-tə brósjıl batínək v palítjıkə.
IPA ktǫ́-tə brǫ́sʲıɫ bɐtʲínək f pɐlʲítʲıkə.

2844

EN I asked her to throw the keys to me from the window,
but when they hit the ground, they fell down a drain.

RU Я попроси́л (♀попроси́ла) её бро́сить мне ключи́
че́рез окно́, но когда́ они́ упа́ли на зе́млю, то
попа́ли в водосто́к.
ROM ja pəprasíl (♀pəprasílə) jıjó brósjıt' mnjɛ kljućí
ćjérjız aknó, no kagdá aní upáljı na zjémlju, to papáljı
v vədastók.
IPA ʲa pəprɐsʲíɫ (♀pəprɐsʲílə) ʲɨʲǫ́ brǫ́sʲıtʲ mnʲɛ klʲütçí
tçérʲız ɐknǫ́, nǫ kɐgdá ɐnʲí ʊpálʲı na zʲémlʲü, tǫ pɐpálʲı
v vədɐstǫ́k.

2845

EN We had a morning meeting and a discussion about
what we should do.

RU У нас бы́ло у́треннее собра́ние и обсужде́ние того́,
что мы должны́ де́лать.
ROM u nas bílə útrjennjejı sabránjıjı i absuždjénjıjı tavó,
što mı dalžní djélət'.
IPA u nas bɨ́lə útrʲınnʲɨʲɨ sɐbránʲɨʲɨ ı ɐpsʊzₔʲénʲɨʲɨ tɐvʷǫ́, ştǫ
mɨ dɐɫzₙí dʲélətʲ.

2846

EN If you're worried about it, don't just sit there, do something about it.

RU Éсли ты беспокóишься об э́том, то не сиди́ сложа́ ру́ки, сде́лай что́-то.

ROM jéslji tı bjıspakójıssjı ab étəm, to njı sjıdí slažá rúkjı, sdjéləj štó-tə.

IPA ʲésłʲɪ tɨ bʲɪspɐkʷǫ́ʲɪɕsʲɪ ɐb étəm, tǫ nʲɪ sʲɪdʲɪ́ slɐzá rúkʲɪ, zdʲéləj ʂtǫ́-tə.

2847

EN He's so selfish that he doesn't care about anybody else.

RU Он настóлько эгоисти́чен, что не забóтится ни о ком другóм, крóме себя́.

ROM on nastól'kə ɛgajıstícm, što njı zabótjıtsjı ni a kom drugóm, krómjı sjıbjá.

IPA ǫn nɐstǫ́łʲkə ɛgɐʲɪstʲítɕɨn, ʂtǫ nʲɪ zɐbʷǫ́tʲɪtsʲɪ nʲi ɐ kʷǫm drʊgʷǫ́m, krǫ́mʲɪ sʲɪbʲá.

2848

EN You're an independent person and can make your
own decisions. I don't care what you do.

RU Ты независимый человек и можешь принимать
свои собственные решения. Меня не волнует, что
ты делаешь.

ROM tı njızavísjımıj ćılavjék i móžıś prınjımát' svaí
sóbstvjınnıjı rıšjénjıjə. mjınjá njı valnújıt, što tı
djéləjeś.

IPA tɨ nʲɪzɐvʲísʲɪmɨj tɕɨlɐvʲék ɪ mʷǫzʲɪɕ prʲɪnʲɪmátʲ svɐʲí
sǫpstfʲɪnnɨʲɪ rʲɪsʲénʲrʲə. mʲɪnʲá nʲɪ vɐɫnúʲɪt, ştǫ tɨ dʲéləʲɪɕ.

2849

EN Would you care for a hot drink or some hot soup?

RU Будешь (Будете) горячий напиток или, может
быть, суп?

ROM búdjeś (búdjetjı) garjáćıj napítək ili, móžıt bıt', sup?

IPA búdʲɪɕ (búdʲɪtʲɪ) gɐrʲǽtɕɨj nɐpʲítək ʲilʲi, mʷǫzɨt bɨtʲ,
sup?

2850

EN My grandfather is already ninety (90) years old and needs somebody to care for him, so we take turns looking after him.

RU Моему́ де́душке уже́ девяно́сто лет, и ну́жен кто́-то, что́бы забо́титься о нём. Поэ́тому, мы следи́м за ним по о́череди.

ROM majımú djéduškjı užjé djıvjınóstə ljɛt, i núžın któ-tə, štóbı zabótjıt'sjı a njóm. paétəmu, mı sljıdím za nim pa óćırjedjı.

IPA mɐʲımú dʲéduşkʲı ʊzʲɨ dʲɪvʲınóstə lʲet, ı núzɨn któ-tə, ştóbɨ zɐbʷótʲɪtʲsʲı ɐ nʲə́m. pɐétəmʊ, mɨ slʲɪdʲím za nʲim pɐ ótɕɨrʲɪdʲɪ.

2851

EN Vikram and Lakshmi both take turns taking care of their elderly parents.

RU Ви́крам и Ла́кшми по о́череди забо́тятся о свои́х пожилы́х роди́телях .

ROM víkrəm i lákšmjı pa óćırjedjı zabótjatsjı a svaíh pažılíh radítjeljıh .

IPA vʲíkrəm ı lákşmʲı pɐ ótɕɨrʲɪdʲɪ zɐbʷótʲɪtsʲı ɐ svɐʲíx pɐzɨlíx rɐdʲítʲɪlʲɪx .

2852

EN I'll take care of all the travel arrangements so you don't need to worry about anything.

RU Я возьму́ на себя́ все обя́занности по организа́ции путеше́ствия, поэ́тому тебе́ не ну́жно ни о чём беспоко́иться.

ROM ja vaz'mú na sjɪbjá vsjɛ abjázənnəstjɪ pa ərganjɪzátsɪjɪ putjɪšjéstvjɪjɪ, paétəmu tjɪbjé njɪ núžnə ni a ćjóm bjɪspakójɪt'sjɪ.

IPA ʲa vɐzʲmú na sʲɪbʲá fsʲɛ ɐbʲázənnəstʲɪ pɐ ərgɐnʲɪzátsɨʲɪ pʊtʲɪşéstʲrʲɪ, pɐétəmʊ tʲɪbʲé nʲɪ núznə nʲi ɐ tɕǿm bʲɪspɐkʷǿɪtʲsʲɪ.

2853

EN Why don't you apply FOR this job? — I'd like to apply TO university instead.

RU Почему́ бы тебе́ не отпра́вить резюме́ на э́ту рабо́ту? — Я бы хоте́л (♀хоте́ла) пода́ть докуме́нты в университе́т вме́сто э́того.

ROM paćɪmú bɪ tjɪbjé njɪ atprávjɪt' rɪzjumjé na étu rɪbótu? — ja bɪ hatjél (♀hatjélə) padát' dakumjéntɪ v unjɪvjɪrsjɪtjét vmjéstə étəvə.

IPA pɐtɕɪmú bɨ tʲɪbʲé nʲɪ ɐtprávʲɪtʲ rʲɪzʲümʲé na étu rɐbʷǿtʊ? — ʲa bɨ xɐtʲéɫ (♀xɐtʲélə) pɐdátʲ dɐkʊmʲéntɨ v ʊnʲɪvʲɪrsʲɪtʲét vmʲéstə étəvə.

2854

EN You should leave FOR work earlier so you get there on time.

RU Тебе́ сто́ит вы́ехать на рабо́ту пора́ньше, чтобы быть там во́время.

ROM tjɪbjé stójɪt víjɪhət' na rɪbótu parán'šɪ, štóbɪ bɪt' tam vóvrjemjɪ.

IPA tʲɪbʲé stǫ́ʲɪt vʲ̩ɪxətʲ na rɐbʷǫ́tʊ pɐránʲʂɨ, ʂtǫ́bɨ bɨtʲ tam vʷǫ́vrʲɪmʲɪ.

2855

EN What kind of person have you dreamed of becoming?

RU Каки́м челове́ком ты мечта́л (♀мечта́ла) стать ?

ROM kakím ćɪlavjékəm tɪ mjɪćtál (♀mjɪćtálə) stat' ?

IPA kɐkʲím tɕɪlɐvʲékəm tɨ mʲɪtɕtáɫ (♀mʲɪtɕtálə) statʲ ?

2856

EN My father heard from an old friend in high school last night.

RU С мои́м отцо́м вчера́ ве́чером связа́лся его́ ста́рый шко́льный друг.

ROM s maím attsóm vćɪrá vjéćɪrəm svjɪzálsjɪ jɪvó stárɪj škól'nɪj drug.

IPA s mɐʲím ɐttsǫ́m ftɕɪrá vʲétɕɪrəm svʲɪzáɫsʲɪ ʲɪvʷǫ́ stárɨj ʂkʷǫ́lʲnɨj druk.

2857

EN You remind me of my mother's kindness.

RU Ты напоминáешь мне о доброté моéй мáмы.

ROM tɪ nəpamjɪnájeś mnjɛ a dəbratjé majéj mámɪ.

IPA tɨ nəpɐmʲɪnáʲɪç mnʲɛ ɐ dəbrɐtʲɛ́ mɐʲéj mámɨ.

2858

EN That's a good idea. Why didn't I think of that?

RU Э́то хорóшая идéя. Почемý я не подýмал
(♀подýмала) об э́том?

ROM étə haróšəjə jɪdjéjə. paćɪmú ja njɪ padúməl
(♀padúmələ) ab étəm?

IPA étə xɐróşəʲə ʲɪdʲéʲə. pɐtɕɪmú ʲa nʲɪ pɐdúmət
(♀pɐdúmələ) ɐb étəm?

2859

EN I'm glad you reminded me about the meeting,
because I'd totally forgotten about it.

RU Я рад (♀рáда), что ты напóмнил (♀напóмнила)
мне о встрéче, потомý что я совершéнно забы́л
(♀забы́ла) о ней .

ROM ja rad (♀rádə), što tɪ napómnjɪl (♀napómnjɪlə) mnjɛ
a vstrjéćɪ, pətamú što ja savjɪršjénnə zabíl (♀zabílə)
a njej .

IPA ʲa rat (♀rádə), ştɔ tɨ nɐpʷómnʲɪt (♀nɐpʷómnʲɪlə)
mnʲɛ ɐ fstrʲétɕɪ, pətɐmú ştɔ ʲa sɐvʲɪrşénnə zɐbɨ́t
(♀zɐbɨ́lə) ɐ nʲej .

2860

EN I'd like to complain to the manager about your service.

RU Я бы хотéл (♀хотéла) пожáловаться мéнеджеру о вáшем обслýживании.

ROM ja bɪ hatjél (♀hatjélə) pažáləvət'sjɪ mjénjedžɪru a vášɪm abslúžɪvənjɪjɪ.

IPA ja bɨ xɐtʲéɫ (♀xɐtʲélə) pɐzáləvətʲsʲɪ mʲénʲɪdzɨrʊ ɐ váʂɨm ɐpslúzɨvənʲɨ́ɪ.

2861

EN Samiya was complaining of a pain in her tummy, so we advised her to see a doctor as soon as possible.

RU Самúя жáловалась на боль в животé, поэ́тому мы посовéтовали ей обратúться к врачý как мóжно скорéе .

ROM samíjə žáləvələs' na bol' v žɪvatjé, paétəmu mɪ pəsavjétəvəljɪ jej əbrɪtít'sjɪ k vrɪcú kak móžnə skarjéjɪ .

IPA sɐmʲɨ́ʲə záləvələsʲ na bʷoɫʲ v zɨvɐtʲé, pɐétəmʊ mɨ pəsɐvʲétəvəlʲɪ ʲej əbrɐtʲítʲsʲɪ k vrɐtɕú kak mʷóznə skɐrʲéʲɪ .

2862

EN I knew he was strange because everybody had warned me about him.

RU Я знал (♀знáла), что он был стрáнным, потомý что меня́ все предупреди́ли об э́том.

ROM ja znal (♀ználə), što on bıl stránnım, pətamú što mjınjá vsjɛ prıduprıdíljı ab étəm.

IPA ʲa znał (♀ználə), ʂtɔ ɔn bʲił stránnɨm, pətɐmú ʂtɔ mʲɪnʲá fsʲɛ prʲɪdʊprʲɪdʲíłʲɪ ɐb étəm.

2863

EN Scientists continue to warn us about the effects of global warming.

RU Учёные продолжáют предупреждáть нас о влия́нии глобáльного потепле́ния.

ROM ućjóniji prədalžájut prıduprıždát' nas a vljıjánjıjı glabál'nəvə patjıpljénjıjə.

IPA ʊtɕɛ́nʲɪ prədɐłʐáʲüt prʲɪdʊprʲɪzdátʲ nas ɐ vlʲɪʲǽnʲɪʲɪ glɐbálʲnəvə pətʲɪplʲénʲɪʲə.

2864

EN She accused me of being selfish.

RU Онá обвини́ла меня́ в эгои́зме.

ROM aná abvjınílə mjınjá v ɛgaízmjı.

IPA ɐná ɐbvʲɪnʲílə mʲɪnʲá v ɛgɐʲízmʲɪ.

2865

EN After discovering he had been wrongly accused of murder, the authorities let him out of prison.

RU После обнаружéния тогó, что он был оши́бочно обвинён в уби́йстве, влáсти вы́пустили егó из тюрьмы́.

ROM pósljɪ əbnaružjénjɪjə tavó, što on bɪl ašíbəćnə abvjɪnjón v ubíjstvjɪ, vlástjɪ vípustjɪljɪ jɪvó iz tjur'mí.

IPA pʷǫ́slʲɪ əbnɐrʊʑɛ́nʲrʲə tɐvʷǫ́, ʂtɔ ɔn bɪɫ ɐʂíbətɕnə ɐbvʲɪnʲǫ́n v ʊbʲíjstfʲɪ, vlástʲɪ vípʊstʲɪlʲɪ ʲɪvʷǫ́ ʲis tʲʊrʲmí.

2866

EN Some students were suspected of cheating on the exam.

RU Нéкоторых студéнтов подозревáли в спи́сывании на экзáмене.

ROM njékətərɪh studjéntəv pədazrɪváljɪ v spísɪvənjɪjɪ na ɛkzámjenjɪ.

IPA nʲékətərɨx stʊdʲéntəf pədɐzrʲɪválʲɪ f spʲísɨvənʲrʲɪ na ɛksámʲɪnʲɪ.

2867

EN His parents don't approve of what he does, but they can't stop him.

RU Его роди́тели не одобря́ют того́, что он де́лает, но они́ не мо́гут останови́ть его́.

ROM jıvó radítjeljı njı ədabrjájut tavó, što on djéləjıt, no aní njı mógut əstənavít' jıvó.

IPA ʲɪvʷó rɐdʲítʲɪlʲɪ nʲɪ ədɐbrʲǽüt tɐvʷó, şto̡ o̡n dʲéləʲɪt, no̡ ɐnʲí nʲɪ mʷógut əstənɐvʲítʲ ʲɪvʷó.

2868

EN The famous actor died OF a heart attack when he was only fifty-one (51).

RU Изве́стный актёр у́мер от серде́чного при́ступа, когда́ ему́ бы́ло всего́ пятьдеся́т оди́н (51) .

ROM jızvjésnıj aktjór úmjır at sjırdjéćnəvə prístupə, kagdá jımú bílə vsjıvó pjıt'djısját adín (51) .

IPA ʲɪzvʲésnɨj ɐktʲőr úmʲɪr ɐt sʲɪrdʲétɕnəvə prʲístupə, kɐgdá ʲɪmú bílə fsʲɪvʷó pʲɪtʲdʲɪsʲát ɐdʲín (51) .

2869

EN He died FROM heart disease.

RU Он у́мер от заболева́ния се́рдца .

ROM on úmjır at zəbaljıvánjıjə sjértsə .

IPA o̡n úmʲɪr ɐt zəbɐlʲɪvánʲɪ̯ʲə sʲértsə .

2870

EN Our meal consisted of seven (7) courses.

RU Наш обéд состоя́л из семи́ блюд.
ROM naš abjéd səstajál iz sjɪmí bljud.
IPA naʂ ɐbʲét səstɐ̯ʲáɫ ʲis sʲɪmʲí blʲut.

2871

EN Water consists of hydrogen oxide.

RU Водá - э́то окси́д водорóда.
ROM vadá - étə aksíd vədaródə.
IPA vɐdá - étə ɐksʲíd vədɐródə.

2872

EN Cake consists mainly of sugar, flour, and butter.

RU Торт в основнóм состои́т из сáхара, муки́ и мáсла.
ROM tort v əsnavnóm səstaít iz sáhərə, mukí i máslə.
IPA tort v əsnɐvnóm səstɐ̯ʲít ʲis sáxərə, mʊkʲí ɪ máslə.

2873

EN I didn't have enough money to pay for the meal.

RU У меня́ бы́ло не достáточно дéнег, чтóбы
    заплати́ть за еду́.
ROM u mjɪnjá bílə njɪ dastátəčnə djénjɪg, štóbɪ zəplatítʲ za
    jɪdú.
IPA u mʲɪnʲá bílə nʲɪ dɐstátətɕnə dʲénʲɪk, ʂtóbɪ zəplɐtʲítʲ za
    ʲɪdú.

2874

EN I didn't have enough money to pay the rent.

RU У меня́ бы́ло не доста́точно де́нег, что́бы
заплати́ть за кварти́ру.

ROM u mjınjá bílə njı dastátəćnə djénjıg, štóbı zəplatít' za
kvartíru.

IPA u mʲɪnʲá bílə nʲɪ dɐstátətɕnə dʲénʲɪk, ʂtɔ́bɨ zəplɐtʲítʲ za
kfɐrtʲíru.

2875

EN When you went to the movies with your boyfriend,
did he pay for the tickets?

RU Когда́ ты с па́рнем ходи́ла в кино́, он плати́л за
биле́ты?

ROM kagdá tı s párnjım hadílə v kjınó, on platíl za bjıljétı?

IPA kɐgdá tɨ s párnʲım xɐdʲílə f kʲɪnó, ɔn plɐtʲíł za bʲɪlʲéti?

2876

EN I couldn't pay the minimum amount on my credit
card bill.

RU Я не смог (♀смогла́) вы́платить минима́льную
су́мму по креди́тной ка́рте.

ROM ja njı smog (♀smaglá) víplətjıt' mjınjımál'nuju
súmmu pa krıdítnəj kártjı.

IPA ʲa nʲɪ smʷɔk (♀smɐglá) víplətʲıtʲ mʲɪnʲɪmálʲnuʲü
súmmu pɐ krʲɪdʲítnəj kártʲı.

2877

EN After doing a homestay in England, I thanked my hosts for their kind hospitality.

RU После прожива́ния в семье́ в А́нглии, я поблагодари́л (♀поблагодари́ла) свои́х хозя́ев за гостеприи́мство.

ROM póslʲɪ praživánjɪjə v sjɪmjé v ángljɪjɪ, ja pəbləgədaríl (♀pəbləgədarílə) svaíh hazjájɪv za gastjɪprɪímstvə.

IPA pʷǿslʲɪ prɐzɨvánʲrʲə f sʲɪmʲé v ánglʲrʲɪ, ʲa pəbləgədɐrʲíɫ (♀pəbləgədɐrʲílə) svɐʲíx xɐzʲǽʲɪv za gɐstʲɪprʲrʲímstfə.

2878

EN It's difficult to forgive a murderer for his crimes.

RU О́чень тру́дно прости́ть уби́йцу за его́ преступле́ния.

ROM óćɪn' trúdnə prastít' ubíjtsu za jɪvó prɪstupljénjɪjə.

IPA ǿtɕɪnʲ trúdnə prɐstʲítʲ ʊbʲíjtsu za ʲɪvʷǿ prʲɪstʊplʲénʲrʲə.

2879

EN No matter how much a murderer apologizes for what he's done, it doesn't bring the victims back.

RU Независимо от того, сколько раз убийца принесёт свой извинения за то, что он сделал, это не вернёт его жертв назад.

ROM njɪzavísjɪmə at tavó, skól'kə raz ubíjtsə prɪnjɪsjót svaí jɪzvjɪnjénjɪjə za to, što on sdjélǝl, étə njɪ vjɪrnjót jɪvó žɪrtv nazád.

IPA nʲɪzɐvʲísʲɪmə ɐt tɐvʷó, skʷólʲkə raz ʊbʲíjtsə prʲɪnʲɪsʲ ə́t svɐʲí ʲɪzvʲɪnʲénʲɪ̯ə za tọ, ştọ ọn zdʲélǝɫ, étə nʲɪ vʲɪrnʲ ə́t ʲɪvʷó zɛrtf nɐzát.

2880

EN The misunderstanding was my fault, so I apologized.
> I apologized for the misunderstanding.

RU Недоразумение было моей ошибкой, поэтому я извинился (♀извинилась). > Я извинился (♀извинилась) за недоразумение.

ROM njɪdərɪzumjénjɪjɪ bílə majéj ašíbkəj, paétəmu ja jɪzvjɪnílsjɪ (♀jɪzvjɪníləs'). > ja jɪzvjɪnílsjɪ (♀jɪzvjɪníləs') za njɪdərɪzumjénjɪjɪ.

IPA nʲɪdərɛzʊmʲénʲɪ̯ɪ bílə mɐʲéj ɐşípkəj, pɐétəmʊ ʲa ʲɪzvʲɪnʲíɫsʲɪ (♀ʲɪzvʲɪnʲíləsʲ). > ʲa ʲɪzvʲɪnʲíɫsʲɪ (♀ʲɪzvʲɪnʲíləsʲ) za nʲɪdərɛzʊmʲénʲɪ̯ɪ.

2881

EN Don't blame your behavior on your sister. You owe her an apology.

RU Не вини́ в своём поведе́нии сестру́. Ты до́лжен (♀ должна́) пе́ред ней извини́ться.

ROM nji vjɪní v svajóm pavjɪdjénjɪjɪ sjɪstrú. tɪ dólžɪn (♀ dalžná) pjérjɪd njej jɪzvjɪnít'sjɪ.

IPA nʲɪ vʲɪnʲí f svɐʲǿm pɐvʲɪdʲénʲrʲɪ sʲɪstrú. tɨ dóɫzɨn (♀ dɐɫzná) pʲérʲɪd nʲej ʲɪzvʲɪnʲítʲsʲɪ.

2882

EN She always says everything is my fault. > She always blames me for everything.

RU Она́ всегда́ говори́т, что э́то всё моя́ вина́ . > Она́ всегда́ во всём вини́т меня́.

ROM aná vsjɪgdá gəvarít, što étə vsjó majá vjɪná . > aná vsjɪgdá va vsjóm vjɪnít mjɪnjá.

IPA ɐná fsʲɪgdá gəvɐrʲít, stǫ étə fsʲǿ mɐʲá vʲɪná . > ɐná fsʲɪgdá vɐ fsʲǿm vʲɪnʲít mʲɪnʲá.

2883

EN Do you blame the government for the economic
crisis? > I think everybody wants to blame the
government for the economic crisis.

RU Ты вини́шь прави́тельство в экономи́ческом
кри́зисе? > Я ду́маю, что ка́ждый хо́чет обвини́ть
прави́тельство в экономи́ческом кри́зисе.

ROM tɪ vjɪníś prɪvítjel'stvə v ɛkənamíćɪskəm krízjɪsjɪ? > ja
dúməju, što ká̆ždɪj hóćɪt abvjɪnít' prɪvítjel'stvə v
ɛkənamíćɪskəm krízjɪsjɪ.

IPA tɨ vʲɪnʲíç prɐvʲítʲɪlʲstfə v ɛkənɐmʲítɕɪskəm krʲízʲɪsʲɪ? >
ʲa dúməʲü, şto kázdɨj xótɕɪt ɐbvʲɪnʲítʲ prɐvʲítʲɪlʲstfə v
ɛkənɐmʲítɕɪskəm krʲízʲɪsʲɪ.

2884

EN The number of people suffering from heart disease
has increased. > The number of heart disease
sufferers has increased.

RU Число́ люде́й, страда́ющих от заболева́ния се́рдца
возросло́. > Коли́чество страда́ющих от
заболева́ния се́рдца возросло́.

ROM ćɪsló ljudjéj, strɪdájuɕɕɪh at zəbaljɪvánjɪjə sjértsə
vəzrasló. > kalíćɪstvə strɪdájuɕɕɪh at zəbaljɪvánjɪjə
sjértsə vəzrasló.

IPA tɕɪsló lʲüdʲéj, strɐdáʲüɕɕɨx ɐt zəbɐlʲɪvánʲrʲə sʲértsə
vəzrɐsló. > kɐlʲítɕɪstfə strɐdáʲüɕɕɨx ɐt zəbɐlʲɪvánʲrʲə
sʲértsə vəzrɐsló.

2885

EN   I think the increase in violent crime is the fault of
     television. > I blame the increase in violent crime on
     television.

RU   Я дýмаю, что увеличéние числá насúльственных
     преступлéний происхóдит по винé телевúдения.
     > Я виню́ телевúдение в увеличéнии числá
     насúльственных преступлéний.

ROM ja dúməju, što uvj ̍ɪljɪćjénjɪjɪ ćɪslá nasíl'stvjɪnnɪh
     prɪstupljénjɪj prajɪshódjɪt pa vjɪnjé tjɪljɪvídjenjɪjə. >
     ja vjɪnjú tjɪljɪvídjenjɪjɪ v uvjɪljɪćjénjɪjɪ ćɪslá
     nasíl'stvjɪnnɪh prɪstupljénjɪj.

IPA ʲa dúməʲü, şt̪o ʊvʲɪlʲɪtɕénʲrʲɪ tɕɪslá nɐsʲílʲstfʲɪnnɨx
     prʲɪstʊplʲénʲɪj prɐʲɪsxód̪ɪt pɐ vʲɪnʲé t̪ʲɪlʲɪvʲíd̪ʲɪnʲrʲə. > ʲa
     vʲɪnʲú t̪ʲɪlʲɪvʲíd̪ʲɪnʲrʲɪ v ʊvʲɪlʲɪtɕénʲrʲɪ tɕɪslá nɐsʲílʲstfʲɪnnɨx
     prʲɪstʊplʲénʲɪj.

2886

EN   I think the increase in suicides recently is to be
     blamed on the economy.

RU   Я дýмаю, что увеличéние самоубúйств в
     послéднее врéмя произошлó из-за эконóмики.

ROM ja dúməju, što uvjɪljɪćjénjɪjɪ səmaubíjstv v
     pasljédnjejɪ vrjémjɪ prəjɪzašló iz-za ɛkanómjɪkjɪ.

IPA ʲa dúməʲü, şt̪o ʊvʲɪlʲɪtɕénʲrʲɪ səmɐʊbʲíjstf f pɐslʲédnʲrʲɪ
     vrʲémʲɪ prəʲɪzɐşló ʲiz-za ɛkɐnómʲɪkʲɪ.

2887

EN My mother suffers from bad headaches.

RU Моя́ мать страда́ет от си́льных головны́х бо́лей.
ROM majá mat' strıdájıt at síl'nıh gəlavníh bóljej.
IPA mɐʲá matʲ strɐdáʲɪt ɐt sʲílʲnɨx gəlɐvnɨ́x bʷólʲɪj.

2888

EN Sunblock protects the skin from the harmful effects of the sun's ultraviolet (UV) rays.

RU Крем от зага́ра защища́ет ко́жу от вре́дного возде́йствия ультрафиоле́товых со́лнечных (УФ) луче́й.
ROM krjem at zagárə zaççıççájıt kóžu at vrjédnəvə vazdjéjstvjıjı ul'trıfjıaljétəvıh sólnjıćnıh (uf) lućjéj.
IPA krʲem ɐt zɐgárə zɐ̞ççi̞ççáʲɪt kʷóʐʊ ɐt vrʲédnəvə vɐzdʲéjstʲʲɪ ʊlʲtrafʲɪɐlʲétəvɪx sólnʲɪtɕnɨx (uf) lʊt̞ɕɨj.

2889

EN The rock star needs a bodyguard to protect him from crazy fans.

RU Рок-звезда́ нужда́ется в телохрани́теле, что́бы защити́ть его́ от сумасше́дших покло́нников .
ROM rak-zvjızdá nuždájetsjı v tjıləhrınítjeljı, štóbı zaççıtít' jıvó at sumassjédšıh paklónnjıkəv .
IPA rɐk-zvʲɪzdá nʊʐdáʲɪtsʲɪ f tʲɪləxrɐnʲítʲɪlʲɪ, ştóbɨ zɐ̞ççɪtʲítʲ ʲɪvʷó ɐt sʊmɐ̞ʂʂétʂɪx pɐklónnʲɪkəf .

2890

EN I don't know when I'll get home, as it depends on traffic conditions.

RU Я не зна́ю, когда́ я прие́ду домо́й, поско́льку э́то зави́сит от движе́ния на доро́гах.

ROM ja njɪ znáju, kagdá ja prɪjédu damój, paskól'ku étə zavísjɪt at dvjɪžjénjɪjə na darógəh.

IPA ʲa nʲɪ znáʲü, kɐgdá ʲa prʲɪʲédʊ dɐmʷój, pɐskʷǫ́lʲkʊ étə zɐvʲísʲɪt ɐt dvʲɪzɛ́nʲɪʲə na dɐrǫ́gəx.

2891

EN Everybody relies on her because she always keeps her promises.

RU Все доверя́ют ей, потому́ что она́ всегда́ де́ржит свои́ обеща́ния.

ROM vsjɛ davjɪrjájut jej, pətamú što aná vsjɪgdá djéržɪt svaí abjɪççánjɪjə.

IPA fsʲɛ dɐvʲɪrʲǽʲüt ʲej, pətɐmú ʂtǫ ɐná fsʲɪgdá dʲérzɨt svɐʲí ɐbʲɪççánʲɪʲə.

2892

EN His salary is so low that he doesn't have enough to live on.

RU Его́ зарпла́та насто́лько мала́, что ему́ практи́чески не на что жить .

ROM jɪvó zarplátə nastól'kə malá, što jɪmú prɪktíćɪskjɪ njɪ na što žɪt' .

IPA ʲɪvʷǫ́ zɐrplátə nɐstǫ́lʲkə mɐlá, ʂtǫ ʲɪmú prɐktʲítɕɪskʲɪ nʲɪ na ʂtǫ zɨtʲ .

2893

EN She is a very simple woman, and lives on just bread and eggs.

RU Э́та же́нщина ведёт о́чень просто́й о́браз жи́зни.
ROM étə žjénççɪnə vjɪdjót óćɪn' prastój óbrəz žíznjɪ.
IPA étə z̞énççɨnə vʲɪdʲ ̞ét ótɕɪnʲ prɛstój óbrəz zʲíznʲɪ.

2894

EN We held a party to congratulate my sister on being admitted to law school.

RU Мы провели́ вечери́нку в честь поступле́ния мое́й сестры́ в юриди́ческую шко́лу.
ROM mɪ pravjɪlí vjɪćɪrínku v ćɪst' pastupljénjɪjə majéj sjɪstrí v jurɪdíćɪskuju škólu.
IPA mɨ prɛvʲɪlʲí vʲɪtɕɪrʲínkʊ f tɕʲestʲ pɛstʊplʲénʲrʲ ̞ə mɛ ʲéj sʲɪstrí v ʲürʲɪdʲítɕɪskʊʲü ̞ ʂkʷólʊ.

2895

EN I congratulated my brother for winning the tennis tournament.

RU Я поздра́вил (♀поздра́вила) моего́ бра́та с побе́дой в те́ннисном турни́ре.
ROM ja pazdrávjɪl (♀pazdrávjɪlə) majɪvó brátə s pabjédəj v ténnjɪsnəm turnírjɪ.
IPA ʲa pɛzdrávʲɪɫ (♀pɛzdrávʲɪlə) mɛ ʲɪvʷó brátə s pɛbʲédəj f ténnʲɪsnəm tʊrnʲírʲɪ.

2896

EN You know you can rely on me if you ever need any help.

RU Зна́ешь, ты мо́жешь положи́ться на меня́, е́сли тебе́ когда́-нибудь пона́добится моя́ по́мощь.

ROM znáješ, tɪ móžɪś pəlažít'sjɪ na mjɪnjá, jésljɪ tjɪbjé kagdá-njɪbud' panádəbjɪtsjɪ majá póməçç'.

IPA zná ᶦɪç, tɨ mʷ ǫ́zɨ̇ç pəlɐzɨ́tᶦsᶦɪ na mᶦɪnᶦá, ᶦéslᶦɪ tᶦɪbᶦé kɐgdá-nᶦɪbʊdᶦ pɐnádəbᶦɪtsᶦɪ mɐ̈á pʷǫ́məçç ᶦ.

2897

EN It's terrible that some people are dying of hunger while others eat too much.

RU Э́то ужа́сно, что не́которые лю́ди умира́ют от го́лода в то вре́мя, как други́е едя́т сли́шком мно́го.

ROM étə užásnə, što njékətərɪjɪ ljúdjɪ umjɪrájut at gólədə v to vrjémjɪ, kak drugíjɪ jɪdját slíškəm mnógə.

IPA étə ʊzásnə, ştǫ nᶦékətərɨ̇ᶦɪ lᶦǘdᶦɪ ʊmᶦɪrá ᶦüt ɐt gʷǫ́lədə f tǫ vrᶦémᶦɪ, kak drʊgᶦíᶦɪ ᶦɪdᶦát slᶦíşkəm mnógə.

2898

EN The accident was my fault, so I had to pay for the repairs.

RU Я был вино́вен (♀была́ вино́вна) в ава́рии, так что я до́лжен был (♀должна́ была́) заплати́ть за ремо́нт.

ROM ja bɪl vjɪnóvjɪn (♀bɪlá vjɪnóvnə) v avárjɪjɪ, tak što ja dólžɪn bɪl (♀dalžná bɪlá) zəplatít' za rɪmónt.

IPA ʲa bɪł vʲɪnǫ́vʲɪn (♀bɪlá vʲɪnǫ́vnə) v ɐvárʲɾʲɪ, tak ștǫ ʲa dǫ́łzʲɪn bɪł (♀dɐłzná bɪlá) zəplɐtʲítʲ za rʲɪmʷǫ́nt.

2899

EN Her speech in English was impeccable, so I complimented her afterwards.

RU Её речь на англи́йском языке́ была́ безупре́чна, поэ́тому я похвали́л (♀похвали́ла) её по́сле.

ROM jɪjó rjeć' na anglíjskəm jɪzɪkjé bɪlá bjɪzuprjéćnə, paétəmu ja pəhvalíl (♀pəhvalílə) jɪjó pósljɪ.

IPA ʲɾʲǫ́ rʲetɕʲ na ɐnglʲíjskəm ʲɪzikʲé bɪlá bʲɪzʊprʲétɕnə, pɐétəmʊ ʲa pəxfɐlʲíł (♀pəxfɐlʲílə) ʲɾʲǫ́ pʷǫ́slʲɪ.

2900

EN Since she doesn't have a job, she depends on her parents for money.

RU Так как у неё нет рабо́ты, то в пла́не де́нег она́ зави́сит от роди́телей.

ROM tak kak u njɪjó njɛt rɪbótɪ, to v plánjɪ djénjɪg aná zavísjɪt at radítjeljej.

IPA tak kak u nʲrʲǫ́ nʲɛt rɐbʷǫ́tɨ, tɔ f plánʲɪ dʲénʲɪg ɐná zɐvʲísʲɪt ɐt rɐdʲítʲɪlʲɪj.

GMS #2901 - 3000

2901

EN They wore warm clothes to protect themselves from the cold.

RU Они носи́ли тёплую оде́жду, что́бы защити́ться от хо́лода.

ROM aní nasíljı tjópluju adjéždu, štóbı zaçҫıtít'sjı at hólədə.

IPA ɐnʲí nɐsʲílʲı tʲɵpluʲü ɐdʲézdʊ, ştҫbɨ zɐçҫɪtʲítʲsʲı ɐt xólədə.

2902

EN All their sweaters and blankets were not enough to prevent them from getting sick though.

RU Одна́ко, всех их сви́теров и одея́л бы́ло не доста́точно, что́бы не заболе́ть.

ROM adnákə, vsjɛh ih svítjırəv i adjıjál bílə njı dastátəҫnə, štóbı njı zəbaljét'.

IPA ɐdnákə, fsʲɛx ʲix svʲítʲırəv ı ɐdʲrʲáɫ bɨlə nʲı dɐstátətҫnə, ştҫbɨ nʲı zəbɐlʲétʲ.

2903

EN I believe in saying what I think.

RU Я ве́рю, что ну́жно говори́ть то, что ду́маешь.

ROM ja vjérju, što núžnə gəvarít' to, što dúməjeś.

IPA ʲa vʲérʲü, ştọ núznə gəvɐrʲítʲ tọ, ştọ dúmə ʲıҫ.

2904

EN Karim is a lawyer who specializes in company law.

RU Кари́м адвока́т, чья специализа́ция - корпорати́вное пра́во.

ROM karím ədvakát, ćja spjɪtsɪaljɪzátsɪjə - kərpərɪtívnəjɪ právə.

IPA kɐrʲím ədvɐkát, tɕʲa spʲɪtsɪɐlʲʲɪzátsɪʲə - kərpərɐtʲívnəʲɪ právə.

2905

EN I hope you succeed in finding the job you want.

RU Я наде́юсь, что ты преуспе́ешь в по́иске рабо́ты, кото́рую хо́чешь.

ROM ja nadjéjus', što tɪ prɪuspjéjeś v pójɪskjɪ rɪbótɪ, katóruju hóćɪś.

IPA ʲa nɐdʲéʲüsʲ, ʂto tɪ prʲɪʋspʲéʲɪɕ f pʷǿ ɪskʲɪ rɐbʷǿtɨ, kɐtórʋʲü xótɕɪɕ.

2906

EN He lost control of his car and crashed it into the highway barrier.

RU Он потеря́л контро́ль над свои́м автомоби́лем и вре́зался в шоссе́йное огражде́ние.

ROM on patjɪrjál kantról' nad svaím əvtəmabíljɪm i vrjézəlsjɪ v šassjéjnəjɪ əgrɪždjénjɪjɪ.

IPA on pɐtʲɪrʲáɫ kɐntrǿlʲ nat svɐʲím ɐftəmɐbʲílʲɪm ɪ vrʲézəɫsʲɪ f ʂɐssʲéjnəʲɪ əgrɐz̥dʲénʲɪʲɪ.

2907

EN Megan and I ran into each other on the subway on Monday.

RU Мы с Мéган столкнýлись друг с дрýгом в метрó в понедéльник .

ROM mɪ s mjégən stalknúljɪs' drug s drúgəm v mjɪtró v panjɪdjél'njɪk .

IPA mɨ s mʲégən stɐɫknúlʲɪsʲ druk s drúgəm v mʲɪtró f pɐnʲɪdʲélʲnʲɪk .

2908

EN His novels have been translated from English into thirty (30) languages.

RU Егó ромáны бы́ли переведéны с англи́йского на три́дцать языкóв.

ROM jɪvó ramánɪ bíljɪ pjɪrɪvjɪdjénɪ s anglíjskəvə na trídtsət' jɪzɪkóv.

IPA ʲɪvʷǫ́ rɐmánɪ bílʲɪ pʲɪrʲɪvʲɪdʲénɨ s ɐnglʲíjskəvə na trʲíttsətʲ ʲɪzɨkʷǫ́f.

2909

EN This book is divided into three (3) parts.

RU Эта кни́га разделенá на три чáсти.

ROM étə knígə rɪzdjɪljɪmá na tri ćástjɪ.

IPA étə knʲígə rɐzdʲɪlʲɪmá na trʲi tɕástʲɪ.

2910

EN I threw the coconut onto the rock again, and it finally split open.

RU Я ещё раз бросил (♀бросила) кокосом в скалу, и он, наконец, раскололся.

ROM ja jıççjó raz brósjıl (♀brósjılə) kakósəm v skalú, i on, nəkanjéts, rıskalólsjı.

IPA ʲa ʲɪççǿ raz brǫ́sʲɪɫ (♀brǫ́sʲɪlə) kɐkʷǿsəm f skɐlú, ɪ ǫn, nəkɐnʲéts, rəskɐlǫ́ɫsʲɪ.

2911

EN A truck collided with a bus on the highway this morning, causing a five-car pile-up.

RU Сегодня утром на шоссе столкнулись грузовик и автобус, что повлекло за собой столкновение ещё пяти автомобилей.

ROM sjıvódnjı útrəm na šassjé stalknúljıs' gruzavík i avtóbus, što pavljıkló za sabój stəlknavjénjıjı jıççjó pjıtí əvtəmabíljej.

IPA sʲɪvǿdnʲɪ útrəm na șɐssʲé stɐɫknúlʲɪsʲ gruzɐvʲík ɪ ɐftóbus, ștǫ pɐvlʲɪkló za sɐbʷój stəɫknɐvʲénʲrʲɪ ʲɪççǿ pʲɪtʲí əftəmɐbʲílʲɪj.

2912

EN Please fill this pot with water and put it on the stove to boil.

RU Пожа́луйста, напо́лни э́ту кастрю́лю водо́й и поста́вь на плиту́.

ROM pažálujstə, napólnjɪ étu kastrjúlju vadój i pastáv' na pljɪtú.

IPA pɐʐálʊjstə, nɐpʷɔ́ɫnʲɪ étʊ kɐstrʲʉ́lʲʉ vɐdɔ́j ɪ pɐstávʲ na plʲɪtú.

2913

EN Our parents provide us with food, clothing, education, healthcare and love.

RU На́ши роди́тели обеспе́чивают нас едо́й и оде́ждой, забо́тятся о на́шем образова́нии и здоро́вье и, наконе́ц, про́сто лю́бят.

ROM nášɪ radítjeljɪ abjɪspjéɕɪvəjut nas jɪdój i adjéždəj, zabótjatsjɪ a nášɪm əbrɪzavánjɪjɪ i zdaróvjɪ i, nəkanjéts, próstə ljúbjɪt.

IPA náʂɨ rɐdʲítʲɪlʲɪ ɐbʲɪspʲétɕɪvəʉt nas ʲɪdój ɪ ɐdʲéʐdəj, zɐbʷɔ́tʲɪtsʲɪ ɐ náʂɨm əbrəzɐvánʲrʲɪ ɪ zdɐrʷɔ́vʲɪ ɪ, nəkɐnʲéts, próstə lʲʉ́bʲɪt.

2914

EN Our teachers provide us with an education necessary for competing in the real world.

RU Háши преподаватели дают нам образование, необходимое, чтобы выжить в реальном мире.

ROM náši prɪpədavátjeljɪ dajút nam əbrɪzavánjɪjɪ, njɪəbhadíməjɪ, štóbɪ vížɪt' v rɪál'nəm mírjɪ.

IPA náṣɨ prʲɪpədɐvátʲɪlʲɪ dɐʲút nam əbrəzɐvánʲrʲɪ, nʲɪəbxɐdʲíməʲɪ, ṣtǫ́bɨ vízɨ̯tʲ v rʲɪálʲnəm mʲírʲɪ.

2915

EN Whatever happened to that murder case? Did the police end up finding the killer?

RU Что случилось с тем делом об убийстве? В конечном итоге полиция нашла убийцу?

ROM što slućíləs' s tjem djéləm ab ubíjstvjɪ? v kanjéćnəm jɪtógjɪ palítsɪjə našlá ubíjtsu?

IPA ṣtǫ slʊtɕíləsʲ s tʲɛm dʲéləm ɐb ʊbʲíjstfʲɪ? f kɐnʲétɕnəm ʲɪtǫ́gʲɪ pɐlʲítsɨ̯ʲə nɐṣlá ʊbʲíjtsʊ?

2916

EN They happened to come across an important piece of evidence, and now he's in prison.

RU Они нашли важную улику, и теперь он в тюрьме .

ROM aní našlí vážnuju ulíku, i tjɪpjér' on v tjur'mjé .

IPA ɐnʲí nɐṣlʲí vázn̪ʊʲü ʊlʲíkʊ, ɪ tʲɪpʲérʲ ǫn f tʲürʲmʲé .

2917

EN I wanted to stay home, but my friends insisted on my coming.

RU Я хотéл (♀хотéла) остáться дóма, но друзья́ настоя́ли на моём прихóде.

ROM ja hatjél (♀hatjélə) astát'sjɪ dómə, no druz'já nəstajáljɪ na majóm prɪhódjɪ.

IPA ʲa xɐtʲéɫ (♀xɐtʲélə) ɐstátʲsʲɪ dómə, nɒ druzʲá nəstɐʲǽlʲɪ na mɐʲǫ́m prʲɪxǫ́dʲɪ.

2918

EN How much time do you spend on your English assignments every day?

RU Скóлько врéмени ты трáтишь на задáния по англи́йскому кáждый день?

ROM skól'kə vrjémjenjɪ tɪ trátjɪś na zadánjɪjə pa anglíjskəmu káždɪj djen'?

IPA skʷǫ́lʲkə vrʲémʲɪnʲɪ tɨ trátʲɪç na zɐdánʲɪ̯ʲə pɐ ɐnglʲíjskəmʊ káz̦dɨj dʲenʲ?

2919

EN If you have trash that can be recycled, throw it away in the proper bins.

RU Если у вас есть му́сор, кото́рый мо́жет быть перерабо́тан, выбра́сывайте его́ в пра́вильные му́сорные ба́ки.

ROM jéslji u vas jest' músər, katórɪj móžɪt bɪt' pjɪrɪrɪbótən, vɪbrásɪvəjtjɪ jɪvó v právjɪl'nɪjɪ músərnɪjɪ bákjɪ.

IPA ʲéslʲɪ u vas ʲestʲ músər, kɐtórɨj mʷózɨt bɨtʲ pʲɪrʲɪrɐbʷótən, vɨbrásɨvəjtʲɪ ʲɪvʷó f právʲɪlʲnɨʲɪ músərnɨʲɪ bákʲɪ.

2920

EN Take your shoes off before coming inside my house, and please don't wake the baby up.

RU Сними́ о́бувь пе́ред вхо́дом в дом, и, пожа́луйста, постара́йся не разбуди́ть ребёнка.

ROM snjɪmí óbuv' pjérjɪd vhódəm v dom, i, pažálujstə, pəstarájsjɪ njɪ rɪzbudít' rɪbjónkə.

IPA snʲɪmʲí óbʊvʲ pʲérʲɪd fxódəm v dom, ɪ, pɐžálʊjstə, pəstɐrájsʲɪ nʲɪ rɐzbʊdʲítʲ rʲɪbʲénkə.

2921

EN The fridge isn't working because you haven't plugged it in properly.

RU Холоди́льник не рабо́тает, потому́ ты не включи́л (♀включи́ла) его́ в розе́тку, как сле́дует.

ROM həladíl'njık njı rıbótəjıt, pətamú tı njı vkljućíl (♀vkljućílə) jıvó v razjétku, kak sljédujıt.

IPA xəlɐdʲílʲnʲɪk nʲɪ rɐbʷǫ́təʲɪt, pətɐmú tɨ nʲɪ fklʲǔtɕíɫ (♀fklʲǔtɕílə) ʲɪvʷǫ́ v rɐzʲétkʊ, kak slʲédʊʲɪt.

2922

EN Xavier went to college but dropped out after a couple semesters. He's what we call a college drop-out.

RU Ксавье учи́лся в ко́лледже, но бро́сил учёбу че́рез па́ру семе́стров. Он из тех, кого́ мы называ́ем недоу́чками.

ROM ksavjɛ ućílsjı v kólljedži, no brósjıl ućjóbu ćjérjız páru sjımjéstrəv. on iz tjɛh, kavó mı nazıvájım njıdaúćkəmjı.

IPA ksavʲɛ ʊtɕíɫsʲɪ f kʷǫ́ɫʲɪdzɨ, nǫ brós'ɪɫ ʊtɕǫ́bʊ tɕérʲɪs páru sʲɪmʲéstrəf. ǫn ʲis tʲɛx, kɐvʷǫ́ mɨ nɐzɨváʲɪm nʲɪdɐútɕkəmʲɪ.

2923

EN What did you get out of your college education? — Besides a professional degree, I also made many friends for life.

RU Что ты получи́л (♀получи́ла) от своего́ вы́сшего образова́ния? — Кро́ме учёной сте́пени, у меня́ та́кже появи́лось мно́го друзе́й на всю жизнь .

ROM što tɪ palućíl (♀palućílə) at svajɪvó vísšɪvə əbrɪzavánjɪjə? — krómjɪ ućjónəj stjépjenjɪ, u mjɪnjá tákžɪ pajɪvíləs' mnógə druzjéj na vsju žɪzn' .

IPA şto tɨ pɐlʊtɕíɫ (♀pɐlʊtɕílə) ɐt svɐʲɪvʷó víşşɪvə əbrəzɐvánʲɪʲɪjə? — krómʲɪ ʊtɕę́nəj stʲépʲɪnʲɪ, u mʲɪnʲá tákşɨ pɐʲɪvʲíləsʲ mnógə druzʲéj na fsʲu zɨ̣znʲ .

2924

EN I'd promised I'd attend her wedding, now there's nothing I can do to get out of it.

RU Я обеща́л (♀обеща́ла), что бу́ду прису́тствовать на её сва́дьбе, тепе́рь я уже́ ника́к не могу́ от э́того отказа́ться.

ROM ja abjɪççál (♀abjɪççálə), što búdu prɪsútstvəvət' na jɪjó svád'bjɪ, tjɪrpjér' ja užjé njɪkák njɪ magú at étəvə ətkazát'sjɪ.

IPA ʲa ɐbʲɪççáɫ (♀ɐbʲɪççálə), şto búdʊ prʲɪsútstfəvətʲ na ʲɪʲó svádʲbʲɪ, tʲɪrpʲérʲ ʲa ʊzɨ̣ nʲɪkák nʲɪ mɐgú ɐt étəvə ətkɐzátʲsʲɪ.

2925

EN The police outsmarted the murderer; he simply couldn't get away with murder.

RU Поли́ция перехитри́ла уби́йцу, он про́сто не мог скры́ться с ме́ста преступле́ния.

ROM palítsıjə pjırıhjıtrílə ubíjtsu, on próstə njı mog skrít'sjı s mjéstə prıstupljénjıjə.

IPA pɐlʲítsɨʲə pʲɪrʲɪxʲɪtrʲílə ʊbʲíjtsʊ, ǫn prǫ́stə nʲɪ mʷǫk skrʲítʲsʲɪ s mʲéstə prʲɪstʊplʲénʲrʲə.

2926

EN You can tell Tomoko works out at the gym every day because she looks great. She jogs, takes a yoga class, does aerobics, and lifts weights.

RU Мо́жно заме́тить, что Томоко хо́дит в спортза́л ка́ждый день, потому́ что она́ вы́глядит великоле́пно. Она́ бе́гает трусцо́й, берёт уро́ки йо́ги, занима́ется аэро́бикой и поднима́ет ги́ри.

ROM móžnə zamjétjıt', što təməko hódjıt v spartzál káždıj djen', pətamú što aná vígljadjıt vjıljıkaljépnə. aná bjégəjıt trustsój, bjırjót urókjı jógjı, zanjımájetsjı aeróbjıkəj i padnjımájıt gírjı.

IPA mʷǫ́znə zɐmʲétʲɪtʲ, ştǫ təmɐkʷǫ xǫ́dʲɪt f spɐrtsáł kázdɨj dʲenʲ, pətɐmú ştǫ ɐná vʲíglʲɪdʲɪt vʲɪlʲɪkɐlʲépnə. ɐná bʲégəʲɪt trʊstsój, bʲɪrʲǫ́t ʊrǫ́kʲɪ jǫ́gʲɪ, zɐnʲɪmáʲɪtsʲɪ ɐɛrǫ́bʲɪkəj ɪ pɐdnʲɪmáʲɪt gʲírʲɪ.

2927

EN It seems that Ludwig and Rita's relationship is having trouble, but we really hope they work it out.

RU Ка́жется, что в отноше́ниях Лю́двига и Ри́ты возни́кли пробле́мы, но мы действи́тельно наде́емся, что у них всё нала́дится.

ROM kážɪtsjɪ, što v ətnašjénjɪjɪh ljúdvjɪgə i rítɪ vazníkljɪ prabljémɪ, no mɪ djɪjstvítjel'nə nadjéjemsjɪ, što u nih vsjó naládjɪtsjɪ.

IPA kázɨtsʲɪ, ştọ v ətnɐşénʲrʲɪx lʲʉdvʲɪgə ɪ rʲítɨ vɐznʲíklʲɪ prɐblʲémɨ, nọ mɨ dʲɪjstfʲítʲɪlʲnə nɐdʲéʲɪmsʲɪ, ştọ u nʲix fsʲǫ nɐládʲɪtsʲɪ.

2928

EN The two (2) companies worked out a cooperation agreement.

RU Э́ти две компа́нии разрабо́тали соглаше́ние о сотру́дничестве.

ROM étjɪ dvjɛ kampánjɪjɪ rɪzrɪbótəljɪ səglašjénjɪjɪ a satrúdnjɪćɪstvjɪ.

IPA étʲɪ dvʲɛ kɐmpánʲrʲɪ rəzrɐbʷǫtəlʲɪ səglɐşénʲrʲɪ ɐ sɐtrúdnʲɪtɕɪstfʲɪ.

2929

EN Nobody believed Sara at first, but she turned out to be right.

RU Никто́ не ве́рил Са́ре снача́ла, но она́ оказа́лась права́.

ROM njɪktó njɪ vjérjɪl sárjɪ snaćálə, no aná əkazáləs' prɪvá.

IPA nʲɪktó nʲɪ vʲérʲɪɫ sárʲɪ snɐtɕálə, n̥ ɐná əkɐzáləsʲ prɐvá.

2930

EN Better find a gas station. We're running out of gas.

RU Лу́чше найти́ запра́вку. У нас зака́нчивается бензи́н.

ROM lúćśɪ najtí zaprávku. u nas zakánćɪvəjetsjɪ bjɪnzín.

IPA lútɕɕɪ nɐjtʲí zɐpráfkʊ. u nas zɐkántɕɪvɐ jɪtsʲɪ bʲɪnzʲín.

2931

EN Please buy more toilet paper before you use it all up.

RU Пожа́луйста, купи́ ещё туале́тной бума́ги пре́жде, чем мы испо́льзуем э́ту.

ROM pažálujstə, kupí jɪɕɕjó tualjétnəj bumágjɪ prjéždjɪ, ćɪm mɪ jɪspól'zujɪm étu.

IPA pɐzálujstə, kʊpʲí ʲɪɕɕɵ tʊɐlʲétnəj bʊmágʲɪ prʲéʑdʲɪ, tɕɛm mɪ ʲɪspʷólʲzʊ jɪm étʊ.

2932

EN I'm sorry, the book you're looking for isn't in stock. It's all sold out.

RU Мне о́чень жаль, но кни́га, кото́рую вы и́щете отсу́тствует на скла́де. Они́ все распро́даны.

ROM mnje óćın' žal', no knígə, katóruju vɪ íççɪtjɪ atsútstvujɪt na skládjɪ. aní vsjɛ rɪspródənɪ.

IPA mnʲɛ ǫ́tɕɨnʲ zalʲ, nǫ knʲígə, kɐtǫ́ruʲü vɨ ʲíɕɕɨtʲɪ ɐtsútstfʊʲɪt na skládʲɪ. ɐnʲí fsʲɛ rɐsprǫ́dənɨ.

2933

EN I've been handing out business cards all day, and now I'm all out of them.

RU Я раздава́л (♀раздава́ла) визи́тки весь день, и тепе́рь они́ зако́нчились.

ROM ja rɪzdavál (♀rɪzdaválə) vjɪzítkjɪ vjes' djen', i tjɪpjér' aní zakónćɪljɪs'.

IPA ʲa rəzdɐváł (♀rəzdɐválə) vʲɪzʲítkʲɪ vʲesʲ dʲenʲ, ɪ tʲɪpʲérʲ ɐnʲí zɐkʷǫ́ntɕɨlʲɪsʲ.

2934

EN Valentina found a beautiful dress at the department store, but she wanted to try it on before she bought it.

RU Валенти́на нашла́ краси́вое пла́тье в универма́ге, но она́ хоте́ла поме́рить его́ пре́жде, чем купи́ть.

ROM valjɪntínə našlá krɪsívəjɪ plát'jɪ v unjɪvjɪrmágjɪ, no aná hatjélə pamjérjɪt' jɪvó prjéždjɪ, ćɪm kupít'.

IPA vɐlʲɪntʲínə nɐslá krɐsʲívəʲɪ plátʲɪ v ʊnʲɪvʲɪrmágʲɪ, nǫ ɐná xɐtʲélə pɐmʲérʲɪtʲ ʲɪvʷǫ́ prʲézdʲɪ, tɕɛm kʊpʲítʲ.

2935

EN Please don't stop telling your story, please go on.

RU Пожа́луйста, продолжа́й расска́зывать исто́рию
    да́льше, не остана́вливайся.

ROM pažálujstə, prədalžáj rısskázıvət' jıstórjıju dál'šı, njı
    əstaná̆vljıvəjsjı.

IPA pɐzálujstə, prədɐɫzáj rɐsskázɨvətʲ ʲıstǫ́rʲɨ̯ʲü dálʲşɨ, nʲı
    əstɐná̆vlʲıvəjsʲı.

2936

EN The concert had to be called off because of the
    typhoon.

RU Конце́рт пришло́сь отмени́ть из-за тайфу́на.

ROM kantsjért prıšlós' atmjınít' iz-za tajfúnə.

IPA kɐntsért prʲışlǫ́sʲ ɐtmʲɪnʲítʲ ʲiz-za tɐjfúnə.

2937

EN Tomorrow I'm off to Paris.

RU За́втра я уезжа́ю в Пари́ж.

ROM závtrə ja ujıžžáju v paríž.

IPA záftrə ʲa ʊʲızzá̆ʲü f pɐrʲíş.

2938

EN Oscar left home at the age of eighteen (18) and went off to Spain.

RU Óскар ушёл из дóма в вóзрасте восемнáдцати (18) лет и отпрáвился в Испáнию.

ROM óskər ušjól iz dómə v vózrəstjı vasjımnádtsətjı (18) ljet i atprávjılsjı v jıspánjıju.

IPA óskər ʊʂɛ́ɫ ʲiz dómə v vʷózrəstʲı vɐsʲımnáttsətʲı (18) lʲɛt ı ɐtprávʲıɫsʲı v ʲıspánʲrʲü.

2939

EN Our plane was delayed on the tarmac and we couldn't take off for an hour.

RU Наш самолёт был задéржан, и мы не моглú вы́лететь в течéние чáса.

ROM naš səmaljót bıl zadjéržən, i mı njı maglí víljetjet' v tjıćjénjıjı ćásə.

IPA naʂ səmɐlʲɛ́t bıɫ zɐdʲérzən, ı mɨ nʲı mɐɡlʲí vílʲıtʲıtʲ f tʲıtɕénʲrʲı tɕásə.

940

EN My parents and friends saw me off at the airport before I embarked on my adventure around the world.

RU Мой роди́тели и друзья́ проводи́ли меня́ в аэропо́рт пе́ред тем, как я отпра́вился (♀ отпра́вилась) в кругосве́тное путеше́ствие.

ROM maí radítjeljı i druz'já prəvadíljı mjınjá v aɛrapórt pjérjıd tjɛm, kak ja atprávjılsjı (♀ atrávjıləs') v krugasvjétnəjı putjıšjéstvjıjı.

IPA mɐʲí rɐdʲítʲɪlʲɪ i druzʲá prəvɐdʲílʲɪ mʲɪnʲá v aɛrɐpʷórt pʲérʲɪt tʲɛm, kak ʲa ɐtprávʲɪɫsʲɪ (♀ ɐtprávʲɪləsʲ) f krʊɡɐsvʲétnəʲɪ pʊtʲɪʂéstfʲɪʲɪ.

941

EN I don't want to keep going on discussing marketing, let's move on to the production issues.

RU Я не хочу́ продолжа́ть обсужда́ть ми́ркетинг, дава́йте перейдём к произво́дственным вопро́сам.

ROM ja njı haćú prədalžát' absuždát' mírkjetjıng, davájtjı pjırıjdjóm k prajızvódstvjınnım vaprósəm.

IPA ʲa nʲɪ xɐtɕú prədəɫʐátʲ ɐpsʊʐdátʲ mʲírkʲɪtʲɪnk, dɐvájtʲɪ pʲɪrʲɪjdʲɵm k prɐʲɪzvʷótstfʲɪnnɨm vɐprósəm.

942

EN Mahmud always dozes off in economics class.

RU Махму́д всегда́ засыпа́ет на уро́ке эконо́мики.

ROM mahmud vsjıgdá zasıpájıt na urókjı ɛkanómjıkjı.

IPA maxmud fsʲɪɡdá zɐsɨpáʲɪt na ʊrókʲɪ ɛkɐnómʲɪkʲɪ.

2943

EN The food was lousy and the service sucked, then they charged us an arm and a leg! We totally got ripped off!

RU Еда́ была́ парши́вой, а обслу́живание отврати́тельным, пото́м они́ ещё содра́ли с нас ку́чу де́нег! Мы оста́лись без копе́йки!

ROM jɪdá bɪlá paršívəj, a abslúžɪvənjɪjɪ ətvrɪtítjel'nɪm, patóm aní jɪççjó sadráljɪ s nas kúću djénjɪg! mɪ astáljɪs' bɪs kapjéjkjɪ!

IPA ʲɪdá bɨlá pɐrʂívəj, a ɐpslúʐɨvən ʲrʲɪ ətfrɐtʲítʲɪlʲnɨm, pɐtóm ɐnʲí ʲɪççɘ́ sɐdrálʲɪ s nas kútçʊ dʲénʲɪk! mɪ ɐstálʲɪsʲ bʲɪs kɐpʲéjkʲɪ!

2944

EN He always buys expensive things to show off.

RU Он всегда́ покупа́ет дороги́е ве́щи, что́бы похва́статься .

ROM on vsjɪgdá pakupájɪt dəragíjɪ vjéççɪ, štóbɪ pahvástət'sjɪ .

IPA ɔn fsʲɪgdá pɐkupáʲɪt dərɐɡʲíʲɪ vʲéççɪ, ʂtóbɨ pɐxfástətʲsʲɪ .

2945

EN Some old houses were torn down to make room for a new housing development. The owners of the houses tried to protest, but it was to no avail.

RU Некоторые старые дома были снесены, чтобы освободить место для нового строительства. Владельцы домов пытались протестовать, но всё было безрезультатно.

ROM njékətərıjı stárıjı damá bíljı snjısjıní, štóbı əsvəbadít' mjéstə dlja nóvəvə straítjel'stvə. vladjél'tsı damóv pıtáljıs' prətjıstavát', no vsjó bílə bjızrızul'tátnə.

IPA nʲékətərɨʲɪ stárɨʲɪ dɐmá bílʲɪ snʲɪsʲɪɲí, ʂtóbɨ əsvəbɐdʲítʲ mʲéstə dlʲa nóvəvə strɐʲítʲɪlʲstfə. vlɐdʲélʲtsɨ dɐmʷóf pɨtálʲɪsʲ prətʲɪstɐvátʲ, nɐ fsʲǿ bílə bʲɪzrʲɪzʊlʲtátnə.

2946

EN One man was so upset by the whole ordeal that he commited suicide.

RU Один человек был так расстроен всеми испытаниями, что покончил жизнь самоубийством.

ROM adín ćılavjék bıl tak rısstrójın vsjémjı jıspıtánjıjamjı, što pakónćıl žızn' səmaubíjstvəm.

IPA ɐdʲín tɕɪlɐvʲék bɨɫ tak rəsstrǿʲın fsʲémʲɪ ʲɪspɨtánʲɪʲrʲɪmʲɪ, ʂtɐ pɐkʷóntɕɪɫ zɨzɲ səmɐʊbʲíjstfəm.

2947

EN The firefighters were able to put the fire out before the house burned down.

RU Пожа́рные смогли́ потуши́ть ого́нь до того́, как дом сгоре́л.

ROM pažárnıjı smaglí patušít' agón' da tavó, kak dom sgarjél.

IPA pɐzárnɨʲɪ smɐglʲí pɐtʊʂítʲ ɐgʷónʲ dɐ tɐvʷó, kak dom sgɐrʲéɫ.

2948

EN However, the firefighters had a hard time trying to calm a woman down. Apparently, her cat perished in the fire.

RU Тем не ме́нее, пожа́рные с трудо́м пыта́лись успоко́ить же́нщину. Су́дя по всему́ её ко́шка поги́бла в огне́.

ROM tjɛm njı mjénjejı, pažárnıjı s trudóm pıtáljıs' uspakójıt' žénççınu. súdjı pa vsjımú jıjó kóškə pagíblə v agnjé.

IPA tʲɛm nʲɪ mʲénʲrʲɪ, pɐzárnɨʲɪ s trʊdóm pɨtálʲɪsʲ ʊspɐkʷóʲɪtʲ zénççɨnʊ. súdʲɪ pɐ fsʲɪmú ʲrʲǿ kʷóʂkə pɐgʲíblə v ɐgnʲé.

2949

EN Talks between Russia and the United States have broken down.

RU Переговóры мéжду Россúей и США потерпéли неудáчу.

ROM pjɪrɪgavórɪ mjɛ́ždu rassíjej i sɪša patjɪrpjéljɪ njɪudáću.

IPA pʲɪrʲɪgɐvʷo̞rɨ mʲɛ́zd̪ʊ rɐssʲíʲɪj ɪ sɨʂa pɐtʲɪrpʲélʲɪ nʲɪʊdátɕʊ.

2950

EN After college, Zahida was turned down from every job she applied for. Finding a job was difficult.

RU Пóсле окончáния кóлледжа Захúде откáзывали в кáждом мéсте, кудá онá отправля́ла резюмé. Ей бы́ло óчень трýдно найтú рабóту.

ROM pósljɪ əkanćánjɪjə kólljɪdžə zahídjɪ atkázɪvəljɪ v káždəm mjéstjɪ, kudá aná ətprɪvljálə rɪzjumjɛ́. jej bílə óćɪn' trúdnə najtí rɪbótu.

IPA pʷo̞slʲɪ əkɐntɕánʲɪʲə kʷo̞ɫʲɪdzə zɐxʲídʲɪ ɐtkázɨvəlʲɪ f kázd̪əm mʲéstʲɪ, kʊdá ɐná ətprɐvlʲálə rʲɪzʲʉmʲɛ́. ʲej bɨ́lə o̞tɕɨnʲ trúdnə nɐjtʲí rɐbʷo̞tʊ.

2951

EN When Ichirou had just arrived in London, a man came up to him in the street and asked for money, so he gave him a few Japanese yen.

RU Когда́ Ичиру то́лько прие́хал в Ло́ндон, како́й-то мужчи́на подошёл к нему́ на у́лице и попроси́л де́нег, так что он дал ему́ не́сколько япо́нских иен.

ROM kagdá ićıru tól'kə prıjéhəl v lóndən, kakój-tə muśśínə pədašjól k njımú na úljıtsı i pəprasíl djénjıg, tak što on dal jımú njéskəl'kə jıpónskjıh ijɛn.

IPA kɐgdá ʲitɕiru tólʲkə prʲrʲéxəl v lóndən, kɐkʷój-tə mʊɕɕínə pədɐʂǫ́ɫ k nʲımú na úlʲıtsɨ ı pəprɐsʲíɫ dʲénʲık, tak ʂtɔ ǫn daɫ ʲımú nʲéskəlʲkə ʲıpʷǫ́nskʲıx ʲịʲɛn.

2952

EN The police are going to ask us a lot of questions, so we need to back each other up.

RU Поли́ция собира́ется зада́ть нам мно́го вопро́сов, поэ́тому мы должны́ прикры́ть друг дру́га .

ROM palítsıjə sabjırájetsjı zadát' nam mnógə vaprósəv, paétəmu mı dalžní prıkrít' drug drúgə .

IPA pɐlʲítsɨ̣ə sɐbʲırájıtsʲı zɐdátʲ nam mnógə vɐprǫ́səf, pɐétəmʊ mɨ dɐɫzņí prʲıkrítʲ drug drúgə .

2953

EN The police set up a special task force to investigate the murders.

RU В поли́ции была́ со́здана специа́льная целева́я гру́ппа для рассле́дования уби́йств.

ROM v palítsıjı bılá sózdənə spjıtsíəl'nəjı tsıljıvájə grúppə dlja rıssljédəvənjıjə ubíjstv.

IPA f pɐlʲítsʲɪ bɨlá sózdənə spʲɪtsíəlʲnəʲɪ tsɨlʲɪvǽʲə grúppə dlʲa rɐsslʲédəvənʲɪʲə ʊbʲíjstf.

2954

EN You should always back up your computer files just in case the hard drive dies.

RU Вы должны́ всегда́ де́лать резе́рвную ко́пию фа́йлов компью́тера на слу́чай, е́сли полети́т жёсткий диск.

ROM vı dalžní vsjıgdá djélət' rızjérvnuju kópjıju fájləv kampjútjırə na slúćəj, jésljı paljıtít žjóstkjıj disk.

IPA vɨ dɐlzní fsʲɪgdá dʲélət rʲɪzʲérvnʊʲü kʷópʲɪʲü fájləf kɐmpʲútʲɪrə na slútɕəj, ʲéslʲɪ pɐlʲɪtʲít zɵstkʲɪj dʲisk.

2955

EN You should always save your files as you're working on them just in case your computer crashes.

RU Сле́дует всегда́ сохраня́ть фа́йлы не́сколько раз по ме́ре рабо́ты на слу́чай, е́сли ваш компью́тер зави́снет.

ROM sljédujɪt vsjɪgdá səhrɪnját' fájlɪ njéskəl'kə raz pa mjérjɪ rɪbótɪ na slúćəj, jésljɪ vaš kampjútjɪr zavísnjɪt.

IPA slʲédʊʲɪt fsʲɪgdá səxrɐnʲǽtʲ fájlɨ nʲéskəlʲkə ras pɐ mʲérʲɪ rɐbʷǫ́tɨ na slútɕəj, ʲéslʲɪ vaʂ kɐmpʲǘtʲɪr zɐvʲísnʲɪt.

2956

EN The police accidentally shot and killed a man. They tried to cover up what really happened, but it became a big scandal.

RU Полице́йский случа́йно вы́стрелил и уби́л челове́ка. Поли́ция пыта́лась скрыть то, что произошло́ на са́мом де́ле, но э́то преврати́лось в большо́й сканда́л.

ROM paljɪtsjéjskjɪj slućájnə vístrjeljɪl i ubíl ćɪlavjékə. palítsɪjə pɪtáləs' skrɪt' to, što prəjɪzašló na sáməm djéljɪ, no étə prɪvrɪtíləs' v bal'šój skandál.

IPA pɐlʲɪtsɨ́jskʲɪj slʊtɕájnə vʲístrʲɪlʲɪɫ ɪ ʊbʲíɫ tɕɨlɐvʲékə. pɐlʲítsɨʲə pɨtáləsʲ skrɨtʲ tǫ, ʂtǫ prəʲɪzɐɕɫó na sáməm dʲélʲɪ, nǫ étə prʲɪvrɐtʲíləsʲ v bɐlʲʂǫ́j skɐndáɫ.

957

EN They couldn't just brush it under the carpet and
expect everything to blow over and go away.

RU Они́ не могли́ про́сто утаи́ть э́то и ждать, что
пра́вда никогда́ не всплывёт.

ROM aní njı maglí próstə utaít' étə i ždat', što právdə
njıkagdá njı vsplıvjót.

IPA ɐnʲí nʲɪ mɐɡlʲí próstə ʊtɐʲítʲ étə ɪ ʐdatʲ, ʂt̪ɔ právdə
nʲɪkɐɡdá nʲɪ fsplɪvʲɵ́t.

958

EN The murder suspect got bad press, but he wasn't the
culprit; he was not the man who did it.

RU Подозрева́емый в уби́йстве подве́ргся напа́дкам со
стороны́ пре́ссы, но он был не вино́вен, он не́ был
челове́ком, кото́рый сде́лал э́то.

ROM pədazrıvájımıj v ubíjstvjı padvjérgsjı napádkəm sa
stəraní prjéssı, no on bıl njı vjınóvjın, on njé bıl
ćılavjékəm, katórıj sdjéləl étə.

IPA pədɐzrʲɪvájɪmɨj v ʊbʲíjstfʲɪ pɐdvʲérgsʲɪ nɐpátkəm sɐ
stərɐní prʲéssɨ, nɔ ɔn bɨł nʲɪ vʲɪnóvʲɪm, ɔn nʲé bɨł
tɕɪlɐvʲékəm, kɐtórɨj zdʲéləł étə.

2959

EN Since he got so much bad press, it wouldn't just blow over. Everybody knew him now.

RU Так как о нём писáли во всех газéтах, то всё э́то не моглó пройти́ бесслéдно. Тепéрь егó все знáли.

ROM tak kak a njóm pjısáljı va vsjɛh gazjétəh, to vsjó étə njı magl ó prajtí bjıssljédnə. tjıpjér' jıvó vsjɛ ználjı.

IPA tak kak ɐ nʲê̞m pʲɪsálʲɪ vɐ fsʲex gɐzʲétəx, tɐ fsʲ ê̞ étə nʲɪ mɐglê̞ prɐjtʲí bʲɪsslʲédnə. tʲɪpʲérʲ ʲɪvʷê̞ fsʲɛ ználʲɪ.

2960

EN So he sued and was awarded compensation for damage to his reputation.

RU Поэ́тому он пóдал в суд, где емý пообещáли компенси́ровать ущéрб, нанесённый егó репутáции.

ROM paétəmu on pódəl v sud, gdjɛ jımú paabjıççáljı kampjınsírəvət' uççjérb, nanjısjónnıj jıvó rıputátsıjı.

IPA pɐétəmu ɐn pʷódəɫ f sut, gdʲɛ ʲɪmú pɐɐbʲɪççálʲɪ kɐmpʲɪnsʲírəvətʲ uççérp, nɐnʲɪsʲ ê̞nnij ʲɪvʷê̞ rʲɪputátsɨʲɪ.

2961

EN We just won a new contract, but completing it will take up the next three (3) months.

RU Мы то́лько что вы́играли но́вый контра́кт, но его́ заверше́ние займёт ближа́йшие три ме́сяца .

ROM mɪ tól'kə što víjɪgrəljɪ nóvɪj kantrákt, no jɪvó zavjɪršjénjɪjɪ zajmjót bljɪžájšɪjɪ tri mjésjɪtsə .

IPA mɨ tó̞l⁽ʲ⁾kə ʂtɔ̞ vʲˠɪgrəl̠ʲɪ nó̞vɨj kɐntrákt, nɔ̞ ʲɪvʷó̞ zɐvʲˠɪrʂén̪ʲr̠ʲɪ zɐjmʲˠé̞t bl̠ʲɨzájʂɨ̠ʲɪ tr̠ʲi mʲˠés̠ʲɪtsə .

2962

EN My parents were away on business when I was a child, so my grandparents brought me up. > My grandparents raised me.

RU Мой роди́тели постоя́нно бы́ли в командиро́вках, когда́ я был (♀ была́) ребёнком, так что меня́ расти́ли (воспи́тывали) ба́бушка с де́душкой. > Меня́ вы́растили (воспита́ли) мои́ ба́бушка и де́душка.

ROM maí radítjeljɪ pəstajánnə bíljɪ v kəmandjɪróvkəh, kagdá ja bɪl (♀ bɪlá) rɪbjónkəm, tak što mjɪnjá rɪstíljɪ (vaspítɪvəljɪ) bábuškə s djéduškəj. > mjɪnjá vírəstjɪljɪ (vaspjɪtáljɪ) maí bábuškə i djéduškə.

IPA mɐˠí red̠ʲít̠ʲr̠ʲɪ pəstɐˠánnə bíl̠ʲɪ f kəmɐnd̠ʲɪró̞fkəx, kɐgdá ʲa bɨɫ (♀ bɨlá) r̠ʲɨbʲˠé̞nkəm, tak ʂtɔ̞ mʲˠɪn̠ʲá rest̠ʲíl̠ʲɪ (vɐsp̠ʲítɨvəl̠ʲɪ) bábʊʂkə s d̠ʲé̞dʊʂkəj. > mʲˠɪn̠ʲá vírəst̠ʲɪl̠ʲɪ (vɐsp̠ʲɪtál̠ʲɪ) mɐˠí bábʊʂkə ɪ d̠ʲé̞dʊʂkə.

2963

EN If you can't find a hotel for the night, you'll end up sleeping on the street.

RU Éсли ты не смóжешь найти́ отéль, в конéчном счёте ты бýдешь спать на ýлице.

ROM jésljɪ tɪ njɪ smóžɨś najtí atél', v kanjéćnəm śśjótjɪ tɪ búdjeś spat' na úljɪtsɪ.

IPA ʲésl̩ʲɪ tɨ nʲɪ smʷózɨ̞ɕ nɐjtʲí ɐtél̩ʲ, f kɐnʲétɕnəm ɕɕótʲɪ tɨ búdʲɪɕ spatʲ na úl̩ʲɪtsɨ.

2964

EN There was a fight on the street and three (3) men ended up in the hospital.

RU На ýлице былá дрáка, пóсле котóрой трóе мужчи́н попáли в больни́цу.

ROM na úljɪtsɪ bɪlá drákə, pósljɪ katórəj trójɪ muśśín papáljɪ v bal'nítsu.

IPA na úl̩ʲɪtsɨ bɨlá drákə, pʷósl̩ʲɪ kɐtórəj tróʲɪ mʊtɕín pɐpál̩ʲɪ v bɐl̩ʲnʲítsʊ.

2965

EN Don't argue with the police officer, or you'll just end up getting arrested.

RU Не спóрьте с полицéйскими или, в конце-концóв, вас прóсто арестýют.

ROM njɪ spór'tjɪ s paljɪtsjéjskjɪmjɪ ili, v kəntsɪ-kantsóv, vas próstə arɪstújut.

IPA nʲɪ spʷór̩ʲtʲɪ s pɐl̩ʲɪtsɨ́jskʲɪmʲɪ ʲil̩ʲi, f kəntsɨ-kɐntsóf, vas próstə ɐrʲɪstúʲüt.

2966

EN There are two (2) universities in the city, and
students make up twenty percent (20%) of the
population.

RU В э́том го́роде два университе́та, а студе́нты
составля́ют два́дцать проце́нтов (20%) населе́ния.

ROM v étəm górədjɪ dva unjɪvjɪrsjɪtjétə, a studjéntɪ
səstavljájut dvádtsət' pratsjéntəv (20%) nasjɪljénjɪjə.

IPA v étəm gʷórədʲɪ dva ʊnʲɪvʲɪrsʲɪtʲétə, a stʊdʲéntɨ
səstɐvlʲǽʲüt dváttsətʲ prɛtséntəf (20%) nɐsʲɪlʲénʲɨ́ʲə.

2967

EN I'll be ready in a few minutes. You go on ahead and
I'll catch up with you.

RU Я бу́ду гото́в (♀гото́ва) че́рез не́сколько мину́т.
Иди́ вперёд, я догоню́.

ROM ja búdu gatóv (♀gatóvə) ćjérjɪz njéskəl'kə mjɪnút.
jɪdí vpjɪrjód, ja dəganjú.

IPA ʲa búdʊ gɐtóf (♀gɐtóvə) tɕérʲɪz nʲéskəlʲkə mʲɪnút. ʲɪdʲí
fpʲɪrʲét, ʲa dəgɐnʲú.

2968

EN My parents dropped me off at the airport two (2) hours before my flight was scheduled to take off.

RU Мои́ роди́тели вы́садили меня́ в аэропорту́ за два часа́ до вы́лета моего́ ре́йса.

ROM maí radítjeljɪ vísədjɪljɪ mjenja v aɛrəpartú za dva ćɪsá da víljɪtə majɪvó rjéjsə.

IPA mɐ^jí rɐdʲítʲɪlʲɪ vísədʲɪlʲɪ mʲenʲa v aɛrəpɐrtú za dva tɕɪsá dɐ vílʲɪtə mɐ^jɪvʷó rʲéjsə.

2969

EN My parents were there again to pick me up when I flew back home.

RU Мои́ роди́тели бы́ли там сно́ва, что́бы встре́тить, когда́ я прилете́л (♀прилете́ла) домо́й.

ROM maí radítjeljɪ bíljɪ tam snóvə, štóbɪ vstrjétjɪt', kagdá ja prɪljɪtjél (♀prɪljɪtjélə) damój.

IPA mɐ^jí rɐdʲítʲɪlʲɪ bílʲɪ tam snóvə, ʂtóbɪ fstrʲétʲɪtʲ, kɐgdá ^ja prʲɪlʲɪtʲéɫ (♀prʲɪlʲɪtʲélə) dɐmʷój.

2970

EN Simon is terribly creative, and is always coming up with great ideas.

RU Са́ймон о́чень тво́рческая ли́чность, ему́ всегда́ прихо́дят в го́лову отли́чные иде́и.

ROM sájmən óćɪn' tvórćɪskəjɪ líćnəst', jɪmú vsjɪgdá prɪhódjɪt v góləvu atlíćnɪjɪ jɪdjéjɪ.

IPA sájmən ótɕɪn^j tfʷórtɕɪskə^jɪ lʲítɕnəstʲ, ^jɪmú fs^jɪgdá prʲɪxódʲɪt v gʷóləvʊ ɐtlʲítɕnʲɪ^jɪ ^jɪdʲé^jɪ.

2971

EN I'm saving my money up for a trip around the world.

RU Я коплю́ де́ньги на кругосве́тное путеше́ствие.
ROM ja kapljú djén'gjɪ na krugasvjétnəjɪ putjɪšjéstvjɪjɪ.
IPA ʲa kɐplʲú dʲénʲɡʲɪ na krʊɡɐsvʲɛ́tnəʲɪ pʊtʲɪʂɛ́stʲɪ̯ʲɪ.

2972

EN The F1 racer caught fire and blew up. Luckily the driver just narrowly escaped.

RU Оди́н из автомоби́лей (боли́дов) «Фо́рмулы оди́н» загоре́лся и взорва́лся. К сча́стью, води́тель вы́брался как раз во́время.
ROM adín iz əvtəmabíljej (balídəv) «fórmulɪ adín» zəgarjélsjɪ i vzarválsjɪ. k śśást'ju, vadítjel' víbrəlsjɪ kak raz vóvrjemjɪ.
IPA ɐdʲín ʲiz əftəmɐbʲílʲʲɪj (bɐlʲídəv) «fʷórmʊlɨ ɐdʲín» zəgɐrʲéɫsʲɪ ɪ vzɐrváɫsʲɪ. k ççástʲü, vɐdʲítʲɪlʲ víbrəɫsʲɪ kak raz vʷóvrʲɪmʲɪ.

2973

EN A friend of mine was attacked and beaten up a few days ago. He's been in the hospital ever since.

RU Не́сколько дней наза́д изби́ли моего́ дру́га. Он до сих пор в больни́це.
ROM njéskəl'kə dnjej nazád jɪzbíljɪ majɪvó drúgə. on da sih por v bal'nítsɪ.
IPA nʲéskəlʲkə dnʲej nɐzád ʲɪzbʲílʲɪ mɐʲɪvʷó drúgə. ɔn dɐ sʲix pʷor v bɐlʲnʲítsɨ.

2974

EN Ludwig and Rita broke up. > Ludwig and Rita split up.

RU Лю́двиг и Ри́та расста́лись.

ROM ljúdvjɪg i rítə rɪsstáljɪs'.

IPA lʲǘdvʲɪg ɪ rʲítə rɛsstálʲɪsʲ.

2975

EN Ludwig and Rita ended up breaking up. > Ludwig and Rita ended up splitting up.

RU Лю́двиг и Ри́та в коне́чном ито́ге расста́лись.

ROM ljúdvjɪg i rítə v kanjéćnəm jɪtógjɪ rɪsstáljɪs'.

IPA lʲǘdvʲɪg ɪ rʲítə f kɛnʲétɕnəm ʲɪtógʲɪ rɛsstálʲɪsʲ.

2976

EN They couldn't get along with each other, so the relationship didn't work out in the end.

RU Они́ ника́к не могли́ пола́дить друг с дру́гом так, что, в конце́ концо́в, их отноше́ния не сложи́лись.

ROM aní njɪkák njɪ maglí paládjɪt' drug s drúgəm tak, što, v kantsjé kantsóv, ih ətnašjénjɪjə njɪ slažíljɪs'.

IPA ɐnʲí nʲɪkák nʲɪ mɛglʲí pɛládʲɪtʲ druk s drúgəm tak, ʂtọ, f kɛntsɨ́ kɛntsóf, ʲix ətnɛʂénʲɾʲə nʲɪ slɛzílʲɪsʲ.

2977

EN Plans to build a new factory have been held up
    because of the company's financial problems.

RU Пла́ны постро́ить но́вый заво́д бы́ли
    приостано́влены из-за фина́нсовых пробле́м
    компа́нии.

ROM plánɪ pastrójɪt' nóvɪj zavód bɨ́lɪ prɪəstanóvljɪnɪ iz-za
    fjɪnánsəvɪh prabljém kampánjɪjɪ.

IPA plánɨ pɐstrój̫ɪt̫ nóvɨj zɐvʷód bɨ́lʲɪ prʲɪəstɐnóvlʲɪnɨ ʲiz-za
    fʲɪnánsəvɨx prɐblʲém kɐmpánʲɪ̫ɪ.

2978

EN We live next to an international airport, so we have
    to put up with a lot of noise.

RU Мы живём ря́дом с междунаро́дным аэропо́ртом,
    поэ́тому нам прихо́дится мири́ться с больши́м
    коли́чеством шу́ма.

ROM mɪ žɪvjóm rjádəm s mjɪždunaródnɪm aɛrapórtəm,
    paɛ́təmu nam prɪhódjɪtsjɪ mjɪrít'sjɪ s bal'ším
    kalíɕɪstvəm šúmə.

IPA mɨ zʲɪvʲǫ́m rʲádəm s mʲɪʐdunɐródnɨm aɛrɐpʷórtəm,
    pɐɛ́təmʊ nam prʲɪxǫ́dʲɪts̫ɪ mʲɪrʲítʲs̫ɪ s bɐlʲşím
    kɐlʲítɕɪstfəm şúmə.

2979

EN The two (2) brothers are identical twins, so everybody gets them mixed up.

RU Бра́тья - иденти́чные близнецы́. Так что их постоя́нно пу́тают.

ROM brát'jɪ - jɪdjɪntíćnɪjɪ bljɪznjɪtsí. tak što ih pəstajánnə pútəjut.

IPA brátʲɪ - ʲɪdʲɪntʲítɕnʲɪ blʲɪznʲɪtsɨ́. tak ʂtǫ ʲix pəstɐʲánnə pútəʲüt.

2980

EN Your house is an absolute mess. When are you going to get this place cleaned up?

RU У тебя́ в до́ме ужа́сный беспоря́док. Когда́ ты собира́ешься здесь прибра́ться?

ROM u tjɪbjá v dómjɪ užásnɪj bjɪsparjádək. kagdá tɪ sabjɪrájeśsjɪ zdjes' prɪbrát'sjɪ?

IPA u tʲɪbʲá v dómʲɪ ʊʐásnɨj bʲɪspɐrʲádək. kɐgdá tɨ sɐbʲɪráʲɪɕsʲɪ zdʲesʲ prʲɪbrátʲsʲɪ?

2981

EN When your language training starts getting tough, it means you're about to make a big breakthrough, so stick with it and don't give up.

RU Когда́ ва́ша языкова́я пра́ктика стано́вится трудне́е, э́то означа́ет, что ско́ро у вас бу́дет большо́й проры́в, поэ́тому продолжа́йте занима́ться и не ду́майте сдава́ться.

ROM kagdá vášə jızıkavájə práktjıkə stanóvjıtsjı trudnjéjı, étə əznaćájıt, što skórə u vas búdjıt bal'šój prarív, paétəmu prədalžájtjı zanjımát'sjı i njı dúməjtjı sdavát'sjı.

IPA kɐgdá vášə ʲɪzɪkɐváʲə práktʲɪkə stɐnóvʲɪtsʲɪ trʊdnʲéʲɪ, étə əznɐtɕáʲɪt, ʂtɐ skʷórə u vas búdʲɪt bɐlʲʂój prɐríf, pɐétəmʊ prədɐłʒájtʲɪ zɐnʲɪmátʲsʲɪ i nʲɪ dúməjtʲɪ zdɐvátʲsʲɪ.

2982

EN Whoever used up all the milk and eggs should go out and buy some more. And get some toilet paper while you're at it.

RU Тот, кто испо́льзовал всё молоко́ и я́йца до́лжен пойти́ и купи́ть но́вые. Заодно́ купи́ туале́тную бума́гу.

ROM tot, kto jıspól'zəvəl vsjó məlakó i jájtsə dólžın pajtí i kupít' nóvıjı. zaadnó kupí tualjétnuju bumágu.

IPA tot, ktɐ ʲɪspʷólʲzəvəł fsʲé məlɐkʷó ɪ ʲǽjtsə dółzɪn pɐjtʲí i kʊpʲítʲ nóvʲɪ. zɐɐdnó kʊpʲí tʊɐlʲétnʊʲü bʊmágʊ.

2983

EN People used to carry pagers around, but they've completely fallen out of use.

RU Ра́ньше все вокру́г по́льзовались пе́йджерами, но тепе́рь они́ практи́чески исче́зли из обихо́да.

ROM rán'ši vsjɛ vakrúg pól'zəvəljıs' pjéjdžırəmjı, no tjɪpjér' aní prıktíćıskjı jıśśjézljı iz abjıhódə.

IPA ránʲṣɨ fsʲɛ vɐkrúk pʷǫ́lʲzəvəɫʲɪsʲ pʲéjdzɨrəmʲɪ, nǫ tʲɪpʲérʲ ɐnʲí prɐktʲítɕɪskʲɪ ʲɪɕɕézlʲɪ ʲiz ɐbʲɪxǫ́də.

2984

EN My manager pointed out a potential problem with our new marketing plan.

RU Мой ме́неджер указа́л на возмо́жную пробле́му с на́шим но́вым марке́тинговым пла́ном.

ROM moj mjénjedžır ukazál na vazmóžnuju prabljému s nášım nóvım markjétjıngəvım plánəm.

IPA mʷoj mʲénʲɪdzɨr ʊkɐzáɫ na vɐzmʷǫ́znʊʲü prɐblʲémʊ s náṣɨm nǫ́vɨm mɐrkʲétʲɪngəvɨm plánəm.

2985

EN A decision has to be made now. We can't put it off any longer.

RU Реше́ние должно́ быть при́нято сейча́с. Мы бо́льше не мо́жем его́ откла́дывать.

ROM rıšjénjıjı dalžnó bıt' prínjıtə sjıjćás. mı ból'šı njı móžım jıvó atkládıvət'.

IPA rʲɪṣénʲrʲɪ dɐɫznǫ́ bɨtʲ prʲínʲɪtə sʲɪjtɕás. mɨ bʷǫ́lʲṣɨ nʲɪ mʷǫ́zɨm ʲɪvʷǫ́ ɐtkládɨvətʲ.

2986

EN I was offered a job at the oil company, but I decided
to turn it down.

RU Я был приглашён (♀былá приглашенá) на рабóту
в нефтянýю компáнию, но я решúл (♀решúла)
отказáться.

ROM ja bıl prıglašjén (♀bılá prıglašıná) na rıbótu v
njıftjınúju kampánjıju, no ja rıšíl (♀rıšílə) ətkazát'sjı.

IPA ʲa bɨɫ prʲɪɡlɐşén (♀bɨlá prʲɪɡlɐşıná) na rɐbʷǫ́tʊ v
nʲɪftʲɪmúʲü kɐmpánʲrʲü, nǫ ʲa rʲışíɫ (♀rʲışílə) ətkɐzátʲsʲı.

2987

EN Several men got angry with Jack in the bar and Jack
told them he wasn't afraid to take them on.

RU Нéсколько человéк в бáре рассердúлись на Джéка,
он сказáл им, что не бойтся их.

ROM njéskəl'kə ćılavjék v bárjı rıssjırdíljıs' na džjékə, on
skazál im, što njı baítsjı ih.

IPA nʲéskəlʲkə tɕılɐvʲék v bárʲı rɐssʲırdʲílʲısʲ na dzɛ́kə, ǫn
skɐzáɫ ʲim, ştǫ nʲı bɐʲítsʲı ʲix.

2988

EN They took it out into the street, and Jack let them have it. Jack put them down one by one, and the spectacle really drew a crowd.

RU Они́ вы́шли на у́лицу и Джек показа́л им, на что спосо́бен. Он положи́л их одного́ за други́м, тако́е зре́лище, есте́ственно, привлекло́ толпу́.

ROM aní víšljɪ na úljɪtsu i džɪk pəkazál im, na što spasóbjɪn. on pəlažíl ih ədnavó za drugím, takójɪ zrjéljɪççɪ, jɪstjéstvjɪnnə, prɪvljɪkló talpú.

IPA ɐnʲí víʂlʲɪ na úlʲɪtsu ɪ dzɛk pəkɐzáɫ ʲim, na ʂtɔ spɐsópʲɪn. ọn pəlɐʐíɫ ʲix ədnɐvʷɵ́ za drʊɡʲím, tɐkʷɵ́ɪ zrʲélʲɪççɨ, ʲɪstʲéstfʲɪnnə, prʲɪvlʲɪklɵ́ tɐɫpú.

2989

EN A man was knocked down by a car when crossing the street and had to be taken to the hospital.

RU Челове́к был сбит автомоби́лем, когда́ переходи́л у́лицу и до́лжен был быть доста́влен в больни́цу .

ROM ćɪlavjék bɪl sbit əvtəmabíljɪm, kagdá pjɪrɪhadíl úljɪtsu i dólžɪn bɪl bɪt' dastávljɪn v bal'nítsu .

IPA tɕɪlɐvʲék bɨɫ sbʲit əftəmɐbʲílʲɪm, kɐgdá pʲɪrʲɪxɐdʲíɫ úlʲɪtsʊ ɪ dóɫzɨn bɨɫ bɨtʲ dɐstávlʲɪn v bɐlʲnʲítsʊ .

2990

EN In the aftermath of the tornado, they discovered a lot of uprooted trees and houses that had been blown down.

RU После торна́до они́ обнару́жили мно́го вы́рванных с ко́рнем дере́вьев и разру́шенных домо́в.

ROM pósljı tarnádə aní əbnarúžıljı mnógə vírvənnıh s kórnjım djırjévjıv i rızrúšınnıh damóv.

IPA pʷǫslʲɪ tɐrnádə ɐnʲí əbnɐrúzʲɪlʲɪ mnǫ́gə vírvənnɨx s kʷǫrnʲɪm dʲɪrʲévʲɪv ɪ rɐzrúṣɪnnɨx dɐmʷǫf.

2991

EN Please calm down. Everything will turn out all right.

RU Пожа́луйста, успоко́йтесь. Всё бу́дет в поря́дке.

ROM pažálujstə, uspakójtjes'. vsjó búdjıt v parjádkjı.

IPA pɐžálujstə, ʊspɐkʷǫjtʲɪsʲ. fsʲǫ́ búdʲɪt f pɐrʲǽtkʲɪ.

2992

EN When the police questioned him, he decided to leave out an important detail.

RU Когда́ поли́ция допра́шивала его́, он реши́л опусти́ть ва́жную дета́ль .

ROM kagdá palítsıjə daprášıvələ jıvó, on rıšíl apustít' vážnuju djıtál' .

IPA kɐgdá pɐlʲítsɨ̯ə dɐprášɨvələ ʲɪvʷǫ́, ǫn rʲɪṣíɫ ɐpʊstʲítʲ váznʊʲü dʲɪtálʲ .

2993

EN When talking with the police, you shouldn't make up stories or lie.

RU Когда́ разгова́риваете с поли́цией, не сто́ит приду́мывать исто́рии или лгать.

ROM kagdá rızgavárjıvəjetjı s palítsıjej, njı stójıt prıdúmıvət' jıstórjıjı ili lgat'.

IPA kɐgdá rəzgɐvárʲɪvəʲɪtʲɪ s pɐlʲítsɨʲɪj, nʲɪ stǫ́ʲɪt prʲɪdúmɨvətʲ ʲɪstǫ́rʲɪ̯ɪ ʲilʲi ɫgatʲ.

2994

EN When Sara decided to move to India and start a new life, she gave away all of her belongings.

RU Когда́ Са́ра реши́ла перее́хать в И́ндию и нача́ть но́вую жизнь, она́ отдала́ (разда́ла) все свои́ ве́щи.

ROM kagdá sárə rıšílə pjırıjéhət' v índjıju i naćát' nóvuju žızn', aná ətdalá (rızdálə) vsje svaí vjéççı.

IPA kɐgdá sárə rʲɪʂílə pʲɪrʲɪ̯éxətʲ v ʲíndʲrʲü ɪ nɐtɕátʲ nǫ́vʊʲü z̦ɨznʲ, ɐná ətdɐlá (rɐzdálə) fsʲɛ svɐʲí vʲéççɪ.

2995

EN Put a smile on your face, and you'll certainly get lots of smiles back.

RU Улыба́йся и ты полу́чишь мно́го отве́тных улы́бок.

ROM ulıbájsjı i tı palúćıś mnógə atvjétnıh ulíbək.

IPA ʊɫɨbájsʲɪ ɪ tɨ pɐlútɕɪɕ mnǫ́gə ɐtfʲétnix ʊlíbək.

2996

EN I waved to the children on the bus, and they waved back.

RU Я помахáл (♀помахáла) дéтям в автóбусе, и они́ помахáли в отвéт.

ROM ja pəmahál (♀pəmahálə) djétjɪm v avtóbusjɪ, i aní pəmaháljɪ v atvjét.

IPA ʲa pəmɐxáɫ (♀pəmɐxálə) dʲétʲɪm v ɐftóbusʲɪ, ɪ ɐnʲí pəmɐxálʲɪ v ɐtfʲét.

2997

EN My first job was at a travel agency, and I didn't like it much. But now, looking back on the experience, I really learned a lot.

RU Моя́ пéрвая рабóта былá в туристи́ческом агéнтстве, и онá мне не óчень нрáвилась. Но тепéрь, оглядываясь назáд, я понимáю, что действи́тельно мнóгому научи́лся (♀научи́лась).

ROM majá pjérvəjɪ rɪbótə bɪlá v turɪstíćɪskəm agjéntstvjɪ, i aná mnjɛ njɪ óćɪn' nrávjɪləs'. no tjɪpjér', agljádɪvəjas' nazád, ja panjɪmáju, što djɪjstvítjel'nə mnógəmu naućílsjɪ (♀naućíləs').

IPA mɐʲá pʲérvəʲɪ rɐbʷótə bɪlá f turʲɪstʲítɕɪskəm ɐgʲéntstfʲɪ, ɪ ɐná mnʲɛ nʲɪ ótɕɪnʲ nrávʲɪləsʲ. nɔ tʲɪpʲérʲ, ɐglʲádɪvəʲɪsʲ nɐzát, ʲa pənʲɪmáü, štɔ dʲɪjstfʲítʲɪlʲnə mnógəmu nɐutɕíɫsʲɪ (♀nɐutɕíləsʲ).

2998

EN When are you going to pay me back the money I lent you?

RU Когда́ ты собира́ешься верну́ть мне де́ньги, кото́рые я одолжи́л (♀ одолжи́ла) тебе́?

ROM kagdá tɪ sabjɪrájeśsjɪ vjɪrnút' mnjɛ djén'gjɪ, katórɪjɪ ja ədalžíl (♀ ədalžílə) tjɪbjé?

IPA kɐgdá tɨ sɐbʲɪrájɪɕsʲɪ vʲɪrnútʲ mnʲɛ dʲénʲɡʲɪ, kɐtórɨ̯ɪ ʲa ədɐɫzíl (♀ ədɐɫzílə) tʲɪbʲé?

2999

EN When you cause problems with the wrong people, those problems will come pay you back, or come back to haunt you.

RU Éсли вы навреди́ли не тем лю́дям, то вас бу́дут постоя́нно пресле́довать пробле́мы .

ROM jésljɪ vɪ navrɪdíljɪ njɪ tjɛm ljudjám, to vas búdut pəstajánnə prɪsljédəvət' prabljémɪ .

IPA ʲéslʲɪ vɨ nɐvrʲɪdʲílʲɪ nʲɪ tʲɛm lʲüdʲám, t̪ə vas búdʊt pəstɐ̯ánnə prʲɪslʲédəvətʲ prɐblʲémɨ .

3000

EN The lone ranger got on his horse and rode off into the sunset.

RU Одино́кий ре́йнджер сел на ло́шадь и уе́хал на зака́т.

ROM adjɪnókjɪj rjéjndžɪr sjɛl na lóšəd' i ujéhəl na zakát.

IPA ɐdʲɪnók̯ɪj rʲéjndzɨr sʲɛɫ na lóʂɨdʲ ɪ ʊʲéxəɫ na zɐkát.

Russian Index

бе́гло [bʲéglə]: 2573, 2630
бе́гу [bʲégʊ]: 2771
бе́дная [bʲédnəʲɪ]: 2059
бе́дным [bʲédnɪm]: 2293, 2298
бежа́ть [bʲɪzátʲ]: 2624
без [bʲɪs]: 2080, 2131, 2132, 2538,
    2943
без [bʲɪz]: 2077, 2084, 2281, 2392,
    2690, ..., +1
безобра́зие [bʲɪzɐbrázʲɪʲ]: 2373
безопа́сности [bʲɪzɐpásnəstʲɪ]: 2473
безрабо́тное [bʲɪzrɐbʷótnəʲɪ]: 2210
безрабо́тный [bʲɪzrɐbʷótnɪj]: 2297
безрезульта́тно [bʲɪzrʲɪzʊlʲtátnə]: 2945
безупре́чна [bʲɪzʊprʲétɕnə]: 2899
бензи́н [bʲɪnzʲín]: 2727, 2930
берегу́ [bʲɪrʲɪgú]: 2390
берёт [bʲɪrʲét]: 2926
беспоко́ил [bʲɪspɐkʷóʲɪɫ]: 2149
беспоко́иться [bʲɪspɐkʷóʲɪtʲsʲɪ]: 2852
беспоко́ишься [bʲɪspɐkʷóʲɪɕsʲɪ]: 2846
беспоря́док [bʲɪspʲɪrʲádək]: 2807, 2980
бессле́дно [bʲɪsslʲédnə]: 2959
би́знес-план [bʲíznʲɪs-plən]: 2543
биле́т [bʲɪlʲét]: 2132
биле́ты [bʲɪlʲétɨ]: 2403, 2875
благодаря́ [bləgədɐrʲá]: 2774
бла́нки [blánkʲɪ]: 2744
ближа́йшие [blʲɪzájʂɨʲɪ]: 2961
бли́зко [blʲískə]: 2599
близнецы́ [blʲɪznʲɪtsɨ́]: 2979
блюд [blʲut]: 2870
бога́тые [bɐgátɨʲɪ]: 2292
бога́тых [bɐgátɨx]: 2298
бо́ится [bɐʲítsʲɪ]: 2987
бои́шься [bɐʲíɕsʲɪ]: 2810, 2811
бо́лее [bʷólʲɪʲɪ]: 2292, 2564, 2798
боле́зней [bɐlʲéznʲɪj]: 2535
боле́зни [bɐlʲéznʲɪ]: 2075
боле́знь [bɐlʲéznʲ]: 2608
бо́лей [bʷólʲɪj]: 2887
болён [bɐlʲén]: 2428
бо́лен [bʷólʲɪn]: 2158
боли́дов [bɐlʲídəv]: 2972

боль [bʷolʲ]: 2861
больна́ [bɐlʲná]: 2428
больни́це [bɐlʲnʲítsɪ]: 2730, 2973
больни́цу [bɐlʲnʲítsʊ]: 2264, 2548,
    2964, 2989
больша́я [bɐlʲʂáʲə]: 2547
бо́льше [bʷólʲʂɨ]: 2026, 2036, 2037,
    2061, 2062, ..., +18
больши́м [bɐlʲʂím]: 2978
большинство́ [bɐlʲʂɨnstfʷó]: 2550,
    2555, 2558
большинство [bɐlʲʂínstfə]: 2430
большо́го [bɐlʲʂóvə]: 2532
большо́е [bɐlʲʂóʲɪ]: 2076
большо́й [bɐlʲʂój]: 2229, 2303, 2304,
    2386, 2583, ..., +3
большо́му [bɐlʲʂómʊ]: 2774
бо́льшую [bʷólʲʂʊʲü]: 2260, 2428, 2436
бо́мба [bʷómbə]: 2198
бори́с [bɐrʲís]: 2179
босс [bʷoss]: 2583
бо́сса [bʷóssə]: 2834
боти́нок [bɐtʲínək]: 2843
бою́сь [bɐʲǘsʲ]: 2173, 2812
боя́лась [bɐʲáləsʲ]: 2174
боя́лся [bɐʲáɫsʲɪ]: 2171, 2174
бо́ясь [bɐʲæsʲ]: 2172
боя́тся [bɐʲætsʲɪ]: 2170, 2284
брак [brak]: 2290
брат [brat]: 2272, 2732, 2796
бра́та [brátə]: 2273, 2895
бра́том [brátəm]: 2516
брать [bratʲ]: 2118
бра́тья [brátʲɪ]: 2979
брита́ния [brʲɪtánʲɪʲə]: 2315
бритья́ [brʲɪtʲá]: 2204
бро́сил [brósʲɪɫ]: 2177, 2843, 2910,
    2922
бро́сила [brósʲɪlə]: 2748, 2910
бро́сить [brósʲɪtʲ]: 2844
бу́дет [búdʲɪt]: 2169, 2180, 2231, 2389,
    2570, ..., +7
бу́дете [búdʲɪtʲɪ]: 2849
бу́дешь [búdʲɪɕ]: 2074, 2161, 2280,
    2670, 2715, ..., +2

будто [búttə]: 2589, 2684, 2685, 2686, 2688, ..., +1
бýду [búdʊ]: 2165, 2395, 2634, 2698, 2924, ..., +1
бýдут [búdʊt]: 2033, 2671, 2999
бýдучи [búdʊtɕi]: 2214
будь [budʲ]: 2714
бýдьте [búdʲtʲɪ]: 2205, 2795
букв [bukf]: 2249
бýквами [búkfəmʲɪ]: 2744
бумáги [bʊmágʲɪ]: 2474, 2931
бумáгу [bʊmágʊ]: 2982
бутýлку [bʊtɨɫkʊ]: 2136
бухáнку [bʊxánkʊ]: 2230
бы [bɨ]: 2007, 2012, 2055, 2056, 2057, ..., +28
бывáет [bɨvájɪt]: 2091, 2460
бывáл [bɨváɫ]: 2313
бывáла [bɨválə]: 2313
был [bɨɫ]: 2051, 2119, 2159, 2163, 2166, ..., +42
былá [bɨlá]: 2040, 2160, 2163, 2166, 2177, ..., +35
бýли [bɨ́lʲɪ]: 2014, 2057, 2123, 2125, 2160, ..., +23
было [bɨlə]: 2034, 2116, 2119, 2121, 2122, ..., +7
было [bɨlọ]: 2384, 2390
бýло [bɨ́lə]: 2058, 2060, 2065, 2078, 2121, ..., +36
бýстро [bɨ́strə]: 2259, 2575, 2618, 2624, 2670
бýстрыми [bɨ́strɨmʲɪ]: 2774
быть [bɨtʲ]: 2033, 2043, 2385, 2386, 2484, ..., +11
в [f]: 2007, 2023, 2030, 2039, 2051, ..., +118
в [v]: 2040, 2050, 2058, 2062, 2069, ..., +142
вадúм [vɐdʲím]: 2046
вáжное [váznəʲɪ]: 2629
вáжную [váznʊʲü]: 2800, 2916, 2992
вáжные [váznɨʲɪ]: 2683
валентúна [vɐlʲɪntʲínə]: 2934
валéрио [vɐlʲérʲɪə]: 2529

валюта [vɐlʲútə]: 2296
вам [vam]: 2023, 2110, 2505, 2820
вас [vas]: 2431, 2613, 2919, 2965, 2981, ..., +1
ваш [vaʂ]: 2955
вáша [váʂə]: 2981
вáше [váʂɨ]: 2744
вáшем [váʂɨm]: 2860
вáшим [váʂɨm]: 2795
вашингтóне [vɐʂɨngtónʲɪ]: 2321
вáших [váʂɨx]: 2830
вверх [vvʲerx]: 2269
вдовá [vdɐvá]: 2514
вегетариáнец [vʲɪgʲɪtɐrʲɪánʲɪts]: 2285
вегетариáнкой [vʲɪgʲɪtɐrʲɪánkəj]: 2214
вéда [vʲédə]: 2153
ведёт [vʲɪdʲǫ́t]: 2893
вéдой [vʲédəj]: 2153
вéжливы [vʲéʐlʲɪvɨ]: 2795
везлó [vʲɪzló]: 2553
вёл [vʲǫ́ɫ]: 2019
велúкая [vʲɪlʲíkəʲə]: 2316
великобритáнии [vʲɪlʲɪkɐbrʲɪtánʲɪʲɪ]: 2726
великодýшно [vʲɪlʲɪkɐdúʂnə]: 2794
великолéпно [vʲɪlʲɪkɐlʲépnə]: 2926
велосипéд [vʲɪlɐsʲɪpʲéd]: 2666, 2737
велосипéда [vʲɪlɐsʲɪpʲédə]: 2188
велосипéде [vʲɪlɐsʲɪpʲédʲɪ]: 2094
велосипéды [vʲɪlɐsʲɪpʲédɨ]: 2322
вéрил [vʲérʲɪɫ]: 2929
вéрить [vʲérʲɪtʲ]: 2016
вернёт [vʲɪrnʲǫ́t]: 2879
вернётся [vʲɪrnʲǫ́tsʲɪ]: 2702
вернёшься [vʲɪrnʲǫ́ɕsʲɪ]: 2033
вернýлась [vʲɪrnúləsʲ]: 2207, 2446, 2521
вернýлся [vʲɪrnúɫsʲɪ]: 2446, 2521
вернýсь [vʲɪrnúsʲ]: 2027, 2711
вернýть [vʲɪrnútʲ]: 2998
вернýться [vʲɪrnútʲsʲɪ]: 2160
вероятно [vʲɪrɐʲátnə]: 2169, 2634
вертолёте [vʲɪrtɐlʲǫ́tʲɪ]: 2766
вéрю [vʲérʲü]: 2903

вес [vʲɛs]: 2756
вести [vʲɪstʲí]: 2775
весь [vʲesʲ]: 2258, 2436, 2462, 2561, 2568, ..., +1
весьма [vʲɪsʲmá]: 2169
вечеринка [vʲɪtɕɪrʲínkə]: 2451, 2687
вечеринке [vʲɪtɕɪrʲínkʲɪ]: 2254
вечеринки [vʲɪtɕɪrʲínkʲɪ]: 2040
вечеринку [vʲɪtɕɪrʲínkʊ]: 2060, 2431, 2894
вечером [vʲétɕɪrəm]: 2063, 2064, 2170, 2283, 2342, ..., +6
вещи [vʲéɕɕɪ]: 2145, 2380, 2944, 2994
взгляды [vzglʲádɨ]: 2434
взлетели [vzlʲɪtélʲɪ]: 2749
взлётной [vzlʲɘ́tnəj]: 2646
взорвалась [vzərvɐlásʲ]: 2198
взорвался [vzɐrváɫsʲɪ]: 2972
взрослые [vzróslɨʲɪ]: 2595
взрыва [vzrívə]: 2218, 2778
взял [vzʲaɫ]: 2068, 2763
взяла [vzʲɪlá]: 2763
взяла [vzʲálə]: 2068
взяли [vzʲǽlʲɪ]: 2686
взять [vzʲætʲ]: 2670
вид [vʲid]: 2341
видел [vʲídʲɪɫ]: 2186, 2187, 2188, 2190, 2510, ..., +3
видела [vʲídʲɪlə]: 2186, 2187, 2188, 2190, 2510, ..., +3
виделась [vʲídʲɪləsʲ]: 2531
видели [vʲídʲɪlʲɪ]: 2057, 2189, 2195
в「делся [vʲídʲɪɫsʲɪ]: 2531
видеться [vʲídʲɪtʲsʲɪ]: 2144
видимся [vʲídʲɪmsʲɪ]: 2461
виды [vʲídɨ]: 2679
вижу [vʲízʊ]: 2466
визитке [vʲɪzʲítkʲɪ]: 2762
визитки [vʲɪzʲítkʲɪ]: 2933
визы [vʲízɨ]: 2123
викрам [vʲíkrəm]: 2851
виктора [vʲíktərə]: 2085
вилма [vʲíɫmə]: 2530
вина [vʲɪná]: 2348, 2480, 2882

винаты [vʲɪnátɨ]: 2347
вине [vʲɪnʲɛ́]: 2784, 2885
вини [vʲɪnʲí]: 2881
винит [vʲɪnʲít]: 2882
винить [vʲɪnʲítʲ]: 2347, 2348
винишь [vʲɪnʲíɕ]: 2513, 2883
виновен [vʲɪnóvʲɪn]: 2898, 2958
виновна [vʲɪnóvnə]: 2898
виновником [vʲɪnóvnʲɪkəm]: 2486
виню [vʲɪnʲú]: 2885
виолетта [vʲɪʊlʲɛ́ttə]: 2640
витале [vʲɪtálʲɪ]: 2562
витаю [vʲɪtájʊ]: 2127
включил [fklʲʊtɕíɫ]: 2921
включила [fklʲʊtɕílə]: 2921
вкус [fkus]: 2566, 2567
вкусно [fkúsnə]: 2565
владельцу [vlɐdʲélʲtsʊ]: 2784
владельцы [vlɐdʲélʲtsɨ]: 2945
владимиру [vlɐdʲímʲɪrʊ]: 2070
власти [vlástʲɪ]: 2778, 2865
влиянии [vlʲɪjǽnʲɪʲɪ]: 2863
влюбился [vlʲʊbʲíɫsʲɪ]: 2496
влюблялась [vlʲʊblʲáləsʲ]: 2745
влюблялся [vlʲʊblʲǽɫsʲɪ]: 2745
вместе [vmʲéstʲɪ]: 2516
вместо [vmʲéstə]: 2083, 2853
вначале [vnɐtɕálʲɪ]: 2718
внедорожнике [vnʲɪdɐrózɣ̩ʲɪkʲɪ]: 2241
внезапно [vnʲɪzápnə]: 2192
внимательно [vnʲɪmátʲɪlʲnə]: 2470
во [vɐ]: 2034, 2108, 2204, 2217, 2228, ..., +10
вовремя [vʷóvrʲɪmʲɪ]: 2148, 2163, 2713, 2714, 2715, ..., +5
вода [vɐdá]: 2288, 2751, 2871
водили [vɐdʲílʲɪ]: 2384
водитель [vɐdʲítʲɪlʲ]: 2473, 2486, 2972
водить [vɐdʲítʲ]: 2002, 2378, 2652, 2670
водой [vɐdój]: 2912
водорода [vədɐródə]: 2871
водосток [vədɐstók]: 2844
воду [vʷódʊ]: 2151

возвраща́ться [vəzvrɐçátʲsʲɪ]: 2588
возвраща́юсь [vəzvrɐçáʲüsʲ]: 2720
возвраща́ются [vəzvrɐçáʲütsʲɪ]: 2738
возде́йствия [vɐzdʲéjstfʲɪ̯ɪ]: 2888
во́здуха [vʷó̯zduxə]: 2255
во́зле [vʷó̯zlʲɪ]: 2552
возмо́жно [vɐzmʷó̯znə]: 2383, 2653
возмо́жное [vɐzmʷó̯znəʲɪ]: 2452
возмо́жность [vɐzmʷó̯znəstʲ]: 2138, 2389
возмо́жную [vɐzmʷó̯znu̯ü]: 2984
возника́ло [vɐznʲɪkálə]: 2419
возни́кли [vɐznʲíklʲɪ]: 2927
возни́кнет [vɐznʲíknʲɪt]: 2401
во́зрасте [vʷó̯zrəstʲɪ]: 2748, 2938
возросло́ [vəzrɐsló]: 2884
возьму́ [vɐzʲmú]: 2852
войны́ [vɐjnɨ́]: 2291
войти́ [vɐjtʲí]: 2364
вокабуля́р [vəkɐbuʲlʲár]: 2250
вокру́г [vɐkrúk]: 2267, 2983
вокру́г [vɐkrúg]: 2267
волейбо́л [vɐlʲɪjbʷó̯ɫ]: 2200
волну́ет [vɐɫnúʲɪt]: 2848
волну́йся [vɐɫnújsʲɪ]: 2838
во́лос [vʷó̯ləs]: 2224
во́лосы [vʷó̯ləsɨ]: 2225
вопро́с [vɐprós]: 2154, 2338, 2474, 2790, 2837
вопро́сам [vɐprósəm]: 2941
вопро́сов [vɐprósəf]: 2952
вопро́сы [vɐprósɨ]: 2152, 2389, 2395
во́ра [vʷó̯rə]: 2677
восемна́дцати [vɐsʲɪmnáttsətʲɪ]: 2938
во́семь [vʷó̯sʲɪmʲ]: 2265
воспита́ли [vɐspʲɪtálʲɪ]: 2962
воспи́тывали [vɐspʲítɨvəlʲɪ]: 2962
воспо́льзоваться [vɐspʷó̯lʲzəvətʲsʲɪ]: 2374
восстано́влено [vəsstɐnóvlʲɪnə]: 2482
восто́чной [vɐstótɕnəj]: 2306
вот [vʷó̯t]: 2024, 2680
вот-вот [vət-vʷó̯t]: 2684
вошёл [vɐʂó̯ɫ]: 2191

вперёд [fpʲɪrʲó̯t]: 2967
впечатлён [fpʲɪtɕɪtlʲó̯n]: 2805
впечатлена́ [fpʲɪtɕɪtlʲɪná]: 2805
впусти́ть [fpustʲítʲ]: 2255
впусту́ю [fpustú̯ü]: 2127
врач [vratɕ]: 2475, 2488, 2489, 2535
врачу́ [vrɐtɕú]: 2861
враща́ется [vrɐɕɕáʲɪtsʲɪ]: 2267
вре́дного [vrʲédnəvə]: 2888
вре́зался [vrʲézəɫsʲɪ]: 2906
вре́менем [vrʲémʲɪnʲɪm]: 2089
вре́мени [vrʲémʲɪnʲɪ]: 2126, 2127, 2133, 2413, 2416, ..., +9
вре́мя [vrʲémʲɪ]: 2083, 2094, 2173, 2184, 2204, ..., +15
вро́де [vróʲdʲɪ]: 2679
вручну́ю [vrutɕnú̯ü]: 2764
все [fsʲɛ]: 2033, 2034, 2040, 2163, 2198, ..., +23
всё [fsʲó̯]: 2083, 2173, 2297, 2315, 2362, ..., +33
всегда́ [fsʲɪɡdá]: 2134, 2509, 2522, 2579, 2626, ..., +13
всего́ [fsʲɪvʷó̯]: 2118, 2424, 2533, 2551, 2762, ..., +2
вселе́нной [fsʲɪlʲɪ̯énnəj]: 2536
всем [fsʲɛm]: 2451, 2655, 2657, 2659
всём [fsʲó̯m]: 2513, 2882
все́ми [fsʲémʲɪ]: 2215, 2946
всему́ [fsʲɪmú]: 2016, 2752, 2948
всех [fsʲɛx]: 2625, 2824, 2902, 2959
всплывёт [fspliˑvʲó̯t]: 2957
вспо́мнить [fspʷó̯mnʲɪtʲ]: 2019
встава́л [fstɐváɫ]: 2701
встава́ла [fstɐválə]: 2701
встава́ть [fstɐvátʲ]: 2045, 2090, 2167
встал [fstáɫ]: 2650
вста́ла [fstálə]: 2650
встре́тил [fstrʲétʲɪɫ]: 2391, 2516, 2517, 2518, 2531, ..., +1
встре́тила [fstrʲétʲɪlə]: 2516, 2517, 2518, 2531, 2631
встре́тилась [fstrʲétʲɪləsʲ]: 2057
встре́тили [fstrʲétʲɪlʲɪ]: 2674
встре́тился [fstrʲétʲɪtsʲɪ]: 2057

встрétимся [fstr^jét^jıms^jı]: 2653
встрétить [fstr^jét^jıt^j]: 2969
встрétиться [fstr^jét^jıt^js^jı]: 2351, 2739
встрéтят [fstr^jét^jıt]: 2391
встрéча [fstr^jétcə]: 2339
встречáл [fstr^jıtcáɫ]: 2563, 2627
встречáла [fstr^jıtcálə]: 2563, 2627
встречáлась [fstr^jıtcáləs^j]: 2754
встречáлись [fstr^jıtcál^jıs^j]: 2366
встречáлся [fstr^jıtcáɫs^jı]: 2754
встречáться [fstr^jıtcát^js^jı]: 2047
встрéче [fstr^jétcɨ]: 2859
встрéчи [fstr^jétcɨ]: 2106
встрéчусь [fstr^jétcʊs^j]: 2054
вступить [fstʊp^jít^j]: 2175
всю [fs^ju]: 2232, 2342, 2456, 2457, 2463, ..., +1
вся [fs^ja]: 2568, 2762
вторóй [ftɐrój]: 2709
вторóм [ftɐróm]: 2725
вторы́м [ftɐrím]: 2166
вхóдом [fxódəm]: 2920
вчерá [ftcɨrá]: 2182, 2283, 2342, 2382, 2428, ..., +3
вы [vɨ]: 2189, 2193, 2346, 2353, 2355, ..., +14
вы́бежал [víb^jızəɫ]: 2202
вы́брался [víbrəɫs^jı]: 2972
выбрácывайте [vɨbrásɨvəjt^jı]: 2919
вы́глядела [vígl^jıd^jılə]: 2288, 2410
вы́глядело [vígl^jıd^jılə]: 2686
вы́глядит [vígl^jıd^jıt]: 2684, 2926
вы́глядишь [vígl^jıd^jıc]: 2466, 2582
вы́дали [vídəl^jı]: 2471
вы́делить [víd^jıl^jıt^j]: 2293
вы́ехать [vɨ^jıxət^j]: 2854
вы́жить [vízɨt^j]: 2914
вызывáют [vɨzɨvá^jʊt]: 2815
вы́играл [vɨ^jıgrəɫ]: 2421, 2771
вы́играла [vɨ^jıgrələ]: 2771
вы́играли [vɨ^jıgrəl^jı]: 2961
вы́йдем [víjd^jım]: 2614
вы́йди [víjd^jı]: 2142

выключáтель [vɨkl^jʊtcát^jıl^j]: 2004, 2005
вы́лезла [víl^jızlə]: 2359
вы́лета [víl^jıtə]: 2968
вы́летел [víl^jıt^jıɫ]: 2646
вы́лететь [víl^jıt^jıt^j]: 2939
вы́нуждены [vínʊzd^jɨnɨ]: 2014, 2023
вы́писал [víp^jısəɫ]: 2773
вы́писала [víp^jısələ]: 2773
вы́платить [víplət^jıt^j]: 2784, 2876
выпускáет [vɨpʊská^jıt]: 2530
выпускникáм [vɨpʊsknʲıkám]: 2772
вы́пустили [vípʊst^jıl^jı]: 2865
вы́пьем [víp^jım]: 2418
вы́растили [vírəst^jıl^jı]: 2962
вырáщивать [vɨráccɨvət^j]: 2375
вы́рванных [vírvənnɨx]: 2990
вы́рос [vírəs]: 2521
вы́росла [vírəslə]: 2093, 2521
вы́садили [vísəd^jıl^jı]: 2968
вы́сказанных [vískəzənnɨx]: 2555
вы́слать [víslət^j]: 2620
высóкие [vɨsók^jı^jı]: 2292
высóкой [vɨsókəj]: 2076, 2660
высотé [vɨsɐt^jɛ́]: 2749
вы́ставку [vístəfkʊ]: 2084
вы́стрелил [vístr^jıl^jıɫ]: 2956
выступлéние [vɨstʊpl^jén^jɪ^jı]: 2803
выступлéнием [vɨstʊpl^jén^jɪ^jım]: 2805
выступлéния [vɨstʊpl^jén^jɪ^jə]: 2802
вы́сшего [víṣṣɨvə]: 2923
вы́терлась [vít^jırləs^j]: 2359
вы́учил [vʊ́ʊtcɨɫ]: 2251
вы́учила [vʊ́ʊtcɨlə]: 2251
выходи́л [vɨxɐd^jíɫ]: 2193
выхóдит [vɨxód^jıt]: 2367
выходи́ть [vɨxɐd^jít^j]: 2612
выходны́х [vɨxɐdnɨ́x]: 2082, 2653
вы́ходом [víxədəm]: 2071
вы́ходу [víxədʊ]: 2162
выхóдят [vɨxód^jıt]: 2465, 2785
выходя́щая [vɨxɐd^jáccə^jə]: 2547
вы́числить [vítcɨsl^jıt^j]: 2677
вы́шла [víṣlə]: 2433, 2827

вы́шли [víʂlʲɪ]: 2988
вы́шлю [víʂlʲü]: 2662
газ [gaz]: 2621
газе́тах [gɐzʲétəx]: 2959
газе́ты [gɐzʲétɨ]: 2632
гастро́ли [gɐstrólʲɪ]: 2752
где [gdʲɛ]: 2122, 2125, 2206, 2390, 2464, ..., +7
ге́рман [gʲérmən]: 2408
гига́нтский [gʲɪgántskʲɪj]: 2813
гид [gʲid]: 2257, 2630
ги́дом [gʲídəm]: 2529
ги́ри [gʲírʲɪ]: 2926
гла́вное [glávnəʲɪ]: 2671
глаза́ [glɐzá]: 2032
глоба́льного [glɐbálʲnəvə]: 2863
глу́пая [glúpəʲə]: 2586
глу́по [glúpə]: 2078, 2156
глу́пой [glúpəj]: 2586
говори́л [gəvɐrʲít]: 2419, 2497, 2537, 2630
говори́ла [gəvɐrʲílə]: 2537
говори́ли [gəvɐrʲílʲɪ]: 2147
говори́т [gəvɐrʲít]: 2016, 2528, 2563, 2573, 2589, ..., +2
говори́ть [gəvɐrʲítʲ]: 2015, 2021, 2078, 2606, 2688, ..., +1
говори́шь [gəvɐrʲíɕ]: 2581
говорю́ [gəvɐrʲú]: 2714
говоря́т [gəvɐrʲát]: 2298
говоря́щий [gəvɐrʲǽɕɕɪj]: 2529
год [gʷɒt]: 2752, 2781, 2783
го́да [gʷódə]: 2030, 2708, 2719, 2720, 2804
года́ми [gɐdámʲɪ]: 2559
году́ [gɐdú]: 2314, 2756, 2785
го́ды [gʷódɨ]: 2786
головны́х [gəlɐvnɨ́x]: 2887
го́лову [gʷóləvʊ]: 2970
го́лода [gʷólədə]: 2897
го́лоден [gʷólədʲɪn]: 2644
голодна́ [gəlɐdná]: 2644
голо́дной [gɐlódnəj]: 2446
голо́дным [gɐlódnɨm]: 2446

го́нки [gʷónkʲɪ]: 2757
го́нок [gʷónək]: 2679
гора́здо [gɐrázdə]: 2090, 2390, 2578, 2608
горди́ться [gɐrdʲítʲsʲɪ]: 2815
гордя́тся [gɐrdʲǽtsʲɪ]: 2814
го́род [gʷórət]: 2144, 2521, 2585
го́рода [gʷórədə]: 2034, 2170, 2472, 2532, 2546, ..., +1
го́роде [gʷórədʲɪ]: 2062, 2257, 2522, 2966
городке́ [gərɐtkʲɛ́]: 2095
го́роду [gʷórədʊ]: 2017
го́ры [gʷórɨ]: 2308, 2310
горя́чий [gɐrʲǽtɕɪj]: 2849
господи́н [gəspɐdʲín]: 2537
гостеприи́мство [gəstʲɪprʲɪʲímstfə]: 2877
гости́ница [gɐstʲínʲɪtsə]: 2721
гости́ницу [gɐstʲínʲɪtsʊ]: 2206
госуда́рство [gəsʊdárstfə]: 2293
гото́в [gɐtóf]: 2967
гото́ва [gɐtóvə]: 2967
граби́тели [grɐbʲítʲɪlʲɪ]: 2073, 2121
гра́дуса [grádʊsə]: 2326
гра́дусов [grádʊsəf]: 2751
гро́мко [grómkə]: 2839
гро́мкой [grómkəj]: 2590
грузови́к [grʊzɐvʲík]: 2911
гру́ппа [grúppə]: 2312, 2953
гру́ппе [grúppʲɪ]: 2435
гря́зной [grʲáznəj]: 2288
гуггенха́йма [gʊggʲɪnxájmə]: 2318
гуд [gud]: 2298
да [da]: 2056, 2082, 2642
дава́й [dɐváj]: 2013, 2064, 2081, 2383, 2418, ..., +1
дава́йте [dɐvájtʲɪ]: 2941
давно́ [dɐvnó]: 2591
даёт [dɐʲét]: 2111, 2536
даётся [dɐʲétsʲɪ]: 2425
да́же [dázɨ]: 2358, 2648, 2649, 2651, 2653, ..., +1
дай [daj]: 2175, 2233, 2396

да́йсукэ [dájsʊkɛ]: 2184
дал [daɫ]: 2458, 2951
дала́ [dɐlá]: 2458
далеко́ [dɐlʲɪkʷó]: 2596
да́ли [dálʲɪ]: 2137
да́льше [dálʲs̞i]: 2116, 2935
дам [dam]: 2665
да́нной [dánnəj]: 2117
дать [datʲ]: 2256
даю́т [dɐjút]: 2511, 2772, 2914
два [dva]: 2014, 2030, 2326, 2546, 2576, ..., +4
два́дцать [dváttsətʲ]: 2249, 2251, 2707, 2782, 2966
два́жды [dvázdɨ]: 2212
две [dvʲɛ]: 2541, 2708, 2804, 2928
двена́дцать [dvʲmáttsətʲ]: 2336
двери́ [dvʲɪrʲí]: 2687
дверь [dvʲerʲ]: 2018, 2056, 2149, 2199, 2208, ..., +4
две́рь [dvʲérʲ]: 2027
две́сти [dvʲéstʲɪ]: 2750
движе́ние [dvʲɪzɛ́nʲɪ̯ɪ]: 2169, 2386, 2726
движе́нию [dvʲɪzɛ́nʲɪ̯ü]: 2092, 2093
движе́ния [dvʲɪzɛ́nʲɪ̯ə]: 2890
дво́е [dvʷóʲɪ]: 2264, 2571, 2827
двумя́ [dvʊmʲá]: 2791
двух [dvux]: 2323, 2328, 2337, 2338, 2442
двухчасова́я [dvʊxtɕɪsɐváʲə]: 2337
двухча́стный [dvʊxtɕásnɨj]: 2338
де́вочке [dʲévətɕkʲɪ]: 2816
девяно́сто [dʲɪvʲɪnóstə]: 2850
девятиста́ [dʲɪvʲɪtʲɪstá]: 2770
де́вять [dʲévʲɪtʲ]: 2030
девятьсо́т [dʲɪvʲɪtʲsót]: 2749
де́душка [dʲédʊşkə]: 2962
де́душке [dʲédʊşkʲɪ]: 2850
де́душкой [dʲédʊşkəj]: 2962
действи́тельно [dʲɪjstfʲítʲɪlʲnə]: 2694, 2793, 2927, 2997
декабре́ [dʲɪkɐbrʲé]: 2707
декабря́ [dʲɪkɐbrʲá]: 2720

дел [dʲeɫ]: 2690
дела́ [dʲɪlá]: 2504
де́лает [dʲélɐ̯ɪt]: 2017, 2201, 2867
де́лаешь [dʲélɐ̯ɪɕ]: 2569, 2848
де́лать [dʲélətʲ]: 2270, 2356, 2569, 2629, 2690, ..., +2
де́лают [dʲélɐ̯üt]: 2330
де́ле [dʲélʲɪ]: 2800, 2956
дели́ть [dʲɪlʲítʲ]: 2372
де́лом [dʲéləm]: 2915
де́нег [dʲénʲɪk]: 2058, 2085, 2102, 2137, 2210, ..., +11
де́нег [dʲénʲɪg]: 2235, 2293, 2900
день [dʲenʲ]: 2237, 2265, 2459, 2462, 2523, ..., +5
деньга́х [dʲɪnʲgáx]: 2156
де́ньги [dʲénʲgʲɪ]: 2028, 2253, 2298, 2404, 2458, ..., +5
дере́вне [dʲɪrʲévnʲɪ]: 2062, 2476
дере́вьев [dʲɪrʲévʲɪv]: 2990
дере́вья [dʲɪrʲévʲɪ]: 2542
держа́ла [dʲɪrzálə]: 2433
держа́ть [dʲɪrzátʲ]: 2032
де́ржит [dʲérzɨt]: 2891
десяти́ [dʲɪsʲɪtʲí]: 2749
де́сять [dʲésʲɪtʲ]: 2077, 2460, 2540, 2714
дета́ль [dʲɪtálʲ]: 2992
дете́й [dʲɪtʲéj]: 2195, 2444, 2827
де́ти [dʲétʲɪ]: 2259, 2814, 2815
детьми́ [dʲɪtʲmʲí]: 2144
де́тям [dʲétʲɪm]: 2289, 2511, 2996
де́ятельности [dʲéʲɪtʲɪlʲnəstʲɪ]: 2341
джама́ла [dzɨmálə]: 2090
джек [dzɛk]: 2988
дже́ка [dzɛ́kə]: 2987
джера́рдо [dzɨrárdə]: 2635
джиёнг [dzɨ̈éng]: 2682
джи́нсы [dzínsɨ]: 2221
джо́ном [dzónəm]: 2698
джулиа́на [dzʊlʲiánə]: 2290
джу́лиус [dzúlʲiʊs]: 2509
дие́го [dʲɪ̯égə]: 2004
дие́ту [dʲɪ̯étʊ]: 2756

ди́паком [dʲípəkəm]: 2434

дипло́м [dʲɪplóm]: 2243

диск [dʲisk]: 2954

дли́нная [dlʲínnəʲɪ]: 2266

дли́нные [dlʲínnʲɪ]: 2225

дли́тельного [dlʲítʲɪlʲnəvə]: 2591

дли́тся [dlʲítsʲɪ]: 2336

для [dlʲa]: 2090, 2134, 2270, 2326, 2328, ..., +10

дней [dnʲej]: 2139, 2265, 2328, 2527, 2973

днём [dnʲǿm]: 2280, 2343, 2707

дни [dnʲi]: 2169

днк [dnk]: 2791

дня [dnʲa]: 2428, 2696, 2709

до [dɐ]: 2019, 2075, 2155, 2383, 2388, ..., +24

доба́вки [dɐbáfkʲɪ]: 2346

добавле́нием [dəbɐvlʲénʲɪrʲɪm]: 2330

доберёмся [dɐbʲɪrʲǿmsʲɪ]: 2614, 2704

добира́ется [dɐbʲɪráʲɪtsʲɪ]: 2766

добира́ться [dɐbʲɪrátʲsʲɪ]: 2767

доби́ться [dɐbʲítʲsʲɪ]: 2037

добрали́сь [dəbrɐlʲísʲ]: 2831

доброжела́тельны [dəbrɐz̠ɪlátʲɪlʲnɪ]: 2649

доброте́ [dəbrɐtʲɛ́]: 2857

довела́ [dɐvʲɪlá]: 2075

доверя́ют [dɐvʲɪrʲǽʲüt]: 2891

дово́льно [dɐvʷólʲnə]: 2423, 2661

догоню́ [dəgɐnʲú]: 2967

доде́лала [dɐdʲélələ]: 2504

дое́хал [dɐʲéxəł]: 2706

дождём [dɐzd̠ʲǿm]: 2743

дождь [dozd̠ʲ]: 2112, 2194, 2260, 2568, 2572, ..., +4

докла́дчик [dɐkláttɕik]: 2688

до́ктору [dóktəru]: 2527

докуме́нты [dɐkumʲéntɪ]: 2853

до́лгая [dółgəʲɪ]: 2160

до́лгий [dółgʲɪj]: 2592

до́лгим [dółgʲɪm]: 2578

до́лго [dółgə]: 2290, 2353, 2609

до́лгое [dółgəʲɪ]: 2531

до́лгой [dółgəj]: 2168

до́лжен [dółz̠ɪn]: 2245, 2350, 2361, 2385, 2473, ..., +13

должна́ [dɐłzná]: 2245, 2350, 2361, 2560, 2666, ..., +9

должно́ [dɐłznó]: 2386, 2985

до́лжность [dółznəstʲ]: 2533, 2540, 2594

должны́ [dɐłzní]: 2026, 2270, 2292, 2348, 2398, ..., +5

до́ллар [dółlər]: 2296

до́лларов [dółlərəv]: 2772

дом [dom]: 2073, 2121, 2364, 2406, 2596, ..., +6

дома́ [dɐmá]: 2945

до́ма [dómə]: 2063, 2083, 2091, 2101, 2165, ..., +8

до́ме [dómʲɪ]: 2385, 2980

домо́в [dɐmʷóf]: 2945, 2990

домо́й [dɐmʷój]: 2033, 2068, 2160, 2207, 2446, ..., +6

до́му [dómu]: 2706

донести́ [dɐnʲɪstʲí]: 2013

до́нна [dónnə]: 2186

доно́сящуюся [dɐnɐsʲáɕɕuʲüsʲɪ]: 2687

допоздна́ [dəpɐzná]: 2669

допра́шивала [dɐpráʂɪvələ]: 2992

допуска́ет [dɐpuskáʲɪt]: 2573

доро́га [dɐrógə]: 2546, 2554

доро́гах [dɐrógəx]: 2169, 2890

доро́ге [dɐrógʲɪ]: 2020, 2542

дороги́е [dərɐgʲíʲɪ]: 2944

дороги́м [dərɐgʲím]: 2439

доро́гу [dɐrógu]: 2437, 2442

доро́же [dɐrózɪ]: 2380, 2611, 2621

доста́в [dɐstáf]: 2208

доста́вил [dɐstávʲɪt]: 2397

доста́вила [dɐstávʲɪlə]: 2397

доста́влен [dɐstávlʲɪn]: 2548, 2989

доста́влены [dɐstávlʲɪnɪ]: 2264

доста́нешь [dɐstánʲɪɕ]: 2132

доста́точно [dɐstátətɕnə]: 2080, 2328, 2573, 2593, 2594, ..., +7

доста́ть [dɐstátʲ]: 2780

дра́ка [drákə]: 2964

друг [druk]: 2365, 2502, 2856, 2907, 2976

друг [drug]: 2353, 2354, 2366, 2367, 2539, ..., +2

друга [drúɡə]: 2353, 2354, 2631, 2706, 2952, ..., +1

другая [drʊɡáʲə]: 2607

другие [drʊɡʲíʲɪ]: 2814, 2897

другим [drʊɡʲím]: 2425, 2988

другой [drʊɡʷój]: 2469

другом [drʊɡʷóm]: 2847

другом [drúɡəm]: 2365, 2907, 2976

другу [drúɡʊ]: 2354, 2366, 2842

другую [drʊɡúʲü]: 2629, 2640

дружелюбны [drʊʐɨlʲúbnɨ]: 2426

друзей [drʊzʲéj]: 2417, 2433, 2923

друзья [drʊzʲá]: 2049, 2603, 2638, 2738, 2785, ..., +2

друзьями [drʊzʲǽmʲɪ]: 2212, 2368, 2638, 2718

думает [dúməʲɪt]: 2178, 2453

думаешь [dúməʲɪɕ]: 2039, 2151, 2328, 2903

думайте [dúməjtʲɪ]: 2981

думал [dúməɫ]: 2615, 2651

думала [dúmələ]: 2615, 2651

думали [dúmələʲɪ]: 2608, 2610

думаю [dúməʲü]: 2089, 2133, 2157, 2246, 2883, ..., +2

думают [dúməʲüt]: 2363, 2838

дыма [dɨ́mə]: 2196

дэ-эн-ка [dɛ-ɛn-ká]: 2791

дэвидом [dévʲɪdəm]: 2678

евгений [ʲɪvɡʲénʲɪj]: 2637

евро [ʲévrə]: 2770, 2773

европе [ʲɪvrópʲɪ]: 2301, 2305, 2310

европейскими [ʲɪvrɐpʲéjskʲɪmʲɪ]: 2792

европу [ʲɪvrópʊ]: 2799

египта [ʲɪɡʲíptə]: 2299

его [ʲɪvʷó]: 2004, 2010, 2042, 2091, 2149, ..., +38

еда [ʲɪdá]: 2747, 2943

едва [ʲɪdvá]: 2584

едем [ʲédʲɪm]: 2721

едешь [ʲédʲɪɕ]: 2799

единственная [ʲɪdʲínstfʲmnəʲɪ]: 2485

единственной [ʲɪdʲínstfʲmnəj]: 2163

единственным [ʲɪdʲínstfʲmnɨm]: 2163

едой [ʲɪdój]: 2913

еду [ʲɪdú]: 2873

еды [ʲɪdɨ́]: 2137, 2253, 2407, 2619, 2825

едят [ʲɪdʲát]: 2897

её [ʲɪ̯ɵ́]: 2012, 2018, 2059, 2079, 2176, ..., +17

ежедневно [ʲɪʐɨdnʲévnə]: 2709

ездил [ʲézdʲɪɫ]: 2094

ездила [ʲézdʲɪlə]: 2094

ездили [ʲézdʲɪlʲɪ]: 2630

ездит [ʲézdʲɪt]: 2241, 2765

ездить [ʲézdʲɪtʲ]: 2061

ездят [ʲézdʲɪt]: 2076

езжу [ʲéʐʐʊ]: 2094, 2765

ей [ʲej]: 2012, 2029, 2079, 2494, 2499, ..., +5

ему [ʲɪmú]: 2037, 2090, 2642, 2643, 2663, ..., +6

если [ʲéslʲɪ]: 2017, 2037, 2064, 2065, 2074, ..., +33

ест [ʲɛst]: 2214, 2285

естественно [ʲɪstʲéstfʲɪnnə]: 2988

есть [ʲéstʲ]: 2017, 2115, 2138, 2226, 2261, ..., +14

ехали [ʲéxəlʲɪ]: 2542

ещё [ʲɪɕɕɵ́]: 2088, 2161, 2418, 2573, 2597, ..., +14

ею [ʲéʲü]: 2115

жаловалась [ʐáləvələsʲ]: 2861

жалость [ʐáləstʲ]: 2809

жаль [ʐalʲ]: 2023, 2042, 2057, 2158, 2179, ..., +4

жара [ʐɨrá]: 2011

жарко [ʐárkə]: 2326, 2742

жаркую [ʐárkʊʲü]: 2648

жару [ʐɨrú]: 2326

ждал [ʐdaɫ]: 2187, 2609

ждала [ʐdɐlá]: 2609

ждать [ʐdatʲ]: 2014, 2048, 2116, 2609, 2824, ..., +1

ждёт [ʐdʲɵ́t]: 2646

ждёшь [zd^jǿɕ]: 2082
жду [zdu]: 2106, 2692
же [zɨ̞]: 2622, 2825
же [zɛ]: 2622
желающие [zɨlá^jüɕɕɨ̞^jɪ]: 2398
железнодорожные [zɨl^jɪznədɐrǿznɨ̞^jɪ]: 2755
женится [zɛ́n^jɪts^jɪ]: 2367
жениться [zɨ̞n^jít^js^jɪ]: 2595
женщина [zɛ́nɕɕɨnə]: 2370, 2475, 2488, 2489, 2492, ..., +4
женщиной [zɛ́nɕɕɨnəj]: 2481, 2491, 2754
женщину [zɛ́nɕɕɨnʊ]: 2948
женщины [zɛ́nɕɕɨnɨ]: 2491
женятся [zɛ́n^jɪts^jɪ]: 2785
жертв [zɛrtf]: 2879
жёсткий [zǿstk^jɪj]: 2954
живём [zɨ̞v^jǿm]: 2095, 2487, 2978
живёт [zɨ̞v^jǿt]: 2086, 2286, 2371, 2406, 2475, ..., +2
живёте [zɨ̞v^jǿt^jɪ]: 2355
живёшь [zɨ̞v^jǿɕ]: 2776
животе [zɨ̞vɐt^jɛ́]: 2861
живу [zɨ̞vú]: 2118, 2390
живут [zɨ̞vút]: 2386, 2476
жизни [zɨ́zn^jɪ]: 2777, 2893
жизнь [zɨ̞zn^j]: 2297, 2457, 2473, 2485, 2923, ..., +2
жили [zɨ́l^jɪ]: 2095, 2505
жить [zɨ̞t^j]: 2026, 2050, 2062, 2087, 2122, ..., +5
за [za]: 2097, 2098, 2100, 2113, 2133, ..., +25
забавная [zɐbávnə^jɪ]: 2838
забавный [zɐbávnɨj]: 2838
забавным [zɐbávnɨm]: 2562
забастовке [zəbɐstófk^jɪ]: 2755
забит [zɐb^jít]: 2605
заблудились [zɐblʊd^jíl^jɪs^j]: 2538, 2780
заболевания [zəbɐl^jɪván^jɪ^jə]: 2869, 2884
заболеть [zəbɐl^jét^j]: 2902
заботится [zɐb^wǿt^jɪts^jɪ]: 2847
заботиться [zɐb^wǿt^jɪt^js^jɪ]: 2850

заботятся [zɐb^wǿt^jɪts^jɪ]: 2851, 2913
забрались [zəbrɐl^jís^j]: 2073, 2121
забудь [zɐbúd^j]: 2020
забыл [zɐbɨ̞ɫ]: 2018, 2029, 2113, 2399, 2663, ..., +1
забыла [zɐbɨ́lə]: 2018, 2029, 2113, 2859
заверешил [zɐv^jɪr^jɪʂɨɫ]: 2771
заверешила [zɐv^jɪr^jɪʂílə]: 2771
завершение [zɐv^jɪrʂén^jɪ^jɪ]: 2961
завидуй [zɐv^jídʊj]: 2816
зависит [zɐv^jís^jɪt]: 2890, 2900
зависите [zɐv^jís^jɪt^jɪ]: 2830
зависнет [zɐv^jísn^jɪt]: 2955
завод [zɐv^wǿd]: 2977
заводов [zɐv^wǿdəf]: 2331
завтра [záftrə]: 2001, 2029, 2065, 2081, 2260, ..., +6
завтракаешь [záftrəkə^jɪɕ]: 2278
завтрашняя [záftrəʂn^jɪ^jɪ]: 2339
загадка [zɐgátkə]: 2484
загара [zɐgárə]: 2888
заглавными [zɐglávnɨm^jɪ]: 2744
загорелась [zəgɐr^jéləs^j]: 2757
загорелся [zəgɐr^jéɫs^jɪ]: 2972
задания [zɐdán^jɪ^jə]: 2918
задать [zɐdát^j]: 2389, 2790, 2952
задержан [zɐd^jérzən]: 2939
задержаться [zɐd^jɪrzát^js^jɪ]: 2669
задних [zádn^jɪx]: 2723
зазвонил [zəzvɐn^jíɫ]: 2676
заинтересован [zɐ^jɪnt^jɪr^jɪsóvən]: 2176, 2537
займёт [zɐjm^jǿt]: 2961
зайти [zɐjt^jí]: 2263
заканчивается [zɐkántɕɪvə^jɪts^jɪ]: 2930
заканчиваешь [zɐkántɕɪvə^jɪɕ]: 2279
закат [zɐkát]: 3000
заключается [zɐkl^jütɕá^jɪts^jɪ]: 2331
закончил [zɐk^wǿntɕɨɫ]: 2243
закончила [zɐk^wǿntɕɪlə]: 2504
закончились [zɐk^wǿntɕɪl^jɪs^j]: 2933
закончилось [zɐk^wǿntɕɪləs^j]: 2713
закончить [zɐk^wǿntɕɪt^j]: 2504

зако́нчу [zɐkʷóntɕʊ]: 2703
закреплено́ [zɐkrʲɪplʲɪnó]: 2373
закрыва́ть [zɐkrɪvátʲ]: 2027
закры́л [zɐkrɨ́ł]: 2018, 2149
закры́ла [zɐkrɨ́lə]: 2018
закры́т [zɐkrɨ́t]: 2503, 2704
закры́ть [zɐkrɨ́tʲ]: 2018, 2056
зали́ть [zɐlʲítʲ]: 2727
замёрзнуть [zɐmʲórznʊtʲ]: 2145
заме́тили [zɐmʲétʲɪlʲɪ]: 2193
заме́тить [zɐmʲétʲɪtʲ]: 2926
замолка́ет [zəmɐłkáʲɪt]: 2563
за́муж [zámʊz]: 2367, 2827
за́муж [zámʊʂ]: 2433, 2785
за́мужем [zámʊzʲɪm]: 2827
занима́ет [zɐnʲɪmáʲɪt]: 2601
занима́ется [zɐnʲɪmáʲɪtsʲɪ]: 2926
занима́л [zɐnʲɪmáł]: 2085
занима́лась [zɐnʲɪmáləsʲ]: 2072
занима́лся [zɐnʲɪmáłsʲɪ]: 2072
занима́ться [zɐnʲɪmátʲsʲɪ]: 2036, 2981
за́нял [zɐnʲáł]: 2028
заня́ла [zɐnʲálə]: 2028
заняли́сь [zɐnʲɪlʲísʲ]: 2206
занята́ [zɐnʲɪtá]: 2416
заня́тие [zɐnʲǽtʲɪʲɪ]: 2052
заня́тия [zɐnʲǽtʲɪʲə]: 2681
заня́тиях [zɐnʲǽtʲɪʲɪx]: 2276
заня́ться [zɐnʲǽtʲsʲɪ]: 2423, 2557, 2585
заодно́ [zɐɐdnó]: 2982
запа́здывает [zɐpázdɨvəʲɪt]: 2685
запа́с [zɐpás]: 2342
за́пах [zápəx]: 2196
за́перта [zápʲɪrtə]: 2364
заплати́ть [zəplɐtʲítʲ]: 2873, 2874, 2898
заплачу́ [zəplɐtɕú]: 2344
заполня́я [zəpɐłnʲǽʲə]: 2744
запомина́нием [zəpɐmʲɪnánʲɪʲɪm]: 2130
запомина́ют [zəpɐmʲɪnáʲüt]: 2259
запра́вку [zɐpráfkʊ]: 2930
запрещена́ [zɐprʲɪɕɕɪná]: 2009
запу́танным [zɐpútənnɨm]: 2558
за́работной [zárəbətnəj]: 2660

за́работную [zárəbətnʊʲü]: 2661
зарегистри́ровать [zərʲɪgʲɪstrʲírəvətʲ]: 2666
зарпла́та [zɐrplátə]: 2622, 2770, 2892
зарпла́ту [zɐrplátʊ]: 2622
заряди́ть [zərʲɪdʲítʲ]: 2038
засну́ть [zɐsnútʲ]: 2111, 2658
заста́вил [zɐstávʲɪł]: 2010
заста́вила [zɐstávʲɪlə]: 2010
заставля́ть [zəstɐvlʲǽtʲ]: 2824
заставля́ют [zəstɐvlʲǽʲüt]: 2048, 2815
заста́л [zɐstáł]: 2197
заста́ла [zɐstálə]: 2197
засыпа́ет [zɐsɨpáʲɪt]: 2942
зате́м [zɐtʲém]: 2842
затра́гивающий [zɐtrágʲɪvɐʲüɕɕɪj]: 2333
затро́нут [zɐtrónʊt]: 2260
затруднено́ [zɐtrʊdnʲɪnó]: 2169
затрудни́ть [zɐtrʊdnʲítʲ]: 2211
затрудня́ло [zɐtrʊdnʲálə]: 2213
затрудня́юсь [zɐtrʊdnʲǽʲüsʲ]: 2154
захи́де [zɐxʲídʲɪ]: 2950
заходи́л [zəxɐdʲíł]: 2673
захоте́л [zəxɐtʲéł]: 2212
захоте́ла [zəxɐtʲélə]: 2212
захо́чешь [zɐxótɕɪɕ]: 2175
зашли́ [zɐʂlʲí]: 2734, 2735
защити́ть [zɐɕɕɪtʲítʲ]: 2270, 2361, 2889
защити́ться [zɐɕɕɪtʲítʲsʲɪ]: 2901
защища́ет [zɐɕɕɪɕɕáʲɪt]: 2888
заявле́ние [zɐʲɪvlʲénʲɪʲɪ]: 2477
зва́ли [zválʲɪ]: 2556
звёзд [zvʲózt]: 2271
звёзд [zvʲózd]: 2536
звезда́ [zvʲɪzdá]: 2536
звёздное [zvʲóznəʲɪ]: 2269
звони́ла [zvɐnʲílə]: 2447
звони́ли [zvɐnʲílʲɪ]: 2697
звони́ть [zvɐnʲítʲ]: 2664
звоню́ [zvɐnʲú]: 2181, 2525
звоня́т [zvɐnʲát]: 2049
зда́ние [zdánʲɪʲɪ]: 2183, 2216, 2334, 2387, 2467, ..., +1
зда́нием [zdánʲɪʲɪm]: 2008, 2009

зда́ния [zdán^jɪ^jə]: 2725
здесь [zd^jes^j]: 2180, 2203, 2223, 2227, 2258, ..., +7
здоро́вье [zdɐróv^jɪ]: 2913
здоро́вьем [zdɐróv^jɪm]: 2329
здоро́вья [zdɐróv^jɪ]: 2329
зелёную [z^jɪl^jǿnʊ^jü]: 2035
земли́ [z^jɪml^jí]: 2267
зе́млю [z^jéml^jü]: 2840, 2844
земля́ [z^jɪml^já]: 2267, 2485
зли́тся [zl^jíts^jɪ]: 2796
зли́ться [zl^jít^js^jɪ]: 2560
зна́ем [zná^jɪm]: 2476, 2575
зна́ет [zná^jɪt]: 2218, 2325, 2453, 2517, 2518, ..., +1
знае́те [znɐ^jét^jɪ]: 2820
зна́ете [zná^jɪt^jɪ]: 2353
зна́ешь [zná^jɪç]: 2286, 2415, 2528, 2896
знако́м [znɐk^wǿm]: 2415
знако́ма [znɐk^wǿmə]: 2415
знако́мы [znɐk^wǿmɨ]: 2353
знал [znał]: 2442, 2592, 2651, 2862
зна́ла [zná lə]: 2592, 2651, 2862
зна́ли [znál^jɪ]: 2066, 2959
знать [znat^j]: 2175, 2233, 2396
зна́чит [znátçɨt]: 2385, 2714
значи́тельно [znɐtçít^jɪl^jnə]: 2380
значи́тельное [znɐtçít^jɪl^jnə^jɪ]: 2782
зна́ю [zná^jü]: 2411, 2617, 2890
зову́т [zɐvút]: 2515
зо́нтик [zǿnt^jɪk]: 2399, 2686
зоопа́рк [zɐɐpárk]: 2523, 2739
зоопа́рке [zɐɐpárk^jɪ]: 2739
зре́лище [zr^jél^jɪçɕɨ]: 2559, 2988
и [ɪ]: 2004, 2022, 2030, 2042, 2080, ..., +98
игра́ть [^jɪgrát^j]: 2069
игра́ющими [^jɪgrá^jüçɕɨm^jɪ]: 2195
игра́я [^jɪgrá^jə]: 2200
игру́ [^jɪgrú]: 2132
иде́и [^jɪd^jé^jɪ]: 2970
иденти́чные [^jɪd^jɪnt^jítçnɨ^jɪ]: 2979

идёт [^jɪd^jǿt]: 2194, 2494, 2513, 2532, 2550
иде́я [^jɪd^jé^jə]: 2858
иди́ [^jɪd^jí]: 2967
идти́ [^jɪtt^jí]: 2063, 2212, 2400, 2596, 2654, ..., +1
иду́щим [^jɪdúçɕɨm]: 2190
иен [^jɪ^jen]: 2951
из [^jiz]: 2202, 2338, 2359, 2405, 2407, ..., +23
из [^jis]: 2162, 2208, 2369, 2409, 2430, ..., +8
из-за [^jiz-za]: 2076, 2085, 2272, 2281, 2544, ..., +8
изби́ли [^jɪzb^jíl^jɪ]: 2973
изве́стно [^jɪzv^jésnə]: 2820
изве́стны [^jɪzv^jésnɨ]: 2294
изве́стный [^jɪzv^jésnɨj]: 2868
извине́ния [^jɪzv^jɪn^jén^jɪ^jə]: 2808, 2879
извини́ [^jɪzv^jɪn^jí]: 2044, 2114, 2181, 2379, 2807, ..., +1
извини́лась [^jɪzv^jɪn^jíləs^j]: 2880
извини́лся [^jɪzv^jɪn^jíłs^jɪ]: 2880
извини́ться [^jɪzv^jɪn^jít^js^jɪ]: 2097, 2098, 2881
извиня́ешься [^jɪzv^jɪn^jǽ^jɪçs^jɪ]: 2448
издалека́ [^jɪzdɐl^jɪká]: 2590
изли́шне [^jɪzl^jíşn^jɪ]: 2578
измени́лась [^jɪzm^jɪn^jíləs^j]: 2582
измени́лся [^jɪzm^jɪn^jíłs^jɪ]: 2582
измени́ться [^jɪzm^jɪn^jít^js^jɪ]: 2026
изнурённой [^jɪznʊr^jǿnnəj]: 2561
изнурённым [^jɪznʊr^jǿnnɨm]: 2561
изнури́тельная [^jɪznʊr^jít^jɪl^jnə^jɪ]: 2160
изнутри́ [^jɪznʊtr^jí]: 2364
изобре́ли [^jɪzɐbr^jél^jɪ]: 2295
изуча́ет [^jɪzʊtçá^jɪt]: 2143
изуча́ть [^jɪzʊtçát^j]: 2575
изуче́ние [^jɪzʊtçén^jɪ^jɪ]: 2425
или [^jil^ji]: 2055, 2066, 2070, 2448, 2643, ..., +5
им [^jim]: 2040, 2066, 2689, 2699, 2987, ..., +1
име́вшиеся [^jɪm^jéfşɨ^jɪs^jɪ]: 2499
име́ли [^jɪm^jél^jɪ]: 2533

имён [ᶨɪmᶨǫ́n]: 2130
и́менно [ᶨímᶨɪnnə]: 2841
име́ть [ᶨɪmᶨétʲ]: 2375, 2444
и́ми [ᶨímᶨɪ]: 2498, 2815
имэ́ил [ᶨméʲɪɫ]: 2834
и́мя [ᶨímᶨɪ]: 2744
и́ндии [ᶨíndᶨɪ̯ɪ]: 2457
и́ндию [ᶨíndᶨɪ̯ü]: 2994
иногда́ [ᶨɪnɐgdá]: 2345, 2758, 2765
иностра́нном [ᶨɪnɐstránnəm]: 2802
иностра́нцам [ᶨɪnɐstrántsəm]: 2819
инспекти́ровании [ᶨɪnspᶨɪktᶨírəvənʲɪ̯ɪ]: 2331
инспе́ктор [ᶨɪnspᶨéktər]: 2331
инстру́кции [ᶨɪnstrúktsɪ̯ɪ]: 2600
интере́сно [ᶨɪntᶨɪrᶨésnə]: 2153, 2177, 2178
интере́сного [ᶨɪntᶨɪrᶨésnəvə]: 2563
интере́сный [ᶨɪntᶨɪrᶨésnɨj]: 2153, 2228
интере́сными [ᶨɪntᶨɪrᶨésnɨmᶨɪ]: 2254
интерне́те [ᶨɪntᶨɪrnᶨétʲɪ]: 2753
информа́цией [ᶨɪnfɐrmátsɪ̯ɪj]: 2257
информа́ции [ᶨɪnfɐrmátsɪ̯ɪ]: 2233
информа́цию [ᶨɪnfɐrmátsɪ̯ü]: 2248
информа́ция [ᶨɪnfɐrmátsɪ̯ə]: 2667, 2762
инциде́нта [ᶨɪntsɨdᶨéntə]: 2215
инциде́нте [ᶨɪntsɨdᶨéntʲɪ]: 2325
иска́л [ᶨɪskáɫ]: 2464, 2495
иска́ла [ᶨɪskálə]: 2464, 2495
иску́сством [ᶨɪskússtfəm]: 2832
испа́нию [ᶨɪspánʲɪ̯ü]: 2938
испа́нцами [ᶨɪspántsəmᶨɪ]: 2435
исполне́нию [ᶨɪspɐɫnᶨénʲɪ̯ü]: 2818
испо́льзовал [ᶨɪspʷǫ́ɫʲzəvəɫ]: 2982
испо́льзование [ᶨɪspʷǫ́ɫʲzəvənʲɪ̯ɪ]: 2103
испо́льзования [ᶨɪspʷǫ́ɫʲzəvənʲɪ̯ɪ]: 2103
испо́льзуем [ᶨɪspʷǫ́ɫʲzuᶨɪm]: 2931
испыта́ниями [ᶨɪspɨtánʲɪ̯ɪmᶨɪ]: 2946
исто́рией [ᶨɪstǫ́rʲɪ̯ɪj]: 2832
исто́рии [ᶨɪstǫ́rʲɪ̯ɪ]: 2478, 2993
исто́рий [ᶨɪstǫ́rʲɪj]: 2562
исто́рию [ᶨɪstǫ́rʲɪ̯ü]: 2935
исто́рия [ᶨɪstǫ́rʲɪ̯ə]: 2287, 2586

исче́зли [ᶨɪççézlʲɪ]: 2983
ита́лии [ᶨɪtálʲɪ̯ɪ]: 2539
ита́лию [ᶨɪtálʲɪ̯ü]: 2738
ита́лия [ᶨɪtálʲɪ̯ə]: 2832
италья́нском [ᶨɪtɐlʲánskəm]: 2529
ито́ге [ᶨɪtǫ́gᶨɪ]: 2915, 2975
их [ᶨix]: 2113, 2220, 2290, 2298, 2504, ..., +11
ицзюа́нь [ᶨɪtssᶨüánᶨ]: 2544
ичиру [ᶨɪtɕiru]: 2951
и́щет [ᶨíççɪt]: 2545
и́щете [ᶨíççɪtᶨɪ]: 2932
йоги [jǫ́gᶨɪ]: 2926
к [k]: 2025, 2087, 2088, 2089, 2091, ..., +27
ка́ждая [kázdəᶨɪ]: 2469
ка́ждое [kázdəᶨɪ]: 2470
ка́ждом [kázdəm]: 2950
ка́ждому [kázdəmu]: 2471
ка́ждую [kázdüᶨü]: 2468
ка́ждые [kázdɪ̯ɪ]: 2460, 2483
ка́ждый [kázdɨj]: 2459, 2466, 2472, 2473, 2474, ..., +6
ка́жется [kázɨtsᶨɪ]: 2035, 2685, 2780, 2927
кайр [kɐᶨír]: 2299
как [kak]: 2018, 2019, 2052, 2057, 2099, ..., +57
ка́к-нибудь [kák-nᶨɪbudᶨ]: 2695
кака́я [kɐkáᶨə]: 2266
каки́е-нибудь [kɐkᶨíᶨɪ-nᶨɪbudᶨ]: 2123, 2161, 2427
каки́м [kɐkᶨím]: 2855
како́е [kɐkʷǫ́ᶨɪ]: 2629
како́й-то [kɐkʷǫ́j-tə]: 2951
како́м [kɐkʷǫ́m]: 2671
каку́ю [kɐkúᶨü]: 2445
калифо́рнии [kɐlᶨɪfʷǫ́rnʲɪ̯ɪ]: 2317
ка́мере [kámᶨɪrᶨɪ]: 2599
ками́ла [kɐmᶨílə]: 2534
кана́дой [kɐnádəj]: 2307
кари́м [kɐrᶨím]: 2904
карма́на [kɐrmánə]: 2208
карма́нам [kɐrmánəm]: 2841

ка́рта [kártə]: 2538

ка́рте [kártʲɪ]: 2876

ка́ртой [kártəj]: 2763

ка́рту [kártʊ]: 2662, 2780

каса́ющиеся [kɐsáʲüȼȼɨ́ɪsʲɪ]: 2329

кастрю́лю [kɐstrʲúlʲü]: 2912

касу́ми [kɐsúmʲɪ]: 2354

ка́честве [kátȼɪstfʲɪ]: 2772

квалифика́цию [kfɐlʲɪfʲɪkátsɨ́ʲü]: 2533

кварти́ра [kfɐrtʲírə]: 2089, 2725

кварти́рой [kfɐrtʲírəj]: 2373

кварти́ру [kfɐrtʲírʊ]: 2874

кейко [kʲejkʷọ]: 2092

кем [kʲɛm]: 2135, 2372, 2531

ке́ния [kʲénʲrʲə]: 2306

кенцзи [kʲentssʲi]: 2146

киломе́тров [kʲɪlɐmʲétrəf]: 2077

киломе́тров [kʲɪlɐmʲétrəv]: 2749, 2750

ки́мико [kʲímʲɪkə]: 2417

кино́ [kʲɪnọ́]: 2063, 2705, 2875

кинотеа́тр [kʲɪnɐtʲɪátr]: 2387

кинотеа́трах [kʲɪnɐtʲɪátrəx]: 2723

кипи́т [kʲɪpʲít]: 2751

кита́е [kʲɪtáʲɪ]: 2316, 2738

кита́йская [kʲɪtájskəʲɪ]: 2316

кита́йцы [kʲɪtájtsɨ]: 2295

кла́дбище [kládbʲɪȼȼɨ]: 2526

кла́ссе [klássʲɪ]: 2277

клие́нтом [klʲʲrʲéntəm]: 2166

клуб [klup]: 2175, 2668

ключ [klʲutȼ]: 2208

ключе́й [klʲütȼɨj]: 2450

ключи́ [klʲütȼí]: 2493, 2844

ключо́м [klʲütȼọ́m]: 2769

книг [knʲik]: 2427, 2468

кни́га [knʲígə]: 2909, 2932

кни́ги [knʲígʲɪ]: 2495

книгопеча́тание [knʲɪgɐpʲɪtȼátənʲrʲɪ]: 2295

кни́гу [knʲígʊ]: 2456, 2471

кно́пку [knọ́pkʊ]: 2035

ко [kɐ]: 2626

когда́ [kɐgdá]: 2033, 2048, 2049, 2057, 2092, ..., +41

когда́-либо [kɐgdá-lʲɪbə]: 2563, 2625, 2627, 2629

когда́-нибудь [kɐgdá-nʲɪbʊdʲ]: 2268, 2278, 2313, 2730, 2731, ..., +2

когда́-то [kɐgdá-tə]: 2275, 2387, 2532

кого́ [kɐvʷọ́]: 2450, 2922

кого́-нибудь [kɐvʷọ́-nʲɪbʊdʲ]: 2528, 2745

кого́-то [kɐvʷọ́-tə]: 2135, 2395

кое-каки́е [kəʲɪ-kɐkʲɨ́fʲɪ]: 2504

кое-кого́ [kəʲɪ-kɐvʷọ́]: 2516, 2531

кое-что́ [kɐʲɪ-ʂtọ́]: 2181

ко́жу [kʷọ́zʊ]: 2888

кокосом [kɐkʷọ́səm]: 2910

коли́чества [kɐlʲítȼɪstfə]: 2782

коли́чество [kɐlʲítȼɪstfə]: 2076, 2781, 2884

коли́чеством [kɐlʲítȼɪstfəm]: 2978

ко́лледж [kʷọ́ɫlʲɪdʂ]: 2256, 2274

ко́лледж [kʷọ́ɫlʲɪdz]: 2371

ко́лледжа [kʷọ́ɫlʲɪdzə]: 2275, 2950

ко́лледже [kʷọ́ɫlʲɪdzɨ]: 2732, 2922

ком [kʷọm]: 2847

командиро́вках [kəmɐndʲɪrọ́fkəx]: 2091, 2962

командиро́вке [kəmɐndʲɪrọ́fkʲɪ]: 2519, 2678

ко́мната [kʷọ́mnətə]: 2226, 2584

ко́мнате [kʷọ́mnətʲɪ]: 2197

ко́мнату [kʷọ́mnətʊ]: 2372

ко́мнаты [kʷọ́mnətɨ]: 2469, 2671, 2728

компа́нии [kɐmpánʲrʲɪ]: 2031, 2333, 2543, 2682, 2772, ..., +4

компа́нию [kɐmpánʲrʲü]: 2030, 2986

компа́ния [kɐmpánʲrʲə]: 2774

компенса́цию [kɐmpʲɪnsátsɨ́ʲü]: 2784

компенси́ровать [kɐmpʲɪnsʲírəvətʲ]: 2960

компью́тер [kɐmpʲútʲɪr]: 2955

компью́тера [kɐmpʲútʲɪrə]: 2954

компью́терную [kɐmpʲútʲɪrnʊʲü]: 2764

коне́чно [kɐnʲétȼnə]: 2056, 2081

коне́чном [kɐnʲétȼnəm]: 2915, 2963, 2975

константи́н [kənstɐntʲín]: 2275

контáктная [kɐntáktnə^jɪ]: 2762
континéнт [kɐnt^jɪn^jént]: 2303
контрáкт [kɐntrákt]: 2961
контрóль [kɐntrój^{lj}]: 2750, 2906
конферéнцию [kɐnf^jɪr^jéntsɨ^jʉ]: 2148, 2800
конферéнция [kɐnf^jɪr^jéntsɨ^jɪ]: 2577
концáми [kɐntsám^jɪ]: 2478
концé [kɐntsɨ́]: 2718, 2720, 2976
конце-концóв [kəntsɨ-kɐntsóf]: 2965
концéрт [kɐntsért]: 2936
концóв [kɐntsóf]: 2718, 2976
копéйки [kɐp^jéjk^jɪ]: 2404, 2943
копировáльный [kəp^jɪrɐvál^jnɨj]: 2035
кóпию [k^wóp^{jɪj}ʉ]: 2954
коплю́ [kɐpl^jú]: 2971
кораблé [kərɐbl^jɛ́]: 2733
кóрнем [k^wórn^jɪm]: 2990
королéвстве [kərɐʋ^{lj}éʋstf^jɪ]: 2314
королéвство [kərɐʋ^{lj}éʋstfə]: 2315
корóче [kɐrótɕɪ]: 2578
корпоратúвное [kərpərɐt^jívnə^jɪ]: 2904
кóсмосе [k^wósməs^jɪ]: 2271
коснýлся [kɐsnúɫs^jɪ]: 2192
котóрая [kɐtórə^jə]: 2475, 2481, 2488, 2530, 2660, ..., +1
котóрого [kɐtórəvə]: 2509, 2515, 2543, 2627
котóрое [kɐtórə^jɪ]: 2494, 2501, 2553, 2629
котóрой [kɐtórəj]: 2485, 2491, 2514, 2525, 2538, ..., +2
котóром [kɐtórəm]: 2051, 2275, 2507, 2539
котóрому [kɐtórəmʊ]: 2335
котóрую [kɐtórʊ^jʉ]: 2492, 2496, 2508, 2519, 2721, ..., +3
котóрые [kɐtórɨ^jɪ]: 2076, 2397, 2439, 2458, 2476, ..., +6
котóрый [kɐtórɨj]: 2166, 2187, 2283, 2330, 2336, ..., +13
котóрым [kɐtórɨm]: 2497, 2510, 2537
котóрыми [kɐtórɨm^jɪ]: 2426, 2430, 2506, 2520
котóрых [kɐtórɨx]: 2342, 2563

кóфе [k^wóf^jɪ]: 2201, 2282, 2283
кóшка [k^wóʂkə]: 2948
кошмáром [kɐʂmárəm]: 2454
крáжи [kráʐɨ]: 2272, 2323
красúвое [krɐs^jívə^jɪ]: 2216, 2934
красúвы [krɐs^jívɨ]: 2429
красноречúвый [krəsnɐr^jɪtɕívɨj]: 2805
кредúтной [kr^jɪd^jítnəj]: 2763, 2876
крем [kr^jem]: 2888
кремль [kr^jeml^j]: 2320
крéпкий [kr^jépk^jɪj]: 2282
крúзисе [kr^jíz^jɪs^jɪ]: 2883
крúками [kr^jíkəm^jɪ]: 2202
критиковáть [kr^jɪt^jɪkɐvát^j]: 2157
критúчески [kr^jɪt^jítɕɪsk^jɪ]: 2818
кричáл [kr^jɪtɕáɫ]: 2839
кричáть [kr^jɪtɕát^j]: 2842
крóме [króm^jɪ]: 2163, 2847, 2923
кругосвéтное [krʊɡɐsv^jétnə^jɪ]: 2940, 2971
круúз [krʊíz]: 2733
ксавье [ksav^jɛ]: 2922
ксéния [ks^jén^{jɪj}ə]: 2192
кто [ktɐ]: 2002, 2161, 2163, 2215, 2217, ..., +10
ктó-нибудь [któ-n^jɪbʊd^j]: 2361, 2431
ктó-то [któ-tə]: 2192, 2193, 2199, 2385, 2399, ..., +4
кудá [kʊdá]: 2232, 2585, 2950
кудá-нибудь [kʊdá-n^jɪbʊd^j]: 2083, 2105
культýрного [kʊl^jtúrnəvə]: 2832
купú [kʊp^jí]: 2931, 2982
купúл [kʊp^jíɫ]: 2088, 2342
купúла [kʊp^jílə]: 2088, 2342, 2494, 2652
купúть [kʊp^jít^j]: 2137, 2176, 2221, 2230, 2253, ..., +3
курс [kurs]: 2336
кýхне [kúxn^jɪ]: 2052, 2053, 2201, 255♀
кýхней [kúxn^jɪj]: 2294, 2832
кýчу [kútɕʊ]: 2943
кэнъúти [kɛn^jít^jɪ]: 2353
лáдили [lád^{jɪlj}ɪ]: 2718

ла́кшми [lákṣmʲɪ]: 2457, 2851
ла́нчем [lántçɨm]: 2185
лати́фа [lɐtʲífə]: 2748
лгать [ɫgatʲ]: 2993
левосторо́ннее [lʲɪvəstɐrónnʲrʲɪ]: 2726
левосторо́ннему [lʲɪvəstɐrónnʲɪmʊ]: 2092, 2093
лёг [lʲǫk]: 2209
легла́ [lʲɪglá]: 2209
лежа́л [lʲɪzáɫ]: 2730
лежа́ла [lʲɪzálə]: 2730
ле́ксики [lʲéksʲɪkʲɪ]: 2103
ле́кции [lʲéktsɨʲɪ]: 2389
лени́в [lʲɪnʲíf]: 2593
лени́ва [lʲɪnʲívə]: 2593
лет [lʲet]: 2030, 2031, 2086, 2335, 2531, ..., +8
лета́ть [lʲɪtátʲ]: 2046
лети́м [lʲɪtʲím]: 2749
ле́тний [lʲétnʲɪj]: 2454
лечь [lʲetç]: 2840
лжи [ɫzɨ]: 2108
ли [lʲi]: 2409, 2504, 2820
ли́нда [lʲíndə]: 2354
листе́ [lʲɪstʲɛ́]: 2474
ли́тинг [lʲítʲɪnk]: 2156
ли́чность [lʲítçnəstʲ]: 2970
лишь [lʲiç]: 2815
ложи́ться [lɐzɨtʲsʲɪ]: 2119
ломи́лся [lɐmʲíɫsʲɪ]: 2199
ло́ндон [lóndən]: 2951
ло́ндона [lóndənə]: 2532
ло́ндоне [lóndənʲɪ]: 2050, 2417, 2698
ло́пез [lópʲɪs]: 2537
лос-а́нджелесе [lɐs-ándzɨɫʲɪsʲɪ]: 2095, 2317
ло́шадь [lóṣɨdʲ]: 3000
луна́ [lʊná]: 2267
лучей [lʊtçíj]: 2888
лу́чшая [lútçҫəʲɪ]: 2747
лу́чше [lútçҫɪ]: 2055, 2063, 2064, 2065, 2066, ..., +9
люби́мая [lʲübʲíməʲə]: 2496
люби́мое [lʲübʲíməʲɪ]: 2052

лю́бит [lʲübʲɪt]: 2062
лю́бишь [lʲübʲɪç]: 2045, 2282
люблю́ [lʲüblʲú]: 2048, 2053, 2061, 2173, 2262, ..., +3
любо́й [lʲübʷój]: 2440
любо́м [lʲübʷóm]: 2449
лю́бят [lʲübʲɪt]: 2913
лю́двиг [lʲüdvʲɪg]: 2974, 2975
лю́двига [lʲüdvʲɪgə]: 2927
люде́й [lʲüdʲéj]: 2076, 2264, 2415, 2476, 2526, ..., +6
лю́ди [lʲüdʲɪ]: 2124, 2170, 2281, 2363, 2384, ..., +6
лю́дно [lʲüdnə]: 2616
людьми́ [lʲüdʲmʲí]: 2047, 2254, 2415, 2694
людя́м [lʲüdʲám]: 2999
лю́дям [lʲüdʲɪm]: 2425
магази́н [məgɐzʲín]: 2129
магази́нов [məgɐzʲínəf]: 2402
магази́нов [məgɐzʲínəv]: 2405
ма́гда [mágdə]: 2358
магна́т [mɐgnát]: 2766
мадри́да [mɐdrʲídə]: 2383, 2388
мала́ [mɐlá]: 2892
ма́леньким [málʲɪmʲkʲɪm]: 2289
ма́леньком [málʲɪmʲkəm]: 2095
мали́ки [mɐlʲíkʲɪ]: 2091
ма́ло [málə]: 2416, 2417, 2420, 2585
ма́льчик [málʲtçɪk]: 2548
ма́ма [mámə]: 2664
ма́ме [mámʲɪ]: 2029
ма́мы [mámɨ]: 2747, 2857
ма́ркетинг [márkʲɪtʲɪnk]: 2754
марке́тинговым [mɐrkʲétʲɪngəvɨm]: 2984
ма́рко [márkə]: 2246
ма́ске [máskʲɪ]: 2677
ма́сла [máslə]: 2872
мать [matʲ]: 2887
мать-одино́чка [mətʲ-ɐdʲɪnótçkə]: 2377
махмуд [maxmud]: 2942
маши́н [mɐṣín]: 2757

маши́на [mɐʂínə]: 2017, 2115, 2150, 2706

маши́нах [mɐʂínəx]: 2473

маши́не [mɐʂínʲɪ]: 2061, 2094, 2337, 2601, 2767

машини́ст [mɐʂinʲíst]: 2750

маши́ну [mɐʂínʊ]: 2019, 2065, 2176, 2186, 2219, ..., +6

маши́ны [mɐʂínɨ]: 2017, 2211, 2384, 2784

ма́я [máʲə]: 2708

ме́бель [mʲébʲɪlʲ]: 2232, 2239, 2530

ме́ган [mʲégən]: 2907

медици́нском [mʲɪdʲɪtsínskəm]: 2732

ме́дленнее [mʲédlʲɪmnʲɪ́ʲɪ]: 2606

ме́жду [mʲéʐdʊ]: 2300, 2307, 2791, 2792, 2949

междунаро́дной [mʲɪʐdʊnɐródnəj]: 2025

междунаро́дным [mʲɪʐdʊnɐródnɨm]: 2978

ме́ксикой [mʲéksʲɪkəj]: 2307

ме́неджер [mʲénʲɪdzɨr]: 2984

ме́неджера [mʲénʲɪdzɨrə]: 2030

ме́неджером [mʲénʲɪdzɨrəm]: 2031, 2682, 2683

ме́неджеру [mʲénʲɪdzɨrʊ]: 2166, 2860

ме́нее [mʲénʲɪʲɪ]: 2616, 2948

ме́ньше [mʲénʲʂɨ]: 2613, 2615, 2617, 2651

меня [mʲenʲa]: 2252, 2812, 2813, 2968

меня́ [mʲɪnʲá]: 2005, 2011, 2016, 2032, 2048, ..., +39

меня́ется [mʲɪnʲǽʲɪtsʲɪ]: 2487

ме́ре [mʲérʲɪ]: 2564, 2955

мест [mʲest]: 2034, 2734

места́ [mʲéstə]: 2122, 2125, 2206, 2227, 2925

места́ми [mʲɪstámʲɪ]: 2260

места́х [mʲɪstáx]: 2211

ме́сте [mʲéstʲɪ]: 2059, 2491, 2492, 2795, 2950

ме́стного [mʲésnəvə]: 2213

ме́сто [mʲéstə]: 2034, 2125, 2134, 2373, 2390, ..., +3

ме́сяц [mʲésʲɪts]: 2258, 2496, 2770, 2788

ме́сяца [mʲésʲɪtsə]: 2961

ме́сяце [mʲésʲɪtsɨ]: 2637

ме́сяцев [mʲésʲɪtsɨf]: 2461, 2712

ме́сяцев [mʲésʲɪtsɨv]: 2028, 2640

метро́ [mʲɪtró]: 2907

ме́тров [mʲétrəf]: 2749, 2771

мечта́л [mʲɪtɕtáł]: 2855

мечта́ла [mʲɪtɕtálə]: 2855

миле́на [mʲɪlʲénə]: 2273

миле́ны [mʲɪlʲénɨ]: 2272

миллио́н [mʲɪłłʲóːn]: 2271

миллио́нов [mʲɪłłʲóːnəv]: 2536

ми́ло [mʲílə]: 2155, 2793

ми́лые [mʲílɨ̈ɪ]: 2520

ми́мо [mʲímə]: 2174

минима́льную [mʲɪmʲɪmálʲnʊ̈ü]: 2876

мину́т [mʲɪmút]: 2460, 2560, 2647, 2710, 2767, ..., +1

мину́тах [mʲɪmútəx]: 2118

мину́тного [mʲɪmútnəvə]: 2343

мину́ту [mʲɪmútʊ]: 2563

мину́ты [mʲɪmútɨ]: 2343

ми́ре [mʲírʲɪ]: 2266, 2303, 2487, 2914

мири́ться [mʲɪrʲítʲsʲɪ]: 2978

ми́ркетинг [mʲírkʲɪtʲmk]: 2941

ми́ру [mʲírʊ]: 2107, 2752

ми́тико [mʲítʲɪkə]: 2214

мла́дший [mlátʂɨj]: 2277

мне [mnʲɛ]: 2001, 2003, 2013, 2015, 2016, ..., +72

мне́ние [mnʲénʲʲɪ]: 2178

мне́нию [mnʲénʲʲü]: 2747

мно́гие [mnóɡʲʲɪ]: 2281, 2434, 2785, 2786, 2815, ..., +1

мно́гим [mnóɡʲɪm]: 2216

мно́гими [mnóɡʲɪmʲɪ]: 2254, 2415, 2792

мно́гих [mnóɡʲɪx]: 2296, 2476

мно́го [mnóɡə]: 2042, 2085, 2126, 2127, 2133, ..., +22

мно́гое [mnóɡəʲɪ]: 2580

мно́гому [mnóɡəmʊ]: 2997

мно́жество [mnóʐɨstfə]: 2340

мной [mnoj]: 2146, 2447, 2488, 2497, 2665, ..., +3

моби́льное [mɐbʲílʲnəʲɪ]: 2780

моби́льном [mɐbʲílʲnəm]: 2779

мог [mʷok]: 2056, 2146, 2194, 2343, 2445, ..., +6

мог [mʷog]: 2019, 2578

могла́ [mɐglá]: 2056, 2150, 2194, 2343, 2445, ..., +5

могли́ [mɐglʲí]: 2034, 2137, 2148, 2450, 2589, ..., +6

могло́ [mɐgló]: 2454, 2959

могу́ [mɐgú]: 2044, 2220, 2223, 2349, 2422, ..., +6

мо́гут [mʷógut]: 2679, 2778, 2867

мо́дой [mʷódəj]: 2832

моё [mɐʲó]: 2052, 2787, 2803

моего́ [mɐʲɪvʷó]: 2197, 2404, 2895, 2968, 2973

мое́й [mɐʲéj]: 2370, 2747, 2762, 2779, 2784, ..., +3

моём [mɐʲóm]: 2224, 2779, 2917

моему́ [mɐʲɪmú]: 2850

мо́жем [mʷóʐɨm]: 2440, 2985

мо́жет [mʷóʐɨt]: 2211, 2484, 2562, 2758, 2795, ..., +2

мо́жете [mʷóʐɨtʲɪ]: 2619

мо́жешь [mʷóʐɨɕ]: 2001, 2027, 2041, 2074, 2117, ..., +10

мо́жно [mʷóʐnə]: 2052, 2121, 2135, 2136, 2151, ..., +9

мой [mɐʲí]: 2039, 2220, 2239, 2603, 2738, ..., +6

мойм [mɐʲím]: 2856

мойх [mɐʲíx]: 2452

мой [mʷoj]: 2015, 2124, 2241, 2242, 2367, ..., +7

мо́края [mʷókrəʲɪ]: 2568

мо́крый [mʷókrɨj]: 2568

мо́лоды [mʷólədɨ]: 2595

молока́ [mələká]: 2330

молоко́ [mələkʷó]: 2566, 2982

моло́чный [mɐlótɕnɨj]: 2330

моме́нт [mɐmʲént]: 2156, 2626

моме́нта [mɐmʲéntə]: 2019

мо́ника [mʷónʲɪkə]: 2416

москве́ [mɐskfʲɛ́]: 2320

моти́вам [mɐtʲívəm]: 2817

мотоци́клах [mətɐtsíkləx]: 2679

мою́ [mɐʲú]: 2374, 2670

моя́ [mɐʲá]: 2239, 2262, 2367, 2371, 2432, ..., +11

муж [muz]: 2091

муж [muʂ]: 2514

мужчи́н [muɕɕín]: 2545, 2964

мужчи́на [muɕɕínə]: 2202, 2335, 2497, 2510, 2951

мужчи́ной [muɕɕínəj]: 2552

мужчи́ну [muɕɕínu]: 2515, 2517, 2518, 2556

музе́й [muzʲéj]: 2318, 2503

му́зыка [múzɨkə]: 2357, 2590

музыка́льному [muzɨkálʲnəmu]: 2818

му́зыку [múzɨku]: 2385, 2687

муки́ [mukʲí]: 2872

му́сор [músər]: 2919

му́сорные [músərnɨʲɪ]: 2919

мы [mɨ]: 2014, 2023, 2026, 2034, 2057, ..., +85

мы́слей [mɨslʲɪj]: 2434

мю́нхен [mʲ̈ɨnxʲɪn]: 2630

мя́со [mʲásə]: 2214, 2285

на [na]: 2020, 2023, 2035, 2049, 2052, ..., +160

наблюда́ется [nɐblʲüdáʲɪtsʲɪ]: 2782

набрала́ [nəbrɐlá]: 2756

наверняка́ [nɐvʲɪrnʲɪká]: 2168, 2388

навести́ть [nɐvʲɪstʲítʲ]: 2273

навреди́ли [nɐvrʲɪdʲílʲɪ]: 2999

на́выки [návɨkʲɪ]: 2074

над [nat]: 2139, 2838, 2906

над [nad]: 2786

надави́л [nədɐvʲíɫ]: 2717

надави́ла [nədɐvʲílə]: 2717

надева́ю [nɐdʲɪváʲü]: 2145

наде́емся [nɐdʲéʲɪmsʲɪ]: 2927

наде́л [nɐdʲéɫ]: 2022

наде́то [nɐdʲétə]: 2501

надéюсь [nɐdʲéʲüsʲ]: 2231, 2314, 2698, 2905

нáдо [nádə]: 2066, 2504

надоéло [nədɐʲélə]: 2806

нажáть [nɐzátʲ]: 2035

назáд [nɐzát]: 2028, 2582, 2621, 2641, 2879, ..., +1

назáд [nɐzád]: 2030, 2640, 2749, 2973

назвáние [nɐzvánʲrʲɪ]: 2502

назнáченная [nɐznátɕɪnnəʲɪ]: 2339

назывáем [nɐzɨváʲɪm]: 2922

назывáется [nɐzɨváʲɪtsʲɪ]: 2333, 2502, 2507

найдя́ [nɐjdʲá]: 2206

найти́ [nɐjtʲí]: 2034, 2125, 2134, 2220, 2512, ..., +4

наконéц [nəkɐnʲéts]: 2206, 2910, 2913

накричáл [nɐkrʲɪtɕáɫ]: 2182, 2808

накричáла [nɐkrʲɪtɕálə]: 2182, 2808

налáдится [nɐládʲɪtsʲɪ]: 2927

налáживать [nɐlázɨvətʲ]: 2764

налúчие [nɐlʲítɕɪrʲɪ]: 2017

налúчных [nɐlʲítɕnɨx]: 2763

налóги [nɐlóɡʲɪ]: 2292

нам [nam]: 2023, 2110, 2112, 2137, 2140, ..., +11

нáми [námʲɪ]: 2645

намнóго [nɐmnóɡə]: 2297, 2380

нанесённый [nɐnʲɪsʲénnɨj]: 2960

наоборóт [nɐɐbɐrót]: 2177

нападёт [nəpɐdʲét]: 2361

напáдкам [nɐpátkəm]: 2958

написáл [nɐpʲɪsáɫ]: 2602, 2642, 2823

написáла [nɐpʲɪsálə]: 2642, 2823

написáть [nɐpʲɪsátʲ]: 2764

напúток [nɐpʲítək]: 2849

напиши́те [nɐpʲɪʂítʲɪ]: 2474

напóлни [nɐpʷóɫnʲɪ]: 2912

напоминáешь [nəpɐmʲɪnáʲɪɕ]: 2857

напóмнил [nɐpʷómnʲɪɫ]: 2859

напóмнила [nɐpʷómnʲɪlə]: 2859

напóмнить [nɐpʷómnʲɪtʲ]: 2001

напóмню [nɐpʷómnʲü]: 2663

напрáвили [nɐprávʲɪlʲɪ]: 2840

напряжённой [nɐprʲɪʐénnəj]: 2758

напугáл [nɐpʊɡáɫ]: 2813

наравнé [nərɐvnʲé]: 2683

наркóзом [nɐrkʷózəm]: 2821

нарóду [nɐródʊ]: 2605

нас [nas]: 2058, 2108, 2147, 2226, 2236, ..., +19

населéния [nəsʲɪlʲénʲrʲə]: 2532, 2966

насúльственных [nəsʲílʲstfʲɪnnɨx]: 2885

наслади́ться [nəslɐdʲítʲsʲɪ]: 2112

наслаждáйся [nəslɐʐdájsʲɪ]: 2231

наслéдия [nɐslʲédʲrʲə]: 2832

настóлько [nɐstólʲkə]: 2590, 2788, 2847, 2892

настоя́л [nəstɐʲáɫ]: 2185

настоя́ли [nəstɐʲǽlʲɪ]: 2100, 2917

настрóена [nɐstrʷóʲmə]: 2818

настроéнии [nəstrɐʲénʲrʲɪ]: 2105

наýка [nɐúkə]: 2287

научи́лась [nɐʊtɕíləsʲ]: 2997

научи́лся [nɐʊtɕílsʲɪ]: 2997

нахóдит [nɐxódʲɪt]: 2086

нахóдится [nɐxódʲɪtsʲɪ]: 2089, 2091, 2300, 2316, 2317, ..., +5

нахóдятся [nɐxódʲɪtsʲɪ]: 2307

нáчал [nátɕəɫ]: 2724

началá [nətɕɪlá]: 2724, 2841

начáле [nɐtɕálʲɪ]: 2719

началóсь [nətɕɪlósʲ]: 2713

нáчался [nátɕəɫsʲɪ]: 2705

начáльником [nɐtɕálʲnʲɪkəm]: 2795

начáть [nɐtɕátʲ]: 2148, 2994

начинáло [nɐtɕɪnálə]: 2022

начинáлось [nɐtɕɪnáləsʲ]: 2675

начинáются [nɐtɕɪnáʲütsʲɪ]: 2169

наш [naʂ]: 2119, 2454, 2583, 2596, 2610, ..., +4

нáша [náʂə]: 2089, 2347, 2348, 2725

нáше [náʂɪ]: 2828

нáшего [náʂɪvə]: 2610

нашёл [nɐʂéɫ]: 2493, 2535

нáшем [náʂɪm]: 2537, 2913

нáши [náʂɪ]: 2913, 2914

нáшим [náʂɪm]: 2112, 2984

нáшими [náʂimʲɪ]: 2368
нашлá [nɐʂlá]: 2131, 2493, 2549, 2640, 2915, ..., + 1
нашлú [nɐʂlʲí]: 2742, 2916
не [nʲɪ]: 2003, 2004, 2005, 2007, 2008, ..., + 248
не [nʲɛ]: 2800, 2821
нé [nʲɛ́]: 2034, 2116, 2119, 2121, 2122, ..., + 14
нéбо [nʲɛ́bə]: 2269
небольшóм [nʲɪbɐlʲʂóm]: 2721
невéжливо [nʲɪvʲézlʲɪvə]: 2775
невероя́тно [nʲɪvʲɪrɐʲátnə]: 2575
невозмóжно [nʲɪvɐzmʷóʐnə]: 2060, 2152
негó [nʲɪvʷó]: 2042, 2090, 2210, 2243, 2246, ..., + 5
недáвний [nʲɪdávnʲɪj]: 2340
недáвно [nʲɪdávnə]: 2521
недéле [nʲɪdʲélʲɪ]: 2323, 2340, 2634, 2698, 2733, ..., + 3
недéль [nʲɪdʲélʲ]: 2336, 2570
недéльный [nʲɪdʲélʲnɨj]: 2342
недéлю [nʲɪdʲélʲü]: 2265, 2342, 2691, 2711
недолю́бливают [nʲɪdɐlʲúblʲɪvɐʲüt]: 2354
недоразумéние [nʲɪdərɐzumʲénʲrʲɪ]: 2880
недостáточно [nʲɪdɐstátətɕnə]: 2058, 2246, 2327
недоýчками [nʲɪdɐútɕkəmʲɪ]: 2922
неё [nʲɪrʲǿ]: 2401, 2416, 2690, 2900
незавúсимо [nʲɪzɐvʲísʲɪmə]: 2879
незавúсимы [nʲɪzɐvʲísʲɪmɨ]: 2830
незавúсимый [nʲɪzɐvʲísʲɪmɨj]: 2848
незнакóмцами [nʲɪznɐkʷómtsəmʲɪ]: 2795
незнáние [nʲɪznánʲrʲɪ]: 2213
незначúтельные [nʲɪznɐtɕítʲɪlʲnʲrʲɪ]: 2792
ней [nʲej]: 2106, 2544, 2754, 2859, 2881
нéкоторые [nʲɛ́kətərʲɪ]: 2259, 2284, 2363, 2426, 2435, ..., + 7
нéкоторым [nʲɛ́kətərɨm]: 2425
нéкоторыми [nʲɛ́kətərɨmʲɪ]: 2694

нéкоторых [nʲɛ́kətərɨx]: 2211, 2866
нельзя́ [nʲɪlʲzʲá]: 2026, 2183
нём [nʲǿm]: 2406, 2797, 2850, 2959
немнóгие [nʲɪmnógʲrʲɪ]: 2421
немнóго [nʲɪmnógə]: 2137, 2255, 2418, 2419, 2606, ..., + 2
немý [nʲɪmú]: 2951
ненавúдел [nʲɪmɐvʲídʲɪɫ]: 2051
ненавúдела [nʲɪmɐvʲídʲɪlə]: 2051
ненавúдит [nʲɪmɐvʲídʲɪt]: 2046
ненавúжу [nʲɪmɐvʲíʐʊ]: 2585
ненарóчно [nʲɪmɐrótɕnə]: 2759
необходúмо [nʲɪɐbxɐdʲímə]: 2079
необходúмое [nʲɪɐbxɐdʲímeʲɪ]: 2914
необходúмости [nʲɪɐbxɐdʲíməstʲɪ]: 2413, 2775
неожúданностью [nʲɪɐzʲídənnəstʲü]: 2381
неподходя́щий [nʲɪpətxɐdʲǽɕɕɪj]: 2626
непрáвильно [nʲɪprávʲɪlʲnə]: 2075
непремéнно [nʲɪprʲɪmʲénnə]: 2164
неприя́тности [nʲɪprʲɪrʲátnəstʲɪ]: 2397
нéрвничал [nʲérvnʲɪtɕəɫ]: 2802
нéрвничала [nʲérvnʲɪtɕələ]: 2802
нéрвничаю [nʲérvnʲɪtɕəʲü]: 2044, 2349
несёт [nʲɪsʲǿt]: 2833
нéсколькими [nʲéskəlʲkʲɪmʲɪ]: 2368
нéскольких [nʲéskəlʲkʲɪx]: 2437
нéсколько [nʲéskəlʲkə]: 2024, 2028, 2031, 2139, 2256, ..., + 10
несмотря́ [nʲɪsmɐtrʲá]: 2655, 2656, 2657, 2658, 2661
несчастлúвыми [nʲɪɕɕɪstlʲívɨmʲɪ]: 2478
несчáстного [nʲɪɕɕásnəvə]: 2217, 2264
несчáстный [nʲɪɕɕásnɨj]: 2189
несчáстных [nʲɪɕɕásnɨx]: 2384
нет [nʲet]: 2029, 2070, 2115, 2117, 2118, ..., + 14
нетерпéнием [nʲɪtʲɪrpʲénʲrʲɪm]: 2082, 2106
неудáчу [nʲɪʊdátɕʊ]: 2949
нефтянóй [nʲɪftʲɪnój]: 2766
нефтяну́ю [nʲɪftʲɪmúʲü]: 2986
нефтяны́е [nʲɪftʲɪmʲrʲɪ]: 2333
нефтяны́м [nʲɪftʲɪnʲím]: 2333

нецензу́рной [nʲɪtsɪnzúrnəj]: 2103
не́чем [nʲétɕɪm]: 2423, 2557, 2585
нече́стно [nʲɪtɕésnə]: 2157
ни [nʲi]: 2343, 2372, 2403, 2404, 2405, ..., +7
ни́ [nʲí]: 2450
нигде́ [nʲɪɡdʲɛ́]: 2034
ни́зкой [nʲískəj]: 2661
ника́к [nʲɪkák]: 2019, 2032, 2220, 2924, 2976
никаки́х [nʲɪkɐkʲíx]: 2535
никогда́ [nʲɪkɐɡdá]: 2366, 2465, 2481, 2632, 2754, ..., +1
никому́ [nʲɪkɐmú]: 2010, 2067, 2408, 2433, 2583
никто́ [nʲɪktó]: 2079, 2109, 2147, 2149, 2176, ..., +8
никуда́ [nʲɪkʊdá]: 2064, 2424, 2465, 2572
ним [nʲim]: 2057, 2088, 2419, 2850
ни́ми [nʲímʲɪ]: 2739
них [nʲix]: 2102, 2161, 2395, 2435, 2437, ..., +8
ничего́ [nʲɪtɕɪvʷó]: 2015, 2044, 2117, 2121, 2407, ..., +4
но [nɐ]: 2018, 2019, 2023, 2032, 2034, ..., +59
но́вая [nóvəʲə]: 2089, 2090, 2252
но́вого [nóvəvə]: 2945
но́вое [nóvəʲɪ]: 2825
но́вой [nóvəj]: 2107
но́вости [nóvəstʲɪ]: 2161, 2234, 2324
но́востью [nóvəstʲü]: 2804
новостя́х [nəvɐstʲáx]: 2753
но́вую [nóvʊʲü]: 2131, 2358, 2994
но́вые [nóvɨʲɪ]: 2088, 2982
но́вый [nóvɨj]: 2216, 2382, 2543, 2583, 2781, ..., +2
но́вым [nóvɨm]: 2984
но́выми [nóvɨmʲɪ]: 2047
но́вых [nóvɨx]: 2251
но́гу [nóɡʊ]: 2200
но́мер [nómʲɪr]: 2146, 2665
номеро́в [nɐmʲɪróf]: 2034
носи́ли [nɐsʲílʲɪ]: 2901

но́сит [nósʲɪt]: 2579, 2648
но́чи [nótɕɪ]: 2199, 2703
ночь [notɕ]: 2463
нра́вилась [nrávʲɪləsʲ]: 2806, 2997
нра́вился [nrávʲɪlsʲɪ]: 2615, 2806
нра́вится [nrávʲɪtsʲɪ]: 2042, 2047, 2049, 2050, 2061, ..., +5
нра́вятся [nrávʲɪtsʲɪ]: 2354, 2506, 2758
нужда́етесь [nʊzdáʲɪtʲɪsʲ]: 2830
нужда́ется [nʊzdáʲɪtsʲɪ]: 2156, 2889
нужда́ются [nʊzdáʲütsʲɪ]: 2039
ну́жен [núzɪn]: 2247, 2850
нужна́ [nʊzná]: 2040, 2041
ну́жно [núznə]: 2036, 2037, 2038, 2039, 2136, ..., +11
нужны́ [nʊznɨ́]: 2220
ну́жны [núznɨ]: 2253
ну́рия [núrʲɪʲə]: 2737
нью-йо́рк [nʲü-jórk]: 2328
нью-йо́рке [nʲü-jórkʲɪ]: 2318
нью-йо́ркского [nʲü-jórkskəvə]: 2244
о [ɐ]: 2010, 2021, 2029, 2070, 2101, ..., +27
об [ɐb]: 2178, 2248, 2398, 2411, 2846, ..., +3
о́ба [óbə]: 2438, 2443, 2635
обвинён [ɐbvʲɪnʲɛ́n]: 2865
обвини́ла [ɐbvʲɪnʲílə]: 2864
обвини́ли [ɐbvʲɪnʲílʲɪ]: 2108
обвини́ть [ɐbvʲɪnʲítʲ]: 2883
обду́мать [ɐbdúmətʲ]: 2422
о́бе [óbʲɪ]: 2443, 2445, 2541
обе́д [ɐbʲét]: 2870
обе́да [ɐbʲédə]: 2695
обе́ду [ɐbʲédʊ]: 2715
обе́им [ɐbʲɛ́ɪm]: 2542
оберну́лся [ɐbʲɪrnúɫsʲɪ]: 2454
обеспе́чивают [ɐbʲɪspʲétɕɪvəʲüt]: 2913
обеща́л [ɐbʲɪɕɕát]: 2924
обеща́ла [ɐbʲɪɕɕálə]: 2924
обеща́ния [ɐbʲɪɕɕánʲʲɪʲə]: 2891
оби́деть [ɐbʲídʲɪtʲ]: 2759
обихо́да [ɐbʲɪxódə]: 2983
облака́х [əblɐkáx]: 2127

обнаруже́ния [əbnɐʊzénʲrʲə]: 2865
обнару́жили [əbnɐʊzʲ́ıˈɪ]: 2990
о́браз [óbrəz]: 2893
образова́ние [əbrəzɐvánʲrʲı]: 2914
образова́нии [əbrəzɐvánʲrʲı]: 2913
образова́ния [əbrəzɐvánʲrʲə]: 2923
обрати́ться [əbrɐtʲítʲsʲ́ɪ]: 2861
обра́тно [ɐbrátnə]: 2092, 2364
обсле́довал [ɐpslʲédəvət]: 2535
обслу́живание [ɐpslúzɪvənʲrʲı]: 2943
обслу́живании [ɐpslúzɪvənʲrʲı]: 2860
обсуди́ли [ɐpsʊdʲílʲı]: 2096
обсужда́ть [ɐpsʊzdátʲ]: 2941
обсужде́ние [ɐpsʊzdʲénʲrʲı]: 2845
обсужде́нию [ɐpsʊzdʲénʲrʲü]: 2025
о́бувь [óbʊvʲ]: 2920
обще́нии [ɐbççénʲrʲı]: 2419
обще́ния [ɐbççénʲrʲə]: 2213
объединенно́м [ɐbʲıdʲınʲmnʲénəm]: 2314
объединённое [ɐbʲıdʲınʲénnəʲı]: 2315
объёмный [ɐbʲémnɪj]: 2250
объясне́ние [ɐbʲısnʲénʲrʲı]: 2558
объяснено́ [ɐbʲısnʲmó]: 2484
объясни́ть [ɐbʲısnʲítʲ]: 2598, 2835
обы́чно [ɐbítɕnə]: 2124, 2279, 2616, 2633
обы́чного [ɐbítɕnəvə]: 2605
обя́занности [ɐbʲázənnəstʲı]: 2852
овоще́й [əvɐçḉj]: 2342
о́вощи [óvəççı]: 2342, 2375
огля́дываясь [ɐɡlʲádɪvəʲısʲ]: 2997
огне́ [ɐɡnʲέ]: 2948
ого́нь [ɐɡʷɡ́nʲ]: 2947
ограбле́ния [əɡrɐblʲénʲrʲə]: 2549
огражде́ние [əɡrɐzdʲénʲrʲı]: 2906
оде́ждой [ɐdʲézdəj]: 2913
оде́жду [ɐdʲézdʊ]: 2579, 2901
оде́лся [ɐdʲétsʲı]: 2352
оде́т [ɐdʲét]: 2579
оде́та [ɐdʲétə]: 2501
одея́л [ɐdʲrʲát]: 2902
оди́н [ɐdʲín]: 2405, 2439, 2442, 2563, 2757, ..., +4

одиннадцати [ɐdʲínnəttsətʲı]: 2703
оди́ннадцатого [ɐdʲínnəttsətəvə]: 2804
одино́кий [ɐdʲınókʲıj]: 3000
одино́ко [ɐdʲınókə]: 2135
одино́чку [ɐdʲınótɕkʊ]: 2376, 2378
одна́ [ɐdná]: 2086, 2087, 2371, 2377, 2536, ..., +1
одна́ко [ɐdnákə]: 2902
одни́м [ɐdnʲím]: 2369
одного́ [ɐdnɐvʷ́ó]: 2403, 2988
одно́й [ɐdnój]: 2012, 2491, 2825
одно́м [ɐdnóm]: 2441, 2449
одному́ [ɐdnɐmú]: 2777
одобря́ет [ɐdɐbrʲǽʲıt]: 2103
одобря́ют [ɐdɐbrʲǽüt]: 2867
одолжи́л [ɐdɐtzʲít]: 2515, 2998
одолжи́ла [ɐdɐtzʲílə]: 2515, 2998
одолжи́ть [ɐdɐtzʲítʲ]: 2374, 2670
оживлённое [ɐzɪvlʲénnəʲı]: 2386
ожида́ется [ɐzɪdáʲıtsʲı]: 2260
ожида́л [ɐzɪdát]: 2381, 2603, 2829
ожида́ла [ɐzɪdálə]: 2381, 2603, 2829
ожида́ли [ɐzɪdáʲı]: 2324, 2421
о́зера [ózʲrə]: 2721
ознако́мил [əznɐkʷ́ómʲıt]: 2257
означа́ет [əznɐtɕáʲıt]: 2210, 2830, 2981
оказа́лась [əkɐzáləsʲ]: 2660, 2798, 2929
оказа́лись [əkɐzáʲısʲ]: 2324
оказа́лось [əkɐzáləsʲ]: 2503, 2651
оказа́лся [əkɐzátsʲı]: 2503
оказа́ться [əkɐzátʲsʲı]: 2059, 2795
океа́н [ɐkʲrán]: 2300, 2304
океа́на [ɐkʲránə]: 2390
о́кна [óknə]: 2018
окно́ [ɐknó]: 2073, 2255, 2844
о́коло [ókələ]: 2312, 2386
оконча́ния [əkɐntɕánʲrʲə]: 2072, 2950
око́нчила [ɐkʷóntɕılə]: 2371
око́нчу [ɐkʷóntɕʊ]: 2274
окружа́ющую [ɐkrʊzáʲüççʊʲü]: 2270
окси́д [ɐksʲíd]: 2871
о́льги [ólʲɡʲı]: 2766

он [on]: 2010, 2016, 2019, 2022, 2031, ..., +74
она́ [ɐná]: 2043, 2075, 2086, 2087, 2091, ..., +42
они́ [ɐnʲí]: 2008, 2066, 2088, 2100, 2108, ..., +35
оно́ [ɐnó]: 2216, 2501
опа́здывает [ɐpázdɨvəˀɪt]: 2636
опа́сна [ɐpásnə]: 2170
опа́сно [ɐpásnə]: 2167
опа́сными [ɐpásnɨmʲɪ]: 2679
опера́ции [ɐpʲɪrátsɨˀɪ]: 2821
опереди́в [ɐpʲɪrʲɪdʲíf]: 2771
опла́те [ɐplátʲɪ]: 2100
опозда́ет [əpɐzdáˀɪt]: 2636
опозда́л [əpɐzdáł]: 2379, 2560, 2618, 2681, 2824
опозда́ла [əpɐzdálə]: 2379, 2560, 2618, 2681
опозда́ли [əpɐzdálʲɪ]: 2163
опозда́ть [əpɐzdátʲ]: 2141
опозда́ю [əpɐzdáˀü]: 2715
определи́ть [ɐprʲɪdʲɪlʲítʲ]: 2833
опроси́ть [əprɐsʲítʲ]: 2323
опусти́ть [ɐpustʲítʲ]: 2992
о́пыт [ópɨt]: 2228, 2229
о́пыта [ópɨtə]: 2246, 2594
о́пытен [ópɨtʲɪn]: 2594
опя́ть [ɐpʲǽtʲ]: 2212, 2479, 2824
ора́тор [ɐrátər]: 2805
организа́ции [ərgɐnʲɪzátsɨˀɪ]: 2852
организо́вана [ərgɐnʲɪzóvənə]: 2577
ору́жие [ɐrúzɨˀɪ]: 2840
оса́дки [ɐsátkʲɪ]: 2260
освободи́ть [əsvɐbɐdʲítʲ]: 2945
о́скар [óskər]: 2938
основа́нии [əsnɐvánʲɪˀɪ]: 2791
основно́й [əsnɐvnój]: 2341
основно́м [əsnɐvnóm]: 2872
осо́бенно [ɐsóbʲɪnnə]: 2424
оста́вил [ɐstávʲɪł]: 2146
оста́вила [ɐstávʲɪlə]: 2146
оста́влю [ɐstávlʲü]: 2664
остаётся [əstɐˀɵtsʲɪ]: 2416

оста́лись [ɐstálʲɪsʲ]: 2281, 2943
оста́лось [ɐstáləsʲ]: 2403, 2420, 2551, 2734
остально́е [əstɐlʲnóˀɪ]: 2416
остальны́е [əstɐlʲnˀɪ]: 2741
остана́вливайся [əstɐnávlʲɪvəjsʲɪ]: 2935
остана́вливаться [əstɐnávlʲɪvətʲsʲɪ]: 2007
останови́лась [əstɐnɐvʲíləsʲ]: 2727
останови́лись [əstɐnɐvʲílʲɪsʲ]: 2505
останови́лся [əstɐnɐvʲíłsʲɪ]: 2727
остано́вимся [əstɐnóvʲɪmsʲɪ]: 2671
останови́ть [əstɐnɐvʲítʲ]: 2867
останови́ться [əstɐnɐvʲítʲsʲɪ]: 2449
остано́вки [əstɐnófkʲɪ]: 2077, 2696
оста́нусь [ɐstánusʲ]: 2063
оста́ться [ɐstátʲsʲɪ]: 2063, 2226, 2917
остаю́сь [əstɐˀúsʲ]: 2424
осторо́жно [əstɐrózpnə]: 2172
осторо́жны [əstɐrózpnɨ]: 2205
о́строве [óstrəvʲɪ]: 2721
острово́в [əstrɐvʷóv]: 2312
от [ɐt]: 2421, 2469, 2496, 2758, 2825, ..., +15
отбира́л [ɐtbʲɪráł]: 2298
отве́т [ɐtfʲét]: 2996
отве́тил [ɐtfʲétʲɪł]: 2642, 2834
отве́тила [ɐtfʲétʲɪlə]: 2834
отве́тить [ɐtfʲétʲɪtʲ]: 2152, 2154, 2395
отве́тных [ɐtfʲétnɨx]: 2995
отве́тственность [ɐtfʲétstfʲɪnnəstʲ]: 2833
отве́ты [ɐtfʲétɨ]: 2474
отвеча́ет [ɐtfʲɪtɕáˀɪt]: 2580
отвеча́ть [ɐtfʲɪtɕátʲ]: 2837
отвеча́ющей [ɐtfʲɪtɕáˀüɕɕɪj]: 2754
отвлека́л [ɐtflʲɪkáł]: 2079
отврати́тельное [ətfrɐtʲítʲɪlʲnəˀɪ]: 2559
отврати́тельным [ətfrɐtʲítʲɪlʲnɨm]: 2943
отда́л [ɐtdáł]: 2499, 2794
отдала́ [ətdɐlá]: 2499, 2994
отда́ла [ɐtdálə]: 2499
отда́ть [ɐtdátʲ]: 2797
отде́ле [ɐtdʲélʲɪ]: 2724

отде́льно [ɐtdʲélʲnə]: 2371
отде́льном [ɐtdʲélʲnəm]: 2474
отдохни́ [ətdɐxnʲí]: 2231
отдохну́ть [ətdɐxnútʲ]: 2343, 2527
о́тдых [ótdɨx]: 2343
оте́ле [ɐtélʲɪ]: 2007, 2505, 2671
оте́лей [ɐtélʲɪj]: 2449
оте́ли [ɐtélʲɪ]: 2034
оте́ль [ɐtélʲ]: 2507, 2611, 2963
оте́ля [ɐtélʲɪ]: 2674
оте́лях [ɐtélʲɪx]: 2248
оте́ц [ɐtʲéts]: 2158, 2766
отказа́лся [ətkɐzálsʲɪ]: 2393, 2837
отказа́ть [ətkɐzátʲ]: 2023
отказа́ться [ətkɐzátʲsʲɪ]: 2924, 2986
отка́зывали [ɐtkázɨvəlʲɪ]: 2950
откла́дывать [ɐtkládɨvətʲ]: 2985
откры́л [ɐtkrɨl]: 2208
откры́т [ɐtkrɨt]: 2405
откры́тыми [ɐtkrɨtɨmʲɪ]: 2032
откры́тых [ɐtkrɨtɨx]: 2402
откры́ть [ɐtkrɨtʲ]: 2136, 2255, 2450, 2722, 2769
отлича́лась [ɐtlʲɪtɕáləsʲ]: 2469
отлича́лся [ɐtlʲɪtɕálsʲɪ]: 2829
отли́чные [ɐtlʲítɕnʲɪ]: 2970
отменена́ [ɐtmʲɪnʲɪná]: 2339
отмени́ть [ɐtmʲɪnʲítʲ]: 2936
отнесла́сь [ɐtnʲɪslásʲ]: 2817
отноше́ние [ətnɐʂénʲɪ̯ɪ]: 2788
отноше́ния [ətnɐʂénʲɪ̯ə]: 2789, 2976
отноше́ниях [ətnɐʂénʲɪ̯ɪx]: 2927
отойти́ [ətɐjtʲí]: 2599
отпра́вил [ɐtprávʲɪl]: 2533
отпра́вилась [ɐtprávʲɪləsʲ]: 2940
отпра́вили [ɐtprávʲɪlʲɪ]: 2540, 2635
отпра́вились [ɐtprávʲɪlʲɪsʲ]: 2368, 2733
отпра́вился [ɐtprávʲɪtsʲɪ]: 2938, 2940
отпра́вить [ɐtprávʲɪtʲ]: 2020, 2594, 2853
отпра́влю [ɐtprávlʲü]: 2699
отправля́ется [ətprɐvlʲǽɪtsʲɪ]: 2710
отправля́л [ətprɐvlʲál]: 2508
отправля́ла [ətprɐvlʲálə]: 2508, 2950

отправля́ются [ətprɐvlʲǽütsʲɪ]: 2752
отпроси́ться [ətprɐsʲítʲsʲɪ]: 2245
отпу́ск [ɐtpúsk]: 2454
о́тпуск [ótpʊsk]: 2058
о́тпуска [ótpʊskə]: 2694
о́тпуске [ótpʊskʲɪ]: 2459, 2588
о́тпуском [ótpʊskəm]: 2112, 2231, 2491, 2492
отремонти́рована [ətrʲɪmɐntʲírəvənə]: 2554
отремонти́рую [ətrʲɪmɐntʲírʊʲü]: 2065
отры́вом [ɐtrɨvəm]: 2771
отсу́тствие [ɐtsútstfʲɪ̯ɪ]: 2211
отсу́тствует [ɐtsútstfʊɪt]: 2932
отсю́да [ɐtsʲúdə]: 2118, 2180, 2596
отцо́м [ɐttsóm]: 2856
о́фис [ófʲɪs]: 2051
офице́ра [ɐfʲɪtsérə]: 2534
очеви́дных [ɐtɕɪvʲídnʲɪx]: 2823
очеви́дцы [ɐtɕɪvʲíttsɨ]: 2842
о́чень [ótɕɪnʲ]: 2023, 2088, 2089, 2090, 2119, ..., +53
о́череди [ótɕɪrʲɪdʲɪ]: 2084, 2850, 2851
очки́ [ɐtɕkʲí]: 2220
оши́бке [ɐʂípkʲɪ]: 2761
оши́бки [ɐʂípkʲɪ]: 2573
оши́бкой [ɐʂípkəj]: 2880
оши́бок [ɐʂíbək]: 2823
оши́бочно [ɐʂíbətɕnə]: 2865
оштрафо́ван [ɐʂtrɐfʷóvən]: 2486
па́бло [páblə]: 2702
па́вел [pávʲɪl]: 2505
паде́ние [pɐdʲénʲɪ̯ɪ]: 2783
пальто́ [pɐlʲtó]: 2022, 2648
па́оло [páələ]: 2290
па́па [pápə]: 2765
пари́ж [pɐrʲíʂ]: 2937
пари́же [pɐrʲíʐɨ]: 2248
паркова́ться [pərkɐvátʲsʲɪ]: 2008
парко́вка [pɐrkʷófkə]: 2009
парко́вки [pɐrkʷófkʲɪ]: 2134
парко́вочное [pɐrkʷóvətɕnəʲɪ]: 2373
па́рнем [párnʲɪm]: 2875
па́ру [párʊ]: 2527, 2551, 2922

паршивой [pɐrʂívəj]: 2943
паук [pɐúk]: 2813
пауки [pɐʊkʲí]: 2810, 2811, 2812
пауков [pɐʊkʷóf]: 2284, 2810, 2811, 2812
пахнет [páxnʲɪt]: 2565
пацифист [pɐtsɨfʲíst]: 2291
певцы [pʲɪftsɨ́]: 2752
пейджерами [pʲéjdzɨrəmʲɪ]: 2983
пекина [pʲɪkʲínə]: 2162
пентагон [pʲɪntɐgʷón]: 2321
первая [pʲérvəʲɪ]: 2997
первого [pʲérvəvə]: 2708, 2804
первой [pʲérvəj]: 2161
первым [pʲérvɨm]: 2161
переведёны [pʲɪrʲɪvʲɪdʲéni]: 2908
переговоры [pʲɪrʲɪgɐvʷórɨ]: 2949
перед [pʲérʲɪt]: 2256, 2940
перед [pʲérʲɪd]: 2008, 2009, 2071, 2881, 2920
передала [pʲɪrʲɪdɐlá]: 2737
передвигаться [pʲɪrʲɪdvʲɪgátʲsʲɪ]: 2017
передвижение [pʲɪrʲɪdvʲɪzɛ́nʲɪ̯ɪ]: 2017, 2211
передвижения [pʲɪrʲɪdvʲɪzɛ́nʲɪ̯ə]: 2322
передвинул [pʲɪrʲɪdvʲínʊɫ]: 2003
передвинула [pʲɪrʲɪdvʲínʊlə]: 2003
передвинуть [pʲɪrʲɪdvʲínʊtʲ]: 2041
переезд [pʲɪrʲɪ̯ézd]: 2629
переезжать [pʲɪrʲɪ̯ɪzʐátʲ]: 2104
переехала [pʲɪrʲɪ̯éxələ]: 2092
переехали [pʲɪrʲɪ̯éxəlʲɪ]: 2144
переехать [pʲɪrʲɪ̯éxətʲ]: 2994
переживать [pʲɪrʲɪzɨvátʲ]: 2117
пережить [pʲɪrʲɪzɨ́tʲ]: 2783
перезвонил [pʲɪrʲɪzvɐnʲíɫ]: 2114
перезвонила [pʲɪrʲɪzvɐnʲílə]: 2114
перейдём [pʲɪrʲɪjdʲém]: 2941
переночевать [pʲɪrʲɪnɐtɕɪvátʲ]: 2034
переполнен [pʲɪrʲɪpʷóɫnʲɪn]: 2735
переполнена [pʲɪrʲɪpʷóɫnʲɪnə]: 2584
переработан [pʲɪrʲɪrɐbʷótən]: 2919
перерыва [pʲɪrʲɪrɨ́və]: 2343
пересекал [pʲɪrʲɪsʲɪkáɫ]: 2268

пересекала [pʲɪrʲɪsʲɪkálə]: 2268
перехитрила [pʲɪrʲɪxʲɪtrʲílə]: 2925
переходе [pʲɪrʲɪxʷódʲɪ]: 2205
переходил [pʲɪrʲɪxɐdʲíɫ]: 2989
перешёл [pʲɪrʲɪʂ̞éɫ]: 2025
пешком [pʲɪʂkʷóm]: 2068, 2400, 2596
пианино [pʲɪɐnʲínə]: 2003
пили [pʲílʲɪ]: 2283
писала [pʲɪsálə]: 2447
писали [pʲɪsálʲɪ]: 2959
письма [pʲɪsʲmá]: 2197
письмо [pʲɪsʲmʷó]: 2020, 2834
питалась [pʲɪtáləsʲ]: 2075
пить [pʲitʲ]: 2151
пишите [pʲɪʂɨ́tʲɪ]: 2744
плавать [plávətʲ]: 2128
план [plan]: 2689
планах [plánəx]: 2408
плане [plánʲɪ]: 2537, 2615, 2900
планета [plɐnʲétə]: 2485
планом [plánəm]: 2984
планы [plánɨ]: 2977
платил [plɐtʲíɫ]: 2344, 2875
платила [plɐtʲílə]: 2344
платить [plɐtʲítʲ]: 2292
плату [plátʊ]: 2661
платы [plátɨ]: 2660
платье [plátʲɪ]: 2494, 2501, 2934
платят [plátʲɪt]: 2580
плеча [plʲɪtɕá]: 2192
плиту [plʲɪtú]: 2912
плохими [plɐxʲímʲɪ]: 2234, 2324
плохо [plóxə]: 2577, 2656
плохой [plɐxój]: 2281, 2783
пляж [plʲaʂ]: 2459
пляж [plʲaz]: 2654
пляже [plʲǽzɨ]: 2462
по [pɐ]: 2017, 2020, 2090, 2190, 2265, ..., +30
по-английски [pɐ-ɐnglʲíjskʲɪ]: 2419, 2573, 2589, 2630
по-итальянски [pɐ-ʲɪtɐlʲǽnskʲɪ]: 2528
по-моему [pɐ-mʷóʲɪmʊ]: 2746
по-новому [pɐ-nóvəmʊ]: 2466

по-францу́зски [pɐ-frɛntsússkʲɪ]: 2528
побе́дой [pɐbʲédəj]: 2895
побе́ды [pɐbʲédɨ]: 2421
побесе́довать [pɐbʲɪsʲédəvətʲ]: 2215
поблагодари́л [pəbləgədɐrʲíł]: 2877
поблагодари́ла [pəbləgədɐrʲílə]: 2877
поблагодори́ть [pəbləgədɐrʲítʲ]: 2113
побли́зости [pɐblʲízəstʲɪ]: 2261
поболта́ть [pəbɐłtátʲ]: 2135
побри́лся [pɐbrʲíłsʲɪ]: 2352
побыва́ть [pɐbɨvátʲ]: 2314
поведе́нии [pɐvʲɪdʲénʲɪʲɪ]: 2881
повлекло́ [pɐvlʲɪkló]: 2911
по́воду [pʷóvədʊ]: 2323, 2802
повреди́ла [pɐvrʲɪdʲílə]: 2200
повреждённая [pɐvrʲɪzdʲénnəʲɪ]: 2554
поги́бла [pɐgʲíblə]: 2948
поговори́ть [pəgəvɐrʲítʲ]: 2247
пого́да [pɐgʷódə]: 2231, 2237, 2258
пого́ду [pɐgʷódʊ]: 2648
под [pɐd]: 2568, 2743, 2781, 2821
по́дал [pʷódəł]: 2960
пода́льше [pɐdálʲşɨ]: 2599
пода́ть [pɐdátʲ]: 2477, 2853
подведёт [pɐdvʲɪdʲét]: 2231
подве́ргся [pɐdvʲérgsʲɪ]: 2958
подéлать [pɐdʲéłətʲ]: 2044
поднима́ет [pɐdnʲɪmáʲɪt]: 2926
поднялась [pɐdnʲɪlásʲ]: 2380
подозрева́емого [pədɐzrʲɪváʲɪməvə]: 2817, 2840
подозрева́емому [pədɐzrʲɪváʲɪməmʊ]: 2790
подозрева́емый [pədɐzrʲɪváʲɪmɨj]: 2839, 2958
подозрева́ет [pədɐzrʲɪváʲɪt]: 2791
подозрева́л [pədɐzrʲɪváł]: 2109
подозрева́ли [pədɐzrʲɪválʲɪ]: 2866
подозре́нием [pədɐzrʲénʲɪʲɪm]: 2817
подошёл [pədɐşéł]: 2951
подру́га [pɐdrúgə]: 2367, 2370, 2501, 2502
подру́ге [pɐdrúgʲɪ]: 2504
подру́гу [pɐdrúgʊ]: 2631

поду́мав [pɐdúməf]: 2078
поду́мал [pɐdúməł]: 2858
поду́мала [pɐdúmələ]: 2858
поду́мать [pɐdúmətʲ]: 2139, 2589
поду́мываю [pɐdúmɨvəʲü]: 2101
подходя́щих [pətxɐdʲǽҫҫɨx]: 2540
по́езд [pʷóʲɪzt]: 2716, 2750
по́езд [pʷóʲɪzd]: 2472, 2710
поезда́ [pɐʲɪzdá]: 2604, 2755
по́езда [pʷóʲɪzdə]: 2418
по́езде [pʷóʲɪzdʲɪ]: 2061, 2601, 2734, 2768
по́ездка [pɐʲéstkə]: 2160, 2236, 2337
по́ездки [pɐʲéstkʲɪ]: 2168
по́ездку [pɐʲéstkʊ]: 2368
пое́л [pɐʲéł]: 2645
пое́ла [pɐʲélə]: 2645
пое́сть [pɐʲéstʲ]: 2645
пое́хать [pɐʲéxətʲ]: 2058, 2654
пожале́л [pəzɨʲéł]: 2022
пожа́ловался [pɐzáləvəłsʲɪ]: 2166
пожа́ловаться [pɐzáləvətʲsʲɪ]: 2860
пожа́луйста [pɐzálujstə]: 2020, 2033, 2148, 2181, 2912, ..., +4
пожа́р [pɐzár]: 2467
пожа́рные [pɐzárnɨʲɪ]: 2947, 2948
пожа́ром [pɐzárəm]: 2482
пожени́лись [pɐzɨnʲílʲɪsʲ]: 2290, 2524
пожени́ться [pɐzɨnʲítʲsʲɪ]: 2712
пожилы́х [pɐzɨlɨ́x]: 2851
позво́лили [pɐzvʷólʲɪlʲɪ]: 2183
позво́ль [pɐzvʷólʲ]: 2013, 2836
позвони́л [pəzvɐnʲíł]: 2071
позвони́ла [pəzvɐnʲílə]: 2071
позвони́ли [pəzvɐnʲílʲɪ]: 2034
позвони́ть [pəzvɐnʲítʲ]: 2001, 2029
позвоню́ [pəzvɐnʲú]: 2029, 2695
поздне́е [pɐznʲéʲɪ]: 2699, 2700
по́здно [pʷóznə]: 2165, 2170, 2181, 2704
поздоро́вались [pəzdɐróvəlʲɪsʲ]: 2649
поздра́вил [pɐzdrávʲɪł]: 2107, 2895
поздра́вила [pɐzdrávʲɪlə]: 2107, 2895
по́зже [pʷózzɨ]: 2055, 2807

позити́вное [pɐzʲɪtʲívnəʲɪ]: 2788
познако́мились [pəznɐkʷómʲɪlʲɪsʲ]:
2254, 2694
по́исками [pʷóʲɪskəmʲɪ]: 2206
по́иске [pʷóʲɪskʲɪ]: 2905
по́иски [pʷóʲɪskʲɪ]: 2099
по́иском [pʷóʲɪskəm]: 2122, 2125,
2401
пои́стинне [pɐʲístʲmnʲɪ]: 2559
поищу́ [pɐʲɪɕɕú]: 2780
пойдём [pɐjdʲóm]: 2064
пойдёт [pɐjdʲót]: 2686
пойду́ [pɐjdú]: 2063, 2672
пойти́ [pɐjtʲí]: 2012, 2081, 2261, 2263,
2431, ..., +5
по́йти [pʷójtʲɪ]: 2585
пока́ [pɐká]: 2089, 2422, 2639, 2640,
2646, ..., +3
показа́л [pəkɐzál]: 2680, 2988
показа́ла [pəkɐzálə]: 2534, 2680
показа́лись [pəkɐzálʲɪsʲ]: 2088
покида́ть [pɐkʲɪdátʲ]: 2183
поки́нуть [pɐkʲínʊtʲ]: 2183
покло́нников [pɐklónnʲɪkəf]: 2889
поко́нчил [pɐkʷóntɕɪł]: 2946
покупа́ет [pɐkʊpáʲɪt]: 2944
поку́пке [pɐkúpkʲɪ]: 2101
покуса́ют [pɐkʊsáʲʊt]: 2173
пола́дить [pɐládʲɪtʲ]: 2976
полети́т [pɐlʲɪtʲít]: 2954
поли́тика [pɐlʲítʲɪkə]: 2843
поли́тики [pɐlʲítʲɪkʲɪ]: 2025
полице́йские [pɐlʲɪtsʲéjskʲɾʲɪ]: 2840
полице́йский [pɐlʲɪtsʲéjskʲɪj]: 2956
полице́йскими [pɐlʲɪtsʲéjskʲɪmʲɪ]: 2965
полице́йских [pɐlʲɪtsʲéjskʲɪx]: 2839
полице́йского [pɐlʲɪtsʲéjskəvə]: 2837
поли́цией [pɐlʲítsɨʲɪj]: 2556, 2993
поли́ции [pɐlʲítsɨʲɪ]: 2015, 2534, 2667,
2953
поли́ция [pɐlʲítsɨʲə]: 2215, 2218, 2219,
2323, 2325, ..., +12
полна́ [pɐłná]: 2823, 2832
полно́ [pɐłnó]: 2831

по́лной [pʷółnəj]: 2381
по́лностью [pʷółnəstʲü]: 2829
полови́на [pəlɐvʲínə]: 2432
полови́не [pəlɐvʲínʲɪ]: 2709
положе́ние [pəlɐzɛ́nʲɾʲɪ]: 2210
положи́л [pəlɐzɨ́ł]: 2988
положи́ться [pəlɐzɨ́tʲsʲɪ]: 2509, 2896
полосе́ [pəlɐsʲɛ́]: 2646
полоте́нцем [pəlɐtʲéntsɨm]: 2359
полу́ [pɐlú]: 2140
полу́дня [pɐlúdnʲɪ]: 2701
получа́ет [pɐlʊtɕáʲɪt]: 2622
получа́лось [pɐlʊtɕáləsʲ]: 2032
получа́ю [pɐlʊtɕáʲü]: 2758, 2785
получе́нием [pɐlʊtɕénʲɾʲɪm]: 2123
получи́л [pɐlʊtɕíł]: 2508, 2655, 2657,
2659, 2923
получи́ла [pɐlʊtɕílə]: 2508, 2655,
2657, 2659, 2923
получи́ли [pɐlʊtɕílʲɪ]: 2576
полу́чит [pɐlútɕɪt]: 2246, 2358
получи́ть [pɐlʊtɕítʲ]: 2248, 2699
полу́чишь [pɐlútɕɪɕ]: 2995
полчаса́ [pəłtɕɪsá]: 2483
по́льзовались [pʷólʲzəvəlʲɪsʲ]: 2983
по́льзуется [pʷólʲzʊʲɪtsʲɪ]: 2583
по́льзуешься [pʷólʲzʊʲɪɕʲɪ]: 2115
помаха́л [pəmɐxáł]: 2996
помаха́ла [pəmɐxálə]: 2996
помаха́ли [pəmɐxálʲɪ]: 2996
поме́дленнее [pɐmʲédlʲmnʲɾʲɪ]: 2606
поме́рил [pɐmʲérʲɪł]: 2574
поме́рила [pɐmʲérʲɪlə]: 2574
поме́рить [pɐmʲérʲɪtʲ]: 2934
помеша́л [pɐmʲɪʂáł]: 2112
помеша́ло [pɐmʲɪʂálə]: 2110
помеще́ние [pɐmʲɪɕɕénʲɾʲɪ]: 2255
по́мнил [pʷómnʲɪł]: 2019
по́мнишь [pʷómnʲɪɕ]: 2523
по́мню [pʷómnʲü]: 2018, 2028
помогли́ [pəmɐɡlʲí]: 2003, 2040
помогу́ [pəmɐɡú]: 2013
помо́чь [pɐmʷótɕ]: 2041, 2437, 2452,
2764, 2793

пóмощь [pʷóməçç̌ʲ]: 2040, 2041, 2113, 2293, 2896

пóмощью [pʷóməçç̌ʲü]: 2136

понáдобится [pɐnádəbʲɪtsʲɪ]: 2233, 2396, 2665, 2896

понедéльник [pɐnʲɪdʲélʲnʲɪk]: 2907

понедéльника [pɐnʲɪdʲélʲnʲɪkə]: 2699

понестú [pɐnʲɪstʲí]: 2013

понимáю [pɐnʲɪmáʲü]: 2997

понимáют [pɐnʲɪmáʲüt]: 2124

понрáвилась [pɐnrávʲɪləsʲ]: 2357, 2451

понрáвились [pɐnrávʲɪlʲɪsʲ]: 2445

понрáвился [pɐnrávʲɪtsʲɪ]: 2283

пóняли [pʷónʲɪlʲɪ]: 2558

понять [pɐnʲǽtʲ]: 2835

пообéдал [pɐɐbʲédət]: 2644

пообéдала [pɐɐbʲédələ]: 2644

пообéдать [pɐɐbʲédətʲ]: 2081, 2206

пообещáешь [pɐɐbʲɪçç̌áʲɪç̌]: 2670

пообещáл [pɐɐbʲɪçç̌át]: 2185

пообещáли [pɐɐbʲɪçç̌álʲɪ]: 2960

пообещáло [pɐɐbʲɪçç̌álə]: 2293

пообещáть [pɐɐbʲɪçç̌átʲ]: 2010

попáл [pɐpát]: 2379, 2568

попáла [pɐpálə]: 2379, 2568

попáли [pɐpálʲɪ]: 2844, 2964

поплáвали [pɐplávəlʲɪ]: 2288

поплáвать [pɐplávətʲ]: 2069

попрóбовал [pɐpróbəvət]: 2567

попрóбовала [pɐpróbəvələ]: 2567

попрóбуем [pɐpróbuʲɪm]: 2825

попрóбуй [pɐpróbuj]: 2035

попросúл [pəprɐsʲít]: 2844, 2951

попросúла [pəprɐsʲílə]: 2844

популярной [pɐpulʲárnəj]: 2816

популярностью [pɐpulʲárnəstʲü]: 2583

попытáлась [pɐpɪtáləsʲ]: 2043, 2360

попытáлся [pɐpɪtátsʲɪ]: 2360

пор [pʷor]: 2524, 2641, 2642, 2778, 2833, ..., +1

поработать [pərɐbʷótətʲ]: 2079

порáньше [pɐránʲşɪ]: 2142, 2148, 2209, 2854

порéзался [pɐrʲézətsʲɪ]: 2204

порекомендовáл [pərʲɪkəmʲɪndɐvát]: 2505

порядке [pɐrʲǽtkʲɪ]: 2991

посетúть [pɐsʲɪtʲítʲ]: 2328, 2503

поскользнýлся [pəskɐlʲznútsʲɪ]: 2673

поскóльку [pɐskʷólʲku]: 2364, 2400, 2677, 2678, 2742, ..., +4

пóсле [pʷóslʲɪ]: 2025, 2040, 2072, 2168, 2207, ..., +12

послéднее [pɐslʲédnʲɪʲɪ]: 2094, 2886

послéдние [pɐslʲédnʲɪʲɪ]: 2782

послéдний [pɐslʲédnʲɪj]: 2129, 2195

послéдняя [pɐslʲédnʲɪʲɪ]: 2806

посмотрéв [pəsmɐtrʲéf]: 2212

посмотрéл [pəsmɐtrʲét]: 2436

посмотрéла [pəsmɐtrʲélə]: 2436

посмотрéли [pəsmɐtrʲélʲɪ]: 2269, 2625, 2689

посмотрéть [pəsmɐtrʲétʲ]: 2120, 2502

посовéтовал [pəsɐvʲétəvət]: 2015

посовéтовали [pəsɐvʲétəvəlʲɪ]: 2861

посредú [pɐsrʲɪdʲí]: 2199

поссóрился [pɐssórʲɪtsʲɪ]: 2369

постáвить [pɐstávʲɪtʲ]: 2232

постáвь [pɐstávʲ]: 2912

постарáйся [pəstɐrájsʲɪ]: 2033, 2920

постарáться [pəstɐrátʲsʲɪ]: 2350

постарáюсь [pəstɐráʲüsʲ]: 2512

постéли [pɐstʲélʲɪ]: 2278, 2428, 2701

постирáть [pɐstʲɪrátʲ]: 2039

постоянно [pəstɐʲánnə]: 2487, 2636, 2962, 2979, 2999

пострáдавший [pəstrɐdáfşɪj]: 2548

пострадáл [pəstrɐdát]: 2217, 2410

пострадáли [pəstrɐdálʲɪ]: 2571

пострóить [pɐstróʲɪtʲ]: 2977

поступáет [pɐstupáʲɪt]: 2156

поступúть [pɐstupʲítʲ]: 2274

поступлéния [pɐstuplʲénʲɪʲə]: 2894

посылку [pɐsɪ̵lku]: 2699

потеплéе [pɐtʲɪplʲéʲɪ]: 2145

потеплéния [pɐtʲɪplʲénʲɪʲə]: 2863

потерпéли [pɐtʲɪrpʲélʲɪ]: 2949

потеря́л [pɐtʲɪrʲáł]: 2179, 2493, 2750, 2906

потеря́ла [pɐtʲɪrʲálə]: 2493, 2640

поте́рянные [pɐtʲérʲɪmnɨ̯ɪ]: 2493

поти́ше [pɐtʲíʂɨ]: 2033

пото́м [pɐtóm]: 2943

потому́ [pətɐmú]: 2088, 2090, 2093, 2140, 2174, …, +13

поторопи́лась [pətərɐpʲíləsʲ]: 2141

поторопи́лся [pətərɐpʲíłsʲɪ]: 2141

потра́тил [pɐtrátʲɪł]: 2126, 2458

потра́тила [pɐtrátʲɪlə]: 2458

потра́тили [pɐtrátʲɪlʲɪ]: 2235, 2412

потуши́ть [pɐtuʂítʲ]: 2947

потяну́лся [pɐtʲmúłsʲɪ]: 2841

поу́жинать [pɐúzɪnɐtʲ]: 2055

похвали́л [pəxfɐlʲíł]: 2899

похвали́ла [pəxfɐlʲílə]: 2899

похва́статься [pɐxfástətʲsʲɪ]: 2944

похо́же [pɐxóʑɨ]: 2165, 2485, 2685, 2687, 2828

почему́ [pɐt͡ɕɪmú]: 2083, 2362, 2374, 2513, 2568, …, +3

по́черк [pʷót͡ɕɪrk]: 2124

почини́ть [pɐt͡ɕɪnʲítʲ]: 2126

по́чте [pʷót͡ɕtʲɪ]: 2762

почти́ [pɐt͡ɕtʲí]: 2394, 2423, 2582, 2583, 2585, …, +1

почто́вый [pɐʂtóvɨj]: 2729

по́чту [pʷót͡ɕtʊ]: 2263

почу́вствовала [pɐt͡ɕúʊstfəvələ]: 2192

пошёл [pɐʂół]: 2060

пошла́ [pɐʂlá]: 2060, 2656

пошли́ [pɐʂlʲí]: 2572

пошло́ [pɐʂló]: 2454

поэ́тому [pɐétəmʊ]: 2040, 2116, 2117, 2127, 2756, …, +9

появи́лось [pɐ̯ɪvʲíləsʲ]: 2923

поя́вятся [pɐ̯ǽvʲɪtsʲɪ]: 2161

права́ [prɐvá]: 2929

пра́вда [právdə]: 2498, 2685, 2957

пра́вду [právdʊ]: 2098

пра́вильно [právʲɪlʲnə]: 2569

пра́вильные [právʲɪlʲnɨ̯ɪ]: 2919

прави́тельство [prɐvʲítʲɪlʲstfə]: 2883

пра́во [právə]: 2904

пра́здничные [prázdnʲɪt͡ɕnɨ̯ɪ]: 2169

пра́ктика [práktʲɪkə]: 2981

практикова́ть [praktʲɪkɐvátʲ]: 2138

практи́чески [prɐktʲít͡ɕɪskʲɪ]: 2892, 2983

преврати́лось [prʲɪvrɐtʲíləsʲ]: 2956

предложе́ние [prʲɪdlɪʐɛ́nʲɪ̯ɪ]: 2240, 2787

предложе́нием [prʲɪdlɪʐɛ́nʲɪ̯ɪm]: 2139

предложе́ний [prʲɪdlɪʐɛ́nʲɪj]: 2470, 2555

предложи́л [prʲɪdlɪʐíł]: 2006

предложи́ли [prʲɪdlɪʐílʲɪ]: 2229

предпочёл [prʲɪtpɐt͡ɕǿł]: 2055, 2063, 2069

предпочита́ю [prʲɪtpɐt͡ɕɪtá̯ü]: 2052

предпочла́ [prʲɪtpɐt͡ɕlá]: 2055, 2063, 2069

предста́вились [prʲɪtstávʲɪlʲɪsʲ]: 2366

предупреди́л [prʲɪdʊprʲɪdʲíł]: 2004

предупреди́ли [prʲɪdʊprʲɪdʲílʲɪ]: 2005, 2016, 2862

предупрежда́ть [prʲɪdʊprʲɪʐdátʲ]: 2863

пре́жде [prʲéʐdʲɪ]: 2931, 2934

президе́нт [prʲɪzʲɪdʲént]: 2025

президе́нта [prʲɪzʲɪdʲéntə]: 2024

преиму́ществ [prʲɪɪ̯ɪmút͡ɕɕɪstf]: 2777

преиму́щество [prʲɪɪ̯ɪmút͡ɕɕɪstfə]: 2776

прекра́сная [prʲɪkrásnə̯ɪ]: 2258

прекрати́тся [prʲɪkrɐtʲítsʲɪ]: 2672

пре́мии [prʲémʲɪ̯ɪ]: 2772

преподава́тели [prʲɪpədɐvátʲɪlʲɪ]: 2914

преподава́ть [prʲɪpədɐvátʲ]: 2289

прерва́ли [prʲɪrválʲɪ]: 2688

пресле́довать [prʲɪslʲédəvətʲ]: 2999

пре́ссы [prʲéssɨ]: 2958

престаре́лых [prʲɪstɐrʲélɨx]: 2797

преступле́ние [prʲɪstʊplʲénʲɪ̯ɪ]: 2545

преступле́нии [prʲɪstʊplʲénʲɪj]: 2667

преступле́ний [prʲɪstʊplʲénʲɪj]: 2782, 2885

преступле́ния [prʲɪstʊplʲénʲɪ̯ə]: 2820, 2878, 2925

преуспе́ешь [prʲɪʊspʲéʲɪç]: 2905
при [prʲɪ]: 2205, 2563, 2611, 2670, 2671, ..., +1
приберу́сь [prʲɪbʲɪrúsʲ]: 2807
прибра́ться [prʲɪbrátʲsʲɪ]: 2980
прибыва́ющий [prʲɪbɨváʲüççɪj]: 2162
прибы́тия [prʲɪbʲítʲrʲə]: 2418
приве́тливы [prʲɪvʲétlʲɪvɨ]: 2795
привлекло́ [prʲɪvlʲɪkló]: 2988
привы́к [prʲɪvʲík]: 2088, 2090, 2093
привыка́ть [prʲɪvɨkátʲ]: 2092
привы́кла [prʲɪvʲíklə]: 2087, 2088, 2091, 2093
привы́кнем [prʲɪvʲíknʲɪm]: 2089
приглашён [prʲɪglɐʂén]: 2986
приглашён [prʲɪglɐʂén]: 2800
приглашена́ [prʲɪglɐʂɪná]: 2800, 2986
приглаше́ний [prʲɪglɐʂénʲɪj]: 2785
придёт [prʲɪdʲǿt]: 2685
придётся [prʲɪdʲǿtsʲɪ]: 2669
приду́мывать [prʲɪdúmɨvətʲ]: 2993
приду́т [prʲɪdút]: 2381
прие́дем [prʲɪrʲédʲɪm]: 2740
прие́ду [prʲɪrʲédʊ]: 2890
приезжа́ет [prʲɪrʲɪzʑáʲɪt]: 2826
прие́ме [prʲɪrʲǿmʲɪ]: 2023
прие́хал [prʲɪrʲéxəɫ]: 2163, 2618, 2768, 2951
прие́хала [prʲɪrʲéxələ]: 2618, 2641, 2768
прие́хали [prʲɪrʲéxəlʲɪ]: 2503, 2603
приземли́лся [prʲɪzʲɪmlʲíɫsʲɪ]: 2647
приземли́ться [prʲɪzʲɪmlʲítʲsʲɪ]: 2647
прийти́ [prʲɪjtʲí]: 2110
прикры́ть [prʲɪkrʲítʲ]: 2952
прилете́л [prʲɪlʲɪtʲéɫ]: 2969
прилете́ла [prʲɪlʲɪtʲélə]: 2969
приложе́ние [prʲɪlɐʐénʲɪrʲɪ]: 2780
приме́рно [prʲɪmʲérnə]: 2461, 2647
принёс [prʲɪnʲǿs]: 2340
принесёт [prʲɪnʲɪsʲǿt]: 2879
принима́ть [prʲɪnʲɪmátʲ]: 2683, 2848
при́нтер [prʲíntʲɪr]: 2479
приняла́ [prʲɪnʲɪlá]: 2803
при́нято [prʲínʲɪtə]: 2985

при́няты [prʲínʲɪtɨ]: 2808
приостано́влены [prʲɪəstɐnóvlʲɪnɨ]: 2977
присе́сть [prʲɪsʲéstʲ]: 2227
пристёгиваться [prʲɪstʲǿɡʲɪvətʲsʲɪ]: 2473
при́ступа [prʲístʊpə]: 2868
прису́тствовать [prʲɪsútstfəvətʲ]: 2924
присци́ллы [prʲɪstsíɫlɨ]: 2541
притормози́л [prʲɪtərmɐzʲíɫ]: 2150
притормози́ла [prʲɪtɐrmɐzʲílə]: 2150
прихо́де [prʲɪxódʲɪ]: 2917
приходи́лось [prʲɪxɐdʲíləsʲ]: 2629
прихо́дит [prʲɪxódʲɪt]: 2626
приходи́те [prʲɪxɐdʲítʲɪ]: 2148
прихо́дится [prʲɪxódʲɪtsʲɪ]: 2090, 2252, 2978
прихо́дят [prʲɪxódʲɪt]: 2970
причи́на [prʲɪtɕínə]: 2525
причи́нах [prʲɪtɕínəx]: 2778
причи́ну [prʲɪtɕínʊ]: 2218
пришёл [prʲɪʂǿt]: 2030
пришли́ [prʲɪʂlʲí]: 2503, 2705
пришло́сь [prʲɪʂlós]: 2092, 2140, 2400, 2675, 2783, ..., +1
прия́тно [prʲɪrʲátnə]: 2803
прия́тными [prʲɪrʲátnɨmʲɪ]: 2694
пробежа́ли [prɐbʲɪzálʲɪ]: 2077
про́бку [própkʊ]: 2379
пробле́м [prɐblʲém]: 2025, 2042, 2080, 2122, 2430, ..., +1
пробле́му [prɐblʲémʊ]: 2096, 2184, 2984
пробле́мы [prɐblʲémɨ]: 2085, 2123, 2125, 2130, 2329, ..., +3
про́бок [próbək]: 2633
провёл [prɐvʲǿt]: 2428
провела́ [prɐvʲɪlá]: 2428
провели́ [prɐvʲɪlʲí]: 2462, 2588, 2894
прове́рю [prɐvʲérʲü]: 2383
прове́трить [prɐvʲétrʲɪtʲ]: 2255
проводи́ли [prəvɐdʲílʲɪ]: 2940
проводи́ть [prəvɐdʲítʲ]: 2155
програ́мму [prɐɡrámmʊ]: 2764
прода́ж [prɐdáʂ]: 2724, 2783

прода́жи   [prɐdáʑɨ]: 2788
прода́ть   [prɐdátʲ]: 2176
продли́лся   [prɐdlʲíɫsʲɪ]: 2290
продолжа́й   [prədɐɫzáj]: 2935
продолжа́йте   [prədɐɫzájtʲɪ]: 2981
продолжа́лась   [prədɐɫzáləsʲ]: 2024
продолжа́ть   [prədɐɫzátʲ]: 2941
продолжа́ют   [prədɐɫzáʲüt]: 2863
продолже́ния   [prədɐɫzénʲɪ̯ə]: 2564
продо́лжил   [prɐdóɫzɨɫ]: 2688
проду́кцию   [prɐdúktsɨʲü]: 2774
прое́хать   [prɐʲéxətʲ]: 2150
прожива́ния   [prɐzɨvánʲɪ̯ə]: 2380, 2877
про́жил   [prózɨɫ]: 2457
проигра́вшего   [prɐʲɪgráfṣɪvə]: 2809
проигра́вшему   [prɐʲɪgráfṣɪmʊ]: 2809
производи́мых   [prəʲɪzvɐdʲímɨx]: 2550
произво́дственным   [prɐʲɪzvʷótstfʲɪnnɨm]: 2941
произоше́дшем   [prəʲɪzɐṣétṣɪm]: 2010, 2070, 2325
произошёл   [prəʲɪzɐṣóɫ]: 2189
произошла́   [prəʲɪzɐṣlá]: 2784
произошло́   [prəʲɪzɐṣló]: 2010, 2643, 2688, 2836, 2886, ..., +1
происхо́дит   [prɐʲɪsxódʲɪt]: 2076, 2885
происше́ствий   [prɐʲɪṣṣéstfʲɪj]: 2781
пройти́   [prɐjtʲí]: 2959
промо́кнешь   [prɐmʷóknʲɪҫ]: 2743
пропа́вших   [prɐpáfṣɨx]: 2195
проры́в   [prɐrɨ́f]: 2981
проси́л   [prɐsʲíɫ]: 2409
проси́ла   [prɐsʲílə]: 2409, 2690
проси́ть   [prɐsʲítʲ]: 2102
просмо́тром   [prɐsmʷótrəm]: 2133
просну́лся   [prɐsnúɫsʲɪ]: 2352
прости́   [prɐstʲí]: 2182, 2397, 2618
прости́ть   [prɐstʲítʲ]: 2878
про́сто   [próstə]: 2373, 2567, 2913, 2925, 2957, ..., +1
просто́е   [prɐstóʲɪ]: 2787
просто́й   [prɐstój]: 2893
протестова́ть   [prət̯ɪstɐvátʲ]: 2945
про́тив   [prótʲɪf]: 2064, 2091

про́тив   [prótʲɪv]: 2053, 2103, 2291
прохо́да   [prɐxódə]: 2736
проходи́ть   [prɐxɐdʲítʲ]: 2174
проце́нтов   [prɐtséntəf]: 2966
проце́сс   [prɐtséss]: 2213
прочита́й   [prɐtɕɪtáj]: 2470
прочита́л   [prɐtɕɪtáɫ]: 2456, 2468, 2753
прочита́ла   [prɐtɕɪtálə]: 2456, 2468, 2753
прошли́   [prɐṣlʲí]: 2084
про́шлой   [próṣləj]: 2323, 2340, 2733, 2737
про́шлом   [próṣləm]: 2287, 2637
про́шлый   [próṣlɨj]: 2258
прошу́   [prɐṣú]: 2808
про́ще   [próҫҫɪ]: 2017, 2425, 2600, 2762
проще́ния   [prɐҫҫénʲɪ̯ə]: 2808
пу́блика   [públʲɪkə]: 2818
пуга́ют   [pʊgáʲüt]: 2811, 2812
пуга́ющие   [pʊgáʲüҫҫɪ̯ɪ]: 2810
пуст   [pust]: 2406
пусты́ня   [pʊstʲínʲɪ]: 2311
пу́тают   [pútəʲüt]: 2979
путеше́ствие   [pʊtʲɪṣéstfʲɪ̯ɪ]: 2940, 2971
путеше́ствия   [pʊtʲɪṣéstfʲɪ̯ɪ]: 2228, 2235, 2852
путеше́ствовал   [pʊtʲɪṣéstfəvəɫ]: 2376
путеше́ствовала   [pʊtʲɪṣéstfəvələ]: 2376
путеше́ствовать   [pʊtʲɪṣéstfəvətʲ]: 2061
путеше́ствуете   [pʊtʲɪṣéstfʊʲɪtʲɪ]: 2613
пути́   [pʊtʲí]: 2631, 2706, 2727
путь   [putʲ]: 2592
пыта́ется   [pɨtáʲɪtsʲɪ]: 2833
пыта́лась   [pɨtáləsʲ]: 2176, 2956
пыта́лись   [pɨtálʲɪsʲ]: 2945, 2948
пыта́лся   [pɨtáɫsʲɪ]: 2176
пыта́ясь   [pɨtáʲɪsʲ]: 2126
пье́тро   [pʲétrə]: 2369
пяти́   [pʲɪtʲí]: 2118, 2700, 2911
пятисо́т   [pʲɪtʲɪsót]: 2770
пятиэта́жное   [pʲɪtʲɪɛtáznə̯ɪ]: 2334
пятна́дцать   [pʲɪtnáttsətʲ]: 2086, 2486, 2582

пя́тницу [pʲǽtnʲɪtsʊ]: 2169
пя́тницы [pʲǽtnʲɪtsɨ]: 2398, 2477
пя́того [pʲátəvə]: 2707
пять [pʲætʲ]: 2276, 2772
пятьдеся́т [pʲɪtʲdʲɪsʲát]: 2868
пятью́ [pʲɪtʲú]: 2334
рабо́та [rɐbʷǿtə]: 2090, 2252, 2297,
   2331, 2758, ..., +3
рабо́тает [rɐbʷǿtəʲɪt]: 2035, 2265,
   2479, 2529, 2530, ..., +3
рабо́таешь [rɐbʷǿtəʲɪɕ]: 2593
рабо́тал [rɐbʷǿtəł]: 2051, 2275, 2561,
   2678
рабо́тала [rɐbʷǿtələ]: 2051, 2275, 2561
рабо́тать [rɐbʷǿtətʲ]: 2037, 2051, 2223,
   2703, 2709, ..., +1
рабо́таю [rɐbʷǿtəʲü]: 2426, 2506, 2520
рабо́тают [rɐbʷǿtəʲüt]: 2786
рабо́те [rɐbʷǿtʲɪ]: 2580, 2669, 2788
рабо́тники [rɐbʷǿtnʲɪkʲɪ]: 2755
рабо́той [rɐbʷǿtəj]: 2107, 2416
рабо́ту [rɐbʷǿtʊ]: 2020, 2023, 2049,
   2094, 2131, ..., +24
рабо́ты [rɐbʷǿtɨ]: 2099, 2156, 2207,
   2281, 2401, ..., +8
рабо́чем [rɐbʷǿtɕɪm]: 2795
рабо́чие [rɐbʷǿtɕɪʲɪ]: 2755
равно́ [rɐvnó]: 2440, 2652, 2656, 2671
рад [rat]: 2395, 2799, 2859
ра́да [rádə]: 2395, 2799, 2859
радж [radʂ]: 2594
ра́дио [rádʲɪə]: 2753
ра́ды [rádɨ]: 2160
раз [raz]: 2195, 2461, 2716, 2717,
   2879, ..., +2
раз [ras]: 2129, 2466, 2574, 2955
ра́за [rázə]: 2621
разби́в [rɐzbʲív]: 2073
разбо́рчиво [rɐzbʷǿrtɕɪvə]: 2744
разбуди́ть [rɐzbudʲítʲ]: 2920
разгова́риваете [rɐzgɐvárʲɪvəʲɪtʲɪ]: 2993
разгова́риваешь [rɐzgɐvárʲɪvəʲɪɕ]: 2345
разгова́ривал [rɐzgɐvárʲɪvəł]: 2481,
   2552, 2754

разгова́ривала [rɐzgɐvárʲɪvələ]: 2481,
   2552, 2754
разгова́ривать [rɐzgɐvárʲɪvətʲ]: 2153
разгова́риваю [rɐzgɐvárʲɪvəʲü]: 2448
разгова́ривают [rɐzgɐvárʲɪvəʲüt]: 2365
раздава́л [rɐzdɐváł]: 2298, 2933
раздава́ла [rɐzdɐválə]: 2933
разда́ла [rɐzdálə]: 2994
разделена́ [rɐzdʲɪlʲɪná]: 2909
разделя́ю [rɐzdʲɪlʲǽʲü]: 2434
раздража́ет [rɐzdrɐʐáʲɪt]: 2089
разли́чия [rɐzlʲítɕɨʲə]: 2792
ра́зные [ráznɨʲɪ]: 2434
ра́зными [ráznɨmʲɪ]: 2469
разобра́ться [rɐzɐbrátʲsʲɪ]: 2778
разочаро́ван [rɐzətɕɪróvən]: 2797
разрабо́тали [rɐzrɐbʷǿtəlʲɪ]: 2928
разреша́ется [rɛzrʲɪʂáʲɪtsʲɪ]: 2378
разреша́ют [rɛzrʲɪʂáʲüt]: 2008
разреши́ли [rɛzrʲɪʂílʲɪ]: 2012
разреши́ть [rɛzrʲɪʂítʲ]: 2184
разруше́ний [rɛzruʂénʲɪj]: 2340
разру́шенных [rɛzrúʂɨnnɨx]: 2990
разу́мными [rɛzúmnɨmʲɪ]: 2555
разы́скивает [rɛzískʲɪvəʲɪt]: 2219
рамо́на [rɐmʷǿnə]: 2086
ране́ния [rɐnʲénʲɪʲə]: 2576
ра́но [ránə]: 2045, 2090, 2119, 2650
ра́ньше [ránʲʂɨ]: 2090, 2094, 2095,
   2245, 2366, ..., +4
раскололся [rɐskɐlʷǿłsʲɪ]: 2910
расплати́ться [rɐsplɐtʲítʲsʲɪ]: 2763
распро́даны [rɛspródənɪ]: 2403, 2932
рассерди́лись [rɛssʲɪrdʲílʲɪsʲ]: 2987
рассе́ржена [rɛssʲérzʲɪnə]: 2798
расска́жет [rɛsskáʐɪt]: 2010
расскажу́ [rɐsskɐʐú]: 2070
рассказа́л [rɐsskɐʐáł]: 2070, 2689
рассказа́ла [rɐsskɐʐálə]: 2070, 2689
рассказа́ть [rɐsskɐʐátʲ]: 2066, 2070,
   2836
расска́зывал [rɛsskázɨvəł]: 2067, 2507,
   2539

рассказывала [rɐsskázɨvələ]: 2067, 2507, 2539
рассказывании [rɐsskázɨvənʲrʲɪ]: 2562
рассказывать [rɐsskázɨvətʲ]: 2010, 2171, 2935
расслабиться [rɐsslábʲɪtʲsʲɪ]: 2349
расследования [rɐsslʲédəvənʲrʲə]: 2953
расследующая [rɐsslʲédʊʲüçcəʲɪ]: 2545
расстались [rɐsstálʲɪsʲ]: 2974, 2975
расстроен [rɐsstróʲɪn]: 2800, 2946
расстроена [rɐsstróʲɪnə]: 2800
растения [rɐstʲénʲrʲə]: 2728
растили [rɐstʲílʲɪ]: 2962
растит [rɐstʲít]: 2377
расширялась [rɐsṣɨrʲáləsʲ]: 2774
рашид [rɐṣíd]: 2796
реакцией [rʲɪáktsɨʲɪj]: 2787
реальном [rʲɪálʲnəm]: 2914
ребёнка [rʲɪbʲénkə]: 2377, 2717, 2920
ребёнком [rʲɪbʲénkəm]: 2962
регионе [rʲɪɡʲɪónʲɪ]: 2341
редко [rʲétkə]: 2632
резервную [rʲɪzʲérvnʊʲü]: 2954
результате [rʲɪzʊlʲtátʲɪ]: 2576
результатов [rʲɪzʊlʲtátəv]: 2791
результаты [rʲɪzʊlʲtátɨ]: 2332
резюме [rʲɪzʲümʲé]: 2508, 2533, 2540, 2594, 2635, ..., +2
рейн [rʲejn]: 2305
рейнджер [rʲéjndzɨr]: 3000
рейс [rʲejs]: 2162, 2383, 2388, 2647, 2740
рейса [rʲéjsə]: 2968
река [rʲɪká]: 2266, 2302, 2305
реки [rʲɪkʲí]: 2195
ремни [rʲɪmnʲí]: 2473
ремонт [rʲɪmʷónt]: 2898
репутации [rʲɪpʊtátsɨʲɪ]: 2960
ресторан [rʲɪstɐrán]: 2382, 2440
ресторана [rʲɪstɐránə]: 2166, 2438
ресторане [rʲɪstɐránʲɪ]: 2510, 2747
ресторанов [rʲɪstɐránəv]: 2439
ресторанов [rʲɪstɐránəf]: 2439, 2441
речи [rʲétçɨ]: 2103

речь [rʲetçʲ]: 2024, 2899
речью [rʲétçʲü]: 2805
решение [rʲɪṣénʲrʲɪ]: 2422, 2629, 2985
решением [rʲɪṣénʲrʲɪm]: 2786
решения [rʲɪṣénʲrʲə]: 2683, 2848
решёткой [rʲɪṣétkəj]: 2731
решил [rʲɪṣíɫ]: 2986, 2992
решила [rʲɪṣílə]: 2986, 2994
решили [rʲɪṣílʲɪ]: 2104
решить [rʲɪṣítʲ]: 2184, 2430, 2445
рискнул [rʲɪsknúɫ]: 2102
рискнула [rʲɪsknúlə]: 2102
рита [rʲítə]: 2974, 2975
риты [rʲítɨ]: 2927
робин [rʲóbʲin]: 2298
родителей [rɐdʲítʲɪlʲɪj]: 2797, 2815, 2830, 2900
родители [rɐdʲítʲɪlʲɪ]: 2012, 2739, 2867, 2913, 2940, ..., +3
родителям [rɐdʲítʲɪlʲɪm]: 2171
родителями [rɐdʲítʲɪlʲɪmʲɪ]: 2789, 2814
родителях [rɐdʲítʲɪlʲɪx]: 2851
родной [rɐdnój]: 2589
розетку [rɐzʲétkʊ]: 2921
розетта [rɐzʲéttə]: 2573
рок-звезда [rɐk-zvʲɪzdá]: 2889
романы [rɐmánɨ]: 2908
росли [rɐslʲí]: 2542
россией [rɐssʲɪʲɪj]: 2949
рубашек [rʊbáṣɨk]: 2445
рублей [rʊblʲéj]: 2327, 2486
ругательств [rʊɡátʲɪlʲstf]: 2103
руки [rúkʲɪ]: 2846
рухнет [rúxnʲɪt]: 2684
рядах [rʲɪdáx]: 2723
рядом [rʲádəm]: 2355, 2497, 2978
с [s]: 2044, 2047, 2054, 2057, 2060, ..., +90
сад [sat]: 2375, 2547
саду [sɐdú]: 2429
саймон [sájmən]: 2970
сам [sam]: 2003, 2066, 2344, 2345, 2356, ..., +1

самá [sɐmá]: 2003, 2066, 2344, 2345, 2356, ..., +1
сáмая [sáməjə]: 2266
самúя [sɐmjíjə]: 2861
сáмого [sáməvə]: 2532
сáмое [sáməjɪ]: 2052, 2629
самолёт [səmɐljǿt]: 2119, 2162, 2646, 2939
самолёте [səmɐljǿtjɪ]: 2497, 2552, 2736, 2766
сáмом [sáməm]: 2800, 2956
самоубúйств [səmɐubjíjstf]: 2886
самоубúйством [səmɐubjíjstfəm]: 2946
самý [sɐmú]: 2019
сáмую [sámʊjü]: 2800
сáмые [sámɨjɪ]: 2495
сáмый [sámɨj]: 2277, 2303, 2304, 2574, 2625, ..., +2
сáмых [sámɨx]: 2563
сáндре [sándrjɪ]: 2001
сáнзит [sánzjɪt]: 2149
сáра [sárə]: 2994
сáре [sárjɪ]: 2929
сáтико [sátjɪkə]: 2691
сатóми [sɐtómjɪ]: 2622
сахáра [sɐxárə]: 2311
сáхара [sáxərə]: 2872
сбúл [sbjíɫ]: 2717
сбúла [sbjílə]: 2717
сбит [sbjit]: 2989
свáдебные [svádjɪbnɨjɪ]: 2785
свáдьбе [svádjbjɪ]: 2924
свéжего [svjéʑɪvə]: 2255
свет [svjet]: 2536
свидéтелем [svjɪdjétjɪljɪm]: 2215
свúтеров [svjítjɪrəv]: 2902
свобóдная [svɐbwódnəjɪ]: 2226
свобóдно [svɐbwódnə]: 2619
свобóдных [svɐbwódnɨx]: 2034
свобóды [svɐbwódɨ]: 2776
своё [svɐjǿ]: 2422, 2533, 2594, 2794
своегó [svɐjɪvwó]: 2534, 2631, 2834, 2923

своéй [svɐjéj]: 2197, 2294, 2374, 2682, 2788
своём [svɐjǿm]: 2881
свой [svɐjí]: 2074, 2375, 2504, 2540, 2848, ..., +3
своúм [svɐjím]: 2511, 2832, 2906
своúми [svɐjímjɪ]: 2814
своúх [svɐjíx]: 2369, 2433, 2851, 2877
свой [svwoj]: 2146, 2375, 2399, 2666, 2689, ..., +1
свою [svɐjú]: 2176, 2177, 2186, 2232, 2372, ..., +2
свяжется [svjǽzɨtsjɪ]: 2447
связáлся [svjɪzáɫsjɪ]: 2856
связáться [svjɪzátjsjɪ]: 2146, 2544, 2665, 2678, 2762
связú [svjɪzjí]: 2491, 2492
связь [svjǽzj]: 2791
сгорéл [sgɐrjéɫ]: 2947
сдавáться [zdɐvátjsjɪ]: 2981
сдал [zdaɫ]: 2394
сдаст [zdast]: 2164
сдать [zdatj]: 2398, 2822
сдéлай [zdjéləj]: 2203, 2846
сдéлал [zdjéləɫ]: 2065, 2409, 2759, 2879, 2958
сдéлала [zdjélələ]: 2759
сдéлать [zdjélətj]: 2117, 2356, 2477, 2680
сдéлаю [zdjéləjü]: 2452
сдержáть [zdjɪrzátj]: 2043
себé [sjɪbjé]: 2221, 2363
себя́ [sjɪbjá]: 2075, 2135, 2344, 2348, 2361, ..., +5
сéвере [sjévjɪrjɪ]: 2311
сéверной [sjévjɪrnəj]: 2301
сегóдня [sjɪvwódnjɪ]: 2063, 2064, 2065, 2105, 2165, ..., +16
сейчáс [sjɪjtɕás]: 2055, 2201, 2371, 2380, 2479, ..., +4
секрéте [sjɪkrjétjɪ]: 2433
сел [sjeɫ]: 2676, 3000
сéла [sjélə]: 2186, 2676
сéли [sjéljɪ]: 2741
семéстров [sjɪmjéstrəf]: 2922

семи́ [sʲımʲí]: 2870
семичасово́м [sʲımʲıtɕısɐvʷǫ́m]: 2768
семна́дцати [sʲımnáttsətʲı]: 2748
семна́дцать [sʲımnáttsətʲ]: 2748
семье́ [sʲımʲɛ́]: 2877
семьёй [sʲımʲǫ́j]: 2054
семьи́ [sʲımʲí]: 2779
сентябре́ [sʲıntʲıbrʲɛ́]: 2691
сентября́ [sʲıntʲıbrʲá]: 2804
серде́чного [sʲırdʲétɕnəvə]: 2868
се́рдца [sʲértsə]: 2869, 2884
серьёзнее [sʲır̝ǫ́znʲr̝ʲı]: 2608
серьёзно [sʲır̝ǫ́znə]: 2571
серьёзной [sʲır̝ǫ́znəj]: 2043, 2410
серьёзности [sʲır̝ǫ́znəstʲı]: 2820
серьёзные [sʲır̝ǫ́znɨʲı]: 2576
сестра́ [sʲıstrá]: 2262, 2371, 2518, 2798
сестру́ [sʲıstrú]: 2881
сестры́ [sʲıstrɨ́]: 2370, 2541, 2894
сесть [sʲestʲ]: 2360, 2756
се́сть [sʲéstʲ]: 2362, 2584
сза́ди [szádʲı]: 2150
сиде́вший [sʲıdʲéfʂɨj]: 2497
сиде́л [sʲıdʲéł]: 2497, 2731
сиде́ла [sʲıdʲélə]: 2497, 2731
сиде́ть [sʲıdʲétʲ]: 2083, 2140, 2723, 2742
сиди́ [sʲıdʲí]: 2846
сидя́т [sʲıdʲát]: 2465
сидя́щим [sʲıdʲǽɕɕim]: 2552
си́лах [sʲíləx]: 2452
си́львии [sʲílʲvʲr̝ʲı]: 2050
си́львио [sʲílʲvʲıə]: 2706
си́льно [sʲílʲnə]: 2089
си́льный [sʲílʲnɨj]: 2572
си́льных [sʲílʲnɨx]: 2887
сингапу́ре [sʲıŋɡɐpúrʲı]: 2726
си́ти [sʲítʲı]: 2216
ситуа́ции [sʲıtʊátsɨʲı]: 2117
ситуа́цию [sʲıtʊátsɨʲü]: 2598
сих [sʲix]: 2641, 2642, 2778, 2833, 2973
скажи́ [skɐʐɨ́]: 2512
скажу́ [skɐʐú]: 2066

сказа́л [skɐzáł]: 2004, 2015, 2021, 2067, 2078, ..., +6
сказа́ла [skɐzálə]: 2021, 2067, 2078, 2097, 2098, ..., +4
сказа́ли [skɐzálʲı]: 2016, 2391, 2498, 2500, 2840
ска́занное [skázənnəʲı]: 2498
сказа́ть [skɐzátʲ]: 2643, 2667
скалу́ [skɐlú]: 2910
сканда́л [skɐndáł]: 2333, 2956
сканда́лом [skɐndáləm]: 2333
скла́де [skládʲı]: 2932
ско́льзким [skʷǫ́lʲskʲım]: 2172
ско́лько [skʷǫ́lʲkə]: 2351, 2353, 2619, 2879, 2918
скоре́е [skɐrʲéʲı]: 2612, 2614, 2620, 2861
ско́ро [skʷǫ́rə]: 2027, 2981
ско́рости [skʷǫ́rəstʲı]: 2076
ско́ростью [skʷǫ́rəstʲü]: 2749, 2750
скрыть [skrɨtʲ]: 2956
скры́ться [skrɨ́tʲsʲı]: 2925
ску́чно [skútɕnə]: 2423, 2557
ску́чный [skútɕnɨj]: 2625
ску́чным [skútɕnɨm]: 2564
ску́чных [skútɕnɨx]: 2563
сла́вится [slávʲıtsʲı]: 2832
следи́м [slʲıdʲím]: 2850
сле́дует [slʲédʊʲıt]: 2097, 2098, 2231, 2643, 2921, ..., +1
сле́дующей [slʲédʊʲüɕɕıj]: 2634, 2698, 2738, 2799
сле́дующем [slʲédʊʲüɕɕim]: 2314, 2795
сле́дующие [slʲédʊʲüɕɕıʲı]: 2570
сле́дующий [slʲédʊʲüɕɕıj]: 2162
сли́шком [slʲíʂkəm]: 2085, 2133, 2223, 2326, 2552, ..., +11
слов [slʷof]: 2251
сло́ва [slǫ́və]: 2463
сложа́ [slɐʐá]: 2846
сложи́лись [slɐʐɨ́lʲıs]: 2976
сложне́е [slɐʐn̝ʲéʲı]: 2297
сло́жно [slǫ́znə]: 2125, 2134, 2154, 2544, 2598, ..., +1
сло́жными [slǫ́znʲımʲı]: 2600

сломáлась [slɐmáləsʲ]: 2706
сломáлось [slɐmáləsʲ]: 2553
сломáлся [slɐmáɫsʲɪ]: 2479
слóман [slǫ́mən]: 2004
слóмана [slǫ́mənə]: 2769
слýчаев [slútɕəʲɪv]: 2384
слýчай [slútɕəj]: 2189, 2662, 2663,
    2664, 2665, ..., +3
случáйно [slʊtɕájnə]: 2760, 2956
слýчая [slútɕəʲə]: 2217, 2264
случи́вшемся [slʊtɕífʂɪmsʲɪ]: 2171
случи́лось [slʊtɕíləsʲ]: 2325, 2480,
    2915
случи́лся [slútɕɪɫsʲɪ]: 2467
слы́шал [slíʂəɫ]: 2191, 2199, 2222,
    2385, 2500
слы́шала [slíʂələ]: 2191, 2199, 2222,
    2385, 2500
слы́шали [slíʂəlʲɪ]: 2198
слы́шать [slíʂətʲ]: 2158, 2194, 2801
слы́шишь [slíʂɪɕ]: 2687
слы́шу [slíʂʊ]: 2581
смéрти [smʲértʲɪ]: 2813
смех [smʲex]: 2043
смешны́х [smʲɪʂníx]: 2562
смея́лись [smʲɪʲǽlʲɪsʲ]: 2838
смог [smʷǫk]: 2360, 2678, 2876
смог [smʷǫg]: 2184, 2437
смоглá [smɐglá]: 2043, 2360, 2678,
    2876
смогли́ [smɐglʲí]: 2364, 2947
смóжем [smʷǫ́ʑɪm]: 2351
смóжешь [smʷǫ́ʑɪɕ]: 2662, 2963
смотрéл [smɐtrʲéɫ]: 2693, 2757
смотрéла [smɐtrʲélə]: 2693, 2757
смотрéть [smɐtrʲétʲ]: 2212, 2502
смóтрит [smʷǫ́trʲɪt]: 2632
смотря́ [smɐtrʲá]: 2573
смы́сла [smíslə]: 2115, 2116, 2117,
    2118, 2119, ..., +1
сначáла [snɐtɕálə]: 2088, 2608, 2929
снесены́ [snʲɪsʲɪní]: 2945
сниже́ние [snʲɪʑénʲrʲɪ]: 2782
сними́ [snʲɪmʲí]: 2920

снóва [snǫ́və]: 2057, 2644, 2969
со [sɐ]: 2089, 2146, 2215, 2254, 2329,
    ..., +11
собáк [sɐbák]: 2173
собáки [sɐbákʲɪ]: 2174
собесéдник [sɐbʲɪsʲédnʲɪk]: 2153
собирáемся [sɐbʲɪráʲɪmsʲɪ]: 2654
собирáется [sɐbʲɪráʲɪtsʲɪ]: 2502, 2594,
    2739, 2952
собирáешься [sɐbʲɪráʲɪɕsʲɪ]: 2070,
    2232, 2502, 2980, 2998
собирáюсь [sɐbʲɪráʲüsʲ]: 2221, 2230,
    2255, 2263, 2356, ..., +1
собирáются [sɐbʲɪráʲütsʲɪ]: 2712
собóй [sɐbʷǫ́j]: 2345, 2686, 2763,
    2911
собрáние [sɐbránʲrʲɪ]: 2675, 2845
собрáнии [sɐbránʲrʲɪ]: 2537, 2555, 2663
сóбственную [sǫ́pstfʲmnʊü]: 2372
сóбственные [sǫ́pstfʲmnʲrʲɪ]: 2848
сóбственный [sǫ́pstfʲmnɨj]: 2375
совершéнно [sɐvʲɪrʂénnə]: 2859
совéт [sɐvʲét]: 2240, 2247
совéта [sɐvʲétə]: 2006, 2525
совéтов [sɐvʲétəf]: 2256
совéтовал [sɐvʲétəvəɫ]: 2007
совéтовала [sɐvʲétəvələ]: 2007
совсéм [sɐfsʲém]: 2029, 2540
согласи́лась [səglɐsʲíləsʲ]: 2660, 2661
соглашéние [səglɐʂénʲrʲɪ]: 2928
содéржится [sɐdʲérzʲɪtsʲɪ]: 2762
содрáли [sɐdrálʲɪ]: 2943
соединённые [sɐʲɪdʲɪnʲǫ́nnʲrʲɪ]: 2307
соединя́ющая [sɐʲɪdʲɪnʲæʲüɕɕəʲɪ]: 2546
сожалéю [səʐɨlʲéʲü]: 2021
сóздана [sǫ́zdənə]: 2953
сознáнии [sɐznánʲrʲɪ]: 2821
созрéли [sɐzrʲélʲɪ]: 2597
сóлнечных [sǫ́ɫnʲɪtɕnix]: 2888
сóлнца [sǫ́ntsə]: 2267, 2522
сóлнце [sǫ́ntsɨ]: 2536, 2742
сообщи́л [sɐɐbɕɕíɫ]: 2408
сообщи́ть [sɐɐbɕɕítʲ]: 2398, 2422

соответствовал [sɐɐtⁱétstfəvəł]: 2655, 2657, 2659

соответствовала [sɐɐtⁱétstfəvələ]: 2655, 2657, 2659

соответствующую [sɐɐtⁱétstfʊⁱüççʊⁱü]: 2533

соревнование [sərⁱɪvnɐvánⁱrⁱɪ]: 2771

сорок [sórək]: 2767

сосед [sɐsⁱéd]: 2241

сосед [sɐsⁱét]: 2242

соседей [sɐsⁱédⁱɪj]: 2369

соседней [sɐsⁱédnⁱɪj]: 2687

соседству [sɐsⁱétstfʊ]: 2286, 2475, 2481, 2488, 2489

сосредоточиться [səsrⁱɪdɐtótçɪtⁱsⁱɪ]: 2350, 2360

составляют [səstɐvlⁱǽⁱüt]: 2966

состоит [səstɐⁱít]: 2872

состоял [səstɐⁱáł]: 2870

состояние [səstɐⁱǽnⁱrⁱɪ]: 2794

состоянии [səstɐⁱǽnⁱrⁱɪ]: 2430

сотрудника [sɐtrúdnⁱɪkə]: 2109

сотрудничестве [sɐtrúdnⁱɪtçɪstfⁱɪ]: 2928

соучастии [sɐʊtçástⁱrⁱɪ]: 2790

сохранять [səxrɐnⁱǽtⁱ]: 2955

сохраняют [səxrɐnⁱǽⁱüt]: 2473

спал [spał]: 2701

спала [spɐlá]: 2701

спальня [spálⁱnⁱɪ]: 2547

спать [spatⁱ]: 2033, 2119, 2209, 2963

специализация [spⁱɪtsɪɐlⁱɪzátsɨə]: 2904

специальная [spⁱɪtsɪəlⁱnəⁱɪ]: 2953

спешить [spⁱɪşítⁱ]: 2413

спешу [spⁱɪşú]: 2740

списывании [spⁱísɪvənⁱrⁱɪ]: 2866

спорта [spʷórtə]: 2679

спортзал [spɐrtsáł]: 2926

спортом [spʷórtəm]: 2036

спорьте [spʷórⁱtⁱɪ]: 2965

способен [spɐsóbⁱɪn]: 2822, 2988

способна [spɐsóbnə]: 2822

спросил [sprɐsⁱíł]: 2006, 2437, 2442

спросила [sprɐsⁱílə]: 2006, 2437, 2442

спросить [sprɐsⁱítⁱ]: 2181, 2525

спросу [sprósʊ]: 2774

спустя [spʊstⁱá]: 2030

сразу [srázʊ]: 2207

средства [srⁱétstfə]: 2322

среду [srⁱɪdú]: 2270

среду [srⁱédʊ]: 2707

ста [sta]: 2751

стабильна [stɐbⁱílⁱnə]: 2297

стал [stał]: 2030, 2031, 2215

стали [stálⁱɪ]: 2718, 2842

стало [stálə]: 2381

становился [stənɐvⁱíłsⁱɪ]: 2564

становится [stɐnóvⁱɪtsⁱɪ]: 2297, 2981

станции [stántsɨⁱɪ]: 2442

старалась [stɐráləsⁱ]: 2032

старался [stɐráłsⁱɪ]: 2032

старшей [stárşɨj]: 2732

старшему [stárşɨmʊ]: 2628

старые [stárɨⁱɪ]: 2945

старый [stárɨj]: 2856

стать [statⁱ]: 2855

стена [stⁱɪná]: 2316

степени [stⁱépⁱɪnⁱɪ]: 2923

стирке [stⁱírkⁱɪ]: 2039

сто [stó]: 2531

стоило [stóⁱɪlə]: 2021

стоимость [stóⁱɪməstⁱ]: 2380

стоит [stóⁱɪt]: 2015, 2016, 2120, 2854, 2993

стоишь [stóⁱɪç]: 2599

стой [stój]: 2203

стол [stół]: 2041

столб [stółp]: 2203

столик [stólⁱɪk]: 2742

столица [stɐlⁱítsə]: 2299, 2309

столкновение [stəłknɐvⁱénⁱrⁱɪ]: 2911

столкнулись [stɐłknúlⁱɪsⁱ]: 2430, 2907, 2911

столкнулся [stɐłknúłsⁱɪ]: 2760, 2761

столько [stólⁱkə]: 2619

стоматолог [stəmɐtólək]: 2262

стоматологам [stəmɐtóləgəm]: 2262

стороной [stərɐnám]: 2542

стороны́ [stərɐní]: 2155, 2157, 2793, 2794, 2958
стоя́ла [stɐʲálə]: 2258
страда́ет [strɐdáʲɪt]: 2887
страда́ющих [strɐdáʲüççɪx]: 2884
стран [stran]: 2296
страна́ [strɐná]: 2301, 2306, 2832
стране́ [strɐnʲɛ́]: 2828
стра́нное [stránnəʲɪ]: 2566
стра́нным [stránnɨm]: 2086, 2862
страну́ [strɐnú]: 2629
страны́ [strɐnɨ́]: 2260
стра́ны [stránɨ]: 2819
страховóй [strəxɐvʷój]: 2773
стра́шно [stráʂnə]: 2174
стра́шные [stráʂnɨʲɪ]: 2810
стра́шный [stráʂnɨj]: 2467
стреля́ть [strʲɪlʲǽtʲ]: 2841
стреми́тельное [strʲɪmʲítʲɪlʲnəʲɪ]: 2783
строи́тельства [strɐʲítʲɪlʲstfə]: 2945
студе́нт [stʊdʲént]: 2275, 2277
студе́нтка [stʊdʲéntkə]: 2164
студе́нтов [stʊdʲéntəf]: 2866
студе́нтов [stʊdʲéntəv]: 2558
студе́нтом [stʊdʲéntəm]: 2244
студе́нту [stʊdʲéntʊ]: 2471
студе́нты [stʊdʲénti]: 2966
стул [stuɫ]: 2167
сту́льев [stúlʲɪf]: 2140
сту́лья [stúlʲɪ]: 2239
стучи́т [stʊtɕít]: 2722
стыда́ [stɨdá]: 2815
стыдя́тся [stɨdʲǽtsʲɪ]: 2814
стэн [stɛn]: 2006
суббо́ту [sʊbbʷótʊ]: 2367, 2702
суббо́ты [sʊbbʷótɨ]: 2702
суд [sut]: 2960
су́дя [súdʲɪ]: 2948
сумасше́дшего [sʊmɐʂʂétʂɪvə]: 2689
сумасше́дших [sʊmɐʂʂétʂɨx]: 2889
сумасше́дшую [sʊmɐʂʂétʂʊʲü]: 2689
су́мка [súmkə]: 2607
су́мку [súmkʊ]: 2013
су́мму [súmmʊ]: 2876

су́мок [súmək]: 2238
суп [sup]: 2849
су́пе [súpʲɪ]: 2224
суперма́ркет [sʊpʲɪrmárkʲɪt]: 2387
суперма́ркете [sʊpʲɪrmárkʲɪtʲɪ]: 2342
существу́ет [sʊççɪstfúʲɪt]: 2777
существу́ют [sʊççɪstfúʲüt]: 2792
схва́тывают [sxfátɨvəʲüt]: 2259
сходи́ли [sxɐdʲílʲɪ]: 2639
сходи́ть [sxɐdʲítʲ]: 2105
схо́дишь [sxódʲɪɕ]: 2083
сча́стью [ɕɕástʲʲü]: 2324, 2410, 2538, 2972
счёте [ɕɕɵ́tʲɪ]: 2963
счита́ешь [ɕɕɪtáʲɪɕ]: 2292
сша [sɨʂa]: 2307, 2949
съел [sʲɛ́ɫ]: 2455
съе́ла [sʲélə]: 2455
съесть [sʲéstʲ]: 2393
сы́на [sɨ́nə]: 2534
сы́ну [sɨ́nʊ]: 2628
сыр [sɨr]: 2490
сэ́ндвич [séndvʲɪtɕ]: 2455
сэр [sɛr]: 2740
сюда́ [sʲüdá]: 2618
та [ta]: 2370
тайва́ня [tɐjvánʲɪ]: 2312
тайла́нда [tɐjlándə]: 2309
тайфу́на [tɐjfúnə]: 2936
так [tak]: 2026, 2044, 2078, 2086, 2090, ..., +35
такахи́ро [tɐkɐxʲírə]: 2201
така́я [tɐkáʲə]: 2586, 2622
та́кже [tákʂɨ]: 2582, 2624, 2923
таки́е [tɐkʲíʲɪ]: 2587
таки́ми [tɐkʲímʲɪ]: 2324
тако́го [tɐkʷóvə]: 2028
тако́е [tɐkʷóʲɪ]: 2988
тако́й [tɐkʷój]: 2168, 2586, 2592, 2746
такси́ [tɐksʲí]: 2068, 2118, 2553, 2765
таку́ю [tɐkúʲü]: 2622
там [tam]: 2051, 2121, 2170, 2375, 2382, ..., +11
тама́ра [tɐmárə]: 2062

таможенное [tɐmʷóʑɪnnəʲɪ]: 2828
твоё [tfɐʲǫ́]: 2776
твоего [tfɐʲɪvʷǫ́]: 2006, 2332, 2525
твоей [tfɐʲéj]: 2054, 2155, 2504, 2793, 2838
твои [tfɐʲí]: 2099, 2404
твоим [tfɐʲím]: 2139
твоими [tfɐʲímʲɪ]: 2789
твой [tfʷoj]: 2158, 2502
творческая [tfʷórtɕɪskəʲɪ]: 2970
твою [tfɐʲú]: 2013, 2065, 2356
твоя [tfɐʲá]: 2041, 2432, 2502
те [tʲɛ]: 2217, 2495, 2511
тебе [tʲɪbʲɛ́]: 2013, 2017, 2028, 2097, 2098, ..., +26
тебя [tʲɪbʲá]: 2002, 2017, 2080, 2115, 2138, ..., +24
телевидение [tʲɪlʲɪvʲídʲɪmʲrʲɪ]: 2885
телевидения [tʲɪlʲɪvʲídʲɪmʲɪʲə]: 2885
телевизор [tʲɪlʲɪvʲízər]: 2632
телевизора [tʲɪlʲɪvʲízərə]: 2133
телевизору [tʲɪlʲɪvʲízərʊ]: 2753
телефон [tʲɪlʲɪfʷón]: 2038, 2664, 2676, 2678
телефона [tʲɪlʲɪfʷónə]: 2146, 2544, 2665
телефоне [tʲɪlʲɪfʷónʲɪ]: 2779
телефону [tʲɪlʲɪfʷónʊ]: 2754, 2762
телохранителе [tʲɪləxrɐnʲítʲɪlʲɪ]: 2889
тем [tʲɛm]: 2075, 2256, 2421, 2612, 2613, ..., +6
темпами [tʲémpəmʲɪ]: 2774
температуре [tʲɪmpʲɪrɐtúrʲɪ]: 2751
тени [tʲɪnʲí]: 2742
теннисном [ténnʲɪsnəm]: 2895
теперь [tʲɪpʲérʲ]: 2021, 2090, 2095, 2387, 2532, ..., +9
тепло [tʲɪplǫ́]: 2536
тёплую [tʲǫ́plʊʲü]: 2901
терпеливый [tʲɪrpʲɪlʲívɪj]: 2627
терпение [tʲɪrpʲénʲrʲɪ]: 2289
терпимы [tʲɪrpʲímɪ]: 2819
теряешь [tʲɪrʲǽʲɪɕ]: 2133
теряю [tʲɪrʲǽʲü]: 2127
тест [tʲɛst]: 2602

тётя [tʲǫ́tʲɪ]: 2739
тех [tʲɛx]: 2286, 2441, 2524, 2533, 2922
течение [tʲɪtɕénʲrʲɪ]: 2337, 2591, 2939
типично [tʲɪpʲítɕnə]: 2824
тихий [tʲíxʲɪj]: 2304
тихо [tʲíxə]: 2581
то [tǫ]: 2067, 2097, 2098, 2184, 2433, ..., +21
тобой [tɐbʷój]: 2247, 2286, 2448, 2634, 2653, ..., +4
товаров [tɐvárəf]: 2550
тогда [tɐgdá]: 2088, 2841
того [tɐvʷǫ́]: 2083, 2085, 2270, 2328, 2409, ..., +10
той [tǫj]: 2825
токио [tǫkʲiǫ]: 2057
толпу [tɐłpú]: 2988
только [tǫ́lʲkə]: 2222, 2363, 2454, 2560, 2567, ..., +12
том [tǫm]: 2007, 2010, 2021, 2115, 2176, ..., +2
томоко [təmək̚ʷǫ]: 2926
тому [tɐmú]: 2091, 2704, 2705, 2706
торговом [tɐrgʷóvəm]: 2616
торжества [tɐrʑɪstfá]: 2785
тормоза [tɐrmɐzá]: 2717
торнадо [tɐrnádə]: 2990
торопишься [tɐrópʲɪɕʲɪ]: 2362
торт [tǫrt]: 2872
тот [tǫt]: 2156, 2285, 2291, 2331, 2507, ..., +6
тратишь [trátʲɪɕ]: 2918
требованиям [trʲébəvənʲrʲɪm]: 2655, 2657, 2659
трёхста [trʲǫ́xstá]: 2327
три [trʲi]: 2696, 2909, 2961
тридцатилетний [trʲɪttsɪtʲɪlʲétnʲɪj]: 2335
тридцать [trʲíttsətʲ]: 2326, 2335, 2647, 2708, 2908
триста [trʲístə]: 2327, 2771
трогал [trógəł]: 2004
трогала [trógələ]: 2004
трогать [trógətʲ]: 2005
трое [trǫ́ʲɪ]: 2964

тройх [trɐʲíx]: 2545
тротуа́р [trɐtʊár]: 2172
труда́ [trʊdá]: 2131, 2132
труди́ться [trʊdʲítʲsʲɪ]: 2252
трудне́е [trʊdnʲéʲɪ]: 2981
тру́дно [trúdnə]: 2878, 2950
тру́дностей [trúdnəstʲɪj]: 2401, 2419
трудо́м [trʊdóm]: 2124, 2581, 2948
трусцо́й [trʊstsój]: 2926
туале́тной [tʊɐlʲétnəj]: 2931
туале́тную [tʊɐlʲétnʊʉ]: 2982
туда́ [tʊdá]: 2704
тури́зм [tʊrʲízm]: 2341
туристи́ческом [tʊrʲɪstʲítɕɪskəm]: 2997
тури́стов [tʊrʲístəf]: 2414, 2831
тури́сты [tʊrʲístɨ]: 2435
турни́ре [tʊrnʲírʲɪ]: 2895
ту́фли [túflʲɪ]: 2088, 2574
ты [tɨ]: 2028, 2029, 2045, 2055, 2056,
     ..., +116
ты́сяч [tɨ́sʲɪtɕ]: 2486, 2749, 2772
ты́сячи [tɨ́sʲɪtɕɨ]: 2708, 2770, 2804
ты́щу [tɨ́ɕɕʊ]: 2692
тюрьме́ [tʲʉrʲmʲɛ́]: 2272, 2731, 2916
тюрьму́ [tʲʉrʲmú]: 2273
тюрьмы́ [tʲʉrʲmɨ́]: 2865
тяжеле́е [tʲɪʐɨlʲéʲɪ]: 2607
тяжело́ [tʲɪʐɨló]: 2090
у [u]: 2017, 2032, 2042, 2058, 2080,
     ..., +68
уби́йств [ʊbʲíjstf]: 2953
уби́йства [ʊbʲíjstfə]: 2833
уби́йствами [ʊbʲíjstfəmʲɪ]: 2791
уби́йстве [ʊbʲíjstfʲɪ]: 2790, 2865, 2915,
     2958
уби́йца [ʊbʲíjtsə]: 2879
уби́йцу [ʊbʲíjtsʊ]: 2878, 2915, 2925
уби́л [ʊbʲíł]: 2956
убира́лись [ʊbʲɪrálʲɪsʲ]: 2559
убира́ться [ʊbʲɪrátʲsʲɪ]: 2052, 2053
убо́рке [ʊbʷórkʲɪ]: 2040
убо́рки [ʊbʷórkʲɪ]: 2053
убра́ться [ʊbrátʲsʲɪ]: 2040
у́быль [úbɨlʲ]: 2532

увеличе́ние [ʊvʲɪlʲɪtɕén̪ʲrʲɪ]: 2885, 2886
увеличе́нии [ʊvʲɪlʲɪtɕén̪ʲrʲɪ]: 2885
увели́чивает [ʊvʲɪlʲítɕɪvəʲɪt]: 2788
увели́чивается [ʊvʲɪlʲítɕɪvəʲɪtsʲɪ]: 2781
увели́чилась [ʊvʲɪlʲítɕɪləsʲ]: 2770
уве́рен [ʊvʲérʲɪn]: 2018, 2028, 2653,
     2822, 2826
уве́рена [ʊvʲérʲɪnə]: 2018, 2028, 2358,
     2653, 2822, ..., +1
уви́дел [ʊvʲídʲɪł]: 2159, 2757
уви́дела [ʊvʲídʲɪlə]: 2757
уви́деть [ʊvʲídʲɪtʲ]: 2492, 2519
уви́деться [ʊvʲídʲɪtʲsʲɪ]: 2491, 2698
уви́димся [ʊvʲídʲɪmsʲɪ]: 2653
уви́жу [ʊvʲíʐʊ]: 2653
уви́жусь [ʊvʲíʐʊsʲ]: 2634, 2669, 2707,
     2708
уво́лилась [ʊvʷólʲɪləsʲ]: 2806
уво́лился [ʊvʷólʲɪłsʲɪ]: 2806
уволня́ясь [ʊvełnʲǽʲɪsʲ]: 2156
углу́ [ʊglú]: 2728, 2729
угости́л [ʊgɐstʲíł]: 2185
угости́ть [ʊgɐstʲítʲ]: 2185
угоща́йтесь [ʊgɐɕɕájtʲɪsʲ]: 2346
удало́сь [ʊdɐlós]: 2184
удивлён [ʊdʲɪvlʲén]: 2159, 2177, 2787
удивлена́ [ʊdʲɪvlʲɪná]: 2177, 2787
удивле́ны [ʊdʲɪvlʲɪnɨ]: 2421
удо́бными [ʊdóbnɨmʲɪ]: 2088
удово́льствие [ʊdɐvʷólʲstfʲrʲɪ]: 2758
удово́льствием [ʊdɐvʷólʲstfʲrʲɪm]:
     2054, 2057, 2060
удруча́ющими [ʊdrʊtɕáʲʉɕɕɪmʲɪ]: 2234
уе́дешь [ʊʲédʲɪɕ]: 2256
уезжа́ет [ʊʲɪʐʐáʲɪt]: 2691
уезжа́ли [ʊʲɪʐʐálʲɪ]: 2674
уезжа́ть [ʊʲɪʐʐátʲ]: 2180
уезжа́ю [ʊʲɪʐʐáʲʉ]: 2719, 2937
уе́хал [ʊʲéxəł]: 3000
уе́хала [ʊʲéxələ]: 2186
уе́хали [ʊʲéxəlʲɪ]: 2706
уе́хать [ʊʲéxətʲ]: 2675
уж [ʊʐ]: 2746
ужа́сен [ʊʐásʲɪn]: 2051

ужа́сно [ʊzásnə]: 2567, 2897
ужа́сный [ʊzásnij]: 2980
уже́ [ʊzɨ́]: 2024, 2033, 2086, 2166, 2212, ..., +17
у́жин [úzɨn]: 2100, 2565
у́жина [úzɨnə]: 2283
у́зкая [úskəʲɪ]: 2546
узна́ет [ʊznáʲɪt]: 2161
узна́й [ʊznáj]: 2178
узна́л [ʊznáɫ]: 2753
узна́ла [ʊználə]: 2753
узна́ть [ʊznátʲ]: 2177, 2178, 2502, 2504
уйти́ [ʊjtʲí]: 2245
указа́л [ʊkɐzáɫ]: 2984
указа́телями [ʊkɐzátʲɪlʲɪmʲɪ]: 2662
укла [ukla]: 2317
укра́денную [ʊkrádʲɪnnʊü]: 2219
укра́денные [ʊkrádʲɪmnɨʲɪ]: 2549
украду́т [ʊkrɐdút]: 2666
укра́сть [ʊkrástʲ]: 2121
уку́сит [ʊkúsʲɪt]: 2174
ули́ку [ʊlʲíkʊ]: 2916
у́лице [úlʲɪtsɨ]: 2089, 2190, 2951, 2963, 2964
у́лицу [úlʲɪtsʊ]: 2988, 2989
у́лицы [úlʲɪtsɨ]: 2205, 2386, 2729
улу́чшить [ʊlútɕɕɪtʲ]: 2074
улыба́йся [ʊlɨbájsʲɪ]: 2995
улы́бок [ʊlɨ́bək]: 2995
ультрафиоле́товых [ʊlʲtrafʲɪɐlʲétəvɨx]: 2888
уме́ет [ʊmʲéʲɪt]: 2652
у́мер [úmʲɪr]: 2514, 2868, 2869
уме́ть [ʊmʲétʲ]: 2361
умира́ют [ʊmʲɪráʲüt]: 2897
умы́лся [ʊmɨ́ɫsʲɪ]: 2352
универма́ге [ʊnʲɪvʲɪrmágʲɪ]: 2934
университе́т [ʊnʲɪvʲɪrsʲɪtʲét]: 2243, 2317, 2853
университе́та [ʊnʲɪvʲɪrsʲɪtʲétə]: 2244, 2966
университе́тов [ʊnʲɪvʲɪrsʲɪtʲétəf]: 2772
университе́тский [ʊnʲɪvʲɪrsʲɪtʲétskʲɪj]: 2243

уничто́женное [ʊnʲɪʂtózɨnnəʲɪ]: 2482
уничто́жено [ʊnʲɪʂtózɨnə]: 2467
уо́лтер [ʊóɫtʲɪr]: 2602, 2632
упа́л [ʊpáɫ]: 2188
упа́ли [ʊpálʲɪ]: 2844
упа́сть [ʊpástʲ]: 2172
управле́ние [ʊprɐvlʲénʲɪʲɪ]: 2828
урага́ном [ʊrɐgánəm]: 2554
уро́ка [ʊrókə]: 2823
уро́ке [ʊrókʲɪ]: 2942
уро́ки [ʊrókʲɪ]: 2926
усе́рдно [ʊsʲérdnə]: 2593
усло́вии [ʊslóvʲɪʲɪ]: 2670, 2671
услы́шал [ʊslíʂəɫ]: 2147
услы́шала [ʊslíʂələ]: 2798
услы́шать [ʊslíʂətʲ]: 2179, 2590
усну́л [ʊsnúɫ]: 2693
усну́ла [ʊsnúlə]: 2693
успе́ли [ʊspʲélʲɪ]: 2716
успе́ть [ʊspʲétʲ]: 2142, 2740
успе́ха [ʊspʲéxə]: 2037
успоко́ить [ʊspɐkʷóʲɪtʲ]: 2948
успоко́иться [ʊspɐkʷóʲɪtʲsʲɪ]: 2362
успоко́йтесь [ʊspɐkʷójtʲɪsʲ]: 2991
уста́вшей [ʊstáfʂɨj]: 2446
уста́вшим [ʊstáfʂɨm]: 2446
уста́л [ʊstáɫ]: 2064, 2168, 2658, 2825
уста́ла [ʊstálə]: 2064, 2168, 2658, 2825
уста́ли [ʊstálʲɪ]: 2443
уста́лость [ʊstáləstʲ]: 2209
утаи́ть [ʊtɐʲítʲ]: 2957
утомля́ет [ʊtɐmlʲǽɪt]: 2011
утра́м [ʊtrám]: 2090
у́треннее [útrʲɪmnʲɪʲɪ]: 2845
у́тро [útrə]: 2464
у́тром [útrəm]: 2119, 2531, 2633, 2708, 2911
уф [uf]: 2888
учёбу [ʊtɕébʊ]: 2360, 2922
учёной [ʊtɕénəj]: 2923
учёные [ʊtɕénɨʲɪ]: 2786, 2863
учи́л [ʊtɕíɫ]: 2002
учи́лся [ʊtɕíɫsʲɪ]: 2922

учи́тель [ʊtɕítʲɪlʲ]: 2650
учи́теля [ʊtɕítʲɪlʲɪ]: 2558
учителя́ми [ʊtɕitʲɪlʲǽmʲɪ]: 2541
у́чится [útɕɪtsʲɪ]: 2732
учи́тывая [ʊtɕítɨvəʲə]: 2169
учи́ться [ʊtɕítʲsʲɪ]: 2143
ушёл [ʊʂǿɫ]: 2637, 2938
ушла́ [ʊʂlá]: 2392, 2496
у́шла [úʂlə]: 2496
ушли́ [ʊʂlʲí]: 2116
уще́рб [ʊɕɕérp]: 2960
уэ́льс [ʊélʲs]: 2315
фа́био [fábʲɪə]: 2185
фа́брике [fábrʲɪkʲɪ]: 2550
фа́йлов [fájləf]: 2954
фа́йлы [fájlɨ]: 2955
факти́чески [fɐktʲítɕɪskʲɪ]: 2777, 2798
фбр [fɛbr]: 2242
фёдора [fʲǿdərə]: 2187
фелисиа́на [fʲɪlʲɪsʲɪánə]: 2635
филлипи́ны [fʲɪɫʲɪpʲínɨ]: 2312
фильм [fʲilʲm]: 2120, 2212, 2357, 2502, 2564, ..., +6
фи́льма [fʲílʲmə]: 2436, 2693
фина́нсово [fʲɪnánsəvə]: 2830
фина́нсовые [fʲɪnánsəvɨʲɪ]: 2085
фина́нсовых [fʲɪnánsəvɨx]: 2977
фи́рме [fʲírmʲɪ]: 2530
флóра [flǿrə]: 2265
фóрмулы [fʷǿrmʊlɨ]: 2757, 2972
фотогра́фии [fətɛgráfʲɪ]: 2779
фотогра́фию [fətɛgráfʲʊ]: 2534
фра́нца [frántsə]: 2197
фра́нции [frántsɨʲɪ]: 2313
францу́зами [frɛntsúzəmʲɪ]: 2435
францу́зском [frɛntsússkəm]: 2529
францу́зы [frɛntsúzɨ]: 2294
ха́нако [xánəkə]: 2059
хвати́ло [xfɐtʲílə]: 2140
хва́тит [xfátʲɪt]: 2342
хидеки [xʲidʲekʲɪ]: 2057
хле́ба [xlʲébə]: 2230
хóббите [xǿbbʲɪtʲɪ]: 2813
ходи́ [xɐdʲí]: 2743

ходи́л [xɐdʲíɫ]: 2129, 2527
ходи́ла [xɐdʲílə]: 2129, 2273, 2527, 2875
ходи́ли [xɐdʲílʲɪ]: 2439, 2459, 2516, 2523
хóдит [xǿdʲɪt]: 2472, 2483, 2926
ходи́ть [xɐdʲítʲ]: 2170, 2262
хóдишь [xǿdʲɪɕ]: 2128
хóдят [xǿdʲɪt]: 2460, 2604, 2755
хожу́ [xɐʐú]: 2424
хозя́ев [xɐzʲǽɪv]: 2877
холл [xoɫɫ]: 2216
хóлода [xǿlədə]: 2901
холода́ть [xəlɐdátʲ]: 2022
холоди́льник [xəlɐdʲílʲnʲɪk]: 2921
холоди́льнике [xəlɐdʲílʲnʲɪkʲɪ]: 2490
хорóнят [xɐrǿnʲɪt]: 2526
хорóш [xɐrǿʂ]: 2562
хорóшая [xɐrǿʂəʲə]: 2164, 2236, 2237, 2858
хорóшее [xɐrǿʂɨɪ]: 2240
хорóшей [xɐrǿʂɨj]: 2231
хорóшие [xɐrǿʂɨʲɪ]: 2438, 2587, 2789
хорóший [xɐrǿʂɨj]: 2237, 2240, 2382, 2746
хорóшим [xɐrǿʂɨm]: 2357
хорóшими [xɐrǿʂɨmʲɪ]: 2638, 2718
хорошó [xərɛʂó]: 2460, 2579, 2580, 2588, 2589, ..., +1
хорóшую [xɐrǿʂʊʲü]: 2579
хоте́л [xɐtʲéɫ]: 2059, 2248, 2256, 2375, 2491, ..., +7
хоте́ла [xɐtʲélə]: 2059, 2215, 2248, 2256, 2323, ..., +10
хоте́ли [xɐtʲélʲɪ]: 2058, 2503, 2588
хоти́те [xɐtʲítʲɪ]: 2346, 2619
хотя́ [xɐtʲá]: 2652, 2655, 2656, 2658, 2659
хотя́т [xɐtʲát]: 2477, 2511
хóчет [xǿtɕɪt]: 2037, 2431, 2444, 2756, 2790, ..., +2
хóчешь [xǿtɕɪɕ]: 2081, 2245, 2374, 2502, 2504, ..., +3
хочу́ [xɐtɕú]: 2274, 2344, 2372, 2732, 2941

хуже [xúzi]: 2602
хэйди [xéjdʲɪ]: 2200
хэнриком [xénrʲɪkəm]: 2355
цветы [tsfʲɪtɨ]: 2429
целевая [tsɨlʲɪvájə]: 2953
целом [tséləm]: 2758
цель [tsʲelʲ]: 2543
цельсию [tsélʲsʲɪʲü]: 2751
центральной [tsɨntrálʲnəj]: 2310
центре [tséntrʲɪ]: 2134, 2616, 2721
ценю [tsɨnʲú]: 2793
цзяньвэну [tssʲænʲvɛnu]: 2071
час [tɕas]: 2472, 2641, 2749, 2750
часа [tɕɪsá]: 2014, 2767, 2968
часа [tɕásə]: 2939
часам [tɕɪsám]: 2700, 2703
часов [tɕɪsóv]: 2265, 2703
часов [tɕɪsóf]: 2024, 2276, 2337, 2700, 2714
частей [tɕɪstʲéj]: 2338
части [tɕástʲɪ]: 2909
часто [tɕástə]: 2091, 2127, 2128, 2461
часть [tɕastʲ]: 2170, 2260, 2428, 2436
часы [tɕɪsɨ]: 2126
чаще [tɕáɕːɪ]: 2052, 2144, 2424, 2604
чего [tɕɪvˠó]: 2136, 2512
чек [tɕek]: 2772, 2773
человек [tɕɪlɐvʲék]: 2323, 2437, 2442, 2509, 2533, ..., +7
человека [tɕɪlɐvʲékə]: 2576, 2956
человеком [tɕɪlɐvʲékəm]: 2855, 2958
чем [tɕem]: 2061, 2062, 2063, 2068, 2069, ..., +22
чём [tɕǿm]: 2409, 2852
чемоданов [tɕɪmɐdánəf]: 2238
через [tɕérʲɪz]: 2031, 2496, 2710, 2711, 2844, ..., +1
через [tɕérʲɪs]: 2647, 2712, 2922
чёрный [tɕǿrnɨj]: 2282
честь [tɕʲestʲ]: 2894
четверо [tɕétfʲɪrə]: 2741
чётко [tɕǿtkə]: 2018
четыре [tɕɪtɨrʲɪ]: 2162
четыреста [tɕɪtɨrʲɪstə]: 2770, 2773

четырнадцатого [tɕɪtɨrnəttsətəvə]: 2708
числа [tɕɪslá]: 2885
численность [tɕɪslʲɪmnəstʲ]: 2532
число [tɕɪsló]: 2884
чистые [tɕɪstɨʲɪ]: 2671
читает [tɕɪtáʲɪt]: 2632
читал [tɕɪtáɫ]: 2427
читала [tɕɪtálə]: 2427
читать [tɕɪtátʲ]: 2074
членов [tɕlʲénəf]: 2668
членом [tɕlʲénəm]: 2668
чтением [tɕtʲénʲɪrʲɪm]: 2197
чтения [tɕtʲénʲɪrʲə]: 2074
что [ʂtɔ]: 2004, 2010, 2015, 2016, 2018, ..., +131
что-либо [ʂtɔ-lʲɪbə]: 2015, 2393
что-нибудь [ʂtɔ-nʲɪbʊdʲ]: 2203, 2396, 2418
что-то [ʂtɔ-tə]: 2136, 2825, 2846
чтоб [ʂtɔp]: 2083
чтобы [ʂtɔbɨ]: 2004, 2006, 2041, 2066, 2067, ..., +44
чувство [tɕúʊstfə]: 2815
чувствовал [tɕúʊstfəvəɫ]: 2209
чувствовала [tɕúʊstfəvələ]: 2209, 2656
чувствуешь [tɕúʊstfʊʲɪɕ]: 2196
чувствую [tɕúʊstfʊʲü]: 2135, 2561, 2809
чуть [tɕutʲ]: 2606
чьим [tɕʲim]: 2516
чья [tɕʲa]: 2331, 2518, 2904
чэндра [tɕéndrə]: 2030
шакира [ʂɨkʲírə]: 2827
швеция [ʂfʲétsɨʲə]: 2301
шёл [ʂǿɫ]: 2068, 2572, 2696, 2750
шёпотом [ʂǿpətəm]: 2147
шестнадцать [ʂɨsnáttsətʲ]: 2628
шесть [ʂɨstʲ]: 2249, 2265, 2461, 2640, 2712
школе [ʂkˠǿlʲɪ]: 2732
школе [ʂkˠǿlʲɪ]: 2816
школу [ʂkˠǿlʊ]: 2274, 2516, 2748, 2894
школы [ʂkˠǿlɨ]: 2072

шко́льный [ʂkʷól̠ʲni̠j]: 2856
шла [ʂla]: 2068
шли [ʂl̠ʲi]: 2172
шоки́рованы [ʂɐkʲírəvəni̠]: 2804
шокола́д [ʂəkɐlát]: 2330
шокола́док [ʂəkɐládək]: 2551
шоссе́ [ʂɐssʲɛ́]: 2911
шоссе́йное [ʂɐssʲéjnəʲɪ]: 2906
шотла́ндия [ʂɐtlánd̠ʲɪ̠ʲɪ]: 2315
шпиона́же [ʂp̠ʲɪɐnázi̠]: 2109
штаны́ [ʂtɐni̠]: 2039
шта́ты [ʂtáti̠]: 2307
шторм [ʂtǫrm]: 2340
што́рм [ʂtǫ́rm]: 2340
шум [ʂum]: 2111, 2222
шу́ма [ʂúmə]: 2978
шу́мно [ʂúmnə]: 2223
шу́мной [ʂúmnəj]: 2089
шу́му [ʂúmʊ]: 2089
шу́ткой [ʂútkəj]: 2838
эгои́зме [ɛgɐʲízm̠ʲɪ]: 2864
эгоисти́чен [ɛgɐʲɪst̠ʲítɕin]: 2847
эгоисти́чны [ɛgɐʲɪst̠ʲítɕni̠]: 2363
э́дриан [édr̠ʲɪən]: 2159
э́йфелевой [éjf̠ʲɪl̠ʲɪvəj]: 2831
эква́тор [ɛkfátər]: 2268
экза́мен [ɛksám̠ʲɪn]: 2164, 2394, 2398, 2822
экза́мена [ɛksám̠ʲɪnə]: 2332
экзаменаци́нные [ɛksam̠ʲɪnɐtsi̠ǫ́nni̠ʲɪ]: 2332
экза́мене [ɛksám̠ʲɪn̠ʲɪ]: 2152, 2866
эконо́мике [ɛkɐnǫ́m̠ʲɪk̠ʲɪ]: 2411
эконо́мики [ɛkɐnǫ́m̠ʲɪk̠ʲɪ]: 2025, 2281, 2886, 2942
экономи́ческом [ɛkɐnɐm̠ʲítɕɪskəm]: 2883
эконо́мия [ɛkɐnǫ́m̠ʲɪ̠ʲə]: 2543
э́кспорт [ékspərt]: 2550
экспре́ссе [ɛkspr̠ʲéss̠ʲɪ]: 2767
электро́нного [ɛl̠ʲɪktrǫ́nnəvə]: 2197
электро́нное [ɛl̠ʲɪktrǫ́nnə̠ʲɪ]: 2834
электро́нной [ɛl̠ʲɪktrǫ́nnəj]: 2762
эли́за [ɛl̠ʲízə]: 2580

э́стебан [ést̠ʲɪbən]: 2579
э́та [étə]: 2170, 2325, 2607, 2832, 2893, ..., +1
этажа́ми [ɛtɐzám̠ʲɪ]: 2334
этаже́ [ɛtɐzí̠]: 2725
э́ти [ét̠ʲɪ]: 2039, 2152, 2404, 2597, 2928
э́тим [ét̠ʲɪm]: 2044, 2177, 2531
э́тих [ét̠ʲɪx]: 2427, 2432, 2449, 2468, 2470
э́то [étə]: 2052, 2060, 2065, 2078, 2086, ..., +64
э́того [étəvə]: 2021, 2544, 2780, 2820, 2853, ..., +1
э́той [étəj]: 2550, 2594, 2635, 2786, 2816
э́том [étəm]: 2178, 2398, 2563, 2611, 2747, ..., +7
э́тому [étəmʊ]: 2087
э́тот [étət]: 2041, 2111, 2154, 2167, 2585, ..., +2
э́ту [étʊ]: 2136, 2151, 2246, 2367, 2533, ..., +8
ю́ге [ʲúg̠ʲɪ]: 2313
ю́жной [ʲúzn̠əj]: 2302, 2308
ю́ко [ʲúkə]: 2674
юлиа́на [ʲül̠ʲɪánə]: 2494
ю́лий [ʲúl̠ʲɪj]: 2509
ю́на [ʲúnə]: 2683
юриди́ческий [ʲür̠ʲɪd̠ʲítɕɪsk̠ʲɪj]: 2732
юриди́ческую [ʲür̠ʲɪd̠ʲítɕɪskʊʲü]: 2894
я [ʲa]: 2003, 2004, 2006, 2007, 2010, ..., +265
я́блоки [ʲáblək̠ʲɪ]: 2597
явля́ется [ʲɪvl̠ʲǽ̠ʲɪts̠ʲɪ]: 2439
явля́ешься [ʲɪvl̠ʲǽ̠ʲɪɕs̠ʲɪ]: 2668
язы́к [ʲɪzí̠k]: 2138, 2589
языка́ [ʲɪzi̠ká]: 2213, 2249
языка́ми [ʲɪzi̠kám̠ʲɪ]: 2792
языке́ [ʲɪzi̠k̠ʲɛ́]: 2250, 2802, 2899
языки́ [ʲɪzi̠k̠ʲí]: 2575
языко́в [ʲɪzi̠kʷóv]: 2425
языко́в [ʲɪzi̠kʷóf]: 2908
языкова́я [ʲɪzi̠kɐvá̠ʲə]: 2981
я́йца [ʲǽjtsə]: 2982

января [ˈɪnvɐrʲá]: 2719
японии [ˈɪpʷónʲrʲɪ]: 2376, 2678, 2726
японию [ˈɪpʷónʲrʲü]: 2092

японских [ˈɪpʷónskʲɪx]: 2951
ящик [ˈǽççɨk]: 2729